READING REFORM RESPONSA

READING REFORM RESPONSA
Jewish Tradition, Reform Rabbis, and Today's Issues

RABBI MARK WASHOFSKY, PhD

Foreword by
Rabbi Joan S. Friedman, PhD

CCAR Press
Central Conference of American Rabbis
5784 New York 2024

Published by CCAR Press
Central Conference of American Rabbis
355 Lexington Avenue, New York, NY 10017
(212) 972-3636 | info@ccarpress.org | www.ccarpress.org

Library of Congress Cataloging-in-Publication Data
Names: Washofsky, Mark, author.
Title: Reading reform responsa: Jewish tradition, Reform rabbis, and today's issues / Rabbi
Mark Washofsky, PhD.
Description: First edition. | New York: Central Conference of American Rabbis (CCAR),
[2024] |
Summary: "Guides readers to understand Reform responsa history, framing, and context"
–Provided by publisher.
Identifiers: LCCN 2023050914 (print) | LCCN 2023050915 (ebook) | ISBN 9780881236439
(trade paperback) | ISBN 9780881236446 (ebook)
Subjects: LCSH: Jewish law–Reform Judaism. | Responsa.
Classification: LCC BM197.W372 2024 (print) | LCC BM197 (ebook) | DDC
   296.1/8541–dc23/eng/20231106
LC record available at https://lccn.loc.gov/2023050914
LC ebook record available at https://lccn.loc.gov/2023050915

Designed and composed by Scott-Martin Kosofsky
at The Philidor Company, Rhinebeck, NY
Printed in U.S.A.

10 9 8 7 6 5 4 3 2 1

CONTENTS

FOREWORD
Rabbi Joan S. Friedman, PhD

I AM DEEPLY HONORED to write this foreword to *Reading Reform Responsa* by my teacher, colleague, and friend Mark Washofsky. Rabbi Washofsky's career was bound up with the Central Conference of American Rabbis (CCAR) Responsa Committee for thirty-five years. He was first appointed to the committee in 1983, becoming its vice chair in 1989 and its chair in 1994. He served the CCAR and the Reform Movement in that capacity for twenty-three distinguished years, until 2017. It was my great privilege and pleasure to serve on the committee for almost his entire tenure as chair. Since stepping into the role of committee chair in 2019, I have come to appreciate even more, if that is possible, his unfailingly learned, wise, insightful, patient, and wickedly witty leadership.

In this book Dr. Washofsky masterfully demonstrates the centrality of responsa for the continued vitality of Reform as an authentic stream of contemporary Judaism. Addressing himself to the everyday Jew-in-the-pew, he explains what halachah is, what responsa are, and what makes "Reform responsa" distinctive. All this he has done before, in the introductions to each of the three volumes of responsa he edited for the CCAR, as well as in his *Jewish Living: A Guide to Contemporary Reform Practice*, though not as expansively as he does here. More importantly, here he draws on his expertise as a scholar both of our tradition and of legal and literary theory to teach the non-specialist reader to become a *critical* reader of responsa. *How* does a responsum take the raw material of existing sources and shape them into a new creation, thereby enabling us Jews to hear the voice from Sinai as refracted through Torah in a new way? He leads the reader on a guided tour through fifteen Reform responsa, showing how the process works: how a question is asked; how a respondent identifies the issues at its heart and determines how to frame the response; how a respondent identifies and consults relevant sources, weighs the circumstances, and reaches a conclusion. Crucially, he shows the reader that the respondent must, all the while, remain aware that theirs is not the only possible answer to the question, that there may well be multiple answers, and so it is essential to argue for why their answer is the best one. Responsa, Washofsky reminds us, are not courtroom verdicts. They are advisory opinions, and they are usually about hard cases with no easy or obvious answers; if the answers were easy or obvious, there would be no need to ask for guidance. It is the process itself—wrestling with the sources and persuading the community that a particular answer, and not any other answer, is the best Torah in this case—that grounds our community in the Jewish legal tradition and thereby validates our claim, as Reform Jews, to Jewish authenticity.

This brings us to his central point, which is that all responsa in all eras, regardless of which rabbi writes them, have always had to meet the same challenge—not to compel but to *persuade* Jews that the best way for a Jew to act in any given situation is *this* way, rather than *that* way. Thus Reform responsa are no different from "traditional" responsa, except that the sources on which they rely for guidance and precedent include the literature of liberal Judaism and incorporate its values, including its willingness to reexamine inherited norms (without necessarily rejecting them). The ongoing process of engaging with the halachah in this way illustrates the absurdity of debating whether Reform is a "halachic" movement. We are halachic, argues Washofsky, by virtue of *doing* the process of halachah.

The earliest Reformers did just this. They turned to the halachic tradition to justify their actions, but as the nineteenth century progressed, the relationship between Reform and the halachah became a matter of contention. Was Reform evolutionary or revolutionary? Was the essence of the Torah legal or ethical? Was Judaism priestly or prophetic? In its early decades the Central Conference of American Rabbis agreed that as rabbis they were free to make changes to Jewish practice as they saw fit. Nevertheless, in 1906 they established a committee to consult the halachic sources to answer "questions that might, from time to time, be submitted concerning Jewish customs and traditions." Thus was the CCAR Responsa Committee born. It received on average barely more than two questions a year in its first forty years of existence, and these asked mostly about liturgical and life-cycle practices.

Rabbi Solomon B. Freehof brought responsa into the mainstream of Reform life in the years after World War II. An influential CCAR leader throughout the war years and after, he was also the most accomplished halachic scholar in the North American Reform rabbinate, and his collaboration with Conservative and Orthodox rabbis in writing responsa for military chaplains raised the profile of the CCAR's Responsa Committee. As its chair he regularly received about two hundred inquiries each year from both rabbis and laypeople. They sought guidance on liturgical and life-cycle practices as Reform congregations continued to reappropriate rituals discarded earlier, on establishing proper boundaries between Jews and gentiles while embracing life in a society with no such formal boundaries, on the new challenges of life on the suburban frontier, on the ethics of new medical advances, and much more. Many rabbis shared Freehof's responsa with their boards and used them as adult education material, thereby increasing awareness of responsa among Reform Jews. These trends continued after the committee chairmanship passed in 1975 to Rabbi Walter Jacob, and then to Rabbi W. Gunther Plaut in 1989, before passing to Rabbi Washofsky.

The Responsa Committee no longer receives two hundred questions annually, because there is no need to ask most of them. As Jews have done for centuries, we now also find information, instruction, and guidance on living our daily lives in written texts—publications of the CCAR such as *Navigating the Journey: The Essential Guide to the Jewish Life Cycle*, *A Guide to the Jewish Seasons*, *Gates of Shabbat*, and a number of other titles, including Rabbi Washofsky's above-mentioned *Jewish Living*, published by the Union for Reform Judaism. And thanks to the internet, all of our responsa are available to everyone. The ready availability of all this guidance means that the questions that come to the Responsa Committee are the hard ones.

Hard questions, many legal scholars will say, make bad law. But hard questions, Rabbi Washofsky shows here, make wonderful responsa. Hard questions force us to articulate just what is bothering us. Hard questions force us to name and justify our values; to identify salient points on our Jewish moral, spiritual, and communal compass; and to explain why, on that compass, we orient ourselves toward Point X rather than to Point Y. No one is better than Rabbi Washofsky at articulating what is at stake in a hard question and explaining to us why, as Jews in this time and this place faced with this dilemma, we are truer to Torah if we orient our actions toward Point Z, rather than toward either Point X or Point Y.

"The personal is political," said the feminists of the 1960s and 1970s. What they meant was that the way we live our daily lives reflects our values and shapes the world we want to live in. That is how Jews have been living ever since Sinai—demonstrating by the way we live our lives that we are faithful to our covenantal commitment. But what does that mean when the possible actions before us are new and unprecedented? How do we live that covenantal commitment when its values may be in conflict with one another? Does honoring a parent mean acceding to their wish to dispose of their body in a way not consonant with the tradition? Should a Reform synagogue, committed to the religious equality of men and women, provide space on its premises for an Orthodox minyan? Does halachic support for workers' rights mean that a synagogue must spend more of its members' money to hire union labor? These, and more, are the hard questions to which my dear, brilliant colleague Mark Washofsky has provided answers for a generation of Reform Jews, enabling them to discern the halachah—the "path"—that runs from Sinai to the very next step they take.

RABBI JOAN S. FRIEDMAN, PhD, Lincoln Professor of Religion and Professor of History at the College of Wooster, was ordained at Hebrew Union College–Jewish Institute of Religion in New York in 1980. She served as a congregational rabbi and as a college chaplain before completing a doctorate in Jewish history at Columbia University in 2003. Her book *"Guidance, Not Governance": Rabbi Solomon B. Freehof and Reform Responsa* was a 2013 National Jewish Book Award finalist.

PREFACE

I WANT TO INVITE YOU to join me in reading some of the most fascinating texts that rabbis have ever written. They are responsa, answers to questions about Jewish religious practice submitted to them by individuals and communities. More specifically, they are *Reform* responsa, composed by Reform rabbis for an audience of progressive Jewish readers.

Fascinating? Okay, I'll admit it: I'm prejudiced. Much of my academic career as a student of the literature of Jewish law (halachah) has involved the study of the genre known as rabbinical responsa (*sh'eilot ut'shuvot*, "questions and answers"), documents dating from the eighth century CE to our own day. And as a member of the Responsa Committee of the Central Conference of American Rabbis (CCAR) from 1985 to 2017, I have taken part in composing many Reform responsa. I have lived for decades with responsa as both a reader and a writer, so it's little wonder that I'm partial to them. Nor should it be surprising that I want you to share my enthusiasm . . . which goes a long way toward explaining the existence of this book.

But *why* should you share my enthusiasm? That's a big question, too big for this preface. Think of the book itself as an extended answer. The introduction will explain what responsa are and their significance in the history of Judaism. It will discuss the nature and history of the genre in general and of Reform responsa in particular. And it will offer suggestions as to why Reform rabbis write responsa, why those responsa legitimately claim importance, and why they deserve to be read carefully and critically. The chapters that follow guide us through the reading of Reform responsa on ten subjects that I hope you will find interesting and that provide good examples of how these texts work and how they seek to accomplish the goals that their authors set for them. In the conclusion, I make some inferences and observations about the role that responsa play in Reform Jewish thought and life.

What I *can* and *should* do in this preface is to name some of the convictions that have brought me to write this book and that will no doubt be evident throughout its pages. First, responsa are an essential literary tool—maybe the most important such tool—through which rabbis (including Reform rabbis) create Torah and create community. Responsa create Torah because they answer new questions, those that the existing texts of halachah do not explicitly address, or hard questions, which the texts do not resolve in any clear and agreed upon way. Responsa create community because they are essays in *persuasion.* Responsa writers do more than simply declare their decisions. They *argue* for those decisions, with the goal of persuading their intended readers to adopt that argument as their own, to form a community around *this* particular understanding of the message of Torah on the question at hand. Second, Reform responsa resemble traditional responsa in that they are halachic texts, drawing their support from the literature of the Jewish legal tradition. The very existence of a genre called "Reform responsa," by far the largest body of writing on issues of Reform religious practice, demonstrates the continuing relevance of halachah to Reform Jewish life. And third, Reform responsa *differ* from traditional responsa. Written by Reform rabbis and speaking to an audience of Reform Jews, they embody a uniquely Reform Jewish discourse, our own way of understanding the halachic tradition and of making meaning within our community. Reform responsa assert our own claim upon the halachic tradition, our refusal to grant to others the exclusive right to interpret that tradition and to say what it means.

One final conviction: this book is but a down payment on the immeasurable debt I owe to my teachers, colleagues, and students.

Among my teachers I give pride of place to Rabbi Solomon B. Freehof, *z"l.* Although I was never granted the privilege of meeting Rabbi Freehof, much less of studying personally with him, his halachic writing has been an inexhaustible source of knowledge and wisdom for me. It was he who insisted that halachah deserves to be a central item in the Reform intellectual curriculum. He is the greatest of all Reform responsa writers; the name "Freehof" to this day is synonymous with our discipline, and we who take part in it stand on his shoulders. Rabbi Walter Jacob, the founder of the Solomon B. Freehof Institute of Progressive Halakhah, succeeded Rabbi Freehof as chair of the CCAR Responsa Committee and invited me to join the committee in 1985. To me (and I'm hardly the only one), he is an exquisite combination of personal qualities: broad learning, compassion, personal integrity, and friendship. I can only hope I have learned something from his example. Professor Ben Zion Wacholder, *z"l,* my dissertation advisor, guided me as I entered the world of traditional halachic scholarship. He taught me to respect that tradition as one of creative brilliance and intellectual rigor equal to that of modern academic scholarship, whose works he insisted I read but urged me to question—always to question. I miss him.

Among my colleagues, I mention first the members of the faculty and administrative staff of the Cincinnati campus of Hebrew Union College– Jewish Institute of Religion. Together we have studied, challenged each other to achieve excellence, and tried to pass our love of learning on to generations of students. We have worked to create and maintain an academic and rabbinical community that I have been proud to call my professional home for many years. I deeply mourn its passing. I am incredibly grateful as well to my fellow members of the Responsa Committee and to those who serve with me on the board of the Freehof Institute. To all these colleagues I say: my life is so much richer for our talks, discussions, learning, and arguments—especially the arguments!

Throughout my career I have been blessed with students whose questions, comments, suggestions, and gentle (well, sometimes not so gentle) criticisms have spurred me to rethink my ideas and to restate them with more clarity and nuance. This book, quite simply, would not exist were it not for them. The Talmud (*Bavli Taanit* 7a) credits Rabbi Chanina with the words, "I have learned much from my teachers and even more from my colleagues, but from my students I have learned the most of all." It's a well-worn and oft-quoted statement. I'd be tempted to dismiss it as trite . . . if it were not so true.

I want to express my gratitude to the staff of CCAR Press who have worked so hard to make this book a reality. These include Rabbi Hara Person, the chief executive officer of the CCAR and past director of CCAR Press (it was she who originally accepted my book proposal, so I owe her big time!); Rafael Chaiken, the director of publications, who has proved most adept at encouraging (read: patiently prodding) at least one distracted author toward completion of a manuscript; Chiara Ricisak, assistant editor; Deborah Smilow, operations manager; Raquel Fairweather-Gallie, marketing and sales manager; Michelle Kwitkin, proofreader; and Scott-Martin Kosofsky, designer. My special thanks go to my editor, Rabbi Annie Villarreal-Belford, whose thoughtful suggestions have contributed immensely to the book's readability, and to Debra Hirsch Corman, my copyeditor, with whom I've worked before and whom I've learned to count on for careful and scrupulous reading of the manuscript. She and Annie have saved me from much error and needless embarrassment.

This book is dedicated to Robin Kosberg: student and teacher of Torah, my wife, and my best friend.

INTRODUCTION

 M Y CONGREGATION does not hold services on Shabbat morning. May we read Torah on Friday night?" "May I take my kids trick-or-treating on Halloween and still be a 'good Jew'?" "My parent wishes to be cremated; may I, as a Reform Jew, object to that?" "My synagogue displays the national flag and the flag of Israel on its bimah; is that an improper mixing of religion and state?" "Is my synagogue obligated to hire union labor for its construction project, even if that results in significant extra expense?" "Is it proper for legal authorities to force-feed political prisoners who have engaged in a hunger strike?" All of these questions, which are addressed in this book, are *Jewish* questions. That is, they touch upon ideas and issues that have been discussed for many centuries in Jewish sacred texts. And like many other questions that are not addressed in this book, they have drawn the attention of Reform rabbis who have endeavored to answer them in Reform responsa.

"Reform responsa" is the name for the Reform Jewish version of "the responsa literature," a vast treasury of rabbinic writing that stretches back nearly fifteen centuries.[1] The Latin word *responsa* originally referred to the ancient Roman practice in which judges and litigants sent difficult questions of law to legal experts who would *respond* in writing with learned opinions. We use the word today to describe a similar genre in Jewish law, the *sh'eilot ut'shuvot*, "questions and answers." That name pretty much says it all. An individual or community sends a *sh'eilah* (question, inquiry) concerning a specific question of halachah (Jewish law) or observance to a recognized rabbinic authority—either one who lives in that community or, frequently, one who lives far away and whose reputation for scholarship has drawn notice. That rabbi writes a *t'shuvah*—responsum (the singular of "responsa")—answering the question. The *t'shuvah* almost always cites the texts of Torah and Jewish law upon which that answer is based, along with the author's reasoning, his or (now) her argumentation supporting that answer. These *t'shuvot* (answers, responses) have been preserved in books or—more recently—in digital form so that future scholars can consult them as part of their learning.[2]

Reform rabbis have been writing their own halachic responsa since the very beginning of the Reform Movement in early nineteenth-century Europe. Those first *t'shuvot* were aimed primarily at offering Jewish legal justification for the various changes that the Reformers introduced into synagogue worship and liturgy.[3] In North America, the Central Conference of American Rabbis (CCAR) established a Responsa Committee in 1906, chaired by Rabbi Kaufmann Kohler, the president of Hebrew Union College, to serve as a central address for Reform Jews seeking thoughtful, source-based answers to questions of religious practice. The leading figure in the history of Reform responsa is indisputably Rabbi Solomon B. Freehof, who chaired the Responsa Committee from 1955 until 1975 and authored eight volumes of *t'shuvot*. More than any other single person, it was Rabbi Freehof who made responsa such a vital and central component of Reform Jewish thought, and for that reason he deserves the title *Rabbeinu*, "our teacher."[4]

"Vital and central"? That description may surprise those Reform Jews who have the impression that their movement is "non-halachic" and believe that Jewish law has little if any role to play in the practice (let alone the "thought") of Reform Judaism. I'll have more to say later about that impression. For the moment, it's enough to point out that in terms of quantity—over thirteen hundred *t'shuvot* have thus far been published by the Responsa Committee (and are available online on the CCAR website)—the responsa are by far the largest body of Reform Jewish writing on issues of practice and observance.[5] The very existence of such a sizable corpus, along with the fact that many prominent Reform rabbis have served on the Responsa Committee during the past hundred or so years, is an argument that we cannot simply dismiss this literature as marginal or idiosyncratic. We should instead accept, as a matter of fact, that Reform rabbis *do* write halachic responsa, and we should ask the proper questions of that reality: *Why* do Reform rabbis write responsa? What makes them specifically *Reform* responsa? What role can these legal texts play in the life of a modern, progressive Jewish movement? And perhaps most importantly: How do Reform responsa *work*? How do they speak to their intended audience, and how do they attempt to exert influence upon the religious practice of Reform Jews today?

The best way to approach these questions is to read the Reform responsa. Now, I'm not proposing that we read all 1,300-plus of them, and this book certainly will not do that. Rather, I've selected a group of *t'shuvot* that, I think, offer a representative sample of this body of work. A critical reading of these *t'shuvot* (I'll explain later what I mean by "critical reading") can help us answer the questions I have asked above and also understand how they seek to make the texts of halachah speak meaningfully to a readership of Reform Jews.

The Halachic Literature

If Reform responsa are an example of halachic literature, we need to begin with a brief discussion of the nature of halachah as that term has functioned in Jewish history and tradition. We usually translate that term as "Jewish law and authoritative practice," but it's more than that. The word is likely derived from the Hebrew root ה-ל-ך, *hei-lamed-chaf*, "to walk," as in "the way that one should walk, the path that one should follow."[6] Halachah therefore defines the Jew's behavior in response to the covenant between God and Israel that was made at Sinai. It speaks to every conceivable aspect of individual and community existence, from prayer, Shabbat, and festival observance, through the realm of personal status (birth and circumcision, marriage, divorce, conversion, burial and mourning), and extending to the conduct of public life (legal practice, commercial and property law, medical ethics, politics and government, and more). Each of these categories comprises countless acts of observance, an intricate complex of rules (*halachot*) and customs (*minhagim*) through which, piece by piece, individuals and communities construct the traditional Jewish world.

Since it concerns itself with the entirety of life, with matters religious as well as conventionally legal, some scholars think that "law" is too narrow a definition for halachah.[7] While they have a point, I use the term "law" in this book because halachah does function like law in some important respects. Like law, halachah contains rules and principles that govern individual and communal conduct. Halachah also resembles law in that it is a *discourse*, a language by which a community creates meaning. Specifically, it is the language of thought and argument that Jews have employed for nearly two millennia to determine how those rules and principles are to be understood and applied. This is why the work of traditional halachic scholarship—locating the applicable rule, interpreting the words of the authoritative texts, and scouring those texts for useful analogies and precedents—closely resembles that of lawyers and judges in other legal systems.

If halachah can be thought of as a tradition of law, then its "constitution" or fundamental legislation is Torah. And by that, we mean the conception of Torah unique to Rabbinic Judaism, the religious legacy of those scholars known as the Rabbis or the Sages who flourished during (roughly) the first five centuries of the Common Era and whose teachings form the foundation of virtually every expression of Judaism today. What set the Rabbis apart from the other Jewish sects of the time was their belief that God, at Sinai, revealed to Moses a twofold Torah—one written, one oral. The Written Torah (*Torah Shebichtav*) is, as that phrase implies, *Scripture*—primarily the Five Books of Moses, which contain most of the Bible's legal content (the mitzvot, God's commandments). The Oral Torah (*Torah Sheb'al Peh*) was to be committed to memory and transmitted in unwritten form by teacher to student from generation to generation. Eventually, this Oral Torah was written down, but it is still called "Oral Torah" to distinguish it from the written one. According to the Rabbis, the Oral Torah defines the mitzvot of the Written Torah and delineates their legal or halachic meaning. Thus, laws transmitted in the Oral Torah are traditionally considered every bit as "Toraitic"—that is, every bit as authoritative—as those appearing in Scripture. The Oral Torah—or, at least, one version of it—was codified in the Mishnah, attributed to Rabbi Y'hudah HaNasi (often referred to simply as "Rabbi") around the year 200 CE. The word *mishnah* means "repetition," which signifies the process of study undertaken by the *Tannaim*, the great Rabbinic teachers of this period who learned and taught their Oral Torah through repetition and memorization. Rabbi edited his Mishnah from among earlier collections of Oral Torah put together by the *Tannaim*. In addition to Oral Torah, the Mishnah contains acts of legislation (*takanot* and *g'zeirot*) attributed to the members of the ancient Great Court (*Beit Din HaGadol*, which exercised legislative as well as judicial powers) as well as rules and practices based upon long-standing custom (*minhag*).

During the next several centuries, Rabbinic scholars in the Land of Israel and in Mesopotamia (Babylonia) engaged in intense study of Rabbi's Mishnah along with other collections of Oral Torah. These sages are called *Amoraim*. The literary product of their study would eventually be redacted by largely anonymous editors into two massive compilations, each called a Talmud: the Jerusalem (or Palestinian) Talmud (*Talmud Y'rushalmi*) and the Babylonian Talmud (*Talmud Bavli*). While the Talmuds are arranged as commentaries on the Mishnah, that description hardly does them justice. The Talmuds investigate, analyze, and debate *all* of the literature of the *Tannaim* (including those texts, called *baraitot*, that Rabbi did not include in his Mishnah), texts created by earlier *Amoraim*, legislative enactments, customs, folklore, nonlegal narrative (aggadah) . . . in short, everything of interest to the Rabbis. They carried on their study in the critical back-and-forth dialectical style (known traditionally by the Aramaic phrase *shakla v'tarya*) that is commonly associated with the adjective "Talmudic." This style is especially evident in the *Talmud Bavli*, a much larger and more extensively edited work than the *Y'rushalmi*. Over time—it's hard to be precise, but certainly by the tenth century CE—the *Talmud Bavli* was redacted (became a book, a fixed text) and accepted by rabbinic scholars as *the* Talmud and, significantly for our purposes, the authoritative source of the halachah.

That Jews turned to the Talmud for legal guidance may seem puzzling, since the Talmud reads nothing at all like a legal code. As its name implies—it is derived from the Hebrew ל-מ-ד, *lamed-mem-dalet*, "to learn"—the Talmud is a study text; it analyzes and debates all aspects of a question of halachah but rarely declares in any explicit way the correct answer. Accordingly, the authoritative halachic decision (*p'sak*) has to be *derived* from the Talmud by its scholarly interpreters, the rabbis who over the course of centuries developed techniques, general principles, and rules of thumb for determining the best interpretations from among the many possibilities arising out of the complex Talmudic discussion. That work—the activity of probing the Talmud in search of the correct understanding of the halachah—produced and continues to produce the voluminous library of post-Talmudic halachic literature: the "codes,"[8] which present the rules of halachah in a more-or-less systematic fashion; the commentaries, works that explicate the Talmud and other halachic texts; and the responsa, the literature of *sh'eilot ut'shuvot*. The codes and commentaries resemble the types of writing that we find in other legal systems. So do the responsa, which we might compare to judicial opinions.

How Responsa Make Meaning
To be precise: a responsum is *not* a judicial opinion, because the rabbi who writes it doesn't usually sit as a judge on a case. The responsum is an "opinion," but it is almost always an *advisory* opinion—the learned essay of a rabbinic scholar whose counsel is sought, perhaps on a case at law between litigants but just as likely on a matter of ritual practice or even, at times, of doctrine and belief. That said, the responsum does resemble the judicial opinion in the way it creates meaning: through *argument*. In the vast majority of responsa, we find not only an answer to the question at hand but also the author's justi-

fication of that answer, arguments as to why this particular answer is the best available solution to the question and why other answers, even if plausible, are not as good. This is so because most *t'shuvot*, like most judicial opinions (especially appellate opinions), are written in response to hard questions, questions for which the authoritative legal sources offer no one obviously correct answer.[9] "Obviously correct" means that the answer is uncontroversial, one that virtually all knowledgeable practitioners of a legal tradition would acknowledge as the right one. Questions that have obviously correct halachic answers are rarely the subjects of responsa, in much the same way that "easy" legal questions don't generally make it to appellate courts. Hard questions arise in the halachah because, for one thing, the circumstances of life are always changing, and the existing halachic texts often do not speak clearly and unequivocally to the new issues that arise from them. But not all hard questions are new ones. Some questions of Jewish practice have been debated for many centuries, yet no general consensus has formed as to their one correct answer. Other issues that seem settled can later become subjects of uncertainty as the community itself changes and the old answers no longer appear sufficient. When confronting a hard question, rabbis—again, like judges—construct their answer by interpreting the existing legal sources, deriving or inferring the solution as it were from between the lines of the texts. And when they find that those texts bear more than one interpretation and thus offer support to more than one answer to the question, rabbis must decide which answer is the best one. That's where argument comes in. Responsa authors do not simply declare that one alternative interpretation is the correct one. They *argue* for that decision, seeking to demonstrate that it represents the best reading of the halachic sources.

As an example of what I mean, let's take a well-known problem of medical ethics: at what point is it morally permissible to discontinue or withdraw life-sustaining medical treatment from a patient who is terminally ill?[10] How does Jewish tradition guide us on this question? Since the biblical and Rabbinic texts make no mention of respirators or any of the other sophisticated lifesaving (or, if you prefer, life-prolonging or death-delaying) technologies of modern medicine, they obviously provide no clear answer to the question. But we do find passages in biblical and Rabbinic literature that, through interpretation, *might* speak to it. One such passage, from the great sixteenth-century halachic code *Shulchan Aruch*, concerns the treatment of the *goseis*, an individual whose death is thought to be imminent. The *goseis*, the text instructs

us, "is like a living person in all respects," which means that we are forbidden to take actions that would hasten their death. Any such action, we are
told, no matter how well-intentioned, is tantamount to murder. On the other
hand, if there exists an "impediment"—some factor that works artificially to
delay the inevitable death of the *goseis*—we are permitted to remove that
impediment and allow the *goseis* to die. Does this passage, which echoes the
distinction we find in modern bioethics between "killing" and "letting die,"
offer a good Jewish textual basis for addressing our problem?[11]

The answer is "yes"—*if* one can make a persuasive analogy between that
text and today's medical situation. And that's a tough call. Here's how the
Shulchan Aruch passage defines an "impediment": "If there is some factor
that delays death [literally, 'that causes a delay in the soul's departure'], for
example a knocking noise close to the house, such as that of a woodchopper,
or if there is salt on their tongue . . . one is permitted to remove it." All this,
of course, strikes us as superstition, since we no longer believe that staccato
sounds or salt on the tongue possesses death-delaying properties. Yet many
contemporary *poskim* (halachic authorities) do draw the analogy. They argue
that today's technologically sophisticated treatments sometimes function
precisely as do the salt and the woodchopper in the *Shulchan Aruch* text. That
is, at a certain point these treatments no longer fulfill a medical purpose but
merely impede the patient's otherwise imminent death. Thus, we can legitimately apply the text to our case: those technologically sophisticated treatments, because they have become the functional equivalent of the salt and
the woodchopper, may be withdrawn. Other authorities, meanwhile, deny
the analogy. In their view, even if we could look past the outdated "science"
of the *Shulchan Aruch* passage, we would have to acknowledge a fundamental difference between the "technologies" described in the text and those in
use today. The woodchopper and salt, however successful in delaying death,
were never considered "medicine," legitimate treatment for disease. They
should not be compared to the respirator and other modern techniques that
are defined as "medicine" and are legitimately part of today's therapeutic
toolbox. Moreover, even if we do accept the analogy, the precedent of the
woodchopper and the salt specifically addresses the situation of the *goseis*,
whose death is expected at any moment. Can it be said to apply to the case
of a terminally ill patient who wishes to discontinue all life-sustaining medical treatment even though they may be weeks or months (or longer) away
from death?

It follows that the "correct" answer to our question—does the *Shulchan Aruch* passage offer useful guidance today for the treatment of the terminally ill?—is controversial, because the text can support either a positive or a negative answer. This doesn't mean that there is *no* answer to the question or that either answer is equally good (or bad). Responsa on this subject, written by rabbis from across the Jewish religious spectrum, do take a stand. They assert that *one* answer—"yes" or "no"—is better than the other, principally because they either accept or reject the analogy between the *Shulchan Aruch* passage and our contemporary situation. The point is that they *justify* that acceptance or rejection. A responsum—at least, a *good* responsum, one that wishes to be taken seriously within the Jewish community of interpretation[12]—doesn't simply declare a position on this or any other hard question of Jewish practice. It supports its ruling with arguments as to why its answer represents the best understanding of the message of Torah and tradition on the question at hand.

We might define a responsum, then, as *an argued claim of meaning* upon the Jewish textual tradition. It sets forth a *claim* that the tradition *means* something, that it answers a question in one particular way and not in some other way. And it *argues* that claim: "This is what I think the texts of Torah mean, and this is why I think so." Argument is characteristic of responsa; we might say that argument is the way these texts make meaning. More than that: argument is essential to the very notion of tradition itself.

As used in this book, the word "tradition" is not a synonym for "old" or "the voice of the past." True, a tradition—Jewish or otherwise—encompasses the past, which expresses itself through the old texts we study and the customs and teachings that we have received from preceding generations. But we do "tradition" a disservice if we imagine it as a set of fixed rules, behaviors, and ideas imposed by the dead upon the living. I prefer to think of "tradition" as it is defined by the philosopher Alasdair MacIntyre: "an historically extended, socially embodied argument, and an argument precisely in part about the goods which constitute that tradition."[13] This argument is *historical* because it extends over time. It is *social* because it takes place within the particular community who engage in it. And the argument is over the *goods*—the ideas, values, and practices through which a particular community constructs its notions of the true, the beautiful, or the right. In our case, the "Jewish tradition" is the never-ending argument, carried out within the Jewish community and people, over the meaning of the texts to which the

Jewish community has historically looked to define the proper way for Jews to live. Accordingly, "Jewish tradition" has never enjoyed a fixed, determinate meaning. As an ongoing argument, it is rather the vehicle by which what we know as Torah has grown and evolved over time. To be sure, Orthodox Jewish doctrine tends to hold that the meaning of the Torah does not evolve but is eternal and unchanging: the meaning of the text lies objectively (if implicitly) *there*, between its lines, and our task as students of Torah is to "turn the Torah over and over again" (*Mishnah Avot* 5:22) until we discover it. But even among the most fervently Orthodox communities (to say nothing of Reform and other non-Orthodox Jewish communities), the *understanding* of the Torah's message always changes, as each generation reads Torah anew, argues the meaning of the texts, and applies those meanings to answer new (and hard) questions.[14]

The rabbinic responsum is a sustained argument or series of arguments (a responsum may offer several reasons), independent of each other, to support its conclusion that its author(s) hope will persuade its intended audience to understand the halachah in *this* particular way, even though the texts could support other interpretations. To the extent that it achieves this goal, the *t'shuvah* will be cited by later scholars as evidence of the correct interpretation of the halachah. On the other hand, the *t'shuvah* may fail to persuade. Frequently the *sho-eil*—the one who asked the question—will respond to the *t'shuvah* by seeking clarification ("I'm not sure that I follow your reasoning") or by contesting the arguments of the *meishiv*, its author. Even if the *sho-eil* seems satisfied with the answer, there's no guarantee that all will be convinced. Other halachic authorities will issue their own responsa, perhaps independently of the original *sh'eilah* (since more than one person or community will seek guidance on a similar question) or perhaps in direct response to it. These responsa may dispute the *meishiv*'s decision, sparking a scholarly dispute—a *machloket*—that can last for generations. Halachic argument, in other words, can play out over a long time, with consensus emerging (if it ever does) only after many years of debate. Yet despite these complications, this ongoing tradition of argument is *the* way in which Jews historically determined and continue to determine just what the texts of Torah have to teach concerning questions of religious practice.

Reform Responsa and the Halachah

Reform responsa resemble traditional responsa in some important ways.

They are written in response to specific questions (*sh'eilot*) of Jewish religious practice, usually hard questions that do not admit of obviously correct answers. A Reform responsum makes an argued claim of meaning upon the tradition, seeking to persuade its intended audience that one particular answer to that hard question represents the best interpretation of what Jewish tradition teaches on the issue. And like a traditional *t'shuvah*, a Reform responsum is a work of halachah, drawing its evidence and constructing its arguments from Jewish legal sources.

This last similarity evokes the question I raised earlier: why do Reform rabbis, members of what some describe as a non-halachic or post-halachic Jewish movement, write halachic responsa?[15] We Reform Jews do not consider ourselves bound to the authority of Jewish law, a corpus of writings mostly composed by an all-male ancient and medieval scholarly elite who did not share the modern and progressive commitments that define our religious outlook. Chief among these commitments is our insistence upon personal religious autonomy—the freedom of individuals and communities to make their own religious decisions—informed by the tradition but not obligated by the rulings of rabbinic jurists. In the words of Rabbi Eugene Borowitz, the preeminent Reform Jewish religious thinker of the twentieth century, Reform Jews "do not believe that God gave the Written and Oral Law and remain unpersuaded that the Jewish desirability of the halachic process should lead them to constrain their freedom by its rulings."[16] Other commitments include (1) our affirmation of gender equality; (2) our recognition of the moral equality of all persons (specifically that the Torah's moral commandments, those involving obligations toward "your neighbor," "your fellow," "your brother," and so on, govern our conduct with all people and not only with other Jews); (3) our acceptance of innovation in religious observance; and (4) our positive attitude toward cultural change. These values, to put it mildly, do not easily square with the outlook of what we call "Orthodox" halachah, and in all cases of conflict we insist that our commitments take precedence. How then can we speak of "Reform Judaism" and "halachah" in the same sentence? What role can halachic responsa play in the life of our movement?

There are, broadly speaking, two answers we can give to these questions.[17] First, we'd note that the concept of "personal religious autonomy," when taken to its logical extreme, leads to conclusions we would find unacceptable. If we are radically free to make whatever religious decisions we please, with no limitations placed upon that freedom by any factor external to ourselves—be it God, Torah, Jewish tradition, or Jewish community—then there are no valid *Jewish* grounds upon which to evaluate, let alone critique, that decision. Reform Judaism would have to accept *any* such personal choice as equally good or correct. And that conclusion does not sit well with serious Reform Jews. Rabbi Borowitz, in particular, doesn't like it: "I am regularly exasperated by an American Jewry that, wallowing in freedom, prates piously of the sanctity of personal choice and uses it mainly to sanction casual nonobservance and flabby ethics."[18] For Borowitz, and for all serious Reform Jews, true Jewish religious autonomy means that we exercise our freedom within *limits*, particularly the limits of *covenant* where God, as it were, is our partner in determining what we shall do. For our part, we would say that a *good* Reform Jewish religious decision is one made by the individual or community exercising their autonomy in thoughtful conversation with the Jewish tradition.

Secondly, we reject the notion that Reform Judaism is "non-halachic." On the contrary: there's no such thing as a "non-halachic" Judaism, because halachah is central to all Jewish observance, including *Reform* Jewish observance. Our teacher Rabbi Solomon Freehof makes this point powerfully in the introduction to the first collected volume of his responsa.[19] There, he draws a sharp contrast between the ideology of the Reform Movement during its "classical" period (roughly from the last decades of the nineteenth century through the first half of the twentieth century) and the facts of Reform Jewish religious life.[20] The classical Reformers, says Freehof, looked upon the Bible as the foundation of their religion, demoting the Talmud and the halachic literature to a marginal status. Yet "the self-description of Reform as being solely Biblical was simply not true. All of Reform Jewish life in all its observances was actually post-Biblical in origin."[21] The *practice* of Reform, the way we have lived out Judaism on a daily, weekly, and seasonal basis, remains firmly rooted in the Rabbinic (that is to say the *halachic*) tradition.

This sweeping insight may be surprising to many readers, so let's unpack it a bit. Consider how we Reform Jews conduct synagogue worship. With all the changes that we have introduced into the traditional prayer service, the framework of Reform synagogue liturgy—the preliminary blessings (*Birchot HaShachar*), the passages of psalms (*P'sukei D'zimrah*), the recitation of the *Sh'ma* and of the *T'filah*, the reading of Torah and haftarah, the recitation of *Kaddish*, the very names of the services (*Shacharit, Minchah, Arvit*)—is the one handed down to us in the Talmudic and halachic literature.

Now let's think about our Shabbat and holiday observance. We Reform Jews have largely departed from the traditional models, especially the specific details of the prohibition against "work" (*m'lachah*) on those days. Still, the many practices that characterize our celebrations as uniquely *Jewish*—lighting Shabbat candles, saying *Kiddush* over wine, making *Havdalah* when Shabbat and holidays end, dwelling in the sukkah, "taking" the *lulav* and *etrog* on Sukkot, celebrating the Passover seder and eating matzah, sounding the shofar, fasting on Yom Kippur, kindling the Chanukah lamp, reading *M'gillat Esther* on Purim—are structured and defined in Talmudic and halachic texts. When it comes to the rituals that mark the important moments of the life cycle, Reform Judaism has introduced a wide range of new ceremonies. But the foundations of our Reform life-cycle rituals and liturgy—circumcision and covenant ceremonies, coming-of-age observances, weddings, funerals, and mourning practices—are set down in the halachic literature. Much the same can be said of Reform Judaism's ethical teachings and practice. As Rabbi Freehof reminds us, while the Bible and especially the prophetic literature offers us stirring words of moral exhortation, the how-to details of Jewish ethical life are worked out in the Talmud, the halachic codes, and the rabbinic responsa. If we want to identify a substantive and detailed *Jewish* teaching on any significant question of business ethics, medical ethics, communal governance, or political obligation, we have no option but to consult the Rabbinic and halachic sources, because that is where substance and detail—and the arguments over the latter—are to be found. In short, halachah is everywhere in our supposedly non-halachic form of Judaism. It is impossible to imagine Reform Jewish practice—ritual or moral—apart from its close connection to the Jewish legal tradition.

What accounts for our continuing attachment to halachah? Two reasons, I think, are essential. The first is the two-sided nature of Reform's approach to Judaism. We often describe our movement in terms of its embrace of religious innovation and creativity. Yet at the same time we want our religious practice to be an authentic expression of Jewish tradition. (What "authentic" means is a subject we'll address below.) It is no coincidence that traditional forms of practice persist in Reform Judaism; it is *intentional*, the natural result of our affirmation of the Rabbinic heritage alongside our acceptance of innovation. This is evident in most of the platforms adopted by the CCAR as broad doctrinal statements for North American Reform Judaism.[22] True, the earliest of these, the Pittsburgh Platform of 1885, takes the opposite stance, declaring that "we recognize in the Mosaic legislation a system of training the Jewish people for its mission during its national life in Palestine, and today we accept as binding only its moral laws, and maintain only such ceremonies as elevate and sanctify our lives, but reject all such as are not adapted to the views and habits of modern civilization." It's hard to imagine a more ringing expression of the classical Reform outlook. But the subsequent platforms (Columbus, 1937; San Francisco, 1976; and Pittsburgh II, 1999) turn away from the radical stance of the first Pittsburgh document by acknowl-edging the importance of traditional Jewish ritual practice to a rich and vital Jewish life. Each of them in its own language asserts that this continuing attachment to traditional practice is integral to our Reform understanding of Judaism. The 1999 (and most recent) platform, for example, includes the following language: "We are committed to the ongoing study of the whole array of mitzvot and to the fulfillment of those that address us as individuals and as a community. Some of these mitzvot, sacred obligations, have long been observed by Reform Jews; others, both ancient and modern, demand renewed attention as the result of the unique context of our own times." Like the 1937 and 1976 platforms, this one seeks to respond to what we might call the essential challenge of Reform: how do we forge a religious practice that is both modern *and* traditional, one that strikes an appropriate balance between these two governing affirmations of Reform Jewish life?

The second reason flows directly from the first: an "authentically" Jew-ish religious practice is one that is grounded in the tradition, a practice that speaks to us from the historical experience of our people. And by "tradition," again, we mean the halachic tradition, because halachah is the discourse of Jewish practice. It is primarily in the halachic literature that the Jews have for the last two thousand years discussed, argued, and reached their (often tentative and temporary) conclusions on all issues of religious observance and sacred action.[23] Halachah is the textual language through which the Jews have worked out their answers to the question "What does God, speaking through the medium of Torah, want us to do?" Therefore, if we want to know how the "Jewish tradition" addresses *any* question of ritual or ethical prac-tice, then we have no option but to consult and to study the halachic liter-ature. Indeed, halachah is the indispensable source of information for the making of "informed choice," which we have declared to be the necessary prerequisite to the exercise of our autonomy. In the words of the CCAR's San Francisco Platform (1976): "Jewish obligation begins with the informed will of every individual. . . . Within each area of Jewish observance Reform Jews are called upon to confront the claims of Jewish tradition, however differently perceived, and to exercise their individual autonomy, choosing and creating on the basis of commitment and knowledge." There can be no autonomous choice in any meaningful sense of the term unless that choice is *informed* by Jewish knowledge. And when it comes to matters of practice, the Jewish knowledge we require is to be found primarily in the texts of the halachah.

For these reasons, halachah does not conflict with our commitment to personal religious autonomy. On the contrary, if we wish to more perfectly realize our autonomy, to meet the prerequisite of informed choice, and to build a Reform practice that is fully conversant with "Jewish tradition," we must take halachah seriously and engage ourselves with its texts.

That's what Reform responsa do. Each *t'shuvah* examines its *sh'eilah* through the lens of the relevant textual sources, centuries of discussion as set forth in the codes, commentaries, and responsa literature. Each *t'shuvah* evaluates this textual material and the arguments supporting both or all potential answers to the question. And each one presents the answer that its author or authors think represents the best understanding of the message of Torah and tradition on the issue under discussion. Every Reform responsum offers a rationale for its answer (some, no doubt, do this better than others), seeking to justify its decision to its readers and to persuade them to adopt this particular understanding of what the tradition would teach us.

How Reform Responsa Are Different

Now it should be clear why Reform rabbis write responsa. We have yet to consider, though, just what makes these texts uniquely *Reform* responsa, as distinguished from responsa that could have been written by rabbis from other Jewish movements. I think that three factors stand out.

The first is the absence of formal authority: Reform responsa exert no obligatory force upon anyone, including the individuals who ask the question. This is in keeping with the personal autonomy doctrine as well as with Rabbi Freehof's famous formulation that, for us, halachah serves as "guidance, not governance."[24] No Reform Jew or Reform Jewish community or organization is bound by the decision (*p'sak*) of any Reform *t'shuvah*. On the other hand, a Reform responsum can exert *informal* authority to the extent that its readers find its argument persuasive and accept it as the sort of "guidance" of which Rabbi Freehof speaks. All of this sets Reform responsa and halachic writing apart from their Orthodox counterparts. While the author of an Orthodox responsum has no way to enforce their *p'sak*, Orthodox communities tend to recognize an obligation of obedience: if one submits a question to a rabbi for halachic adjudication, one is expected to accept the answer as binding. Reform responsa differ, too, from those published by the Committee on Jewish Law and Standards (CJLS) of the Conservative Movement's Rabbinical Assembly. The *t'shuvot* of the CJLS are seen as official halachic positions of the Conservative Movement, although ultimate halachic authority in Conservative congregations rests formally with the *mara d'atra*, the local rabbi acting as ultimate halachic decisor (*poseik*). Reform responsa do not enjoy such "official" status.

The second thing unique to Reform responsa is their authorship and audience. Reform responsa are written by Reform rabbis for a Reform Jewish readership, even though others may find interest in them. This point may seem obvious, but it's of critical importance. One of the first principles of rhetoric (speech or writing aimed at persuasion) is that an argument is always directed toward a particular audience composed of individuals who, in the opinion of the speaker or writer, will be open to this argument and may find it convincing.[25] The primary audience for Reform responsa consists of those Reform Jews who are committed to the progressive values that define our movement and at the same time care deeply about what Jewish tradition teaches concerning issues of religious practice. This twofold characterization helps explain why our responsa are halachic texts. As we've indicated, the "Jewish tradition" on matters of religious practice is the Jewish *legal* tradition, expressed in the literature of the halachah. It also helps explain why Reform responsa almost never base their conclusions *exclusively* upon those halachic texts. Unlike an audience of Orthodox Jews, a Reform audience will not likely be persuaded to accept an answer simply because "the Torah says so" or "thus it is written in the *Shulchan Aruch*." They will want to know why *this* answer, as opposed to some other, is the best answer for *Reform* Jews— the answer that best reflects the values that we associate with the Reform Jewish outlook. Reform responsa are written with the goal of persuading this specific readership. Whether a particular responsum actually achieves that goal is another matter. But its language and its arguments will be framed so that such an audience *can* be persuaded by them and, at any rate, will take them seriously.

The third factor that distinguishes our *t'shuvot* as "Reform" is their engagement with the tradition of Reform Judaism. In addition to traditional and Orthodox halachic literature, our responsa cite the halachic writings of the Reform Movement itself: earlier Reform responsa, resolutions of the CCAR and of the Union for Reform Judaism (URJ), guidebooks to Jewish practice published by those organizations, the various CCAR rabbis' manuals, the halachic writings of Liberal and Progressive rabbis from countries outside of North America, and articles and studies on halachic issues published in the *CCAR Yearbook*. (Orthodox responsa, as you might imagine, tend to show no interest in these Reform sources.) This literature was written by authors we regard as our teachers, and it serves us as a vital resource of thought and direction. That doesn't mean that we are obligated to follow their rulings. As a matter of theory, Jewish law doesn't recognize a formal doctrine of binding precedent. Although present-day *poskim* are as a general rule expected to show humility and deference before the words of their predecessors, they are not required to follow a previous decision merely because some past authority decided that way, particularly when they disagree with the reasoning upon which that ruling was based.[26] And as a matter of practice, Reform responsa writers will not hesitate to disagree with prior Reform *t'shuvot* that they believe to be outdated, faulty, or poorly reasoned, just as they dissent from rulings of the traditional halachah that are irreconcilable with our most deeply held beliefs and commitments. Still, *all* halachic study takes place within an atmosphere of respect for the past, with the acknowledgment that we are able to do what we do because we stand upon the shoulders of giants. And among *our* giants are the scholars of our own movement.

How to Read a Responsum

You need no special training or preparation to read Reform responsa, which are written to be accessible not only to rabbis but also to the educated non-specialist. But as this book's title suggests, I have in mind a particular way of "reading Reform responsa." I call it a *critical* reading, which does not mean that you disagree with a responsum's decision (though you very well might), but rather indicates an approach that resembles "literary criticism."

At first glance, we probably don't think of rabbinic responsa as "literature," a term we usually associate with novels, poetry, and drama. By that same token, we also don't think of legal texts as literature. Yet in recent decades legal scholars associated with the academic movement called "Law and Literature" have sought to bring the tools of literary criticism to bear upon the study of those texts. A favorite object of their attention is the judicial opinion, which as we've seen is similar to the responsum in some important ways. While most readers are interested in the judicial opinion primarily for its decision—its bottom line—and the reasons the opinion gives for it, Law and Literature scholars hold that the judicial opinion is much more than that. As one of them puts it:

> But what are a court's "reasons"? Not just reified propositions, but its whole method of thought as it is exemplified in the opinion, its ways of imagining the world and its own role within it, its intellectual and literary procedures, its sense of the shape of a proper argument, including what counts as a conclusion. It invites lawyers and judges in the future to think and speak as it does. For in every case, the court is saying not only "this is the right outcome for this case," but also "this is the right way to think and talk about this case, and others like it." ... Action with words is after all a form of action, in relation both to a cultural inheritance and to other people, and it is charged with ethical and political significance. The excellence of the opinion is not one of "mere style," but an excellence of thought, represented and enacted in language in such a way as to live in the minds of others.[27]

That is, in reading the judicial opinion we ought to look past its technical verbiage, its footnotes, and citations, and perceive it as a *composition*—a crafted essay that seeks to create community with other minds. It acts out a way of thinking and speaking about the question at hand and about the law in general, seeking to bring others to its point of view. In this sense a judicial opinion is "literature," a literary *performance* of the judicial role, and it can be evaluated on that basis—does it perform its role well, not so well, or badly?—even if the criteria for its evaluation are necessarily different from those we use for novels and poems.

My claim is that, in a similar way, a rabbinic responsum is much more than the decision it reaches. It too is a composition, a work of literary artifice, a model of how to think and speak about the issue at hand. The authors seek to persuade us, the readers, to share that model, to view the question in this way rather than in some other way. Like all authors, they employ a literary strategy designed to bring us along, to invite us to enter their world and to share this particular understanding of Torah and Judaism. That's what I mean when I describe a responsum as "literature." To read this literature critically means, as with literary criticism generally, that we read the text in a reasoned way, searching out the techniques it uses to create meaning, with the goal that we might "make what is implicit in a book finely explicit."[28] What we're after here is to discover not just what the responsum *says* but how it *works*— its thought process, the way it thinks about the question, and the literary, intellectual, and rhetorical techniques it utilizes to bring us to share its way of thinking and persuade us to accept its conclusion.

Three of these techniques deserve special mention.

FRAMING

What is a responsum "about"? The simple answer is that it's about the *sh'ei-lah*, the question being asked. But that simple answer overlooks the degree to which the responsum actually chooses its subject, characterizing it in one way rather than any other way. We can call this process "framing," the making of a lens through which the responsum perceives the question. Framing is a necessary element of any act of communication. Before we can talk intelligently about a subject, we need to know what that subject *is*; we must define its terms and set its parameters for ourselves and our conversation partners. Framing is a necessity, but it always involves a choice that the speaker or writer makes between or among alternatives. By choosing one way rather than another, the *t'shuvah* shapes the direction of the argument and prepares us for the answer it will reach. Like the judge's opinion, a responsum "makes a fundamental decision about the question . . . and the wording in that first decision controls all others."[29]

NARRATIVE

Rabbis, like all of us, tell stories. Just as lawyers and judges resort to narrative to organize their data into meaningful form, a *t'shuvah* uses story to arrange the otherwise disorganized factoids of Jewish law—the mass of texts, rules, principles, commentary, and decisions of past authorities—into a pattern that suggests direction and purpose. Sometimes this story is told explicitly; sometimes it's implied or hinted at in the text. And as with framing, such a narrative is the product of *choice*, because the author(s) could reasonably have told other stories that would have given a different shape to their material and have supported different conclusions. That a rabbi tells *this* story, as opposed to some other story about Torah and halachah, often has to do with the rabbi's deeply held value commitments, be they theological, ethical, cultural, or ideological. And it is largely through those values that a rabbi will understand the meaning and message of the texts upon which the decision is formally based. The critical reader's job is to uncover and identify the stories and the value commitments at work in the responsum, either openly or between the lines.

ARGUMENT

A responsum, as we've said, is all about argument, the effort to persuade its readers that its *p'sak* (ruling, decision) is the correct one, or at least the best available one. Critical readers will examine the quality of that argument. They will ask, for example: Is the argument *cogent*: does the responsum's conclusion follow smoothly from the texts and sources that it cites? Is the argument *strong*: does the text show confidence in it, or does it admit to serious uncertainty? Finally, is the argument *generous*: does the responsum present the opposing position fully and treat it with respect? On the simplest level, this generosity is a matter of self-interest. It's easy to knock down a weak argument. But if a responsum is to win over its intended readers, it must refute the best and strongest version of the position it opposes. Otherwise, those readers may dismiss its argument as naïve or trite. Yet "generosity" has deeper implications. Respect breeds respect: when we treat the other side's position as a reasonable one that deserves serious consideration, we build community. When a *t'shuvah* argues with generosity, it tells the reader that both sides—"they" no less than "we"—are engaged in a common intellectual and religious enterprise, and that both are willing to be persuaded if the other side's argument proves stronger and more convincing. Not all responsa meet this test. Sometimes a *t'shuvah* will simply declare its truth and brusquely dismiss the opposing position as weak, not to be taken seriously. A responsum might use such language in all sincerity, but critical readers should ask whether this lack of generosity toward the opposing point of view masks the responsum's uncertainty that its own arguments can withstand the scrutiny of fair debate. Besides, we should remember that *dis*respect breeds disrespect and that a lack of generosity toward the other viewpoint and its supporting argumentation is destructive of the sort of community and open dialogue that a healthy responsa process seeks to build.

In examining these trees, however, let us not lose sight of the forest. A responsum uses these and other literary and rhetorical techniques not only to justify a particular answer but also to invite us to define our Judaism in that particular way. To put this differently, a responsum speaks to an audience composed of readers who, it hopes, will accept "its ways of imagining the world," who are open to *this* framing, to *this* story, and to *these* arguments.[30] Whether or not the *t'shuvah* persuades us that its decision is correct, its real goal is something more: it seeks to create community. It calls upon us to share its way of thinking and speaking about Torah and Judaism. Accordingly, one who reads a responsum critically should focus upon this larger issue: what sort of Jew—indeed, what sort of *person*—is this responsum asking us to be?

The Plan of This Book
In the ten chapters that follow, we'll apply this sort of close and critical reading to fifteen Reform responsa. I've chosen these *t'shuvot* both because I think their subject matter is intrinsically interesting (I hope you'll agree) and because I think they are good material for the sort of reading strategy that I've described—namely, to discover a responsum's thought process. My discussion will follow the text of each responsum, which you can access either online or in this book's Appendix. These texts, like all responsa, are full of citations to the Talmud, Jewish legal works, and earlier responsa, but they don't quote those references in full. In this book, I often bring forward the full texts of these citations, especially when they are central to the responsum's argument, so that you can see and explore the original references. Our goal will be to inquire as to how responsa make meaning and create Torah: how they change the tradition from what it was to something new, how they make the old texts speak to questions that the authors of those texts could scarcely have imagined. And though we shall be reading *Reform* responsa, let's remember that this is how Jews have always created Torah. This is how for two thousand years Torah has constantly renewed itself, how its texts have spoken to new questions and changing times, and how they have never become stagnant, reduced to a single, fixed meaning.

It's what the responsa literature is all about.

CHAPTER ONE
EMBRACING REFORMS
Torah Reading on Friday

Rabbi Solomon B. Freehof is the leading figure in the history of Reform responsa writing. The eight volumes of his collected *t'shuvot* continue to serve as an important resource for all who are interested in questions of Jewish religious practice. Much of the guidance he sets forth in those books remains relevant and compelling today. And even when his successors find themselves disagreeing with his conclusions, they continue to regard him as *Rabbeinu*, "our teacher," because it is Freehof more than anyone else who shows us just what it means to write a Reform responsum and how to uncover the deep connections between Reform Jewish religious life and the Jewish legal tradition.

For an example, let's read his response to the following question (the responsum can be read in full on pages 169–71):

> At one of the smaller American colleges, because of the heavy student schedule it seems impossible to have services other than on Friday night. The students, therefore, have services at that time and also read the Torah. The local rabbi prohibits the reading of the Torah on Friday night (which is not a traditional Torah-reading time) and declares that reading the Torah at this traditionally unauthorized time would make the Torah unfit for proper use at regular services. Is this judgment of the rabbi justified by the legal tradition?[1]

While this *sh'eilah* speaks of a Jewish college student group, the situation it describes is familiar to many Reform congregations that have experienced difficulty holding Shabbat services on Saturday morning. The problem was especially acute during the late nineteenth and early twentieth centuries, when most Jews were employed in occupations that required Saturday work. Facing sparse attendance on Saturday, a growing number of Reform congregations, among them some of the largest in the movement, began to schedule their major weekly worship services on Sunday mornings.[2] These synagogues took pains to emphasize that they were not imitating Christian religious practice. They were not, they insisted, observing a "Sunday Sabbath"; with rare exceptions, these services used a weekday liturgy and did not include passages specific to Shabbat worship. Most Reform communities, however, while agreeing that something must be done in response to anemic attendance on Saturday mornings, preferred to keep their principal worship on Shabbat rather than move it to the Christian holy day. Following the suggestion of Rabbi Isaac Mayer Wise, they established instead a "late" Friday evening service—that is, a service scheduled after dinnertime, when the entire family could attend—that featured a sermon and, not infrequently, a Torah reading. The late Friday evening service quickly became a familiar feature of Reform worship, and it remains so in many congregations.[3] But this raises a problem: as the *sh'eilah* indicates, the public Torah reading (*k'riat haTorah*) does not traditionally take place on Friday night, let alone on Sunday morning. Does Jewish law permit the reading of Torah at Friday evening services? The local rabbi in this case thinks it does not and has gone so far as to prohibit the reading of Torah on Friday night. Our *sh'eilah*, submitted by a prominent Reform rabbi named Rabbi Stanley R. Brav,[4] asks Freehof whether the local rabbi's ruling is justified by "the legal tradition"—the halachah.

This question poses an interesting challenge. There is no text in any of the authoritative legal codes that permits the reading of Torah at a Shabbat evening service. But there is no text that explicitly forbids that practice either. And while the local rabbi has prohibited the Torah reading, our *sh'eilah* doesn't provide his source or explain his reasoning. How then can we test the soundness of his decision and determine whether it is in fact "justified"? Relying upon his deep knowledge of the traditional responsa literature, Rabbi Freehof locates a *t'shuvah* that, like the decision of the local rabbi in our case, prohibits the reading of Torah at non-customary times and that does offer sources and arguments. Its author is Rabbi Naftali Tzvi Yehudah Berlin (1816–93), also known as "the Netziv," an acronym formed from the initials of his name. Given Berlin's stature as a halachic authority—he was head of the storied Lithuanian yeshivah of Volozhyn and the author of several well-regarded works of Talmudic scholarship—we can presume that he will bring forth the strongest possible halachic reasoning in support of his ruling. If it then turns out that his arguments are not persuasive, Freehof will be able to claim that the widespread Reform practice to read Torah on Friday night is *not* prohibited by halachah.

The question addressed to Rabbi Berlin (*Responsa Meishiv Davar*, vol. 1, no. 16) by coincidence originated in Cincinnati, where Rabbi Brav would later serve a congregation. A local synagogue held a dedication ceremony for its new ark on a Sunday. At the ceremony, which involved a procession of Torah scrolls, one of the synagogue's members wanted to open one of the scrolls and read from it. A rabbi in attendance (who appears not to have been the rabbi of that synagogue) objected to the reading on various grounds and has submitted the issue to Rabbi Berlin. The objecting rabbi based his argument on the principle *bal tosif*, according to which we are not permitted to add to the stock of observances that the Torah commands. The principle is founded upon Deuteronomy 13:1, "Be careful to observe only that which I enjoin upon you: neither add to it nor take away from it." From that verse, the Rabbis learn (Babylonian Talmud, *Rosh HaShanah* 28b and *Sifrei* to Deuteronomy 13:1) that a *kohein* (priest) who blesses the congregation is forbidden to add anything to the text of the Priestly Benediction prescribed in the Torah (Numbers 6:24–26) and that we are not to add a fifth thread to the tzitzit (the fringes at the four corners of garments; Numbers 15:37–41) or a fifth species of plant to the four specified for the *lulav* and *etrog* (Leviticus 23:40). Accordingly, the Cincinnati rabbi argues that it is also forbidden to add any days to the traditional schedule of Torah readings. But Rabbi Berlin rejects this argument. He notes that the prohibition *bal tosif* applies only to commandments of the Torah itself (*d'oraita*), whereas the public reading from the Torah is based upon an enactment of the ancient Rabbis (*d'rabanan*) described in Babylonian Talmud, *Bava Kama* 82a. In other words, reading Torah on a Sunday (or on a Friday night) may be an addition to traditionally accepted Jewish ritual, but it is not the sort of "addition" prohibited under the category of *bal tosif*. Still, Berlin declares that the Sunday Torah reading should be forbidden on different grounds, namely the prohibition against reciting a *b'rachah l'vatalah*, a blessing that is "unnecessary," out of place, or repetitious. The "unnecessary blessing" is a serious transgression in traditional ritual law; some opinions hold that it violates the Torah's commandment against taking God's name in vain (Exodus 20:7).[5] And since we recite blessings both before and after the formal public reading of the Torah, to read it at a time when the reading is not required by halachah necessarily means that we would recite "unnecessary blessings." For this reason, Rabbi Berlin concludes, the Cincinnati rabbi was right in objecting to the Sunday morning Torah reading. He expresses puzzlement that the man who insisted on the reading would take such an action in the absence of any halachic sources that would support him. If he is at all knowledgeable about Jewish law, says Rabbi Berlin, let him cite a source. "At any rate, at present I know of no source that would support him."

This ruling, at first glance, does nothing to help Rabbi Freehof's case. Rabbi Berlin, after all, comes out *against* reading the Torah at nontraditional times, which seemingly reinforces the prohibition issued by the rabbi of the college town. But as Freehof reads that ruling, Rabbi Berlin is in fact unsure of his decision. Freehof stresses this point three times:

1. "But even so [Berlin] is not too firm on the matter, since he asks the rabbi whether the lay leader is a learned man. If he is, then he may have a reason for this or some other precedent. But if the man is ignorant, he should be brushed aside for wanting such a novelty."

2. "It can be seen from [Berlin's] responsum that it is far from certain in the mind of this great scholar whether the reading of the Torah and the recital of the Torah blessings are really prohibited. He admits the possibility that the man who wanted it may have had some justification. But, of course, in accordance with the general Orthodox mood, he objects to any unauthorized novelty (that is, if it really is unauthorized)."

3. "To sum up: While Orthodoxy naturally objects to any new custom, it is far from clear (judging by Naftali Berlin's response) that it is forbidden to read the Torah at other than the regular times."

If Berlin is uncertain that the halachah actually forbids this practice, then the only real basis for rejecting it is the "Orthodox mood," the tendency within Orthodoxy that objects to any novelty or innovation in ritual practice. A "mood," of course, is not identical to the "law." And since we Reform Jews do not share in that mood, that Orthodox opposition to new customs, we are not bound by the prohibition. Freehof has therefore defended the common Reform practice: to read Torah on Friday night does not violate any rule or principle of Jewish law. And while we don't know whether the college group that originally asked the question is a *Reform* student community, Rabbi Freehof's conclusion may be reassuring to them too.

The problem, though, is that the "local rabbi" (perhaps of a congregation that is not connected with the college) has ruled against the Friday evening Torah reading. Again, since that rabbi doesn't provide any sources for his prohibition, there is no way to determine its halachic basis. However, we'll recall that the local rabbi has declared that the Torah becomes ritually unfit for use (*pasul*) should it be read on Friday night. This, it turns out, is a major blunder; the statement, says Freehof, "with all due respect to him, is absurd." The conditions that render a Torah scroll ritually unfit are spelled out in the sources, and reading the scroll at an improper time is not one of these conditions. He refers to the Talmudic statement "words of Torah do not contract impurity" (Babylonian Talmud, *B'rachot* 22a), which leads to the statement in the *Shulchan Aruch* (*Yoreh Dei-ah* 282:9) that "any person who is ritually impure . . . is permitted to touch a Torah scroll and to read from it." The upshot is that, in Rabbi Freehof's words, "The Torah scroll . . . is not so easily made unfit." The rabbi's ruling is "totally unjustified," and "it is hard to believe that he actually made such a baseless statement." Freehof here cannot resist an ironic reference to Rabbi Berlin's responsum: "I would say to him exactly what Naftali Berlin said concerning the layman in Cincinnati: If he is a learned man (and in the case of a rabbi, we assume he is), then we would like to know the reason for his statement that the Torah can be made unfit by an irregular reading." Of course, since Freehof has already branded the statement as "absurd," it's clear he doesn't think the rabbi has such a reason.

None of this, in fact, proves that the local rabbi's original ruling is "baseless." The halachah may prohibit the reading of Torah on Friday night even if doing so does *not* render the scroll ritually unfit. Those are two separate issues. Still, his "absurd" claim that the Torah scroll becomes *pasul* if read at a nontraditional time allows Freehof to question his halachic knowledge and competence. The implication is that the members of the college group need pay no attention to the rabbi's prohibition, particularly given that the outstanding halachic authority who has addressed this question is uncertain that such a prohibition exists. The conclusion: Jewish law raises no clear objection to the practice of reading Torah on Friday night.

We Reform Jewish readers are no doubt happy with this conclusion. But as *critical* readers, we have to ask whether Rabbi Freehof's reasoning stands up under scrutiny. And when we do, we find the results decidedly mixed. Specifically, our reading uncovers three significant problems in his argument.

First, Rabbi Freehof overreaches when he suggests that Rabbi Naftali Berlin is "uncertain" that the halachah prohibits Torah reading at nontraditional times. His evidence is the fact that Berlin asks his correspondent "whether the lay leader is a learned man" and can supply a halachic source to support his position. But let's look at what Berlin actually says:

> Truly, I have no idea on what basis your adversary could justify [reading Torah on Sunday], a practice for which there is no known halachic source. If he is not an ignoramus [*katil kanya*, literally "a reed chopper"; see Babylonian Talmud,

Shabbat 95a], it would be proper for him to provide some source. But if he has
no relevant source, his act is nothing but nonsense [sh'tut] and boorishness
[gasut ruach], the desire to puff himself up in the eyes of the crowd. At any
rate, at present I know of no source that would support him.

Berlin's challenge to the lay leader to provide a source is hardly a polite
request for information or a suggestion that the latter may be a "learned
man." His language is that of irony, much like Freehof's own request that
the presumably learned rabbi of the college town offer a source to defend a
ruling that Freehof has already described as "absurd." Nothing in these lines
indicates "uncertainty" on Rabbi Berlin's part. Rabbi Freehof's interpretation
of them, to put it mildly, is forced.

Second, Rabbi Freehof does not directly critique Berlin's halachic argument that Torah reading at nontraditional times violates the prohibition
against b'rachah l'vatalah. He could have faulted it as overly complex, con-
voluted, and unpersuasive.[6] Perhaps he does not want to burden the text of
his responsum with a lengthy, technical legal analysis. Either way, he leaves
Berlin's halachic theory standing, with no refutation. And from this the reader
might well conclude that silence signals consent, that Freehof concedes that
Berlin is correct as a matter of halachah.

Third, Rabbi Freehof provides no positive justification for the Reform
practice. This omission is significant. Surely Rabbi Brav and the college group
would have wanted to hear him argue that Jewish law permits the reading of
Torah on Friday night. Such arguments, in fact, were available to him. Against
Rabbi Berlin's position, he could have responded that the blessings recited
over a Friday-night Torah reading are hardly "unnecessary" or repetitious
when the community does not hold services or read Torah on Shabbat morning. He could also have made the case that since the Rabbis established the
institution of public Torah reading precisely at times that were convenient
for the community to assemble, the college community's observance is fully
in keeping with the spirit (if not the letter) of the halachah. He does mention
that point elsewhere in his writings, but he does not do so in this responsum.[7]

In short: our critical reading shows that Rabbi Freehof neither refutes
Rabbi Berlin's argument against Torah reading on Friday night nor provides
a cogent argument in favor of that custom. From this, we might reasonably
conclude that his responsum is a failure, that it does not prove what it needs
to prove in order to accomplish its intended task. But that conclusion would
be hasty. A closer look at this t'shuvah reveals that these weaknesses are mar-

ginal to the agenda that Freehof has set for it. As he frames the *sh'eilah*, the question is not whether there exists a halachic justification for this specific reform of traditional observance, but rather is about the general tendency among Orthodox Jews to oppose *any* innovation, *any* new practice, that the Reform Movement has introduced into Jewish religious life. He stresses this repeatedly in his responsum:

1. "Although [Torah reading at nontraditional times] is not prohibited, he is against it as a novelty."
2. "But if the man is ignorant, he should be brushed aside for wanting such a novelty."
3. "But, of course, in accordance with the general Orthodox mood, he objects to any unauthorized novelty (that is, if it really is unauthorized)."
4. "To sum up: While Orthodoxy naturally objects to any new custom. . . ."

With these remarks, Rabbi Freehof radically transforms the *sh'eilah* from a question of halachah to one of ideology. No longer a traditional rabbinic-style dispute over the interpretation of Jewish law, it is now a theological standoff between Orthodoxy—which as he portrays it opposes any and all change in the inherited body of Jewish ritual practice—and the more liberal communities that look upon ritual innovation as a positive response to changing times and conditions. This doesn't mean that halachah plays an unimportant role in this dispute. The rabbis whom Freehof cites in this *t'shuvah* express themselves in the language of Jewish law and construct their arguments as halachic ones. But it does allow Freehof to suggest that those these arguments are artificial, manufactured in order to provide a covering of legal language to a point of view that has much more to do with "the general Orthodox mood" than with what the halachic texts have to say about this particular question.

We might add that when Rabbi Freehof speaks of "the general Orthodox mood," he taps into a narrative familiar to many Reform Jews: the story of the rise of both Reform and Orthodox Judaism in the early nineteenth century. This narrative begins with the historical fact that the founders of the Reform Movement, who introduced changes into the pattern of Jewish ritual observance so as to accommodate it to aesthetic and ethical values of modernity, presented these innovations as halachicly permissible.[8] On issue after issue—the use of instrumental music at services, the recitation of prayer in the vernacular language, reading Torah without using the traditional chant, the architecture of the synagogue, holding wedding ceremonies in the synagogue sanctuary, and others—rabbis sympathetic to the Reform Movement cited halachic sources to demonstrate that the innovation was justifiable (or, at least, not explicitly prohibited) according to Jewish law. The opponents of religious reform, who were eventually designated as "Orthodox," countered with their own, sometimes quite innovative halachic theories in defense of the status quo. The dueling responsa emanating from both sides are written primarily in traditional rabbinic-halachic language. Eventually, the battle over halachic interpretation died down, possibly because each side had argued its case without persuading the other and thus there was nothing more to say. But, as the Reform narrative has it, something else was happening too. As the anti-Reform camp crystallized into a distinct Orthodox denomination, the nature of its rhetoric shifted. Those who called themselves Orthodox rallied around a program of total rejectionism, symbolized by the slogan "everything new is forbidden by the Torah," coined by Rabbi Moshe Sofer (the Chatam Sofer) of Hungary.[9] The new Orthodoxy committed itself to the "sanctification of the tradition": the entirety of the inherited body of Jewish ritual practices was now to be defended as *the* correct structure of observance and preserved against any changes whatsoever, even if those changes could be halachicly justified.[10] Under these circumstances, halachic argumentation was pointless. It no longer mattered that Reform rabbis could cite halachic support for their ritual innovations. Their Orthodox opponents would find *some* halachic impediment to them (or, as in this case, they would create such an impediment if none could be readily identified) precisely because they were new and precisely because *we* had introduced them. Reform Jewish readers, familiar with the general outline (if not the details) of this narrative, are likely to be persuaded by Freehof's assertion that Orthodox rabbis oppose *this* innovation not so much because it violates some existing halachic prohibition, but because it is a Reform practice and because Orthodoxy opposes *all* changes in traditional Jewish ritual life.[11]

Let's keep in mind that this is a *narrative*, not an exercise in academic history. It is a story that seeks to give order to the data of experience, a tale based in a particular perspective and directed toward a particular audience or community of readers that the author believes will share that perspective. It's a story told from a Reform perspective to a specifically Reform audience (Orthodox Jews would likely tell a very different story about those nineteenth-century events). Aside from the *sho-eil*, that Reform audience consists of two groups. The first are the members of the college student organization who prompted the *sh'eilah*. These students, who had already decided to read the Torah at their Friday evening service, are now troubled by the ruling of the local rabbi. They seek reassurance that their *minhag* is acceptable, and Freehof gives it to them partially by depicting the objections to it as rooted in an "Orthodox mood." The second (and larger) audience is the wider community of Reform Jews who may one day read this *t'shuvah*, as we are doing now. These Reform Jews, whether or not their congregations read Torah on Friday night, may wish to think of Reform Judaism's contributions to Jewish religious life as authentic expressions of Jewish tradition. To that audience Freehof signals that none of the stated halachic arguments against Friday-night Torah reading should be taken seriously, because Orthodoxy's real objection is based not upon halachah but upon its ideological opposition to all "novelties" and ritual innovation. Arguments grounded in Orthodox ideology speak exclusively to an Orthodox audience. A Reform Jewish audience, which does not share this antipathy to ritual change, is not likely to find them persuasive.

Rabbi Freehof's conclusion, then, is firm. But there's a deeper message to his responsum, one that will not be lost on the critical reader. To say, as Freehof says here, that Orthodox opposition to Torah reading on Friday night is a matter of ideology rather than halachah is to make three separate claims. The first is a claim of legitimacy: Jewish law either permits (or at least does not explicitly prohibit) the Reform practice of Friday-night Torah reading. The second is a claim of ownership: the halachah, Rabbi Freehof tells his readers, belongs to us—the Reform Jewish community—no less than it belongs to Orthodox Jews, and in this case *our* reading of the halachic sources is arguably better than theirs. And the third is a claim of meaning: *this*, says Rabbi Freehof, is how the halachah works, how it is meant to be understood. We've seen that the Jewish legal sources do not speak explicitly to whether Torah may be read publicly at nontraditional times. Legal thinkers describe this sort of situation, where the law is silent, as a "gap" in the law.[12] How should we understand the message of halachah when the sources are silent? Orthodoxy, particularly that version of Orthodoxy that follows the lead of the Chatam Sofer, answers this question with its own claim of meaning: anything that the existing texts do not explicitly approve must therefore be forbidden. Rabbi Freehof's claim, the one he would have us adopt, is precisely the contrary: what the halachah does not explicitly prohibit is thereby permitted. This expansive understanding of the halachah enables the Jewish legal tradition to respond positively and affirmatively to the changing conditions of modern life. And that, to this day, has been the foundation of the entire Reform halachic enterprise.

CHAPTER TWO

PRINCIPLES IN CONFLICT
Orthodox Minyan in a Reform Synagogue

THIS NEXT RESPONSUM, like the previous one, addresses the relationship between Reform and Orthodox Judaism. But while the previous responsum dealt with the ways in which Reform halachic thinking both resembles and differs from that of Orthodoxy, this one arises from the meeting between people, between members of the two groups. It asks: how do we negotiate our differences so that we might live together as Jews—united, and not only divided, by our religious commitments? The answer to that question, it suggests, will require that we take a good hard look at the nature of the Judaism that we teach and preach.

The question to the CCAR Responsa Committee comes from the rabbi of a Reform congregation in Jackson, Mississippi (the responsum can be read in full on pages 171–79):

> A few years ago a young man converted to Judaism at our congregation, which is the only one in the city. He subsequently underwent an Orthodox conversion, left the community, and attended a yeshivah in New York. During a recent visit to Jackson, he requested the use of our facilities for an "Orthodox" minyan. By this he means that women, though they may attend the service, will not count as part of the minyan and will be denied any opportunity to participate in the service.
>
> My initial response to this request was "no," on the grounds that the minyan would not be egalitarian and therefore contrary to our communal custom (*minhag hamakom*). On the other hand, I wonder if the Judaic value of hospitality to guests (*hachnasat orchim*) argues in favor of accommodating Orthodox visitors? Does the answer differ when these visitors ask for space for a minyan that meets on a regular or permanent basis? How forthcoming should we be, especially in view of the numerous incidents at the Western Wall, where, to put it mildly, no accommodations are made for liberal practice and "mixed" minyanim?[1]

A Hard Case

Let's note that the rabbi seeks a *principled* answer to this question. Perhaps this is too obvious a point to mention; after all, why would anyone submit a *sh'eilah* for a rabbinic responsum if they did not want an answer based upon principle or, in the language of this *sh'eilah*, "Judaic values"? But it's worth our attention nonetheless, because the rabbi and the congregation could have approached this issue quite differently. They might have defined the young man's request as a question of *policy* rather than principle, something to be decided on pragmatic grounds. Which decision serves the best interests of the synagogue? Which decision will spark the least opposition and prove the least disruptive to congregational harmony? The rabbi and the synagogue leadership could have informally consulted some of the congregation's most prominent members, to gauge their sentiment and determine just which responses would be more acceptable or less distasteful to them. There's nothing wrong with pragmatism, of course, and the wise rabbi will invariably take the political temperature of the congregation before rendering any important decision. We must presume that whatever the Responsa Committee might advise, the congregation's actual decision will be based in large part on factors we would call "political." At the same time, the rabbi is searching for the best *Jewish* answer to this question, and it's likely that many of the members of this synagogue, an organization dedicated to Jewish life and learning, will be interested in how the Jewish tradition in general and the Reform Jewish tradition in particular would answer it. That answer might help them move toward consensus on a potentially divisive issue such as this one.

The responsum agrees with the rabbi's description of the *sh'eilah* as one of principle—better, a conflict between principles—rather than pragmatics. The conflict, it tells us, involves "a fundamental tension between two important Reform Jewish principles, both of which we proudly affirm" and each of which represents "a range of values and commitments that express themselves throughout our personal and communal observance." That tension makes this a "hard case" (what in this book we call a "hard question"[2]), one for which "the existing law offers no single clear and obviously 'correct' solution," because "the applicable rules, principles, and precedents of [the Jewish] tradition pull in conflicting directions." But where the rabbi describes a conflict between the value of hospitality and our concern for local custom, the responsum identifies the clashing values as "Jewish pluralism" and "Reform Jewish integrity." In other words, the responsum declares at the outset that it will rewrite the *sh'eilah*, proposing to address a question that the rabbi did not ask. The critical reader should take note of this and ask why.

Could it be that the responsum's authors for some reason wish to avoid the rabbi's actual question? No, because endnote 4 of the responsum *does* answer the question. (This is a good reminder to always read the endnotes!) The note tells us that the mitzvah to welcome visitors (*hachnasat orchim*) has never been understood to require us to alter our established communal custom (*minhag hamakom*) on their behalf. On the contrary, it is the responsibility of the guests to respect our worship practices and to follow them so long as they are with us. It turns out, then, that the *sh'eilah* as the rabbi words it is not a "hard" question at all: respect for our communal custom clearly outweighs this young man's right to an Orthodox minyan in the synagogue building. Had the responsum been satisfied with addressing this relatively easy and straightforward question, it could have stopped right here. Instead, it wants to tackle a more difficult—and therefore more interesting—question. The responsum agrees that the *sh'eilah*—whether to approve or reject the young man's request for an Orthodox minyan—is a "hard case" not for the reasons the rabbi supplies, but because at its root lies a conflict between two essential principles of Reform Judaism, "both of which we proudly affirm." It is hard because it admits of no "clear and obviously 'correct' solution." And since it is a truly hard question, we should not expect a simple, straightforward answer to it. In the words of the responsum: "We have no choice but to think our way toward an answer that, while recognizing the ambiguities of the situation, nonetheless represents our best and most coherent understanding of that tradition as a whole."[3] The emphasis upon coherence and "the whole" indicates that the responsum will tend toward complexity rather than simplicity. It will seek to encompass both conflicting principles, to draw a proper balance between them rather than adopt one of them at the expense of the other.

The responsum justifies this course on the grounds that both of these conflicting principles are indispensable to any adequate definition of Reform Judaism. The first principle, that of "Jewish pluralism," is a product of liberalism, a term that refers not to contemporary politics but to the intellectual and cultural outlook within which the Reform Movement came into being in Europe and America during the nineteenth and twentieth centuries. That outlook places the personality and the conscience of the individual at the center of its concern.[4] The doctrine of pluralism holds that individuals and communities must be as free as possible to set their own course on matters of religious belief and practice. *Jewish* pluralism, it follows, would assert that there is more than one legitimate approach to Jewish religion. Accordingly, we Reform Jews have every right both to choose our own Jewish path *and* to regard that path as an *authentic* interpretation of the covenant of Sinai; we therefore reject Orthodoxy's claim to represent the one and only "Torah true" Judaism. But pluralism, if we are serious about it, cuts both ways: just as we demand the freedom to define *our* Judaism, we must grant that right to other Jews. To "bar our doors" to other Jews unless "they adhere to our own version of 'the correct way'" would amount to "rank intolerance," a denial of our own founding ideals. By allowing this young man to engage in his preferred form of Jewish worship within our building, we affirm the heritage of Reform Judaism and the ideals that have always defined it.

The second principle, that of "Reform Jewish integrity," includes those substantive beliefs ("core values") that form "the irreducible content of our approach to Judaism," affirmations without which "Reform Judaism" as we know it could scarcely exist. Among these is our commitment to gender equality. A Reform congregation cannot in honesty and good conscience compromise upon the commitment to gender equality and still think of itself as "Reform." Similarly, a Reform congregation cannot deny (as Orthodoxy denies) the Jewish status of those who have converted to Judaism under Reform Jewish auspices without questioning the Jewish legitimacy of its own movement. A minyan that refuses to include as equals women and those whom we have converted to Judaism would certainly violate these core values, and for that reason we must not open our building to it. This stand does not contradict our pluralism. Even the broadest conceptions of Reform Judaism accept the need for boundaries, for reasonable limits upon the ideas, teachings, and practices that we define as "Reform." As the responsum declares, "No religious community, no matter how liberal, could possibly exist if it were unable to draw lines. . . and to agree upon at least the most minimal definitions of what it does and does not believe." To allow this minyan on our property is to signal that either we endorse its governing theology or we regard it as a legitimate option for our community. No self-respecting Reform community should send that message.

The responsum therefore insists that the issue cannot be resolved "simply by invoking 'Reform religious principles,' because more than one such principle speaks to it and because those principles draw us in contradictory directions." Any decision favoring one of them while denying the other would reflect at best a partial (and at worst a distorted) picture of Reform Jewish faith.

This is what the responsum means when it describes our *sh'eilah* as a hard case. Of course, not all Reform Jewish readers will agree with that characterization. They will view the question as an "easy" one, readily resolved, because one of these principles outweighs the other. Some will think the core values expressed under the heading "Reform Jewish integrity" take priority, so that a Reform synagogue most assuredly should not permit an Orthodox minyan on its premises. Others will say that "Jewish pluralism" is the principle that ought to govern our thinking, meaning that the congregation ought to allow this Jew to organize a service that meets his Jewish religious needs. Either way, these readers will think that the question admits of one clear and obviously correct answer.

The responsum, for its part, does not attempt to argue against either of those positions. Instead, it asks us to imagine ourselves as a different kind of Reform Jewish community, one whose members wish to uphold both principles. That is, they are deeply committed to a vision of Jewish pluralism and tolerance, *and* they insist upon Reform Judaism's core values and its integrity as a Jewish religious movement. Holding that *both* principles are central to Reform Judaism, they do not wish to choose between them. *This* is the responsum's "intended audience," the audience for whom the depiction of the question as a "hard" one will resonate, the readers to whom the text addresses itself in the sentence that begins section 2: "How then shall we proceed in this situation, in which Jews deeply divided over matters of religious outlook and practice seek to live together within the same institutional framework?" Put differently, how do we maintain our Reform religious integrity while yet extending a hand of friendship to the Jews in our midst who do not believe or practice as we do? There is nothing about being a Reform Jew that *requires* us to view the question in this way. But to the extent that we readers accept the responsum's invitation and perceive that we belong to its "ideal audience," we are more likely to accept its framing of the question and to be persuaded by the answer it ultimately reaches.

A Precedent in Jewish Law

That answer is based upon "a helpful precedent" from the Talmud. It centers upon one of a long series of disagreements (*machlokot*) between the students (or "houses," schools) of Hillel and Shammai, two leading sages of the first century CE. This particular disagreement (*machloket*) deals with a detail of the Bible's law of levirate marriage (Deuteronomy 25:5–10). The issue is a significant (if complicated) one, as the responsum explains in endnote 7. For purposes of the Talmud's discussion (Babylonian Talmud, *Y'vamot* 13b–14a), however, the important point is that the disagreement exists at all.

Mishnah Y'vamot 1:4 tells us that both schools acted upon their opinion; that is, they practiced the laws of marriage in accordance with their position on this matter. But how could the school of Shammai do this? Since the students of Hillel were more numerous than they, the actions of the school of Shammai would seem to transgress the rule that the halachah usually follows the majority opinion. Moreover, as we read in a well-known text:

> Rabbi Abba said in the name of Sh'muel: For three years the schools of Shammai and Hillel disputed, each one claiming that "the halachah is according to our interpretation."
>
> A *bat kol* [divine voice] came forth and declared, "The opinions of both (schools) are the words of the living God, but the halachah is in accordance with the school of Hillel." (Babylonian Talmud, *Eiruvin* 13b)

This text is often cited to demonstrate Judaism's capacity for pluralism in the interpretation of Torah. But it also informs us that while heaven itself can accommodate the conflicting and often contradictory opinions of the two schools, as a practical matter the law we follow is that of the school of Hillel. Thus, if the school of Shammai practiced marriage law according to their own understanding, they would be in violation of this heavenly ruling.

This difficulty can be resolved, though, by appeal to an equally famous text. In Babylonian Talmud, *Bava M'tzia* 59b, the colleagues of Rabbi Eliezer all dispute his opinion concerning a detail of the laws of ritual purity and impurity. Rabbi Eliezer performs a series of miracles as evidence that his opinion is the correct one, but the Sages refuse to accept miracles as proof of the correctness of an interpretation of Torah. Finally, a *bat kol* issues forth and declares that the halachah is in accordance with Rabbi Eliezer, to which Rabbi Y'hoshua retorts by quoting Deuteronomy 30:12: "It [that is, the Torah] is not in heaven!" He understands this to mean, "We do not heed the opinion of heaven in matters of halachah, because in Your Torah You have already told us to decide such matters on our own."[5] Thus, if the school of Shammai indeed practiced the laws of marriage according to their own opinion, perhaps they did so because they agreed with Rabbi Y'hoshua that we are entitled to ignore heaven's declaration that "the halachah is in accordance with the school of Hillel."

But there is a second objection to the actions of the school of Shammai, based upon Deuteronomy 14:1, "You are children of the Eternal your God. You shall not gash yourselves [*lo titgod'du*; from the root *g-d-d*, 'to cut'] or shave the front of your heads because of the dead." The literal sense of this verse in all likelihood prohibits Israelites from adopting pagan Canaanite rituals of self-mutilation as mourning practices.[6] The Rabbis, however, read the words *lo titgod'du* to mean "you shall not divide yourselves into separate sects [*agudot agudot*]," a prohibition against needless and excessive disputes over religious practice among the Jewish people. How then could the students of Shammai have insisted upon practicing their own version of marriage law without transgressing this prohibition, especially given that they were the minority compared to the school of Hillel? The Talmud answers by quoting Rava, a fourth-century Babylonian Rabbinic scholar:[7] "The rule 'do not divide yourselves into separate sects' applies only to disputes among the members of the same *beit din* [court], where some judges rule according to the school of Hillel and others according to the school of Shammai. But it does not apply to two separate courts in the same community" (Babylonian Talmud, *Y'vamot* 14a).

The responsum reads Rava's statement as an effort to strike a careful balance between the twin goals of unity and diversity within a community of Torah learning. We seek unity because, as the responsum teaches, "We are, after all, one people, in possession of one Torah, who ought to be united in service to the one God." "One Torah," of course, implies that we know the one correct understanding of what that Torah requires of us. The school of Hillel certainly thought that it possessed the one correct understanding; after all, didn't the heavenly voice tell them as much? But we also prize diversity, because it is "inevitable." We will always disagree among ourselves as to the correct understanding of Torah, just as the schools of Hillel and Shammai disagreed, because disagreement is an inherent element of the human—and perhaps especially the *Jewish*—condition. The *t'shuvah* might have added that diversity is also desirable, because disagreement, debate, and argument are essential tools (certainly for the Rabbis) in the search for knowledge and truth. Rava's position is therefore a "compromise" that allows more than one "court"—or school of thought, or "interpretive community"[8]—to function within the structure of the larger community, each one following its own understanding of Torah and halachah.

This compromise becomes the pattern for the Responsa Committee's solution to the present case. In this arrangement, the Reform congregation serves as "the school of Hillel," while the young man and those who would help compose his minyan are "the school of Shammai." The congregation, as the majority, could insist that the young man observe the principle *lo tit-god'du*: you are welcome to join our religious services, but you must not create a separate sect, particularly one that stands in contradiction to our Reform Jewish core values, within our building. But rather than follow a course that so sharply contrasts with our liberality and our pluralistic commitments, we create space for two separate "courts" to operate within the larger community, so that each can interpret the law (which in this case refers to the laws of prayer) as it sees fit. And "so long as the nascent Orthodox minyan enjoys a separate organizational identity from our own," a separate existence "acknowledged and made clearly visible to all," we will not give the impression that we endorse that group's discrimination against women and against those who have entered Judaism through our doorway. This accommodation can be reached by several different procedures, which are discussed at the conclusion of the responsum. In the end, though, the message is clear: "Jewish unity *and* diversity—integrity *and* pluralism—are equally worthy goals, and . . . our tradition would have us make room for both."

On Precedent and Analogy
Our responsum frames the *sh'eilah*'s central issue as a clash between the principles of Jewish pluralism and Reform Jewish integrity, and it argues that the best answer is one that incorporates both of them rather than favoring one over the other. It supports its argument by means of "a halachic precedent" involving the schools of Hillel and Shammai. The responsum *works*, in other words, if that precedent speaks persuasively to our case. Its authors claim that it does. The critical reader must examine that claim.

First, a technical point. In the language of law, a precedent is an existing decision that is considered authoritative for deciding future cases that involve similar facts or legal issues. That authoritative force may be either *binding* (future decision-makers *must* follow them) or *persuasive* (future decision-makers may use the precedent's reasoning as a guide, but they aren't obliged to follow its result). These precedents are identified by way of *analogy*, the mode of reasoning from case to case commonly utilized in law, halachah, and ethics, as well as in many of the decisions we are called upon to make in our everyday lives.[9] Analogy is a form of comparison. The decision-maker seeking an answer to case A notices that case B, which was already decided, resembles case A in some of its aspects. The decision-maker therefore draws an analogy between the two cases, concluding that the existing answer to case B should apply as a solution for case A. The major difficulty with this method of reasoning is "the problem of importance." By their nature, the two cases are not identical. (If they were identical, we wouldn't need to compare them!) They share similarities with each other, but there will be differences between them as well. The decision-maker must determine whether the similarities are more "important" than the differences; if they are, then we can say that the comparison is a *good* analogy. But that determination is a matter of judgment rather than "proof." This is how reasoning by analogy differs from methods of deductive reasoning, like mathematical equations or logical syllogisms. For example: $2 + 2 = 4$ in a base 10 numerical system; the number 4 is the one and only correct answer. Or: If all men are mortal (major premise), and if Socrates is a man (minor premise), then the conclusion of this syllogism *must* be that Socrates is mortal. Equations or syllogisms are true or valid because they adhere to the appropriate structure or formula. No such structure or formula distinguishes between analogies that work and analogies that don't. Decision-makers must *argue* that their analogies are cogent, because they can't demonstrate cogency through any formal method. This doesn't mean that the analogy is nothing more than a literary device that doesn't count as substantive evidence, for were that the case jurists, ethicists, rabbis, and the rest of us would not use it when we make our arguments. It does mean, though, that since the cogency and power of an analogy demands argument, it is the job of the critical reader of any legal, ethical, or halachic decision to put that argument to the test. To put this differently, an analogy's "fit" or appropriateness is a matter of the interpreter's judgment. The beauty of an analogy is in the eye of the beholder; one either finds it persuasive or one doesn't. Ultimately, this responsum will succeed or fail in its effort at persuasion to the extent that its intended audience recognize themselves as the sort of Reform Jews that it describes, those who see no necessary contradiction between Jewish pluralism and Reform Jewish integrity. In that sense it resembles all responsa, which seek through their argumentation to assemble a community around a particular understanding of what Torah and Jewish tradition would have us do.

In our case, the critical reader can and should consider the "problem of importance" as a way of testing the judgment that underlies the analogy. It's certainly true that the ancient "schools" of Hillel and Shammai were deeply divided over issues of thought and practice. But despite their differences, they recognized each other as "rabbis"—that is, as members of the Rabbinic community (even if that title was not yet in widespread use during their time). Both groups accepted the existence of something called Oral Torah or halachah, and even as each rejected many of the opinions of the other "school," they viewed those opinions as legitimate, if mistaken, understandings of a common tradition. The responsum argues that this classic Rabbinic disagreement is a fitting analogy to the divisions between Reform and Orthodox Judaism, the "schools" represented here by the congregation and the young man, respectively. But one could argue just as plausibly that the differences between Reform and Orthodoxy today are more religiously significant than those that separated the two ancient "schools." Most Orthodox Jews, at any rate, most definitely would deny the analogy. Orthodoxy holds that our two communities are divided by a chasm of theology (let alone practice) much wider and deeper than the one that separated the students of Hillel and Shammai. The responsum acknowledges this, and it is instructive to cite its words on that subject:

> We are aware of the irony of this position. We know that, were the situation of our *sh'eilah* to be reversed, an Orthodox congregation would not likely grant permission to a Reform group to hold services in its synagogue building. This is because Orthodox Judaism is not a liberal creed. It proclaims that there is but one correct version of Jewish practice and that Reform Jewish worship is not an acceptable variation of that correct version. They do not regard our disagreements as similar to the conflict between the schools of Hillel and Shammai, two legitimate if conflicting interpretations of the same Torah. On the contrary: they condemn us as heretics, they cast us outside the pale, they deny the Jewish validity of our practice.

In short, the analogy certainly would not persuade an Orthodox audience. Orthodox Jews would not be inclined to compare us to a separate "court" or *beit din* operating alongside them within the larger community, because they regard the version of Jewish law and practice carried out by our "court" as false rather than simply mistaken. Orthodox Jews do not accept the validity of the conversions that we administer, because in their eyes our *beit din* is not a valid court of Jewish law. As far as they are concerned, the two poles of the analogy—the *machloket* between the "schools" of Hillel and Shammai on the one hand and the disagreements between Reform and Orthodoxy on the other—are more unlike than they are similar. Accordingly, the analogy fails, at least if we're trying to persuade an Orthodox audience to accept our compromise.

But the responsum is not addressed to an Orthodox audience. It speaks not to the young man who wants an Orthodox minyan, but to the Reform congregation that has to decide whether to grant his request. For that matter, it directs its words to *all* Reform Jews who, facing a question that concerns their relationship to Orthodox Jews, are in search of a solution or solutions that speak the language of sacred text, the authentic voice of Jewish tradition. In this view, the fact that an Orthodox audience would reject the analogy to the "schools" of Hillel and Shammai is irrelevant. The responsum offers that analogy to its intended Reform readership in the hope that *they* will find it persuasive and so look favorably upon the solutions set forth in the conclusion. Indeed, it does more than simply "offer" the analogy. Aware that the analogy is (at the least) questionable, it supports it with an argument aimed specifically at its readers' identity and commitments as Reform Jews. The argument begins with a reference to the words of the *sh'eilah*: "How forthcoming should we be, especially in view of the numerous incidents at the Western Wall, where, to put it mildly, no accommodations are made for liberal practice and 'mixed' minyanim?" Put simply, if *they* wouldn't be "forthcoming" to us, why should *we* "accommodate" them? The responsum answers that question with some rhetorical passion:

> It may be tempting to respond in kind, to reject them in return, to deny them space within our precincts as they would surely deny it to us. Yet our religious principles forbid us the path of retaliation. The conduct of the Orthodox Jews who drive us from our rightful place at the Western Wall cannot serve as a model for our own behavior. If they are not liberals, *we* are; if their conception of Judaism cannot make room for diversity, ours does and must. We look upon Orthodox Jews not as enemies but as friends. We greet them not as aliens and heretics but as our brothers and sisters. And whether or not they would do the same for us, our liberal Jewish faith demands that we reach out to them in a spirit of fellowship and generosity.

The responsum urges Reform Jews to accept the analogy, ironically, precisely because Orthodox Jews probably *won't* accept it. It reminds us that Reform is a *liberal* creed, shaped by the values of pluralism, tolerance, and respect for interpretations of Judaism that differ from our own. Orthodox

Jews, and certainly those Orthodox Jews who violently disrupt egalitarian minyanim at the Western Wall, do not share that worldview, and we cannot expect them to apply that analogy to define the differences between us. But our own principles, the values that make us who and what we are, require that we make room for the practices of the other "school"—the Orthodox minyan—in our building. To be sure, our commitment to our Reform Jewish integrity is another component of who and what we are, and that commitment imposes some limitations upon the operation of the Orthodox minyan in our building. As the responsum's concluding paragraphs suggest, our grant of permission to them must be made in such a way that it is clear to all that, first, the building itself is a *Reform* synagogue and, second, the Orthodox group that meets within our precincts is a separate and independent entity and not a subgroup of our Reform congregation practicing an accepted version of Reform Judaism.

In this way, the responsum argues that the analogy between our *sh'eilah* and the "schools" of Hillel and Shammai is a proper way to understand our relationship to Orthodox Jews and to respond to the challenge of this *sh'eilah*. And again, we will be persuaded by that argument to the extent that we accept the responsum's invitation to define our Reform Judaism in the way that it does.

CHAPTER THREE

REFORMING REFORMS, EMBRACING TRADITION
When a Parent Requests Cremation

Reform responsa differ from those of Orthodox rabbis, as we note in the introduction to this book, in that they work simultaneously within more than one tradition. Besides the age-old tradition of Torah learning that they share in common with all other Jews, Reform responsa writers draw from the tradition of our own movement. During the two centuries of our movement's history, Reform rabbis have produced many responsa and other texts dealing with matters of Jewish religious practice, and we look to those writings for guidance. And as is the case with that broader Jewish tradition, the meaning of our specifically Reform tradition cannot be fixed once and for all time or set down as a body of fixed rules. Rather, it must be determined through a process of argument. From this, we learn that we cannot say with confidence just what either of these traditions is teaching us until we have participated in that argument.

Our next responsum, from 2006, centers upon arguments over what both those traditions have to say (the responsum can be read in full on pages 180–92):

> A man, who is approaching death, has instructed that his body be cremated. His children are very uncomfortable with this request. They ask whether, under Jewish tradition, they are obliged to honor it, or are they entitled to bury him intact,[1] in contradiction to his express wishes? Rabbi Solomon B. Freehof has ruled that in such a case we apply the Talmudic dictum "It is a mitzvah to fulfill the wishes of the deceased" (Babylonian Talmud, *Gittin* 40a and elsewhere). I wonder, however, if a more nuanced approach is better suited to a case such as this, where the children have strong religious objections to their father's instruction?[2]

The *sh'eilah* invokes both of the traditions we have mentioned. First, there is the historical Jewish tradition, which according to the *sh'eilah* prohibits cremation of the dead and therefore supports the children's "strong religious objections" to their father's request. Then there is the specifically Reform Jewish tradition, embodied in the responsum of Rabbi Freehof, that permits cremation and supports the father's wishes. At first glance it appears that the issue is open-and-shut: the present responsum ought to recommend that the children follow the practice of our own Reform tradition, and it could cite Rabbi Freehof's *t'shuvah* as a precedent for that decision. The difficulty, though, is that Freehof's responsum, which the rabbi who submits the *sh'ei-lah* has presumably shared with the children, apparently has not persuaded them to set aside their convictions and fulfill their father's wishes. For this reason, the rabbi seeks "a more nuanced approach" than that taken by Free-hof.

The present responsum is indeed an essay in nuance. As it works toward an answer, it will note complexity at every step of the way. This is particularly true because, it asserts, the meaning of *neither* of our two traditions—the general Jewish tradition and the specifically Reform tradition—is crystal clear when it comes to cremation.

The Freehof Responsum

The responsum's first order of business is the 1974 *t'shuvah* of Rabbi Freehof cited in the *sh'eilah*.[3] The question in that instance was: "A Jew had died and left instruction in his will that his body is to be cremated; but the next of kin, either for religious or other reasons, wish to have a burial instead. Whose wish is to be carried out?" His decision is that the next of kin should allow the cremation, based upon the Talmudic principle (Freehof calls it a "maxim") *mitzvah l'kayeim divrei hameit*, "it is a mitzvah to fulfill the wishes of the deceased." As Freehof acknowledges, there is a major limitation upon this principle: the deceased's wishes are binding upon us only "in ordinary circumstances," but *not* in cases where they would have us transgress Jewish law. Freehof cites some examples,[4] and the Responsa Committee buttresses the point (in responsum endnote 2) with a text that begins with Leviticus 19:3, "You shall each revere your mother and your father, and keep My Sabbaths: I am the Eternal your God."

A midrash on this verse (cited in Babylonian Talmud, *Y'vamot* 5b) notes that it imposes two separate and apparently equal duties: the mitzvot of reverence for our parents and observance of Shabbat. This raises a difficulty: suppose my father instructs me to transgress the laws of Shabbat—for example, to perform for him an act of prohibited "work" (*m'lachah*) on that day. Which duty takes precedence? The midrash responds, "This is why the verse ends with the words 'I am the Eternal your God': that is, all of you are obligated to honor Me." "All of you" here includes your father and your mother. Therefore, the reverence due to God takes precedence over the reverence we owe to our parents; we must obey the instruction of the Torah even when a parent tells us otherwise.[5] It follows that we are not obligated to fulfill the wishes of the deceased if those wishes contradict a mitzvah. This makes sense; if my father instructs me to rob a bank, I am certainly not obligated to do so because of the commandment to revere him!

For this reason, says Freehof, an Orthodox rabbi would rule that one is not obligated to fulfill the wish of the deceased in our case, "since cremation is contrary to Jewish law." But for a Reform rabbi, he continues, "the answer cannot be so clear-cut," because Reform Judaism does not regard cremation as a violation of Jewish law. He bases this conclusion on two grounds. First, the Central Conference of American Rabbis (CCAR) resolved in 1892 that "we should not refuse to officiate [at a cremation]" should we be invited to do so. And second, it is not altogether obvious that Jewish law *does* prohibit cremation. No explicit prohibition can be found in the Bible or the classical Rabbinic sources. Moreover, while Orthodox opponents of cremation do cite various halachic arguments, Freehof dismisses them as "forced." The real source of this opposition is the "mood" of contemporary Orthodoxy. We've seen Rabbi Freehof use this term in chapter 1 to account for the general tendency of Orthodox Judaism to resist all change and "novelty" in Jewish ritual observance. This explains, he says, the Orthodox "agitation" against cremation that began in the nineteenth century as a reaction to the spread of the practice. Since Reform Jews do not and need not share in that Orthodox mood, of course, it should not serve in this case as a barrier to fulfilling the deceased's wishes.

The present responsum, however, takes issue with Rabbi Freehof. Borrowing his language, it writes that the situation today "is no longer 'so clear-cut'; the Reform position on cremation is more complex today than it was" in 1974, so that the dying man's children deserve the "more nuanced approach"— that is, another responsum—that they have requested. It's clear that the authors of this new responsum feel some trepidation. The *sh'eilah* "is asking that we rule against our teacher, and we are ordinarily reluctant to do so." True, "reluctant" is not the same as "forbidden." As we've discussed in the introduction to this book, Jewish law does not recognize a formal doctrine of binding precedent, and the Responsa Committee (see responsum endnote 4) does not consider itself bound to follow the rulings of Rabbi Freehof or other predecessors. Rather, the words "our teacher" suggest that the real issue here is not precedent but the Judaic value of *k'vod harav*, the obligation to treat one's Torah teacher with honor and deference. As the Talmud explains, this duty means that students should refrain from openly criticizing a ruling of their teacher; when one does so, "it is as though one has openly disputed the *Shechinah*," the Divine Presence (Babylonian Talmud, *Sanhedrin* 110a). This statement, to be sure, is hyperbole. The halachic tradition may tell us to honor our teacher, but it also prizes the search for truth, and in fact it encourages students to argue matters of Torah with their teachers so long as they express their disagreements with humility and respect.[6] For this reason, this responsum sets aside Rabbi Freehof's decision without openly declaring it wrong. It claims that because "the Reform position on cremation" and our attitudes toward "the maintenance and encouragement of traditional forms of Jewish observance" have changed substantially since he wrote his *t'shuvah*, a new responsum is needed. The implication, of course, is that "our teacher," were he alive today, would agree.

Cremation in Jewish Law

This responsum may be "new," but it covers much of the same ground as did Rabbi Freehof in 1974. It begins with the status of cremation in Jewish law and, concurring with Freehof, finds that while intact burial is the long-standing normative Jewish practice, there exists no explicit prohibition of cremation in the biblical or the Rabbinic sources. (The present responsum adds more documentation, especially in the endnotes.) Not only are the major halachic codes—Maimonides's *Mishneh Torah* (twelfth century) and the *Shulchan Aruch* of Rabbi Yosef Karo with Rabbi Moshe Isserles's commentary *HaMapah* (sixteenth century)—silent on the subject, but one can even argue that cremation, though exceptional, is *permitted* under halachah. Consider a famous responsum, cited by both Rabbi Freehof and the present *t'shuvah*, of Rabbi Sh'lomo ben Adret, also known as Rashba (Spain, d. 1310), one of the outstanding *rishonim* ("early"—that is, medieval—Talmud commentators) and the author of over 3,500 *t'shuvot*:

> Reuven, at the time of his death, left instructions that he be buried with his ancestors in the family gravesite.[7] When he died, [his children] were unable to transport him to that gravesite immediately, so they buried him in a temporary grave at the location of his death. Now the children are ready to transport the body, but it is impossible to do so, due to the deterioration of the remains and

the stench resulting from decomposition. You ask whether it is permissible to cover the entire body with quicklime in order to hasten the decomposition. Is this prohibited on the grounds that it is an act of contemptible treatment [*bizayon*] of a corpse?

T'shuvah. It is permissible to perform such an action, one that hastens decomposition, in order to transport the body to the place the deceased specified for his burial. This is not an instance of *bizayon*.[8]

There is more to Rashba's responsum, but the section quoted here shows that there is no absolute prohibition against using chemicals to cause the corpse's rapid decomposition. And since fire, a more efficient agent of rapid decomposition, is an obvious analogy to quicklime, we could say that cremation is also not an act of *bizayon* (disrespectful treatment of a corpse), and as such it is not prohibited by the halachah. This, at any rate, is what Rabbi Freehof argues: the well-known "prohibition" of cremation is the invention of those nineteenth-century halachic authorities (*poskim*) who manufacture a series of "forced" arguments to support it.

The problem with his analysis, the present responsum tells us, is twofold. First, while Rabbi Freehof dismisses the Orthodox arguments against cremation as "forced," that's *his* perception. Readers may find some of those arguments "more persuasive than others." Second, he draws a sharp distinction between the rules laid down in the classical sources of Jewish law—the Bible, the Talmud, and the leading codes—and the writings of more recent Orthodox *poskim*. The former, he tells us, represent the real content of the halachah, while the latter are less authoritative. This distinction is correct, as far as it goes, but we shouldn't exaggerate its significance. If the classical sources do not explicitly prohibit cremation, the reason may be that the question never arose in those days. Jews buried their dead and did not burn them; that practice was presumed to be the law, and that presumption was ratified by centuries of custom (*minhag*). If some subsequent authorities permit the use of chemical agents to speed the decomposition of the body, their rulings speak to special or exceptional situations. We cannot logically derive from those rulings a permit for cremation as an alternative to burial in ordinary cases.[9] Besides, we know that in halachah, as in law, the authoritative rule is not limited to what is stated explicitly in the classical texts, because those texts cannot speak to contemporary reality until they are read and applied by those living in the here and now. Thus, "tradition" must consist of *both* the original texts *and* the record of their interpretation.

The 2006 responsum, surveying this tradition in all its complexity, tries to make sense of it by telling a story of halachic change. According to this narrative, the original texts—for whatever reason—never clearly addressed the question of cremation as a ritual means of disposing of human remains, and it was the nineteenth-century Orthodox rabbis, reacting to cultural trends they perceived negatively, who declared that the halachah prohibits the practice. This is essentially the same story that Rabbi Freehof tells. The difference is that while he attributes this historical development to the Orthodox "mood" (based upon weak or "forced" halachic evidence), the 2006 responsum sees it as a normal instance of law changing to meet changing social conditions. This is crucial, because if the prohibition is not "forced," then the children in this case have substantive traditional backing for their "strong religious objections" to cremation.

Cremation in the Literature of the CCAR

What of the position of Reform Judaism, and particularly of the CCAR, the parent body of the Responsa Committee? It's true, as Rabbi Freehof notes, that the CCAR resolved in 1892 that Reform rabbis should not refuse to officiate at cremation ceremonies, but that resolution was hardly its last word on the subject. The present responsum lists in chronological order seven separate statements on cremation found in CCAR halachic publications. Using these statements, the responsum tells a story of gradual change in the stance of the Reform rabbinate, from one of acceptance and even affirmation toward disapproval and discouragement. Rabbi Freehof's 1974 *t'shuvah* is the third statement in this list. Given that the two prior statements—dating from 1892 and 1961—accept or endorse cremation as an acceptable option for Reform Jews, Freehof was thoroughly justified in summarizing the Reform position as he did. He can't be faulted for not predicting the turn that began with the publication of *Gates of Mitzvah* in 1979, the fourth of those seven CCAR statements. By that token, though, the list suggests that his decision is outdated: it does not reflect the Reform Jewish teaching on cremation as it has developed since his time.

The responsum now takes an additional step, giving an explanation for that development—the "why" that accounts for the "what." Strictly speaking, this step is unnecessary. The *t'shuvah* could simply have noted that Reform Jewish attitudes toward cremation have changed over the years (or at least since 1974). But the responsum clearly wishes to make a more general point. It ties the subject of cremation to the larger narrative of change and development in Reform religious practice as a whole. Thus, it claims that the changing Reform position on cremation "is based upon two threads of argument" that not only deal with this specific issue but "reflect two important transformations in the way that many Reform Jews have come to think about their religious lives and decisions."

The first transformation is the positive reevaluation of traditional observance (the so-called and much talked about "return to tradition") that has characterized our movement since the latter part of the twentieth century. In practical terms, this means that "tradition" in and of itself is a positive factor in our thinking. We will tend to prefer and choose a traditional standard of practice (for example, intact burial) in the absence of any overriding moral or aesthetic objection to that observance. This is a dramatic departure from earlier American Reform Jewish thought. As the quotation from the 1885 Pittsburgh Platform reminds us, there was a time when Reform Jews were inclined to eliminate all traditional ritual practices "not adapted to the views and habits of modern civilization" and that "fail to impress the modern Jew with a spirit of priestly holiness."[10] We should not overlook the truly radical implications of that statement, which enthrones the values of "modern civilization" (as opposed to halachah or "tradition") as a sort of default position, the supreme criterion by which we determine our religious practices. The responsum cites the words of Rabbi Bernard Felsenthal, spoken during the 1892 CCAR debate that led to the original resolution on cremation, as an expression of this position: the living should not look to the dead (that is, to the Bible and the other texts of the Jewish legal tradition) to discover "the spirit of Judaism." This stands in marked contrast to the intellectual climate of today's Reform, for whom, according to the responsum, the traditional practice is the default position: "we are now more inclined than ever before to adopt or to preserve a ritual observance precisely because it is 'Jewish.'" This new inclination is itself the product of a long historical development. By 1999, in the words of a responsum on "The Second Festival Day and Reform Judaism," Reform had reclaimed many of the ritual practices that our predecessors abandoned, not because we thought those predecessors wrong or misguided, but because of our generation's "divergent religious agenda."[11] As that responsum has it, if our predecessors' neutral (to put it mildly) attitude toward traditional observance stemmed from their push for "acculturation into the surrounding society," we who no longer have to engage in that struggle "are more concerned with taking active measures to preserve our distinctive Jewishness."

As an example of this new thinking, the 2006 responsum considers the argument, raised by some of those nineteenth-century Orthodox opponents of the practice, that cremation is an act of *nivul hameit* (a synonym for *bizayon hameit*), contemptible treatment of a corpse. The answer, the responsum tells us, will turn upon what we mean by concepts such as "disgrace" and "honor" that resist objective definition and take on meaning within a particular social context. Reform Jews have alternatives here. They can choose to work within the specific context of contemporary Western culture ("the views and habits of modern civilization"), which regards cremation as an honorable means for disposing of human remains. "Yet to say that we are not obligated to adopt the traditional definition does not entail that we are *forbidden* to do so." A Reform Jew "who finds special and satisfying meaning in the values and affirmations of Jewish tradition" can choose to accept the traditional Jewish definition of *nivul* or *bizayon* precisely because it *is* traditionally Jewish, and can therefore favor burial over cremation.

The responsum continues with the second transformation, "our sensitivity to the experience of the Shoah (Holocaust)." The ways in which we think about and practice our religion cannot help but respond in some significant ways to the murder of six million of our people. This, the responsum concedes, is a dicey argument. The Holocaust is used all too often as "a facile justification" for changes in contemporary Jewish religious life (our next responsum will discuss this phenomenon), and we could be making that mistake here.[12] Still, it is undeniable that the intimate association of crematoria with the Nazi genocide makes it difficult for "many liberal Jews" to regard cremation as a proper Jewish way of dealing with our dead, and several of the CCAR statements that discourage cremation make this point explicitly.

By invoking these two transformations in our religious thinking, the responsum makes a claim of meaning upon recent Reform Jewish history: while the 1892 resolution is still on the books as its "formal policy," the CCAR's statements on cremation issued between 1979 and 1990 reflect the direction of contemporary Reform attitudes about observance in general. Our opinion on cremation has changed because over the last several decades we as a movement have changed in the way we think about the forms of our Jewish life and about the tragic experiences of our recent history.

This is the story—a historical narrative that supports the major part of its argument—the responsum tells. As with any such story, critical readers ought to ask two questions of this one. First, is it an accurate representation of the facts? And second, whether accurate or not, does it justify the conclusions that the responsum draws from it? Let's begin with the first question. The *t'shuvah* speaks as though the Reform Movement in its entirety has experienced these "transformations." Using the language of first-person plural—"*We* are more likely to regard a practice's traditional pedigree as a reason for maintaining it"; "The second transformation in *our* religious thinking concerns *our* sensitivity to the experience of the Shoah" (emphasis added)—it implies that these views are shared universally by Reform Jews. It offers no data or evidence to support that impression; it simply asserts it as fact. Wouldn't it be more plausible to say that these new ways of thinking describe the approach of *many*—but not *all*—within the movement? (Rabbi Freehof, to cite one obvious example, wrote his *t'shuvah* nearly thirty years after the end of the Second World War, yet he expresses no tendency to discourage cremation in response to the experience of the Shoah.) The second question, however, is more important. Even if we grant that these transformations have occurred and that they accurately describe "us"—the preponderant majority of the movement—this proves nothing, for neither of these changes *requires* that we alter our stance on any *particular* religious observance. Many Reform Jews today do favor a more traditional style of Jewish practice than did their predecessors. But this does not entail that they will prefer—let alone that they *must* prefer—*all* traditional practices, including intact burial, over alternatives. Similarly, it may be true that the Shoah has made an indelible and even "transformative" impression upon the way Reform Jews look at the world. But that does not obligate them to reject cremation simply because the Nazis utilized it to dispose of their victims' bodies. One might as well argue that we should stop riding trains because the Nazis utilized the railroad to transport Jews to the death camps. In other words, even if we concede that these transformations have affected all or most of us, it does not logically follow that the CCAR was *required* to alter its original, approving stance on cremation.

The responsum is aware of this difficulty. The citation (in responsum endnote 30) of Justice Holmes's remark that "general propositions do not decide concrete cases" signals that it wishes to avoid such sloppy thinking. In this instance, the "general proposition" is that our movement has experienced the "two important transformations" the responsum describes, while the "concrete case" is the specific question of cremation. The former does not determine the latter. Instead, the responsum argues that we reverse the thought process, beginning with the case and not the proposition: "in this particular concrete case, the CCAR has moved decisively away from its previous acceptance of cremation." The goal is not to demonstrate that recent Reform Jewish history *required* this move, but simply to explain it, to provide it with context. A new rule, practice, or statement of preference most likely doesn't happen by coincidence but reflects some change in a community's cultural habits or ways of thought. By linking the fact of change (the CCAR's more recent support for intact burial over cremation) to the two "transformations," the responsum seeks to account for that change in a way that lends it a larger meaning.

This is how narrative works, not only in responsa but in all legal thought. As the legal scholar Robert Cover writes in one of the most famous law-review articles ever published:

> No set of legal institutions or prescriptions exists apart from the narratives that locate it and give it meaning. For every constitution there is an epic, for each decalogue a scripture. . . . In this normative world, law and narrative are inseparably related. Every prescription is insistent in its demand to be located in discourse—to be supplied with history and destiny, beginning and end, explanation and purpose. And every narrative is insistent in its demand for its prescriptive point, its moral. History and literature cannot escape their location in a normative universe, nor can prescription, even when embodied in a legal text, escape its origin and its end in experience, in the narratives that are the trajectories plotted upon material reality by our imaginations.[13]

If every law ("prescription") comes to us wrapped in a web of "discourse" that provides it with point and purpose, then we needn't speak of cause and effect. In this responsum, the narrative (the "two important transformations") supplies "explanation and purpose" to the prescription—that is, the position on cremation embodied in the CCAR's more recent statements on cremation. The prescription is an *expression* of the narrative, not its logically necessary result.

The Question before Us

As the responsum summarizes its conclusions in this section, we should note that while it takes issue with Rabbi Freehof's 1974 decision, it does not stray far from his reasoning and approach. That is to say, the Freehof responsum establishes a paradigm, a framework within which the 2006 *t'shuvah* works toward its own answers. In the first paragraph ("a") of the section "The Question before Us," the present responsum accepts Freehof's central argument: since the Reform Movement has been on record since 1892 that cremation is not a "sin," the halachah according to our understanding would permit the children to honor their father's request. The second paragraph ("b"), to be sure, departs from Freehof, declaring that the children are "not obligated" to fulfill that request should it violate "their sincerely held Judaic religious principles." But it justifies this conclusion in precisely the same way Freehof justified his own—on the basis of the then-current policy of the CCAR as expressed in its official pronouncements on cremation. One might well read this as a suggestion that, had Freehof written in 2006, he (like the Responsa Committee) would have found that the CCAR's 1892 resolution is no longer its last word on the subject and would have agreed that "when a Reform Jew has serious and substantive religious objections to cremation, he or she may refuse a loved one's request for it." In paragraph "d," the *t'shuvah* argues that children who wish to refuse a parent's request for cremation must discuss their refusal openly with the parent. The failure to explicitly say "no" may reasonably be understood as an implied promise, which would impose "an ethical responsibility" upon the child to fulfill its terms. This ethical responsibility evokes Freehof's citation of Babylonian Talmud, *Gittin* 40a, "it is a mitzvah to fulfill the wishes of the deceased." That mitzvah continues to govern our actions in the absence of any other mitzvah—that is, a serious and sincerely held religious value—that would argue against doing what the deceased asks us to do. Rabbi Freehof's influence and guidance are palpable throughout this concluding section, even though the responsum has reached a decision that differs from his.

We began this chapter by mentioning that this responsum, like Reform responsa in general, draws guidance from two traditions of halachic thought: the wider Jewish tradition as expressed in the Talmud, codes, and responsa literature, and the specifically Reform tradition set down in the writings of our predecessors. On this particular question, the message of either of these traditions is equivocal and uncertain. The halachic tradition, depending on how we choose to read it, either prohibits or does not prohibit cremation. Similarly, the specifically Reform Jewish tradition has issued statements both supportive and critical of the practice. The task of the interpreter, then, is to construct what they consider the *best* reading of the message of each. This responsum does this by telling stories that account for the historically changing attitudes toward cremation in both traditional halachah and Reform halachah. And it does this by telling a third story, one of continuity, hewing closely to the 1974 responsum of our teacher Rabbi Solomon B. Freehof even as it decides (against his decision) that the children are entitled to uphold their own religious standards against their father's request. From this we should learn never to discount the role played by storytelling in the understanding of law or halachah. The critical reader should identify these narratives and recognize that role. Whether these particular stories succeed in persuading their intended reader is, of course, another question.

Or, we might say, another story.

CHAPTER FOUR
HONORING MEMORY AND HALACHAH
A Defective "Holocaust" Torah Scroll

THE RESPONSUM we read in the preceding chapter identifies the memory of the Shoah, or Holocaust, as one of the significant "transformations" in contemporary Reform Judaism and in our Jewish consciousness. Our world, and certainly our Jewish world, has changed radically after Auschwitz, so that it is difficult and perhaps impossible for us to think about our Judaism and to tell its story without confronting in some meaningful way the horrors of the Nazi genocide. This confrontation is expressed, among other ways, in the changes we have introduced into our public ritual and synagogue life. We mark Yom HaShoah and Kristallnacht with liturgy and ceremony; we place memorials to the victims of the Holocaust in our buildings; we refer to the memory of the murdered six million when as a congregation we recite the Mourner's *Kaddish*; the list goes on. These changes have seemed entirely appropriate to us, for how can we continue to recite our prayers and perform our rituals as though the Shoah never happened?

Yet are these changes *always* appropriate? At times, the ritual actions we take to preserve the memory of the Shoah's victims clash with established rules and customs, religious practices that existed long before the Second World War and that testify to other memories and other Jewish responsibilities. In those cases, we must decide whether our desire and duty to remember the Shoah take precedence over the demands that those other responsibilities make upon us.

Our next *sh'eilah*, dating from 2000, poses such a conflict (for the full text of the responsum, see pages 192–202):

> Our congregation possesses one of the Czech Torah scrolls that were taken by the Nazis and then rescued and cared for by London's Westminster Synagogue Memorial Trust. There are over one thousand scrolls now on "permanent loan" to synagogues around the world. Ours comes from the town of Kolin, near Prague. Some synagogues have scrolls that are fragmentary or incomplete. Our scroll is a complete *sefer Torah*, but sections of script have flaked away. A

sofer stam (i.e., a scribe qualified to write Torah scrolls, *t'fillin*, and mezuzot) has told us that the parchment will not hold new ink. The scroll, since it cannot be repaired, is technically *pasul*, disqualified for public reading.

Our congregation has decided to use the scroll for Shabbat Torah readings, in places where the script is perfect or at least very clear. In addition, we have allowed many *b'nei mitzvah* to read their *parashah* from the scroll. This enables our youngsters to make a tactile connection between themselves and the vanished community of Kolin. We have taken synagogue and youth trips to Kolin and have prayed at its synagogue, which still stands. The scroll and its history have therefore become a significant part of our congregation's life.

A question has been raised: is it proper for us to read from this scroll, inasmuch as it has been declared *pasul*? How shall we answer this question, in light of both our tradition and the value we have found as a congregation in the public reading of the scroll?[1]

As we learn from this richly detailed *sh'eilah*, the congregation has already made a considered decision to depart from established ritual rules in response to the Shoah. To be sure, it called in a *sofer* to repair its Czech *sefer Torah* so that it might conform to the rules that define a ritually fit (*kasher*) Torah scroll. But upon hearing from him that the scroll cannot be made *kasher*, they have determined nonetheless to read from it during public worship. But now, "a question has been raised" about this practice. We aren't told exactly who raised the question, although the *sh'eilah*'s language suggests it has come from a small minority. After all, as the text makes clear, most congregants seem to be happy with the way the scroll is being used. Still, the "question" (objection?) has become insistent enough to prompt the congregation to turn for guidance to the CCAR Responsa Committee. How shall it resolve this conflict between "our tradition," which would argue against public reading from this *sefer Torah*, and "the value" and meaning its members have found in doing just that?

It's quite possible that the congregation is hoping that the Responsa Committee will declare quickly and decisively in favor of this practice. Such a decision, presumably, would rest upon the finding that for a Reform congregation in a case like this one, the duty to remember the Shoah and to honor the memory of its victims clearly outweighs the importance of adhering to the details governing the ritual fitness of a *sefer Torah*. But that's definitely not the answer the congregation will receive. The responsum frames the question as a close call: "a conflict between two profoundly important Jewish religious values": the remembrance of the Shoah on the one hand and the honor due to the Torah scroll (*k'vod sefer Torah*) on the other. This assertion of a conflict may surprise the congregation, which likely believes that it is *honoring* its Czech Torah scroll by reading from it at services. But the text notes that the phrase *k'vod sefer Torah* has a specific meaning in Jewish tradition. It is a formal ritual observance defined by halachic rules, one of which "demands that the formal public reading of the Torah (*k'riat haTorah*) be performed from a *sefer Torah kasher*, a scroll that meets the strict requirements of ritual fitness." The congregation's practice certainly violates that rule. And since the responsum tells us that *both* of these conflicting values "make powerful claims upon our attention," it is asking us to regard the formal rules of *k'vod sefer Torah* as bearing the same weight as our responsibility for remembering the Shoah.

This, for many (most?) Reform Jews, is a difficult ask indeed. We are accustomed to the claim that in Reform Judaism the details of halachah (often labeled, pejoratively, as "minutiae") are of secondary importance and that we may freely set them aside whenever observing them would prevent us from achieving some important goal. By framing the *sh'eilah* this way, the responsum wants its readers to think of those rules in a different way and see them as an important goal of our religious life. Indeed, as we shall see, the responsum will argue that rules like this one *define* the essential Jewishness of our ritual observance. We cannot simply dismiss them as trivial or as marginal to our concern. Calling upon us to acknowledge the centrality and importance of those rules, the responsum characterizes this question as a hard one, a conflict that allows of no clear and obviously correct solution. Its resolution requires that we "accommodate"—that is, find an appropriate balance between—these two values.

The Reading of the Torah from a Ritually Unfit Scroll

The responsum immediately turns to a discussion of the halachic rules that define a *sefer Torah*. Until now, the message of those rules has seemed painfully obvious from the viewpoint of the congregation: this Torah scroll is ritually unfit for public reading. It turns out, though, that the issue is not so cut and dried. In fact, it's complicated, which makes this an even harder—and more interesting—question than we may have thought.

As is often the case in the halachic literature, the clearest statement of "the rules" (as opposed to the arguments and debates that produce those rules) is provided by Rambam (Maimonides, 1138–1204) in his great code the

Mishneh Torah. He begins the tenth and final chapter of its section "Laws of T'fillin, Mezuzah, and the *Sefer Torah*" with a list of the defects that ritually disqualify a *sefer Torah* for public reading:

> We learn that any one of twenty defects will render a Torah scroll *pasul*. A scroll that displays any one of them has the status of a *Chumash*, which is suitable for teaching children but does not enjoy the sanctity of a *sefer Torah* and is not read in a public worship service. . . .
>
> If the form of [even] one letter is spoiled so that it cannot be read at all or that it resembles another letter, whether this is due to an error in the writing, to a perforation or tear in the parchment, or to blurring of the text.

A valid (*kasher*) Torah scroll must contain the *entire* text of the Five Books of Moses. If even a single letter is missing, imperfectly written, or illegible, the scroll loses its sanctity (*k'dushah*) as a Torah scroll and is reduced to the status of a *Chumash*. Nowadays, the word *Chumash* refers to a printed text of the Pentateuch, often including translation and/or commentary; the volumes used by synagogue worshipers to follow along with the Torah reading are called *Chumashim*. In Rabbinic times, as the responsum's endnote 6 explains, a *Chumash* (the word literally means "one-fifth") was a handwritten scroll containing the text of one of the Five Books. A *Chumash* would not be used to perform *k'riat haTorah b'rabim*, the reading of the Torah on Shabbat, festivals, or other days when the Torah is read during formal public worship. The reason for this is stated in the Talmud (Babylonian Talmud, *Gittin* 60a): "We do not read from *Chumashim* to perform the public Torah reading because this would insult the dignity of the congregation [*k'vod tzibur*]."[2]

This raises a question: what is the *real* objection to reading the Torah from a ritually defective scroll? Rambam seemingly gives two answers. The first is that, by definition, we can fulfill the mitzvah to read from the Torah only by reading from a scroll that is a complete *sefer Torah*, one that meets all the ritual requirements. The second answer, based on his comparison of a defective Torah scroll to a *Chumash*, is that to read from such a scroll is insulting to the community. This second answer implies that a defective scroll *is* a real *sefer Torah* and that, theoretically, we could fulfill the mitzvah by reading from it, but we don't use it for that purpose because to do so would offend our dignity. This second answer will become significant later. For now, though, it is clear that Rambam rules that a scroll like our Czech *sefer Torah*, which is missing some sections and cannot be repaired, is *pasul* and disqualified from public reading.

And yet, this same Rambam is also the author of a responsum that takes the opposite position.[3] He is asked the following question: "Instruct us, our teacher, on a matter concerning the public Torah reading. May a community that does not possess a *sefer Torah* read the assigned portion from *Chumashim* and recite the appropriate blessings both before and after the reading? Or should it abstain from reading Torah altogether? Similarly, if the Torah scroll is defective in a way that renders it ritually *pasul*, is it permissible or forbidden for the reader to recite the blessings over it?"

The *sh'eilah* offers no details about the community from which it originates, but we can easily imagine it to be a small one, in a province distant from any Jewish metropolis. The congregation cannot afford or easily obtain a ritually fit *sefer Torah*. Should Rambam answer that it is forbidden to read from a *Chumash* or from a *pasul* scroll, they will not be able to engage in the public reading of the Torah. But he answers that it is *permissible* to read from such texts *and* to recite the blessings. He explains his reasoning:

> The blessing for the Torah reading is not like the blessing for taking the *lulav* or for dwelling in the sukkah. In those cases, if either the *lulav* or the sukkah is defective [*pasul*], the blessing would be a *b'rachah l'vatalah* [an improper or unnecessary blessing]. This is because the mitzvah is to take the (actual) *lulav* or to dwell in (an actual) sukkah, and if either of these is ritually defective, one has not fulfilled the mitzvah. Here, however, the mitzvah is the reading from a *sefer Torah*, whether it is *kasher* or *pasul* . . . because the blessing is recited over the reading [that is, the text, and not the scroll].

In other words, the reading itself—the actual recitation of the words of the text—is what counts, and that recitation is valid even if performed from a *sefer Torah pasul*. Why then does the Talmud object to reading from a "defective" Torah scroll? The answer, says Rambam, is the second of the two answers we discuss above: reading from such a scroll, equivalent in ritual status to a *Chumash*, insults the dignity of the congregation. But that concern would not apply in the case he is addressing here, where the congregation's only *sefer Torah* happens to be *pasul*. To read from that scroll would not insult the honor of that community.

Rambam's ruling in his *t'shuvah* therefore contradicts what he tells us in his great code. Which opinion takes precedence? The CCAR responsum tells us that as far as the history of the halachah is concerned, the *t'shuvah*'s "permissive ruling remains very much a minority view." Indeed, the *t'shuvah* receives overwhelmingly negative reviews from subsequent halachic author-

ities, almost all of whom hold that the authoritative halachah follows his ruling in the *Mishneh Torah*. They stress that there is no support in the Talmudic
sources for his theory that the reading of Torah has more to do with the words
that are read than with the scroll that contains them. Rambam appears to
have invented this theory out of whole cloth. Since no other authorities support his theory, the ruling in his *t'shuvah* has the status of *daat yachid*, the
opinion of a single individual against the preponderant majority (which, of
course, includes his own ruling in the *Mishneh Torah*). While this, as we'll see,
does not prove that the ruling in his *t'shuvah* is *wrong*, it does mean that,
legally speaking, it's a curiosity. Out of a desire to account for that curiosity,
some authorities go so far as to deny the *t'shuvah*'s authenticity: somebody
else must have forged it, for surely a great scholar like Rambam could never
have written such nonsense! Others resolve the problem chronologically:
Rambam authored the responsum in his "youth," while the *Mishneh Torah*
conveys his more mature, considered (and correct) understanding of the law.
The CCAR responsum makes its own contribution to the scholarly debate: we
can accept both rulings as genuine and noncontradictory, because each may
speak to a different set of circumstances. As evidence, the responsum cites
the concluding words of Rambam's *t'shuvah*: "It is proper for every community to possess a Torah scroll that is *kasher* in all respects, and it is preferable
[*l'chat'chilah*] to read from that scroll.[4] If this is not possible, however, let
them read in public even from a *pasul* scroll and recite the blessings, on the
basis of the reasoning I have supplied."

In other words, Rambam's ruling in the *Mishneh Torah* corresponds to
the ideal or best standard of observance (if one has a choice, *this* is how one
ought to perform the mitzvah), while his *t'shuvah* offers a standard that,
while certainly not preferable, is at least minimally acceptable and fulfills
the mitzvah. Thus, while a congregation *should* read Torah from a scroll that
meets all the ritual requirements and must do so if it has that option, a congregation that possesses only a defective scroll may use it to fulfill the mitzvah of public Torah reading, so that, as some commentators explain, "the
practice of reading the Torah not be forgotten" in that community.[5]

The Issue from a Reform Jewish Perspective

What does all this mean for us? Why does this Reform responsum engage
in this extensive discussion of a medieval halachic controversy? We find a
possible answer in this next section, where the responsum builds a case for

each of the two possible answers to our *sh'eilah*: "Yes, you may read publicly from this *pasul* scroll" and "No, you should not read publicly from this *pasul* scroll." The "yes" answer, as we'll see, is what we might call a classic Reform halachic argument, one that begins with the Jewish legal sources (in this case, the controversy we have just discussed) and reads them through the lens of Reform Jewish thought and concerns. The "no" answer is more theological or doctrinal than halachic in nature. The responsum will ultimately side with "no," which might seem odd, given that this is a halachic responsum. As critical readers, our task (among others) is to inquire as to why this *t'shuvah* follows doctrine rather than law.

The "yes" answer begins with the words "We could make a good case to support this congregation's desire to conduct its Shabbat Torah readings from the Czech scroll." (Notice that word "could," as in "we *could* make this argument, but we won't." The responsum signals us here that it will ultimately reject this "good case.") This halachic argument consists of three stages. The first stage—quite appropriately, given the responsum's discussion until now—is Rambam's *t'shuvah* that permits Torah reading from a *sefer Torah pasul*. Granted, that ruling is a minority opinion, but the prestige of its author demands that we pay it attention. As a matter of fact, as the responsum's endnote 26 explains, Rambam's *t'shuvah* exerts a lasting influence upon subsequent halachah, defining to this day the procedure followed in many Orthodox congregations when an error is discovered in a Torah scroll during the reading. This allows us to conclude that Rambam's ruling has the sort of "gravitational force" that makes it a reliable precedent and definitely *not* a legal curiosity.[6] The second stage considers the nature of Reform halachah, which holds that a minority opinion is not necessarily "wrong" just because it is outvoted. Given that Rambam's *t'shuvah* corresponds to what Rabbi Freehof has called the "liberally affirmative" position,[7] we have reason to adopt it as the basis of our own practice. And the third stage: the concern that reading from a *pasul* scroll insults "the dignity of the community" does not apply to *this* congregation, which finds great meaning in reading from its Czech *sefer Torah* at worship services. Rambam's "minority" opinion, in other words, is the better fit for Reform Jewish practice.

The "no" answer ("Yet this 'good' case is insufficient") avoids technical halachic considerations and goes directly to the nature of ritual practice in Reform Judaism. The congregation should not read Torah from its *pasul* scroll because to do so violates our own standard, the one we Reform Jews have historically set for our ritual observance—namely, to read from a scroll that meets the traditional definition of a *sefer Torah*. The rules that define the ritual fitness of a Torah scroll are binding upon us, not because the halachah itself is binding upon us, but because we Reform Jews have bound ourselves to observe them. These rules are "not mere technicalities, nor are they standards of 'Orthodox' practice," but also *our* standards—standards that determine what counts as an authentic *sefer Torah* for *all* Jews, us included. To put this another way, there is no such thing as a "Reform" Torah scroll or an "Orthodox" Torah scroll; all Jews read from a scroll that meets the same rules and specifications. If, therefore, a Torah scroll is *pasul* according to those rules, it is *pasul* for us as well as for other Jewish communities. True, Rambam's *t'shuvah* permits the reading of Torah from a *sefer Torah pasul*. But that permit was aimed specifically at communities who do not possess a *kasher* scroll and have no other way to practice the public reading of the Torah. It is therefore not a precedent for a congregation that possesses other Torah scrolls. In a rather blunt rhetorical flourish, the responsum declares, "To exalt this stopgap device to the status of a permanent and weekly observance . . . is to suggest that we are satisfied with an ersatz standard of Jewish practice, that appearances count more than reality, that we are perfectly content to read from a scroll that looks like—but is not—a real *sefer Torah*." The responsum challenges the congregation, and by extension all its Reform Jewish readers, to reject that path: "This is not the sort of statement that *any* Jewish community, Reform or otherwise, ought to make; we should consider it an affront to the dignity of our congregation."

This point—that we should not be satisfied with an "ersatz standard" of ritual practice—is reminiscent of a *t'shuvah* issued by the Responsa Committee in 1995 entitled "A Non-Traditional Sukkah."[8] (It is cited in the responsum's endnote 30, which goes to show just how footnotes and endnotes are crucial for the critical reader!) In that case, the *sh'eilah* asks whether a "liberal Jewish" definition of *sukkah* might include a nontraditional structure (say a tent), or even if the mitzvah could be fulfilled simply by eating meals outdoors. The 1995 responsum frames the issue as reflecting the ongoing Reform *machloket* over the place of ritual observance in our religious life. It recognizes that Reform Judaism has always been ready to eliminate "ceremonies" it considers outdated or "objectionable on moral or aesthetic grounds." But since there are no such objections against the practice of sukkah, Reform rabbis ought to encourage people to observe that mitzvah in its traditional form.

The choice, as we see it, is between two definitions of rabbinic responsibility. On the one hand, we can decide that our role is to tell our people that they may be satisfied with *ersatz* [emphasis added] Jewish rituals or with whatever level of observance they are able to reach at the moment. On the other, while we validate their good intentions, we can resolve to teach, to lead, and to encourage them to adopt into their lives those forms of Jewish observance that, while resonating with our modern temperament, have become emblematic of Torah, of our people's particular religious experience in its search for God.

The word "ersatz," of course, appears in the present responsum as well, and it suggests two points. First, unless there is some overriding objection that we Reform Jews would make to it, the traditional definition of a ritual mitzvah is the *real* definition, the *Jewish* definition. Second, a ritual observance is more than an external shell that can be discarded once we perceive its essential content. The ritual is just as "essential" as the content; it is the indispensably *Jewish* way of bringing that content into our lives through action. As the 1995 responsum puts it:

It is through these concrete observances, rituals by which the Jewish people has come to express its understanding of itself as an historical religious community, that we identify ourselves with their experience. Surely we would not suggest that liberal Jews could somehow "fulfill" the mitzvot of Shabbat and Passover by stripping these special times of the very rituals that make them special, that make them Jewish. And just as surely, we do not think that liberal Jews can "fulfill" the mitzvah of *sukkah* by substituting some non-traditional approximation for the age-old Jewish observance.

In this view, a traditional Jewish ritual practice is not merely a symbol of some greater spiritual truth. It is an inextricable element of that truth, the concrete expression that conveys the essential Jewishness of that truth. Accordingly, observance of the mitzvah in its traditional form should be the default standard.

This, of course, is not the only way that Reform Jews have understood the role of ritual observance in our religious practice. The competing understanding is that ritual is a means to an end, a vessel that conveys ethical and spiritual meaning and is of secondary importance to that meaning. As we've seen in the introduction, that understanding is a predominant message of the 1885 Pittsburgh Platform, and though the subsequent platforms of the CCAR have, each in its own way, sought to moderate that message, it continues to reflect the religious worldview of many Reform Jews. The 1995 responsum, in its argument that ritual practice is an essential element of Reform Jewish life and not simply an auxiliary to some more important element of it, poses a direct challenge to that worldview. The present responsum applies that argument to our *sh'eilah*: to read Torah from a scroll that does not adhere to the traditional definition of a *sefer Torah*, in the absence of sufficient cause, is to depart from the default standard of observance that we ourselves recognize. What it does not mention, but what critical readers ought to keep in mind, is that it is taking up one side of that ongoing *machloket* over the proper place of ritual in Reform Judaism. This, then, is a responsum that can be adequately understood only within the context of Reform Jewish history, from the Pittsburgh Platform to our own day.

The phrase "in the absence of sufficient cause" in the preceding paragraph demands attention. Even if we accept this responsum's approach to ritual practice in Reform Judaism and its definition of the "default standard" for such practice, doesn't our congregation have "sufficient cause" to modify that standard? Why can't we say that the duty to remember the Shoah outweighs this particular requirement of ritual halachah? The responsum offers two answers to this objection. First, it is *unnecessary* to make an exception in this case. We already fulfill the obligation to remember the Shoah through numerous rituals and commemorations that we have introduced into our communal life. Second, it is *unwise* to make an exception in this case. It is one thing to create and add new rituals, such as the observance of Yom HaShoah and the observance of Kristallnacht, to remember the Shoah. But it is another thing to allow that memory an excessive role in defining our religious practice. As the responsum puts it, "To change, detract from, or abandon essential religious observances *because* of the Shoah, to read from a *pasul* Torah scroll—something we would otherwise not do—*because* the Nazis murdered the Jews who once possessed it, is to proclaim that the crimes of Hitler take precedence over the 'voice of Sinai,' the proper conduct of Jewish religious life" (emphasis in original). This sentence evokes the debate among some prominent late twentieth-century Jewish religious thinkers over Emil Fackenheim's notion of "the commanding voice of Auschwitz," the divine demand upon the Jews to survive as a people so as to deny Hitler any posthumous victories. Fackenheim calls this demand "the 614th commandment," suggesting that it enjoys the same status as the traditional mitzvot of the Torah. Fackenheim's critics deny that the Holocaust is a "commanding voice" for us, insisting that Sinai remains the one true source of Jewish religious obligation.[9] The responsum's language places it on the side of the critics. The "crimes of Hitler" may stir us to acts of remembrance, but they are not a commanding voice for us; we therefore should not alter our established patterns of observance in response to them. Here the text makes its plea for the *balance* of which we spoke at the beginning of this chapter: let us remember the Shoah, but let that memory not distort our Judaism and the standards of religious practice that we, along with all other Jews, have historically accepted.

To summarize: the responsum's "no" argument, the case against reading from the Czech Torah scroll, is built not upon halachic considerations (as is the case in favor of reading from the scroll), but upon a particular understanding of the role of ritual observance in Reform Judaism and upon a particular understanding of the proper Jewish religious response to the Shoah. A "particular" understanding is by its nature controversial, since other interpretations of Reform Judaism and of the meaning of the Shoah are available to us. Accordingly, when choosing one or the other interpretation, we shall have to *argue* for it to establish that it is better or more persuasive than the alternatives. The responsum for its part argues vigorously for each of its own interpretations, inviting its readers to share in them and to define their Jewish worldview accordingly.

The Decision

Having made the case for two plausible answers to the *sh'eilah*, the responsum adopts the second one: "We should insist, instead, that our regular weekly, Shabbat, and holiday Torah portions be read from a *sefer Torah kasher*." This brief paragraph concludes with three sentences: "This is the standard bequeathed to us from Jewish tradition. This was the standard observed by the Czech community from which the scroll in question originated. And it remains the standard that informs Reform Jewish life, the standard to which we educate our children and to which we ought to aspire." These sentences may strike us as superfluous, a mere rhetorical embellishment that adds nothing to the decision itself. In fact, though, they are part of the argument for that decision. The rhythmic emphasis upon the word "standard" calls the reader to a sense of obligation: a "standard" is something we ought to live up to. We ought to aspire to read Torah from a ritually fit scroll because that is the criterion of correctness that all Jews have established for themselves and have "aspired" to pass on to their descendants—and we are included in that group. If the reader accepts the call, it is a clinching argument; who, after all, would want to claim that their Judaism is "substandard"? Again, we see how a responsum, as a species of persuasive writing, uses language and rhetorical art to convince us that its answer, originally one of two plausible responses to the *sh'eilah*, is the unquestionably correct one.

The text now makes a sharp turn. After stating its decision in unequivocal language—"we should insist" upon reading a scroll that is *kasher*—it backtracks: "The above does not mean that the congregation should *never* read from its Czech *sefer Torah*." The two paragraphs that follow offer suggestions as to how the congregation might continue reading from the scroll in such a way as to remove "the traditional objections" to doing so. Essentially, the responsum recommends that the congregation conduct its regular weekly reading from a *kasher* scroll and then use its Czech scroll for an *additional* reading. As endnote 31 informs us, once the congregation has performed the mitzvah of *k'riat haTorah* by means of the *kasher* scroll, there is no halachic objection to its reading an additional section of text from the *sefer Torah pasul* (provided that the traditional *b'rachot* are not recited).[10] This procedure, certainly, would lengthen the service, and that's no small thing. Still, it allows the congregation to make significant use of its Czech scroll, just as it does now, while maintaining the "standard" that we fulfill the mitzvah of reading the Torah from a scroll that is ritually fit and textually whole.

What's going on here? Some readers will likely conclude that the responsum is searching for technical loopholes to permit what it has just forbidden. Maybe, but let's remember two things. First, the responsum has framed this *sh'eilah* as a conflict between two values that demand our loyalty: the importance of rendering honor to the Torah scroll and the duty to render honor to the memory of the victims of the Shoah. It should thus be no surprise that the text wishes to find a solution or solutions that will accommodate both of those values. Second, these so-called loopholes are an intrinsic element of the halachic rules that define a *sefer Torah* and regulate its ritual use. That is, the very same rules that prohibit the public Torah reading (*k'riat haTorah*) from a *sefer Torah pasul* do *not* prohibit reading from that scroll once the regular weekly reading is concluded. Crucially, the responsum sees no reason to extend the prohibition beyond its formal limits; it does not wish to forbid what the rules technically permit. Here too we see evidence of the "liberally affirmative" tendency of Reform responsa, the positive effort to expand the boundaries of the halachah so as to make room for options and interpretations that other (Orthodox?) approaches would not accept. In the end, this Reform responsum wishes to empower the congregation to realize its wish to read from its Czech *sefer Torah*, so long as it does so in ways that are coherent with the standards—*our* standards—that define what a *sefer Torah* is.

CHAPTER FIVE

THE CHANGING REFORM "MOOD"
Three Responsa on Shabbat

Four mitzvot are stated concerning Shabbat: two emanate from the Torah and two are based in the enactments of the Sages as spelled out in the prophetic literature.[1] The Toraitic mitzvot are *zachor*, "remember the Sabbath day" [Exodus 20:8], and *shamor*, "observe the Sabbath day" [Deuteronomy 5:12]. The mitzvot spelled out in the prophetic literature are *kavod*, "honor the Sabbath," and *oneg*, "delight" in the Sabbath, as it is said (Isaiah 58:13), "If you call the Shabbat 'delight,' the day of *Adonai* 'honored.'"
—RAMBAM, *Mishneh Torah, Hilchot Shabbat* 30:1

IF SOMEONE WERE TO ASK us for a concise, standing-on-one-foot definition of the Jewish Sabbath, we'd probably reply that it is a day of "rest" (*m'nuchah*) on which one is to abstain from "work" (*m'lachah*). But if someone asked what those concepts mean to us as *Reform* Jews, the answer would be much less obvious. According to the Rabbis, the "work" prohibited by the Torah on Shabbat consists of thirty-nine general categories of activity called *avot* (*Mishnah Shabbat* 7:2), each of which is subdivided into many subcategories called *tol'dot*. (That list is the same for Yom Kippur and, with some important exceptions, for festival days.) To this, the Rabbis themselves added other prohibitions. This highly detailed system of rules and principles constitutes the bulk of what Orthodox Jews mean when they speak of *sh'mirat Shabbat*, the *observance* of the Sabbath. Reform Judaism, from its early days in Germany, has largely rejected that system and has never replaced it with a single, officially sanctioned alternative definition of "work" and "rest." For this reason, one may reasonably wonder whether Reform Judaism offers any substantive teaching on the subject. And if not, then doesn't it follow that Reform Judaism has abandoned the observance of the Jewish Sabbath?

"Abandoned"? Readers may point to the bustling activity on Friday nights and Saturdays in Reform synagogues as evidence that Shabbat is alive and well in our movement. But it's certainly true that we have ignored the major part of the tradition that over many centuries has characterized the day.

Let's take a quantitative measurement. Look at the quotation that begins this chapter. The "Laws of Shabbat" (*Hilchot Shabbat*) in Rambam's *Mishneh Torah* is divided into thirty chapters. The commandment to "remember" Shabbat—which refers to the recitation of *Kiddush* and *Havdalah*—is detailed in the twenty-ninth chapter.[2] The instructions to "honor" the Sabbath (by wearing nice clothes, setting a beautiful table, etc.) and "delight" in it (by eating at least three meals on Shabbat with especially good food and drink) are found in chapter 30. The remaining twenty-eight chapters—the preponderance of Rambam's material—are devoted to the prohibitions against *m'lachah* on Shabbat, which characterize the mitzvah of *shamor*, "observe the Sabbath." Measured in these purely quantitative terms, the traditional Jewish Sabbath is defined much more by its "thou shalt not" prohibitions than by its ritual "thou shalt" elements. But in Reform Judaism, these proportions are reversed: our literature concentrates upon the ritual aspects of *zachor*, *kavod*, and *oneg* and has very little to say about *shamor*, actions prohibited on Shabbat.

It's not difficult to understand why. Traditional Shabbat law includes many prohibitions (concerning travel, commerce, and technology, to name just a few) that render it nearly impossible for the Jew to take part in the surrounding society's economic, social, and cultural life. Traditionalists would insist that this is the very point of Shabbat: to take a break from *chol*, the "secular" weekday world in order to devote ourselves to *kodesh*, "holy" activities such as prayer, Torah study, family time, and *m'nuchah*. However, we Reform Jews—who regard equal participation in the life of the wider world as a crowning achievement of Jewish modernity—tend not to see this enforced separation as a blessing. Besides, we have never been comfortable with the Rabbinic definition of *m'lachah*. The Rabbis derived the thirty-nine *avot* (general categories) of *m'lachah* by way of tortuous analogies to labors involved in the building of the ancient Tabernacle;[3] most of us fail to understand why these activities—many of which we simply do not think of as "work"—should prevent us from doing things on Shabbat that we find convenient or meaningful. Why, for example, should we be forbidden to use an umbrella on a rainy Shabbat just because someone once decided that opening an umbrella resembles *boneh*, the prohibited act of "building" a structure? And why should we be prevented from turning on electric lights and other appliances on Shabbat just because Orthodox rabbis over the last two centuries have compared the use of electricity to actions prohibited in ancient texts?[4] We have found it more useful to concentrate upon the positive, ritual elements of Shabbat that *do* strike us as meaningful rather than upon the negative ones that are devoid of significance to us.

This isn't to say that Reform has paid no attention whatsoever to Shabbat observance. Although for many years "neither rabbinic nor lay Reform bodies were interested in tackling this vexing question,"[5] that situation has changed in recent decades.One sign of this change is CCAR's publication of *A Shabbat Manual* and *Gates of Shabbat*, books that offer officially sanctioned guidance how Shabbat might be observed.[6] Another is the *sh'eilot* addressed to the CCAR Responsa Committee asking for guidance on *sh'mirat Shabbat*. But how should Reform responsa writers formulate such guidance? Lacking clear standards for determining "what we do and what we don't," how can Reform rabbis argue that a particular act ought to be forbidden on Shabbat? Do their opinions represent anything more than subjective preferences or personal taste? If we have renounced the halachic system of Shabbat observance, how can we write halachic *t'shuvot* on that subject, particularly when the goal of our responsa is to offer arguments that a Reform Jewish audience could find persuasive?

In this chapter, we will read three responsa that take up this challenge. Each raises the question of our attitude toward the traditional Shabbat prohibitions. More than that: each involves an activity that we would regard as a mitzvah but that runs afoul of the traditional halachah of Shabbat. Should this activity be permitted in a Reform community, whose members do not consider themselves bound by that halachah? How *can* a Reform responsum answer such a question? To do so requires a *language* for talking and arguing about Shabbat observance in a way that makes sense to us. Each responsum attempts to develop such a language. How well they do that, of course, is left to the judgment of the critical reader.

1. Gift Corner Open on the Sabbath

Our first *sh'eilah* was submitted to Rabbi Solomon B. Freehof and published in 1960 (the full text of the responsum can be found on pages 202–205):

> The congregational gift corner provides books and prayer books, candles and candlesticks, Chanukah menorahs; in other words, it serves a religious purpose. Should this fact not justify keeping the gift corner open on Friday night? It is only on Friday night that large numbers of people coming for the Sabbath service can conveniently make use of the gift corner.[7]

Rabbi Freehof opens his *t'shuvah* by acknowledging the problem that Shabbat observance poses for Reform Jews. Unlike Orthodox and Conservative rabbis, who would approach the issue from the standpoint of traditional halachah, a Reform rabbi does not enjoy the option of such a "simple" response.[8] This is because, as he puts it, "the Sabbath laws of prohibited work are no longer clear with us," a situation he attributes to what he calls "the rather undefined mood of Reform." Many traditional Shabbat prohibitions, such as driving, carrying in the public domain, and cooking, "are no longer contrary to our general Sabbath mood."

But if that's the problem, it is also the beginning of a solution. If this "mood" in fact determines our standards our practice, then we ought to use it in principle as our starting point for thinking about questions like this one. "Generally," he writes, "we feel that those observances that are gone cannot now be easily restored. The effort to restore them would require an overemphasis on ritual matters," practices in which Reform Jews find relatively little meaning. On the other hand, traditional observances that do fit in with our Shabbat mood are worth keeping; "what we can preserve, and without too much overemphasis [on ritual matters] restore as a natural mood of the people, that we would endeavor to do."

That this "Reform Sabbath mood" replaces halachah as the criterion to decide our Shabbat observance is Freehof's *chidush*, his unique contribution to the discussion of the issue. Like most innovative ideas, this one has roots in the past. Freehof's "mood" bears a family resemblance to *minhag*, the community's long-standing custom and accepted patterns of behavior. While other scholars regard *minhag* as one of several sources of Jewish law,[9] Freehof considers it the ultimate source: "The Minhag created by the masses was the raw material which the law took up and shifted, rearranged, justified and embodied as legal practice. The law itself did not create. The people created and the law organized."[10] If Freehof's conception of *minhag* is controversial, he is correct that communal custom has always exerted a powerful influence upon the development of the law.[11] His notion of "mood" is also a close cousin to what the eminent historian Jacob Katz calls the "ritual instinct" of the people—their general sense of what constitutes proper religious conduct in any particular situation, which often influences the rulings of the *poskim*, the recognized halachic authorities.[12] Still, Freehof's "mood" exceeds the scope of both *minhag*, which in traditional Jewish law does not have the power to nullify rules based in the Torah, and of the "ritual instinct," which operates informally and behind the scenes. His Sabbath mood, by contrast, is a halachic principle, the official, formal reference point for all matters of Shabbat observance within a Reform community.

Another criticism is that while Rabbi Freehof cites the "Reform Sabbath mood" as a basis for making decisions, he never offers evidence for its existence. That is, he produces no empirical data, like the findings of a sociological study, to prove that a significant number of Reform Jews share this attitude about Shabbat observance. He simply *declares* that the Reform Sabbath mood exists. But then, perhaps that is all he needs to do. Consider his repeated use of the first-person plural: "Generally we feel that those observances that are gone cannot now be easily restored"; "what we can preserve . . . that we would endeavor to do"; "we are justified in making a distinction between what the people do outside the temple . . . and what we would permit on the Sabbath or on other occasions on the temple premises"; "It is from this point of view that we must consider the question." The "we" in these sentences signifies Freehof's intended audience: that body of those Reform Jews who take the question of Shabbat observance seriously and who share his particular vision of how Shabbat is and ought to be observed within the movement. They share, in other words, his notion of a Reform Sabbath mood. Through this act of language, the repeated use of "we," Freehof calls this audience into being, inviting us to identify as its members. To the extent that we accept his invitation and recognize in his words our own attitude toward Shabbat observance, we *already* accept the existence of this Reform Sabbath "mood" and will tend to agree with him that this mood forms the standard for what our practice ought to be.

Rabbi Freehof, we might say, *chooses* the audience for his words, speaking intentionally to *some* Reform Jews but not to those who would deny either the existence or the significance of the Reform Sabbath mood. Students of rhetoric say there is nothing unusual or devious about this. Persuasive speech, as I discuss in the introduction to this book, "is always directed toward a particular audience composed of individuals who, in the opinion of the speaker or writer, will be open to this argument and may find it convincing." And to a great extent, the speaker or writer *constructs* this audience; it exists because of choices the speaker makes.[13] Freehof's "we" language invokes his particular, intended audience of Reform Jews who accept as a general rule the traditional prohibition of commercial activity on Shabbat, especially in the synagogue. Note that the rabbi who has submitted the *sh'eilah* identifies as a member of this audience. The rabbi presumably accepts the traditional prohibition against conducting commercial activity in the synagogue on Shabbat and asks whether the benefits of the gift corner "justify" waiving that prohibition in this case. Freehof's audience, then, understands this to be a halachic question, and they are asking him for a halachic answer. They wish to know whether traditional Jewish law, as read and debated by a community of committed Reform Jews, is able to permit the operation of the gift corner on Shabbat. Speaking to *this* audience, and operating within the boundaries of these assumptions, Freehof's halachic argument is entirely appropriate and to the point.

That argument begins with the traditional textual basis for the rule banning commerce on Shabbat.[14] While the Torah never mentions that prohibition, the Rabbis (in Babylonian Talmud, *Shabbat* 150a) locate it in Isaiah 58:13: "If you refrain from trampling the Sabbath, from pursuing your affairs [*chafatzecha*, literally 'your desires'] on My holy day; if you call the Sabbath 'delight,' the Eternal's holy day 'honored'; [v. 14: then you can seek the Eternal's favor, etc.]." The Rabbis interpret the phrase "refrain from . . . pursuing your affairs" as a prohibition of commerce, "even though," as Rambam puts it in the *Mishneh Torah*, "the act of buying and selling does not resemble one of the forms of forbidden 'work.'"[15] But notice that the Isaiah text reads "*your* affairs." The Talmud applies a strict construction to these words: "The verse says 'from pursuing your affairs' . . . this means that though your affairs are prohibited, the affairs of heaven are permitted." "The affairs of heaven," obviously, are mitzvot. Thus, the Talmud continues:

> Rav Chisda and Rav Hamnuna said, "It is permissible on Shabbat to make calculations for the purpose of mitzvah."
>
> And Rabbi Elazar said, "It is permissible on Shabbat to decide allocations of *tzedakah* to the poor."
>
> And Rabbi Yaakov bar Idi reported in the name of Rabbi Yochanan, "We may attend to activities necessary for saving a life or for communal needs on Shabbat, and we may go to a synagogue to attend to communal affairs on Shabbat."
>
> And Rabbi Sh'muel bar Nachmani reported in the name of Rabbi Yochanan, "We may go to theaters, circuses, or public buildings on Shabbat to discuss and make decisions on communal affairs."

Rambam (*Mishneh Torah, Hilchot Shabbat* 24:5) codifies the above as decided law: "It is permitted on Shabbat to make allocations of *tzedakah* to the poor, and to go to synagogues and study halls and even to theaters and other non-Jewish places of entertainment to supervise communal affairs on Shabbat."

The halachah thus allows wide latitude to transact "communal affairs" on Shabbat. As Rabbi Freehof argues, the temple's gift corner most definitely serves a community purpose, both by supporting the synagogue financially and by supplying Judaica to the members of the congregation. On that basis, it would seem logical to allow the gift corner to conduct business as usual on Friday night. But Freehof does not draw that conclusion, because Rambam's ruling doesn't stretch that far. In the words of a leading commentator to the *Mishneh Torah*, "Bear in mind that no Rabbinic prohibition is waived for the sake of public business . . . all that is permitted is the *discussion* of these matters" (emphasis added).[16] While it is permissible to *discuss* public affairs and even to make financial decisions concerning those matters on Shabbat, says Freehof, one may *not* perform any "definitely prohibited actions," such as monetary exchange, to that end. He adds that even in our Reform context the exchange of money is "violative of the mood of the Sabbath, especially in the synagogue."

Does this mean that the gift corner should remain closed on Friday night? Rabbi Freehof says that this would be the "simplest" answer, particularly in the absence of any "pressure" within the congregation to open it. But the *sh'eilah* itself indicates that there is real division over this issue within the congregation. We therefore cannot say that the existing "Sabbath mood" offers a definitive answer in this case. For disputed questions such as this one, we must use "judgment," especially "under our present vague relationship with the Sabbath laws." The "best procedure" is to forge an accommodation that speaks to the concerns of both sides: the gift shop may operate on Friday night, provided that it doesn't handle money. Congregants attending services can select items for purchase and pay for them once Shabbat is over.

Some readers will object that this solution is not a real "accommodation" but rather a legal fiction—a transparent ruse designed to disguise the reality that the gift corner is in fact doing business on Friday night. Those readers have a point, but let's consider a more generous reading of the decision. Rabbi Freehof argues that the only sure criterion by which a Reform community can make decisions about Shabbat observance is the prevailing "Sabbath mood." It follows that in cases like this one, where that criterion does not decide "yes" or "no" in a clear and unambiguous way, the best decision is a pragmatic compromise between those two possible answers. One may find fault with this compromise, but one cannot call it unreasonable.

Still, pragmatic compromise is not the *tachlit* (the ultimate goal) of this *t'shuvah*. As Rabbi Freehof remarks in his conclusion, the requirement that the gift corner operate differently on Shabbat than on weekdays might "remind [the congregants] of the Sabbath traditions and perhaps influence them to do less purchasing in general on the Sabbath, whenever such self-restraint is practical." Here Freehof abandons the descriptive tone he has used until now in favor of more normative and even aspirational language. At this moment, given our "vague" relationship with the traditional Shabbat halachah, the prevailing Sabbath mood argues for accommodation and compromise. But Rabbi Freehof urges us to look forward to a day when that mood will transform into something more definite: a higher and more demanding standard of Shabbat observance.

2. Delayed *B'rit Milah* on Shabbat

Like Rabbi Freehof's responsum, our next *t'shuvah* involves a situation in which a traditional Shabbat prohibition interferes with the achievement of another religious purpose (the full text of the responsum can be found on pages 205–208):

> The *b'rit milah* of a newborn baby was delayed past his eighth day. His parents now wish to schedule that ceremony on a Shabbat, since Shabbat is a day when family and friends can attend the *simchah* [joyous event]. According to tradition, a delayed *b'rit milah* may not take place on Shabbat. Is that the position of Reform Judaism as well?[17]

This *sh'eilah* poses a question about the acceptable religious grounds that permit a Reform community to deny the family's request to schedule the delayed *b'rit milah* on Shabbat. If the only objection to their request is a detail of traditional Shabbat halachah, which as Freehof might say is "no longer clear with us," perhaps there is no good Reform Jewish reason to stand in their way. Yet the responsum will decide otherwise, as it hints in its introductory paragraph: "This question, as we understand it, concerns the nature and standing of both *b'rit milah* and Shabbat as they are observed or ought to be observed in our communities. Is the celebration of the mitzvah of circumcision, truly a powerful Jewish moment, so important and central that it should supersede the restrictions that customarily define Shabbat? Or does the reverence we accord Shabbat demand that other mitzvot, should they interfere with its observance, be set aside?"

Once again, a responsum frames the sh'eilah as a conflict between two meaningful Jewish practices. Noteworthy here is its depiction of Shabbat as a day for which we feel "reverence," an observance "customarily define[d]" by its "restrictions," a clear reference to the prohibitions against m'lachah and other activities. This language is quite a departure from the ambivalence of Rabbi Freehof's "Reform Sabbath mood." In this responsum, Shabbat observance is not a problem desperately seeking a solution, but rather a mitzvah equal in status to others. As we'll see, this descriptive language makes all the difference in the responsum's ultimate decision.

B'RIT MILAH ON SHABBAT IN JEWISH LAW

The responsum is divided into two sections, the first surveying the traditional halachic literature and the second setting forth an explicitly Reform Jewish viewpoint. The halachic section, which discusses the tradition's rule concerning b'rit milah on Shabbat, begins with Leviticus 12:3, "On the eighth day [of the newborn boy's life] the flesh of his foreskin shall be circumcised."

A Rabbinic midrash (Babylonian Talmud, *Shabbat* 132a) interprets the verse as follows: "The phrase 'on the eighth day [*uvayom hash'mini*]' implies: even if that day is Shabbat." This midrash, as the responsum's first endnote explains, employs a common Rabbinic approach to "superfluous" language (*yitur lashon*) in the Torah. It begins with the assumption that the Torah does not use language merely for literary or stylistic effect. Thus, an apparently "superfluous" word or phrase in its text—one not necessary to convey the text's literal sense—is not superfluous at all; rather, say the Rabbis, it's there to convey information that goes beyond that literal sense. In this case, the word *uvayom*, "on the day," seems unnecessary. Why? Because the previous verse (Leviticus 12:2) tells us that "when a woman at childbirth bears a male, she shall be impure seven days [*shivat yamim*]." The word *hash'mini*, "the eighth," in verse 3 obviously means "the eighth *day*" and by itself would have been sufficient to inform us that the circumcision is to occur on the eighth day of the boy's life. The word *uvayom* is therefore "superfluous" to the literal meaning of the verse. The midrash therefore deduces that it comes to communicate a detail that we don't learn from the literal meaning: the circumcision must take place on *that* day, the eighth day, *even* if it falls on Shabbat. This instruction is necessary because the surgical procedure of *milah* (circumcision) involves actions defined as *m'lachah* and normally prohibited on Shabbat. From *uvayom*, the Rabbis learn that when the eighth day of a boy's life falls on Shabbat, the circumcision "overrides" the Shabbat prohibitions (*dochah et haShabbat*). This applies, of course, *only* if Shabbat is his eighth day. Should the *milah* be delayed for any reason beyond the eighth day, the circumcision does *not* override the prohibitions and therefore may not take place. According to traditional halachah, then, the answer to our question is straightforward: the family may not schedule their ceremony on Shabbat.

The responsum now takes up a Rabbinic text that appears tangential to our *sh'eilah*. *Mishnah Shabbat* 19:1 recounts a *machloket* (dispute) between two Tannaim (sages of the Mishnaic period) concerning the proper procedure for a *b'rit milah* that takes place on Shabbat:

> Rabbi Eliezer says, "If one [the mohel, the person who will perform the circumcision] did not bring a circumcision knife on the day before Shabbat, he may bring it on Shabbat. . . ." Rabbi Eliezer says further, "One may cut wood [on Shabbat] in order to make charcoal so as to manufacture an iron knife."
>
> Rabbi Akiva, however, states a general principle: "If a prohibited labor [*m'lachah*] could have been performed on the day before Shabbat, it does not override Shabbat; if it could not have been performed on the day before Shabbat, it does override Shabbat."

The two sages agree that *b'rit milah* takes precedence over the Shabbat prohibitions when a boy's eighth day falls on Shabbat. They disagree, however, on just how far that "precedence" extends. Rabbi Eliezer thinks that since the circumcision itself overrides Shabbat, *any* action necessary to its performance may also take place on that day. Thus, he allows the mohel to carry his knife through the public thoroughfare or even to manufacture a knife—activities normally prohibited by traditional halachah on Shabbat—when those activities are essential to the circumcision. Rabbi Akiva takes what the responsum terms a "more stringent position": an activity necessary for the performance of *b'rit milah* overrides Shabbat *only* when that activity must take place on the day of the procedure itself (for example: the surgery, the dressing of the wound, etc.). Other prohibited actions, even though essential to the circumcision, remain prohibited if they could have been performed prior to the onset of Shabbat. Since the mohel could have—and should have—prepared his knife and brought it on Friday to the house where the circumcision is to take place, he may not do so on Shabbat, even though the circumcision cannot occur without it and will have to be delayed until the following day.

Rabbi Akiva's position is the accepted rule in the halachah, as we read in the *Shulchan Aruch* (*Yoreh Dei-ah* 266:2):

> Circumcision performed at its proper time [on the eighth day of a boy's life] overrides the prohibitions associated with festivals and Shabbat. But a delayed circumcision does not override the prohibitions.
>
> And even when performed at the proper time, it overrides [festivals and Shabbat] only for the surgical procedure and its constituent elements. . . . But other actions performed in support of the circumcision do not override, because they could have been performed the day before Shabbat or the festival. Therefore, it is not permitted either to manufacture the circumcision knife [on Shabbat] or to transport [the knife on Shabbat] from place to place.

The responsum concludes that Rabbi Akiva's general principle "teaches an important point": even when we are allowed to set aside Shabbat prohibitions in order to fulfill another mitzvah, such allowances are to be kept "to a minimum." We may do so *only* when the mitzvah must be performed on that day. Shabbat does not disappear simply because another mitzvah is performed on that day. "Shabbat continues to make its legitimate demands upon the Jew, demands that cannot be ignored or forgotten."

REFORM APPROACHES

This *machloket*, it turns out, is not so tangential at all. Rabbi Akiva's principle, the responsum claims, has guided the CCAR Responsa Committee's thinking for decades. "We have held that Shabbat is a sacred span of time, an institution of Jewish life that makes its own legitimate demands [note the repetition of this phrase] upon us." As precedents, it cites several earlier Reform responsa on questions concerning weddings and social action projects.[18] Although these activities qualify as mitzvot, traditional halachah prohibits them on Shabbat because they involve actions that violate Shabbat law. Those earlier responsa hold that we, too, should not schedule these activities on Shabbat since, in keeping with Rabbi Akiva's principle, they could be performed on other days. Similarly, this responsum concludes that a *b'rit milah* postponed beyond a boy's eighth day should not take place on Shabbat because we are not required to hold it then. What's new in this responsum—its *chidush*, its new idea or contribution to Reform halachah— is that it identifies Rabbi Akiva's principle as the unifying rationale behind those earlier rulings and as a theory of Reform Shabbat observance. The theory defines Shabbat as a mitzvah in its own right and not simply a means to achieve other desirable goals. "Put differently, Shabbat is more than merely a good day on which to schedule good deeds. It is *Shabbat kodesh*, a holy day; we do not violate or trespass upon it, even for the sake of mitzvot, unless those mitzvot must be performed on it."

Like Rabbi Freehof's *t'shuvah*, this one does its work by constructing a language, a way of talking about *sh'mirat Shabbat* that also invokes its intended audience. To speak of the Reform Sabbath as *Shabbat kodesh*—an occasion of "reverence" that makes "demands" upon our attention and our loyalty—is to declare that Shabbat is a mitzvah (at least) equal in importance to other worthy activities, including (in this case) *b'rit milah*. If we recognize our Shabbat in these words, we are more likely to share the responsum's determination: "The fact that Shabbat 'conflicts' with another mitzvah or worthy cause does not mean that it is *Shabbat* that must give way. Indeed, the reverse is often the case."

We may agree with this conclusion, but it's hard to escape the impression that it is based upon incomplete reasoning. We Reform Jews, we are told, should observe the traditional halachic rule that prohibits a delayed *b'rit milah* on Shabbat because Shabbat is a day of holiness and a mitzvah in its own right. But what we are not told is just why a delayed *b'rit milah* would violate the holiness of Shabbat for us. It's all well and good to talk about *Shabbat kodesh*, but what do we mean by that phrase? Why must Reform Jews define the sanctity of Shabbat as the traditional halachah does, according to rules that we no longer regard as authoritative? Why can't we define that *k'dushah* in a way that that speaks to our contemporary religious consciousness quite apart from the traditional prohibitions? Were we to do so, we might very well say "yes" to this family and permit them to hold the delayed *b'rit milah* in the synagogue on Shabbat. The responsum doesn't address these questions. It would have been more successful—and, potentially, more persuasive—had it done so.

The next *t'shuvah*, issued just one year later, attempts to do just that.

3. Presenting a Check for *Tzedakah* at Shabbat Services

Our final responsum presents, once again, a conflict between a mitzvah (the giving of *tzedakah*) and the traditional rules of Shabbat observance, which as we'll see prohibit the making of monetary gifts on that day (the full text of the responsum can be found on pages 208-15):

> Our congregation plans a special Shabbat service to honor the work of a charitable agency. As we have raised funds for that cause, we wonder whether it

would be permissible to give a check to a representative of that agency during the service.[19]

The problem for this responsum is therefore the same that faced the previous two: while an Orthodox rabbi would certainly prohibit the making of this gift on Shabbat, the answer in a Reform context is not at all clear and obvious. "On the one hand," it notes, "we dispense in our practice with many of the traditional [Shabbat] prohibitions," so we might well dispense with *this* one and permit the giving of the check at Shabbat services. "On the other hand, it is inaccurate to say that we Reform Jews have no concept of Shabbat observance." Indeed, "the seventh day is for us, as it is for other Jews, *Shabbat kodesh*, a sacred time, possessing a character that differentiates it from other days." That character involves "the recognition that certain activities ought not to be performed" if they are out of step with "the essence and spirit of the holy day." It follows that we Reform Jews, who "regard the issue of Shabbat observance with the utmost seriousness," have "our list of 'forbidden' activities," even though it "may differ from and be markedly smaller than that maintained by the traditional halachah." Perhaps *this* activity, making a monetary gift on Shabbat, should be on that list, even if that gift is to *tzedakah.*

The language of *Shabbat kodesh*, of course, reminds us of the language of the previous *t'shuvah*. And it raises the same difficulty that we encountered when reading that *t'shuvah*: Why must the sanctity of Shabbat necessarily involve, for Reform Jews, the observance of the traditional halachic prohibitions? Why can't we say that *for us*, holding a delayed *b'rit milah* or making a donation to *tzedakah* on Shabbat actually enhances the day's holiness? The previous responsum, as we saw, did not address that difficulty. This one, by contrast, points the way toward an answer in its first paragraph. The key phrase is "The seventh day is for us, as it is for other Jews, *Shabbat kodesh*, a sacred time." When the responsum mentions "Shabbat," it means the *Jewish* Sabbath, which we share in common with "other Jews"—that is, the rest of the Jewish people. The "sanctity" of that Sabbath is not some unspecified feeling of spiritual exaltation, but rather holiness as defined by the sources of Jewish tradition and Jewish history. (Note how the responsum repeatedly uses the first-person plural—"we," "our," "us"—throughout this first paragraph to drive home the point that *this* Sabbath is *our* Sabbath too.) "An inescapable component" of that Shabbat—*our* Shabbat—is the reality that certain activities are prohibited. Simply put, there is no *Jewish* Sabbath without both *shamor* (prohibitions) and *zachor* (positive ritual acts).

Thus, the responsum has filled in the gap left by its predecessor. We now know that *Shabbat kodesh* necessarily involves prohibitions. But which prohibitions are those? That's unclear, since "our list of 'forbidden activities'" differs from that of the halachic tradition. But to the extent that ours is the *Jewish* Sabbath and to the extent that "we regard the issue of Shabbat observance with the utmost seriousness," it is essential that we find a way to decide just which activities belong on that list.

In its second paragraph, the *t'shuvah* proposes a three-step process for making that decision: we should "consider the nature of the halachic prohibition, the extent to which it continues to speak to us as Reform Jews, and the possibility that a gift to *tzedakah* counts for us as an exception to the rules laid down by Jewish law and tradition." Note that the process begins with "the rules," the traditional halachic prohibitions. While those rules no longer bind us, they act as the default position (the text will later describe it as "the starting point" for our thinking). Readers can recognize this as an argument from "authenticity." We do not design our Shabbat observance as it were from the ground up. Rather, we begin with the "authentic" *Jewish* Sabbath, the one that has come down to us with its existing prohibitions— in this case, the prohibition against making a gift of money on Shabbat. We then consider whether circumstances exist that would lead us to modify or discard that traditional rule. This approach has something in common with Rabbi Freehof's invocation of the Reform "Sabbath mood" as the basis for determining our standards of observance: "What we can preserve, and without too much overemphasis restore as a natural mood of the people, that we would endeavor to do."

COMMERCIAL ACTIVITY (SALE AND GIFT) ON SHABBAT

The first step, then, is to consider just what the halachah forbids and why it forbids it. Why is commercial activity—including gifts—prohibited on Shabbat, given (as we've seen) that it doesn't violate the Torah's injunction against "work" on the seventh day? One line in the tradition, as Rabbi Freehof wrote, traces the rule to Isaiah 58:13, where the prophet describes Shabbat as a day on which we do not "pursue our own affairs." Others say that it is the ancient Rabbis who forbade commerce as a *sh'vut*. That word, derived from the Hebrew root, *shin-bet-tav* (as in *Shabbat*), carries the sense of "rest"—

of refraining from activity the Rabbis deemed inappropriate even though it does not fall into the category of "work." As Rambam explains in his *Mishneh Torah* (*Hilchot Shabbat* 23:1):

> The Torah says (Exodus 23:12): "Six days shall you work, and on the seventh day you shall rest [*tishbot*]"—meaning that you are obligated to "rest" from doing some things that are not *m'lachah*.

The Rabbis prohibited many activities as *sh'vut*. Some are prohibited because they resemble acts of "work," while others are prohibited as a precautionary measure, lest in doing them one come to perform an action that *is* forbidden as "work."

Why did the Rabbis see fit to add to the list of actions already prohibited by the Torah? One of Rambam's leading commentators explains: "What our teacher means is this: though the Torah prohibits acts of *m'lachah*, one could toil all day long on Shabbat performing acts that are not technically 'work.' For this reason, the Torah adds the command: *tishbot*, 'you shall rest.'"[20]

Nachmanides (Ramban; thirteenth-century Spain) expresses much the same idea in his commentary to Leviticus 23:24 (as the responsum indicates in its endnote 10): the positive commandment "you shall rest" is the necessary complement to the negative commandment "you shall do no manner of work." Otherwise, "one could weigh produce, fill casks of wine, move utensils and stones from place to place . . . the stores would be open for business and the moneychangers would sit with their coins in front of them. The festivals and Shabbat would become like weekdays, for none of these activities is defined as *m'lachah*."

Through these texts, the responsum emphasizes that there is more to the observance of Shabbat than merely avoiding "work." "Shabbat, as idea and experience, demands that we separate ourselves from other inappropriate preoccupations as well." The ancient Rabbis prohibited monetary transactions because "they comprise a realm of effort, of striving after gain, which is out of place on a day devoted to holiness, destructive of the goal of *m'nuchah*, of Shabbat rest and spiritual renewal." It is for this reason that even though the halachah does not prohibit *all* gifts on Shabbat (the responsum cites numerous exceptions to the general rule), gifts of *money* are not allowed, even when directed toward *tzedakah*. The monetary aspect of such gifts violates the tradition's sense of the meaning and purpose of Shabbat.

SHABBAT OBSERVANCE AND REFORM JUDAISM

Now for step two of the decision-making process: is this prohibition still relevant "in the context of a contemporary Reform congregation"? As the responsum has indicated in its introductory paragraph, two answers are available to us, each one based upon a different—and conflicting—interpretation of Reform Judaism's stance on Shabbat observance and toward traditional ritual practice in general. The first interpretation begins with the fact that, according to Reform doctrine, we are not bound by the traditional halachah of *sh'mirat Shabbat* and that we may set its rules aside "when we find them irrelevant to our conception of Shabbat or when we believe that the sanctity of the day will be nurtured and encouraged thereby." Should this be our view of Reform Shabbat observance, we will be more likely to approve the congregation's plan to make its gift at Shabbat services, because the act of donating to *tzedakah* in such a public way "would serve to strengthen in our congregants the sense of holiness and the commitment to Jewish life." The second interpretation, "the other side of our attitude toward religious observance," stresses our ongoing connection with traditional ritual practice. Since it is a goal of Reform Judaism "to balance our creativity in practice with the desire to conserve and adapt what speaks to us from the past," then traditional practice "ought to enjoy a considerable presumptive weight in our thinking." In practical terms, this means we will tend to side with a traditional form of practice "in the absence of a compelling reason to abandon or alter it." If we take this stance toward Shabbat observance, we will be more likely to affirm the traditional prohibition against making monetary gifts on Shabbat even when the object of those gifts is the mitzvah of *tzedakah* and social justice.

Both of these interpretations are plausible for Reform Jews. Indeed, the text provides support for each of them with quotations from *Gates of Shabbat* (see the responsum's endnotes 18 and 19), which at the time was the CCAR's most recent official statement on the subject of Shabbat observance. To answer our *sh'eilah*, then, we shall have to choose between them. The responsum opts for the second interpretation. To support that choice, it cites a line of its recent decisions (responsum endnotes 21–24) that portray Shabbat as "a mitzvah in its own right" that often takes precedence over other "worthy causes." Those worthy causes include weddings, congregational business meetings, a *b'rit milah* held after a boy's eighth day (the preceding responsum that we've read in this chapter), and relevant to our own question, a *tzedakah* project that involves labor traditionally prohibited on Shabbat. In each case the Responsa Committee has ruled that the observance of Shabbat preempts the other mitzvah because "the traditional practice expresses a sense of the sanctity of Shabbat that maintains its attraction to Reform Jews." The motivating idea in those decisions is clear: "Shabbat is not simply a day on which we do good deeds. It is *Shabbat kodesh*, a holy day. . . . We do not trespass upon Shabbat, even for the sake of mitzvot, unless those mitzvot must be performed on that very day," perhaps a reference to the "general principle" of Rabbi Akiva that the previous responsum cited approvingly. We shouldn't be surprised that the present responsum has chosen this interpretation of Reform Shabbat observance, because the text has taken care to prepare us for it. It has told us that by "Shabbat" it means the *Jewish* Sabbath, the Sabbath we share in common with all other Jews. The sanctity of that Jewish Sabbath (*Shabbat kodesh*) has always been expressed through prohibited activities (*shamor*) as well as positive ritual acts (*zachor*). Since the making of monetary gifts, even to good causes, has been one of those prohibitions, our position should be to observe the rule unless a "compelling reason" exists to modify or to do away with it.

CONCLUSION

This brings the responsum to the third step of its decision-making process, posing the "simple" question: "Must the donation be made to the charitable organization on Shabbat?" Phrased in that way, the answer is clearly "no"; there is no emergency involved, and the gift can easily be made on Friday or Sunday. Therefore, "we doubt that any good purpose is served by abandoning the traditional prohibition against the transfer of money on the Sabbath." That assertion may strike us as somewhat tone deaf, since the congregation had a very "good purpose" in mind when it planned the ceremony. Handing over the check during the service, we must presume, would be a moment of great teaching value and spiritual uplift for those in attendance. The responsum, though, is not unaware of this presumption and speaks directly to it: an equal or greater meaning can be achieved if the congregation honors the social service agency during Shabbat worship but does *not* make the actual gift at that time. In this way, it can fulfill *two* good purposes—emphasizing the central importance of both *tzedakah* and the observance of Shabbat in Reform Jewish life. With this pragmatic accommodation, the responsum urges us to reimagine the *sh'eilah* entirely. Shabbat is no longer a problem, something that interferes with our other religious objectives, but a mitzvah in its own right that must not and need not give way to the achievement of those objectives.

The word "problem" recalls the issue with which we began this chapter: how can Reform Judaism in general, and the Reform responsa in particular, speak of the observance of Shabbat when the rules of traditional halachah no longer bind us? What does *sh'mirat Shabbat* even mean in our Reform context? Our three responsa address this problem not by creating a new set of halachic rules, but by developing a *language* of Shabbat observance. That language enables each *t'shuvah* to maintain a traditional Shabbat prohibition, grounding itself in the halachic tradition without claiming obligatory authority for the halachic rules themselves. Rather, each begins by locating a starting point for discussion and argument. For Rabbi Freehof, that starting point is the "Sabbath mood," the existing state of our communal observance. For the responsum on a delayed *b'rit milah* and the responsum on giving *tzedakah* on Shabbat, it is the acknowledgment that Shabbat is a mitzvah in its own right that makes legitimate demands upon us. From that starting point, each responsum attempts to construct a framework within which Reform Jews, exercising their considered judgment, might arrive at decisions that have the power to persuade.

This doesn't mean, of course, that they *do* persuade all who read them. On this subject, as on all other subjects, Reform Jews are entitled to disagree. But at the very least, these *t'shuvot* demonstrate that it is possible for Reform responsa, drawing upon the resources of the halachic tradition, to speak coherently and to argue forcefully about one of the central mitzvot of Jewish religious life.

CHAPTER SIX
NATIONALISM, ZIONISM, AND REFORM
Flags on the Bimah

WE THINK of our synagogues as places of holiness because it is there that we Jews express our ultimate religious commitments. These commitments find their physical expression in the Jewish symbols that adorn the bimah, the platform at the front of the sanctuary from which we lead our prayers and read the Torah. The *aron kodesh* (the ark that holds the Torah scrolls), the *ner tamid* (eternal light), and the seven-branch menorah testify that this is a place dedicated to the worship of the God of Israel. Yet many American synagogues add the national flag and the flag of the State of Israel to the bimah's furnishings (or elsewhere in the sanctuary). These flags are also symbols of commitments that most of us take with deep seriousness. But is it proper to mix our commitments in this fashion? Is it appropriate to display the flags of *secular* nation-states in proximity to the *religious* symbols in the sanctuary?

The answer requires that we balance between our religious values, our patriotism, and our sense of connection to the State of Israel. Reform responsa have attempted to strike such a balance four times over a period of four decades. As we read those *t'shuvot*, we'll consider just how each one tells its own story about who we are as Jews and as citizens of our country. We'll see that the stories differ because both the world and we ourselves, the storytellers, change with the times.

1. National Flags at Religious Services
In 1954, the CCAR Responsa Committee received the following question (the text of the full responsum can be found on pages 215–16):

> In our temple we have two flags on the pulpit: one is the United States flag and the other is the flag of Israel. Some members of the congregation seem much disturbed by the practice. They feel that these flags have no place in the auditorium where religious services are held and should therefore be removed to the social hall. The matter has been referred to our Committee on Religious Practice. We are anxious to avoid unnecessary emotional conflicts among our

members. We should like to bring to them a proposal that would rest on sound principle and could be followed by all factions.[1]

The responsum was written by Rabbi Israel Bettan, a native of Lithuania and professor at Hebrew Union College–Jewish Institute of Religion, who served at the time as the chair of the Responsa Committee. Bettan makes his direction absolutely clear in his one-sentence opening paragraph: "In Judaism, devotion to the welfare of the country in which one lives has long assumed the character of a religious duty." When we translate his phrase "religious duty" into its obvious Hebrew equivalent—mitzvah—we see immediately what he means. For Bettan, there is no daylight between the "religious" and the "secular" on this topic; patriotism simply *is* a matter of Jewish religious concern. The paragraph means to deny any uncertainty. This is not, it tells us, a hard question; its answer is obvious, unambiguous, beyond doubt.

Rabbi Bettan bases his sweeping assertion upon a text from Rabbi David Abudarham, the fourteenth-century Spanish author of an important treatise on the halachah of Jewish prayer:

> It is customary [following the reading of the Torah] to bless the king and to pray that God will help him prevail over his enemies, for thus it is written (Jeremiah 29:7): "Seek the welfare [*shalom*] of the city to which I have exiled you and pray to the Eternal on its behalf; for in its prosperity you shall prosper." To seek the city's "well-being" means to pray that the king will vanquish his enemies. . . . Moreover, we learn in the Mishnah (*Avot* 3:2): Rabbi Chanina, the second to the High Priest, said, "Pray for the welfare of the government [*malchut*, literally "kingdom"], for were it not for the fear of the government, we humans would swallow each other alive."[2]

Abudarham's purpose is to provide biblical and Rabbinic support for the custom, already known in medieval times, of praying for the welfare of the king or government. Rabbi Bettan, who claims that this prayer "is recited in all the synagogues of the world," reads it as an expression of patriotism: "In every country the Jew thus affirms his faith from week to week that loyalty to the institutions of the particular country of which he is a citizen is a solemn religious obligation."[3]

This ringing endorsement of patriotism as a Jewish value should give us pause. It may well be that Jews feel a deep sense of "loyalty" or devotion to the countries in which they reside. As a factual matter, Rabbi Bettan's language may describe the attitude of the preponderant majority of Jews in the

United States, particularly during the early postwar period (more about this later). It's less certain, of course, that the Jews "in every country" would have felt the same way. (For example, what would the Jews of the Soviet Union in 1954 have said about "love of country"?) Moreover, it is difficult to accept his claim that this message derives from the sources he cites. Jews living under the Babylonian Empire (as in the Jeremiah verse), the Roman Empire (as in *Mishnah Avot*), or a medieval Christian monarchy (as in Abudarham's time) may have recognized that their personal safety depended upon both the stability of the government in power and their ability to remain in that government's good graces. They may also have grasped that it would be advisable to demonstrate in a public way—say, through prayers for the "welfare of the government"—that they did not constitute a hostile alien element within the society and posed no threat to the regime. But can we identify it with "love of country"? Those Jews prayed for their governments out of pragmatism, not patriotism. It's hardly likely that Jeremiah, Rabbi Chanina, and Abudarham imagined that displaying "loyalty" to their governments constituted a "solemn religious obligation"—that is, a mitzvah.

Nonetheless, Rabbi Bettan reads a mitzvah of patriotism into these texts, which leads to the next step in his argument. If loyalty to one's country is a Jewish religious obligation, displaying its flag in the synagogue as a demonstration of that loyalty can be construed as a fulfillment of the obligation. "The presence of the American flag in the synagogues of the land, far from being an intrusion, may well serve to strengthen in us the spirit of worship" and "partakes, therefore, of the sanctity of our religious symbols." Again, Bettan's sources would never have followed him this far. Would the Jews of Abudarham's day have said the same about the flag of the king of Castille? Later CCAR responsa, indeed, will either implicitly or explicitly criticize Bettan's language as excessive. But Bettan was writing not for later generations but for an American Jewish audience in the early 1950s. In considering the nature of that audience, let's remember that the classical Reform Judaism that predominated at the time saw in America the fulfillment of its theological hopes and dreams. In the words of historian Michael A. Meyer, "The mission of Israel demanded a providential Diaspora that would never end, and America was the land in which that religious and moral mission could be best carried out. Reform Jews placed American flags in their synagogues, put 'America the Beautiful' into their hymnal, and dwelt on similarities between Judaism and the republican form of government."[4]

Let's remember, too, that in 1954 America had just fought a world war against a truly evil enemy, a broadly popular struggle that had united the nation in a way that those later generations might find difficult to appreciate. The United States was at that time embroiled in the Cold War, with its attendant fears of Communist domination abroad and subversion at home. It was a time of investigations, blacklists, and loyalty oaths. Open displays of flag-waving patriotism, whether as an expression of true sentiment or as a defensive measure to ward off suspicions of disloyalty, were more commonplace than they are now. We might look askance at Bettan's patriotic rhetoric today, but it would have sounded much more reasonable to his intended readers in the 1950s.

As for the flag of the State of Israel, founded a mere six years before this *sh'eilah* was submitted, the author again states his position in no uncertain terms: "The American flag has no proper place in the synagogues of Israel, even as the Israeli flag is quite out of place in an American synagogue." Israel is a foreign country for American Jews, and its flag should accordingly be treated like the flag of any foreign country. Bettan refers to the US Army regulations "governing the display of any national flag other than our own." Those rules tell us that we may display the flag of a foreign nation on special occasions, such as when an official of that nation visits our community or on a "notable" holiday of that nation, such as its day of independence, "as a token of respect."

"Respect"? Is that what we Jews feel for Israel? What about love, passion, pride? The responsum's language concerning the Jewish state strikes us as odd, if not distant and cold. Again, though, this kind of expression wasn't out of place at its time. Zionism had long been a deeply controversial subject within the Reform Movement. The 1885 Pittsburgh Platform had firmly renounced any conception of Jewish nationalism: "We consider ourselves no longer a nation, but a religious community, and therefore expect neither a return to Palestine, nor a sacrificial worship under the sons of Aaron, nor the restoration of any of the laws concerning the Jewish state."[5] And immediately prior to the First Zionist Congress in Basel (1897), the CCAR declared, "We totally disapprove of any attempt for the establishment of a Jewish state."[6] Opposition to Zionism remained a powerful element within the American Reform Movement during the succeeding decades.[7] However off-putting it sounds to us today, Bettan's unequivocally non-Zionist language, besides conveying his own position, would have found a substantial receptive audience at the time.

Yet on this very point Bettan is open to criticism. Zionism, to repeat, was a *machloket*—a deep controversy in the American Reform Movement during this period—as a growing number of Reform Jews began to reconsider their relationship with Jewish nationalism during the interwar period and particularly after the founding of the State of Israel.[8] By 1954, many Reform Jews would decidedly *not* have agreed with Bettan that Israel was simply another foreign country. Bettan, presumably, was aware of the controversy, but his responsum refuses to argue the point. He simply declares that one side of that *machloket* is correct while ignoring the existence of the other. The implication, in fact, is that there *is* no *machloket*, that his point of view is the only one that an intelligent Reform readership could adopt. But, of course, there *were* many Reform Jews at the time who would have argued that the flag of Israel possesses a meaning for American Jews that is fundamentally different from that of the flag of any other state. By speaking as though there was no debate, by refusing to engage the other side of the question, Rabbi Bettan's responsum fails the test of generosity, and its persuasive power is therefore reduced. Those more favorable to Zionism and the State of Israel could dismiss his responsum, both then and now, as a simple statement of ideology rather than a serious attempt at argument and persuasion.

2. Israeli Flag on a Synagogue Pulpit

In 1977, a congregational rabbi asked the CCAR Responsa Committee:

> Should an Israeli flag be displayed on the pulpit of an American Reform synagogue? In this case, an American flag is already so displayed.[9]

The committee's responsum answers "yes," reversing Rabbi Bettan's 1954 decision concerning the Israeli flag. And while this responsum never mentions that earlier *t'shuvah*, a careful reading shows that it is aware of Rabbi Bettan's argument and tracks it closely, refuting it and at times co-opting it in support of its own conclusion. (The 1977 responsum can be read in its entirety on pages 217–18.)

The 1977 responsum begins with a direct and conclusive opening statement that neatly parallels that of Rabbi Bettan: "The six-pointed Star of David is now commonly recognized as a symbol of Jews and Judaism throughout the world, both by ourselves and by our non-Jewish neighbors. There is no clear distinction between Jews and Judaism, between our religious and our national aspirations." As with the 1954 responsum, this one indicates its direction from the very beginning. And note how it frames the question: we are dealing here not with the flag of the State of Israel, the emblem of a political entity other than the one to which we owe allegiance, but rather with the Magen David, the symbol of the Jewish people. Since Jewish peoplehood is an inseparable element of Jewish religious belief, there is nothing "foreign" about that symbol. If Rabbi Bettan's language is reminiscent of the 1885 Pittsburgh Platform, the introductory paragraph of this responsum evokes the 1937 Columbus Platform of the CCAR, which opens with the statement "Judaism is the historical religious experience of the Jewish people."[10]

To prove the point, the responsum uses Rabbi Bettan's own source: the siddur, the traditional Jewish prayer book. While it is true that the Shabbat liturgy contains a prayer "for the gentile government under which we live," it has also "constantly contained petitions for the return to Zion and the reestablishment of Israel." These prayers declare that we Jews constitute a nation as well as a community of religious believers. The implication is that Rabbi Bettan and his responsum cannot have it both ways. If as he says we learn from the siddur that Jews owe a duty of loyalty to the country in which they live, we also learn from it that we are a people with "national aspirations" extending beyond the borders of a particular country. And where Bettan says that the national flag is a physical expression of the loyalty to our country that our sources demand of us, the flag of Israel is likewise a symbol of "the prayers that have always been said in the synagogue." If so, the 1977 responsum concludes, it is appropriate to display that flag alongside the American flag "on the pulpit," pursuant to the "specific secular regulations about the placement of such flags that should be followed"—a clear allusion to Bettan's reference to the "United States Army regulations."

Rhetorically, then, the 1977 *t'shuvah* is a close, point-by-point refutation (or better, perhaps, a co-optation) of Rabbi Bettan's language from 1954. It shadows every step of his argument, utilizing his own sources and reasoning to support a conclusion he categorically rejects, as if to suggest that had he thought more deeply about it, Bettan would have agreed with the decision of this responsum. It does this without ever explicitly referring to him, perhaps to avoid the impression that it is disputing the words of an eminent predecessor.

As a matter of substance, the 1977 *t'shuvah*'s conclusion rests upon its argument that the Israeli flag is a *Jewish* symbol as well as an Israeli one. How persuasive is that argument? The text provides a "historical background" of the Magen David, ostensibly to demonstrate that the six-pointed star is in fact a symbol of the Jewish people. Yet that background yields, at best, a mixed message. We are told that "there is no ancient record of a Jewish flag or symbol for the entire people of Israel," that "the six-pointed star was rarely used by the early Jewish community," and that with a few isolated exceptions "we have no record of the use of a flag by any Jewish community, and, of course, the six-pointed star now so commonly used was rarely used as a Jewish symbol before the late eighteenth century and early nineteenth century." These details of history would seem to weaken the responsum's case: does a symbol of such recent vintage truly convey the national aspirations of a people whose existence spans millennia? We might ask, moreover, whether the congregation, when they look upon the flag with the six-pointed star on their bimah, actually see the flag of the Jewish people? It's much more likely that they view it as the flag of Israel, which of course is the reason the synagogue displays the flag in the first place. Its members wish to express their sense of love and devotion to the Jewish state. If so, then Bettan was right, and the framing of this responsum is wrong: the real question is whether it is appropriate to place upon the bimah the flag of a country other than the one of which we are citizens. By translating the Israeli flag into a symbol of Jews and Judaism, the 1977 responsum seeks to neutralize Rabbi Bettan's concern about "foreign" flags and political loyalty. It's far from clear, however, that the translation succeeds: we all recognize that flag as the flag of the State of Israel. And by speaking approvingly about the "national aspirations" of the Jewish people, the responsum kicks open the door to a recognition of Zionism's legitimacy, the door that Rabbi Bettan had slammed shut.

Still, its approval of the flag's placement is less than enthusiastic. In its final paragraph, the responsum declares the display of national flags in synagogue sanctuaries acceptable but not obligatory. Some congregations display them; others don't. And either way, "both the loyalty of our communities to the United States and our common concern for Israel are clear with or without the placement or possession of flags." In other words, the issue is no big deal and certainly not worth a serious controversy. This sentiment strikes the reader as an effort to tone down Rabbi Bettan's rhetoric of enthusiastic patriotism: what he saw as the expression of "a religious duty" has become a matter of little real importance. Here we should bear in mind that the 1977 responsum addresses an American Reform Jewish community that has just lived through the deep national divisions over the Vietnam War and the social upheavals of the 1960s. To many in this audience, patriotism of the "flag-waving" variety had sadly become identified with right-wing extremism, and Rabbi Bettan's language would likely have struck them as over-the-top. (The next responsum, from 1993, will make this point explicitly, and it isn't unreasonable to imagine that this thought was present in the minds of the authors of this *t'shuvah*.) As for Israel, by 1977 the Reform community had become much more uniformly supportive of the Jewish state than was the case in 1954, and relatively few would view the synagogue's display of the flag of Israel alongside that of the United States as an affront to their patriotic obligations. The responsum, speaking of "our common concern for Israel," presumes the pro-Israel sentiments of its audience. But the moderate tone of its language suggests that this audience has become less than enthusiastic about flag-waving devotion of any variety.

3. Flags on the Bimah

In 1993 the Responsa Committee turned once again to a question concerning the display of national flags (the responsum can be found on pages 219–22):

> It is customary in many synagogues to place flags on the bimah, both the national flag and that of the State of Israel. Is it appropriate for Reform synagogues to exalt national symbols to the same rank as the symbols of Jewish worship? Specifically, does this practice border upon idolatry (*avodah zarah*)?[11]

That last sentence may strike us as outlandish. We may display flags in our synagogue sanctuaries, but we certainly do not imagine that in doing so we are worshiping them. But, as the responsum informs us in its first three paragraphs, it's not all *that* outlandish. The synagogue, after all, is a place of worship whose furnishings and ritual accoutrements are patterned after the *Beit HaMikdash*, the ancient Temple in Jerusalem. No national or dynastic symbols were displayed in the Temple, for the presence of such symbols "would have invited the suspicion that we were equating devotion to the nation with the service of God. This, in turn, would have been seen as idolatry." If this concern applied to the *Beit HaMikdash*, it should logically apply as well to the *beit k'neset*, the synagogue, our own "small Sanctuary." That's not a bad argument for removing the national flags on the bimah.

The responsum, however, rejects the argument, citing an incident recounted in the Talmud: "There was a synagogue that had been destroyed and rebuilt in [the town of] Nehardea. In this synagogue there stood a statue [of the king, according to Rashi]. Yet Rav, Sh'muel, Sh'muel's father, and Levi [notable Babylonian rabbis] would enter it and pray there, and they were not concerned that this would raise a suspicion of idolatry" (Babylonian Talmud, *Rosh HaShanah* 24b). From this, the responsum learns that "the presence of a national symbol, even a graven image that might otherwise create the suspicion of idolatry, is not necessarily prohibited in a synagogue on the grounds of *avodah zarah*, idolatry."

This answers one part of the *sh'eilah*: since flags are not graven images and since (we can assume) our congregants do not actually worship them, their presence on the bimah is not prohibited *on grounds of idolatry*. But our *sh'eilah* is motivated by a broader concern: is it "appropriate" to display the flags so as to "exalt" them "to the same rank as the symbols of Jewish worship"? We can well imagine that had those four Babylonian rabbis been asked their opinion, they would have said that it is *not* appropriate to place the statue of an earthly monarch in a synagogue, even if (for understandable political reasons) the Jewish minority had to acquiesce in its presence once it was there. (The responsum alludes to this point in its endnote 9.) We can as easily imagine that they would have said the same about national flags. So the responsum must tackle this broader question: should the flags be on the bimah at all?

HALACHIC PERSPECTIVES

Unlike the 1977 responsum, this one acknowledges that it is not the first to address the issue. It points explicitly to three precedents: the 1954 and 1977 decisions of the Responsa Committee that we have read and a 1957 *t'shuvah* of Rabbi Moshe Feinstein, the preeminent twentieth-century Orthodox halachic authority in North America. These earlier rulings demonstrate that rabbinical authorities from across the ideological spectrum have accepted (with varying degrees of enthusiasm) the display of national flags in synagogue sanctuaries. This acceptance—and remember that our *sh'eilah* also recognizes that the practice "is customary in many synagogues"—testifies that the presence of flags on the bimah has become a widespread *minhag* (custom). As we saw in the previous chapter, *minhag* is a powerful force in the shaping of Jewish religious observance. For its part, the present responsum regards the existence of such a *minhag* as an argument for its acceptability on Jewish grounds, and it sees no reason to criticize this particular custom: "we would certainly not urge [the flags'] removal."

Still, these precedents do not *require* that synagogues place flags on the bimah, nor do they declare that a congregation is forbidden to change its custom and remove the flags. Rabbi Feinstein, in particular, defines the flags as *chulin*, "secular" symbols, which though not ritually forbidden in the synagogue's sacred precincts are certainly inappropriate there. This is especially true, he says, of the Israeli flag, which represents the achievements of the founders of the State of Israel, secular Zionists whom he calls *r'shaim* (literally "evildoers"), a term that extreme Orthodox writers often use to describe halachicly nonobservant Jews. The flags are *hevel ush'tut*, which the responsum translates as "nonsense" but which might also be rendered as "meaningless": the flags serve no legitimate religious purpose and ought to be removed if that can be done without creating too much controversy within the congregation. Feinstein's rhetoric marks quite a contrast with that of Rabbi Bettan, for whom the American flag is for all intents and purposes a religious symbol for American Jews. The 1977 CCAR responsum "strikes a different chord" from Bettan and, for that matter, from Feinstein. Neither praising nor disparaging national flags, it depicts them as material expressions of legitimate religious sentiments that a congregation may—or may not—choose to display in its sanctuary.

The 1993 responsum declares that it "reaffirms the ruling and the attitude" of the 1977 decision: "the flag serves as an expression of a religiously legitimate devotion, a devotion that may be expressed, should the congregation so choose, by the placement of national flags in the sanctuary." At the same time, it breaks new ground in two major respects.

First, it explicitly critiques the language of both Rabbi Feinstein and Rabbi Bettan as extreme. It objects to Feinstein's putdown of the flag as *hevel ush'tut*—"We care deeply about the welfare of our societies; their symbolic representations must not be dismissed as 'nonsense.'" Bettan, meanwhile, isn't so much wrong as outdated. "While it may have been proper at one time to speak of the flag as a religious symbol"—an allusion to Bettan's 1950s—such rhetoric (of "God and King" and "God and Country") "connotes for many of us today some of the most disturbing historical tendencies of our time: chauvinism, racism, and ethnic intolerance." Here the responsum clearly reflects its own social and cultural context. By 1993, it would seem, the generation of Reform rabbis that had experienced the war in Vietnam and the ensuing domestic discord had tired of intense patriotic language. Unlike the 1977 responsum, this one is willing to express its discomfort with Bettan's rhetoric in unmistakable terms.

Second, the responsum explicitly refers to "our love for the State of Israel," a theme that doesn't appear in its predecessors. Even the 1977 *t'shuvah*, which approves the display of Israeli flags on the bimah, speaks of "honoring" Israel and of our "common concern" for the Jewish state; it doesn't mention "love." This language marks a clear reversal of Rabbi Bettan's cool neutrality toward the existence of the Jewish state. Declaring American Jews' "love" for Israel to be a fact, it is certainly more "Zionistic" or "pro-Israel" than either of its predecessors. But that declaration, that expression of our feelings, fails to confront Bettan's most powerful argument against the display of the Israeli flag, namely that Israel is still legally and formally a foreign state for American Jews, so that the permanent display of its flag on the bimah next to the flag of our own country is most definitely not "appropriate."

The next responsum responds directly to that argument.

4. "HaTikvah" and "The Star-Spangled Banner"
A *sh'eilah* from 1998 adds another perspective (the responsum can be found on pages 222–27):

> It is the custom at our congregation to conclude our Yom HaAtzma-ut service with the singing of "HaTikvah." In addition, since this past year was the fiftieth anniversary of the founding of the State of Israel, three *b'nei mitzvah* as well as our confirmation class requested that "HaTikvah" be sung at their services. The vice president of the synagogue criticizes this practice on the grounds that "HaTikvah," as the national anthem of a foreign country, should always be accompanied by "The Star-Spangled Banner." Is it proper for us to sing "HaTikvah" unaccompanied by our own national anthem?[12]

It's worth noting, first of all, that this Reform congregation holds an annual Yom HaAtzma-ut service, celebrating the birth of the State of Israel as part of its religious calendar. We have definitely come a long way from Reform's anti-Zionist or non-Zionist past. Yet the synagogue vice president appears to agree with Bettan in defining Israel as a foreign country. Thus, times have changed, but not necessarily in the same way for every single member of the community. It's critical to keep this context in mind as we read this responsum.

OF FLAGS AND ANTHEMS

Like the 1993 *t'shuvah*, this one begins with a consideration of its precedents. If those earlier rulings deal with flags rather than anthems, the responsum argues that the analogy is apt: those *t'shuvot* speak "not only to the specific issue of national flags but also to the more general one of patriotism, of our sense of commitment to our own countries and to the State of Israel"—the very issue behind the vice president's objection. What they have to say about flags, then, has a direct bearing on how we should think about anthems. The responsum lists three conclusions—"observations" it draws from its survey of the earlier decisions. The third of these addresses our relationship to Israel:

> The State of Israel is the political embodiment of the age-old Jewish dream of national redemption, a dream that we have expressed in our prayers for two millennia. The survival and welfare of the Jewish state are therefore matters of our utmost religious as well as political concern. It follows that the symbols of the Israeli state are not simply Israeli symbols; they reflect and convey a powerful Jewish meaning to us. Should we choose to display the Israeli flag in our synagogues, we do not thereby declare political allegiance to the Israeli state; we rather affirm that the Jewish ideas and ideals that that flag symbolizes are present in the religious life of our community.

Much of this restates the language of the 1977 responsum ("Israeli Flag on a Synagogue Pulpit"), reaffirmed in the 1993 responsum ("Flags on the Bimah"): Israel's national symbols are *Jewish* symbols, representing the historical national aspirations of the Jewish people. But this responsum takes a crucial additional step when it identifies the State of Israel as "the political embodiment" of those aspirations. We need no longer pretend that the flag of Israel that stands on our bimah is simply the material symbol of an age-old religious hope. It is in fact the flag of the political state that has fulfilled that hope. The gap between the political and the religious is thus eliminated or at least radically reduced. If, as our prayer books have always testified, we care for the welfare of the Jewish people, we must also care for the welfare of the Jewish state, which is now a matter "of our utmost religious as well as political concern." We might argue that this conclusion is already implied in the 1977 and 1993 *t'shuvot*, but this responsum makes it explicit and unequivocal. No previous Reform responsum has gone this far.

"HATIKVAH": THE NATIONAL ANTHEM OF A "FOREIGN" STATE?

Since "HaTikvah" is by analogy the musical equivalent of the Israeli flag ("It thus expresses, quite literally, our hope for the restoration of our people to

Zion . . . a central and quite legitimate theme of Reform Jewish worship"),
then just as we may display an Israeli flag on our bimah, so may we without
reservation sing the Israeli national anthem at our services. Still, as a matter
of law, the synagogue's vice president is correct. Israel is indeed a foreign
country, a state other than the one to which American Jews owe political
allegiance. The question is whether Israel's "foreign" status entails, as the
vice president thinks, that American congregations ought not to treat its
national symbols as though they are our own.

To this, the text claims that the real basis of the vice president's objection
is not law but ideology, a set of political beliefs. This obviously weakens the
objection, for while we are bound to accept a reality based upon facts of law,
we are not required to accept arguments that flow from "an ideology that we
categorically reject" and that would lead us to "define our Judaism in a way
that is surely foreign to us." Notice how the responsum turns the rhetorical
tables! The word "foreign" no longer describes the State of Israel but rather
the vice president's ideologically skewed understanding of our relationship
to it.

How do we know that the objection is ideological rather than legal? The
t'shuvah asks its Reform Jewish readers to consider, by way of an "illustration" (we might call it a thought experiment) whether they feel toward Israel
the way they feel toward any other foreign country. Do we respond to the
anthem of, say, the Czech Republic with the emotional resonance that we
feel when we hear and sing "HaTikvah"? Of course not; the very suggestion
is absurd. The reason for this difference, the responsum asserts, is that when
we sing "HaTikvah," we do not imagine that we are pledging allegiance to the
Israeli state. We sing it as an expression of our own "religious and cultural
identity as Jews," a *people* and not merely a religious community, for whom
"*M'dinat Yisrael*, the State of Israel, is the political structure through which
this people unites to give concrete expression to its national existence."

In short, *our* attitude toward Israel, like that which the responsum attributes to the synagogue's vice president, is also based in ideology. We call
that ideology "Zionism." In the paragraph that begins, "The Reform movement in North America has long recognized these facts," the text sets forth
an extensive list of platforms, prayer services, customs, and celebrations as
evidence of "our acknowledgment of the religious significance of the Zionist movement and of the State of Israel." The list culminates in the CCAR's
"Platform on Reform Religious Zionism," adopted just one year before the

publication of this *t'shuvah*, which proclaims in no uncertain terms that Israel, whose establishment constitutes "an historic triumph of the Jewish people," is "unlike all other states" but rather "serves uniquely as the spiritual and cultural focal point of world Jewry."[13] All of this is geared, obviously, to prove that Zionism is part of *our* ideology: the Reform Movement recognizes Zionism as a thoroughly legitimate expression of Jewish religion.

But *does* it? The synagogue's vice president could criticize this argument in the same way that we criticized that of Rabbi Bettan, namely that it is a one-sided presentation of an ongoing *machloket*. The responsum's list of sources omits those like the 1885 Pittsburgh Platform (the only North American Reform platform until that time that it does *not* mention!) that portray Reform Judaism as a purely religious community that has abandoned all its "national aspirations." That is certainly true; as we've discussed, Zionism was once the subject of deep controversy within the movement, and this responsum, like that of Rabbi Bettan, can be faulted for a lack of generosity, for ignoring the other side of the debate, for not offering a balanced treatment of Reform Jewish history on the subject. The responsum's argument would have been stronger had it acknowledged that history and then claimed that the debate is now over. According to this more nuanced narrative, what was once a lively *machloket* over our attitude toward the Jewish national movement and the state it created has been decided, as attested by the *t'shuvah*'s list of platforms, prayer services, customs, and celebrations that have arisen within our community *since* 1885 (and 1948). While we may have been divided in the past, today we (and note the responsum's repeated use of the first-person plural) affirm Zionism and "categorically reject" the opposing ideology.

The responsum may ultimately suffer because it does not offer that broader, more inclusive account of Reform Judaism's history on Zionism. On the other hand, and ironically just like Rabbi Bettan's responsum, this one succeeds to the extent that its intended audience accepts its invitation to tell *this* particular story about themselves and their Judaism. The reader who accepts this invitation will resonate with the responsum's conclusion, which flows inexorably from it: Israel is "emphatically not a 'foreign' country to us."

Responsa Sources

The goal of these discussions is not, as it were, to wave the flag. Our intention here has not been to comment upon the substance of these four *t'shu-*

vot, to decide whether their conclusions about the display of national flags, expressions of patriotism, and Zionism and love of Israel are right or wrong. The point of this chapter, as throughout this book, is to inquire how responsa make meaning through the interpretation of relevant traditional sources. That poses a special challenge in this instance, where there is a paucity of traditional source material on our subject. The responsa we've read cite only two such texts, and neither one of them—the prayer for the government in *Sefer Abudarham* and the Talmudic story of the four Babylonian rabbis— mentions the display of national flags in the synagogue sanctuary. Still, these responsa, because they *are* responsa, do rely upon sources, albeit of a different type. We can classify these sources into three groups: *minhag*, previous responsa, and the temper of the times.

MINHAG

Rabbinic authorities, as we've noted, ascribe significant weight to long-established customary practice as evidence for what the law is, especially when, as in our case, the more technical halachah expressed in Jewish legal texts is either silent or ambiguous on a particular question. The Reform responsa we've read in this chapter rely heavily upon the data of customary practice. And since many American congregations customarily display flags on their bimah, these responsa conclude with confidence that the practice is a legitimate one, by no means required but certainly not forbidden by Jewish law.

PREVIOUS RESPONSA

Beginning with "Israeli Flag on a Synagogue Pulpit" (1977), each of the responsa we've read draws upon the discussions found in its predecessors. The earlier responsa thus serve as precedents for the later ones. But, as we suggest in the introduction, they function as *guiding* as opposed to binding precedents, since the authors of the later *t'shuvot* do not regard themselves "bound" by the conclusions of the earlier ones. While all of the later responsa follow Rabbi Bettan in accepting as legitimate the display of a national flag in the synagogue sanctuary, they do not cite his responsum as their "authority." Indeed, they dissent either implicitly or explicitly from his patriotic rhetoric and from his stance concerning Israel. But Bettan *guides* the later responsa in the sense that they all *respond* to him. Though his conclusions have been "overruled" several times, it is he who frames the issues and sets the intellectual agenda within which the later responsa writers operate. To borrow a phrase from the field of philosophy, the later *t'shuvot* can be seen in part as a series of footnotes to his own.[14]

THE TEMPER OF THE TIMES

Responsa, like all texts, are products of a particular time and place, display-ing the influence of the social, political, and cultural environment in which they are written. We don't usually refer to such influence as a "source," but we make an exception in this case, where the tone of each responsum is so clearly shaped by the events of recent history. We should not exaggerate: history and environment do not *determine* what responsa will say, just as no single text determines just what meaning any particular scholar will draw from it. The authors whose work we have read in this chapter could very well have arrived at different conclusions. Still, as we read these decisions, we can't help but think it obvious that Rabbi Bettan is "responding" to the situ-ation of postwar America as experienced by classical Reform Jews and that the subsequent *t'shuvot* are "responding" to the world created by the Viet-nam War and the growing identification among Reform Jews with Israel and Zionism. It's difficult to imagine these particular responsa in isolation from the world of their time. In that sense, environment is most definitely a *source* that guides the writing of each.

CHAPTER SEVEN

JEWISH FAITH AND SECULAR CULTURE
St. Valentine's Day and Other "Secular" Holidays

WE NORTH AMERICAN JEWS enjoy citizenship in our countries of residence and participate as equals in their public life. Unlike Jews in other times and places, for whom the surrounding culture was an alien and even threatening world, we experience our present-day culture—its ways of life, institutions, arts, customs—as fully our own. Still, we tend to feel that some aspects of that culture do not truly belong to us. This is especially the case with those rituals, folkways, and celebrations that are rooted in other religions, primarily Christianity. Thus, questions such as the following inevitably arise (the responsum can be read in full on pages 227–34):

> Is it acceptable for Jews to participate in the customs and celebrations of St. Valentine's Day and other non-Jewish holidays that are currently regarded as "secular" but that originated as religious observances?[1]

The t'shuvah begins by suggesting a potential framing for the sh'eilah. It proceeds from the Talmudic statement Pok chazi mai ama dabar, "Go out and see what the people are doing" (Babylonian Talmud, B'rachot 45a and elsewhere); that is, in cases where the correct observance isn't clear to us, let the popular minhag (custom) be an indication of what the law is. According to this framing, then, this is a question to be decided by minhag. As we've seen several times in this book, minhag is an important source of law in rabbinic thought, and halachic authorities, like jurists in other legal traditions, pay it great deference. Since, as the responsum notes, "Jews in our communities take full part in the activities" of many of the holidays to which the sh'eilah refers, we could simply conclude that popular custom has already decided our question in the affirmative. The responsum describes this approach as "the quick and easy way to answer our sh'eilah," and with good reason. If most of our people see nothing wrong with celebrating "St. Valentine's Day, Halloween, Thanksgiving, New Year's, and Mardi Gras," and if we allow the accepted custom to define the proper observance, then "yes" is the clear and obvious response to our question.

The responsum, however, rejects this framing. The question, it insists, is one of halachah and not *minhag*, of the *ought* rather than the *is*. The fact that many Jews observe St. Valentine's Day or any similar "secular" holiday does not by itself prove that they are doing the right thing. Here we see the other side of the coin of *minhag*. While rabbis have traditionally respected popular custom and recognized it as evidence of the proper practice, they have never done so automatically. Frequently, they have regarded it their role to challenge that practice, to subject it to "careful Judaic scrutiny," and to determine whether it is in accord with our sources. The first paragraph of the *t'shuvah* announces that this is precisely what the responsum will attempt to do, thus framing the question as one of *Jewish authenticity*. Whatever answer we reach (spoiler alert: the responsum will say "yes" to participation in these holidays), it is not to be derived by taking a survey of popular practice. It's not enough to know what the people are doing; we should want to know that their action is defensible according to our best understanding of what Jewish tradition has to say about the subject.

This marks quite a departure from the responsa we read in chapter 6, which accept the popular custom (to display national flags in the sanctuary or on the bimah) as evidence for the right answer. Why the difference? The responsum doesn't say, and that lack of explanation is certainly not a point in its favor. The best explanation would seem to lie with the availability of source material. We noted in the previous chapter that the traditional texts do not speak directly to the subject of national flags. In such a situation, the absence of a clear halachic rule or standard, we can't say that *minhag* contradicts the message of "tradition." On the contrary, *minhag* may be our only or best evidence of what that message is. By contrast, as we shall see, there is extensive discussion in the sources about the participation of Jews in non-Jewish ritual and cultural life. In this case, custom may very well contradict the halachah. It's necessary, then, to examine those sources to see just what the halachah is and whether a contradiction exists.

The Prohibition of *Chukot HaGoyim*

The responsum begins its examination with the "most obvious" halachic rule that applies to our *sh'eilah*. We read in Leviticus 18:3, "You shall not copy the practices of the land of Egypt where you dwelt, or of the land of Canaan to which I am taking you; nor shall you follow their laws [*uv'chukoteihem lo teileichu*]."

The literal meaning of the verse is clear enough, but obviously there are questions: which Canaanite "laws" (*chukot*) are prohibited to us, and does the prohibition extend beyond Canaan to cover the *chukot* of other nations? A halachic midrash on Leviticus 18:3 suggests an answer: "Does this mean that we are forbidden to build houses and to plant fields as they do? No; the text says 'you shall not follow their *chukot* [laws],' meaning their *nimusot*" (*Sifra, Acharei Mot*). The word *nimusot*, derived from the Greek *nomos*, refers to social, cultural, and religious practices. As examples, the midrash specifies "theaters, circuses, and arenas." And since those venues are common to Roman society, we see that the Rabbis do not restrict the prohibition of Leviticus 18:3 to biblical Canaan but apply it to their own time and cultural milieu. Jews are therefore forbidden to adopt the social practices of any non-Jewish peoples (*chukot hagoyim*). As Maimonides (Rambam) formulates the rule in his legal code the *Mishneh Torah*, "We are not to follow the laws of the gentiles [*chukot hagoyim*][2] or seek to resemble them in their manner of dress, haircut, and the like. . . . Rather, the Jew should remain separate from them, recognizable (as a Jew) by their manner of dress and by their other deeds, just as they are recognizable by their philosophy and beliefs" (*Hilchot Avodat Kochavim* 11:1). This is indeed a demand for strict cultural separation. While to us, the concept of a distinctive Jewish mode of dress and appearance may conjure memories of the yellow six-pointed star forced upon us by the Nazis and other persecutors, for Rambam and his Rabbinical sources it has a much more positive connotation: Jews should strive to be distinct in their ways so that they do not lose their special and specific identity through assimilation into the surrounding peoples.

Historically, though, the rule was never applied literally; the responsum cites several "significant exceptions" to it in the halachic literature. These exceptions stretch back to the days of the *Tannaim*, the Sages of the first two centuries of the Common Era: "It was taught: one who trims the front of his hair (in the Roman fashion) transgresses the prohibition against adopting gentile 'laws' [literally, 'he follows the ways of the Amorites']. But Avtolmus bar Reuven was permitted to cut his hair in this fashion, because he was in close contact with the government [*karov lamalchut*]" (Babylonian Talmud, *Bava Kama* 83a). That is, some individuals are exempt from the requirements of Leviticus 18:3 because, due to their professional role, they must adopt the cosmetic or sartorial style of the surrounding culture. Moreover, some gentile practices came to be regarded as acceptable, while others remained prohibited. How is this determination to be made? The fifteenth-century Italian rabbi Yosef Colon (known as Maharik) formulated a theory that was adopted by later authorities, such as Rabbi Moshe Isserles (sixteenth-century Poland), who writes in his authoritative Ashkenazic glosses to the *Shulchan Aruch*, "The only things prohibited under the category of 'laws of the gentiles' are: (1) customs in which the gentiles engage for licentious or obscene purposes . . . and (2) a custom or 'law' [*chok*] for which there is no rational purpose [*taam*], for such a practice may contain the traces of forbidden activities, perhaps idolatrous rites that they have inherited from their ancestors. But a practice that serves a rational and acceptable purpose . . . is permitted" (*Yoreh Dei-ah* 178:1).

The halachah therefore prohibits *chukot*, those gentile practices that (like the *chukot* of biblical Israel)[3] have purely ritual or religious implications. The only reason that Jews would want to imitate those *chukot*, writes Maharik, is to shed their distinctive Jewish identity and to assimilate into the surrounding society. The prohibition comes to forestall that possibility. Other practices, though non-Jewish in origin, are nonreligious in nature. It is acceptable to adopt those practices when they serve some recognizably utilitarian purpose.

"Secular" versus "Religious" Celebrations

The responsum now applies this halachic standard to our question. If Jewish law, in discussing the prohibition of *chukot hagoyim*, distinguishes between "religious" and "nonreligious" practices, that same distinction is the foundation of our specifically "Reform Jewish approach to Leviticus 18:3": the prohibition "does not apply to aspects of our contemporary surrounding culture that we experience as secular." The suggestion that traditional Jewish law recognizes the realm of the "secular" is very much a *chidush*, a new halachic idea. The very notion of secularity is a concept born in modernity that was unknown in ancient and medieval times. The Rabbis of the Talmud and the medieval halachic authorities (like their Christian and Muslim intellectual counterparts) did not perceive a field of human social experience that is independent of religious concern and that serves as a "common space in which all of us can meet . . . uniting the members of a disparate and multicultural society into a common bond." If Maharik believed that some non-Jewish practices filled a "rational and acceptable purpose" and were therefore permissible to Jews, he did not refer to those practices as "secular"—a concept that he, as a premodern, would not have recognized. The responsum's *chidush* is therefore an act of translation, one that transforms the vocabulary of the traditional halachic texts into a new language that speaks to the modern temperament.

We find a similar translation in the paragraph of the responsum beginning "Second, in the positive sense. . . ." The term *karov lamalchut* (cited above) in its original Talmudic context refers to "one who is in close contact with the government"—that is, a sort of lobbyist for the Jewish community to the Roman authorities. The responsum understands *karov lamalchut* as describing not a special emissary but *all* of us: "for we *are* the *malchut*; the government and the culture belong to us, they are of us, and we do not regard them as alien entities." Again, the Rabbinic authors and redactors who invented the term never contemplated the possibility of a political community in which the people are the sovereign power, let alone that the Jews might be full and equal citizens of a non-Jewish society.

Some observers argue that this kind of "translation" is invalid, because it intentionally reads into these texts meanings that were not present in the minds of their authors. Others disagree. These arguments will be familiar to you if you are acquainted with the long-running debates over the nature and limits of literary and legal interpretation.[4] We're not going to decide those debates here, if such a decision is even possible. What we can say is that many contemporary theorists point to a similarity between translation and interpretation. Both of these activities involve the rendering of a text into a different set of words that purport to replicate the meaning of that original text.[5] In this sense, the work of a jurist is much like that of a translator. "Like the linguistic translator, the judge is faced with a text . . . written in an original or source context . . . ; she too must write a text (a decision, or an opinion) in a different context. . . . This decision, in its context, is to have the *same meaning* as the original text in its context."[6] Rabbis do the same thing when they interpret and apply texts of Torah and halachah to situations that did not exist when those texts were composed. Like the judge, the rabbi claims that "*this* is what the text is saying," even when the text's author(s) never contemplated the reality to which the rabbi refers. We can criticize this sort of "translation" as illegitimate, but if we do, we are saying that the work of lawyers and rabbis—let alone of philosophers and ethicists and literary critics—is also illegitimate. We probably don't want to go that far. We presumably want our legal and religious texts to speak to us and to our present-day concerns even though they were written long ago. If so, then we have no choice but to interpret—that is, to "translate"—our texts. Still, we should at least be aware of what the translator/interpreter is doing: attributing to the text a meaning that was not in the mind of its author at the time of its writing.

On the basis of this translation, the responsum draws what it considers an authentically Jewish distinction between the secular customs that the halachah accepts and the religious influences it would have us reject. The word "secular" describes those aspects of our culture that pertain to *all* citizens and in which they participate as equals, while "religious" refers to customs and observances not shared in common but are properly specific to separate and distinct religious communities. As an example, the responsum cites (in endnote 14) several previous decisions of the CCAR Responsa Committee holding that we do not adopt prayers and hymns clearly identified with Christianity (such as the Lord's Prayer and "Amazing Grace") into our own worship because "we regard it a mitzvah to preserve the distinctly Jewish elements of our identity."

Among the acceptable "secular customs" that the responsum identifies are two categories of non-Jewish holidays. The first includes national patriotic holidays, which are "nonreligious" and "speak equally to all the citizens of the state." This immediately raises the problem of the "civil religion." Social scientists have noted that the rituals and ceremonies of patriotism often function like a "nonsectarian faith" or a "cult of the nation" (see the responsum's endnote 15). If we take this language literally, we would have to define patriotic holidays (Independence Day, Memorial Day, and the like) as religious rather than secular observances, so that according to the responsum's own logic we Jews should not observe them ourselves. The *t'shuvah*, however, chooses to "resist this conclusion" and to read that language metaphorically. The "civil religion" is not a *real* religion, even if patriotism can at times be "twisted into the form of a quasi-religion"—a worrisome development that, as another responsum has already warned us, we must guard against.[7] Otherwise, national holidays fall into the category of customs that, as Maharik put it, serve a "rational and acceptable purpose."

The second group of "secular" holidays, the ones about which our *sh'eilah* inquires, are "Valentine's Day, Halloween, Thanksgiving, New Year's, Mardi Gras," which—with the possible exception of Halloween (see the responsum's endnote 18)—originated as Christian religious observances. The responsum sees "no reason" to declare these holidays off-limits to Jews because *now*, despite their origins, they are secular observances; "neither we nor the vast majority of our fellow citizens perceive them as religious festivals." Origins, in other words, don't count. Once a holiday has passed in the public mind from the realm of the religious to that of the secular, it enters that category of customs shared by all citizens of the community, including the Jews.

At this point, the responsum takes the opportunity to distinguish its position from that of Rabbi Moshe Feinstein, the eminent Orthodox halachic authority whom we met in the previous chapter. In a 1981 responsum, Feinstein prohibits Jews from celebrating "the Thanksgiving Day of American gentiles."[8] It's important to note that he does *not* base his prohibition on "religious" grounds. Indeed, he regards Thanksgiving as a nonreligious observance. The creators of the holiday may have had religious intentions, Feinstein writes, but that fact is no longer relevant, for nowadays the holiday has nothing to do with *avodah zarah*, a term that literally means "idolatry" but that he uses here to refer to all non-Jewish religions. If so, then why does he oppose the celebration? Feinstein thinks that when Jews observe Thanksgiving, they transgress the rule of Leviticus 18:3, *uv'chukoteihem lo teileichu*, "do not follow their laws." Thanksgiving is one of "their laws," a non-Jewish cultural practice that is prohibited to us not because it is a non-Jewish religious idolatrous celebration, but simply because it is non-Jewish, and for that reason good Jews should not observe it. From this, the responsum concludes that "Rabbi Feinstein does not recognize the existence of the cultural realm that we have defined as 'secular,'" as opposed to the Reform position: "We, by contrast, do recognize the existence of the secular."

This may (or may not) be an interesting digression, but it raises two problems. First, the responsum's inference may be overstated. We really don't know that Rabbi Feinstein "does not recognize" the concept of secularity. He never mentions the word "secular" in his text, and it's quite possible that he wasn't thinking about that cultural concept when he wrote it. We also have to ask why this Reform responsum takes the time to discuss Feinstein at all. It doesn't attempt to argue against him on the facts, to prove him "wrong." It simply notes its disagreement: he doesn't believe in the "secular," while we do—and perhaps that's just the point. The responsum discusses Rabbi Feinstein's ruling because it wants to demonstrate that there is clearly more than one way to read the halachah on this question. Rabbi Feinstein bases his view upon a literal interpretation of the biblical phrase "do not follow their laws." He makes no distinction between religious and nonreligious customs. He sees no middle ground; holidays are either Jewish and permitted or non-Jewish and forbidden. To put this differently, whatever Rabbi Feinstein thinks of Maharik's exemption of activities that serve a "rational and acceptable purpose" from the prohibition, he does not translate that exemption into the existence of something called "secularity," a religiously neutral space in our social and cultural world.[9] The Reform responsum obviously reads the halachah differently, and it leaves it to us, its intended audience, to choose between these alternative understandings. The implication seems clear: to choose the reading offered by this outstanding Orthodox authority would require that American Jews cease to participate in all "secular" holidays—patriotic festivals as well as Thanksgiving—a conclusion that most of them, presumably including many Orthodox Jews, likely would find extremist and absurd. In arranging this contrast, then, the responsum argues not only for its own interpretation of Jewish tradition, but also for the larger claim that lies at the foundation of the whole Reform responsa enterprise: the "correct" or best understanding of the halachah is not necessarily its "Orthodox" version. We Reform Jews, too, can read the sources, and our reading of them just might be the better one.

Secular versus Religious Holidays

The responsum's case assumes that we can tell the difference between "secular" and "religious," so that we are able to say that holidays that originated as religious observances but have now lost their religious character may be defined as secular. To show that Jewish law recognizes this sort of change, the text (in responsum endnote 21) cites an example from the Talmud:

> Sh'muel said: in the Diaspora, it is forbidden to do commerce with non-Jews on the day of their festivals.[10]
>
> [An objection was raised:] But is it really forbidden? Didn't Rav Y'hudah permit Rav Bruna to trade in wine and Rav Gidel to trade in grain on the festival day of the caravan merchants?
>
> [This objection is resolved:] The festival of the caravan merchants is different, because it is not a fixed one. (Babylonian Talmud, *Avodah Zarah* 11b)

Sh'muel, a leading Babylonian scholar of the early amoraic period, prohibited trade with non-Jews on their festival day. Classical Rabbinic tradition explains this rule on the grounds that the non-Jews, who in those days were presumed to be pagans (idol worshipers), would likely render thanks to their gods for the successful transaction made on a day when their religious fervor was at its peak. This would be a case of "aiding and abetting" the practice of idolatry, which Jews are forbidden to do. So why did Rav Y'hudah, a disciple of Sh'muel and who would certainly follow his teacher's instruction, permit his own students to do business with non-Jews on the festival day of the caravan merchants? The Talmud resolves the difficulty by declaring that the caravan merchants' festival day has lost its status as an idolatrous festival because it is not fixed on the same day every year. The assumption is that a movable festival, whose date depended upon the scheduling of trade fairs, was taken less seriously by the idol worshipers. Since their religious fervor on that day would also be lessened, there would be no concern that they would worship their idols *because* of their transactions with Jewish traders. From this, the responsum infers that the halachah recognizes the possibility of his-torical development: "holidays with religious origins can lose their religious connotations over time," even as "other holidays are and remain essentially religious in nature." On this basis, we can distinguish between "Christmas, Easter, and other obviously religious holidays" and those non-Jewish holi-days that were once religious observances but have now lost their religious character.

We can object that the Talmudic text is *not* a precedent for our case. If the Talmud minimizes the religious origins and nature of the caravan mer-chants' festival, that doesn't turn the festival into a secular one. As we've seen, "secularity" is a modern development, and it certainly wasn't around in Talmudic Babylonia. But for the sake of argument, let's suppose that hol-idays that began as religious observances "can lose their religious connota-tions over time." The difficulty then, as the responsum acknowledges, is that "for many non-Jews in our society," Christmas and Easter themselves "have become nonreligious celebrations." Since many mark these holidays with "tinsel and reindeer and Santa Claus and bunny-and-egg displays," without ever going to church or participating in explicitly religious rituals, perhaps we should conclude that Christmas and Easter have become like St. Valen-tine's Day—holidays "currently regarded as 'secular' but that originated as religious observances." If so, according to the responsum's reasoning, there should be no objection to Jews' observing those holidays as well.

The responsum rejects this conclusion. Instead, it argues, we should define a non-Jewish holiday as "religious" not by the percentage of non-Jews who observe it as such, but by its "central role in the doctrine and practice of non-Jewish faiths." This approach is problematic for two reasons. The first, as the responsum concedes, is that decisions like this require judgments that are necessarily "controversial," not least because it may be improper for a committee of rabbis to decide just what is a "central" belief of another religion. Still, the Responsa Committee believes that we can confidently make this judgment, given that "many of our Christian neighbors" would feel "insulted" were we to declare Christmas and Easter to be secular holidays. The second problem is that Jews already participate in many of the non-religious aspects of Christmas and Easter—"office parties, gift exchanges, watching parades" and other activities. In endnote 19, the responsum recognizes that this sort of thing is unavoidable; it happens in a free and open society. Again, though, a line is to be drawn. Even if we cannot escape the public celebrations connected with these essentially religious holidays, we Jews should not celebrate them—even the nonreligious elements of them—at home. The Jewish home, in other words, should remain "a 'Christmas-free zone' during the holiday season."

Conclusion

The responsum rules in favor of Jews taking part in secular holidays that "originated in other religious traditions," even as, in "A Final Note," it encourages them not to neglect Jewish holidays in so doing. This conclusion may well strike the Reform Jewish reader as entirely reasonable and, given that so many of us already participate in the activities surrounding these holidays, entirely predictable. But for critical readers, the more important feature of this responsum is the fact that its conclusion is *not* inevitable. The decision is the product of *choices* that it has made along the way, moments at which its authors' reasoning moves in one direction when it just as easily could have gone in another:

- The responsum could have reached its conclusion by simply following popular *minhag*, "go out and see what the people are doing." This would have made the *sh'eilah* an easy question, one that admits of a single, clearly correct answer. Instead, it chooses to make the question a hard one by delving into the thorny problem of distinguishing between "secular" and "religious" observances.
- The responsum reads our modern concept of "secularity"—that part of culture we share in common with all other citizens—into the halachah, specifically the *t'shuvah* of Rabbi Yosef Colon (Maharik). This act of translation, as we've seen, rests on uncertain ground.

Neither Maharik nor any other medieval halachist imagined Jews as "citizens" of the surrounding societies, nor would they have recognized a "secular" realm of experience.

- The responsum defines St. Valentine's Day, St. Patrick's Day, Mardi Gras, and Halloween as "secular" holidays. It could just as readily have argued that those holidays still retain some religious meaning so that, therefore, we do *not* share them equally with all other citizens.

- The responsum defines the "civil religion" as a secular matter. Alternatively, it could have defined it as a real religion, one that like all religions demands our ultimate devotion, so that its patriotic rituals would be examples of non-Jewish religious observances that we should not adopt for ourselves.

- The responsum defines Christmas and Easter as religious holidays because of their central role in Christian doctrine and practice. It might have instead proceeded on grounds of sociology rather than theology. If millions of our fellow citizens celebrate these holidays as secular celebrations, devoid of explicit religious content, why shouldn't Jews celebrate them, too, even in their homes?

In each of these cases, the responsum makes a choice that is not required by logic or by the obvious meaning of the textual sources. In each case, it could have chosen differently, and that alternative choice would have supported a very different answer (or, at least, a very different approach) to the *sh'eilah*. As we've noted before in this book, choices like this are common in rabbinic responsa, particularly those that address hard questions that admit of more than one plausible answer. But that doesn't mean that the choices are arbitrary. It's the task of a responsum to identify the *best* of those plausible answers and to offer arguments to show why it is better than the others. In this responsum, the arguments proceed from a particular understanding of American secular culture and of Jews' relationship to it. To the extent that the intended readers share that understanding, they will likely find in those arguments a description of a Jewish religious and intellectual outlook they can identify with their own. If so, then the responsum has likely succeeded in its task of persuasion. If not, the readers might consider it an invitation to respond, to pursue the argument, and to arrive at a better understanding of our relationship to the culture that surrounds us.

CHAPTER EIGHT

MODERN VALUES, JEWISH TRADITION
Privacy and the Disclosure of Personal Medical Information

THE RESPONSA we have read thus far deal with Jewish ritual practice. The next three chapters focus on *t'shuvot* that address questions of ethics.

Jewish tradition distinguishes between mitzvot that characterize our relationship with God (*mitzvot bein adam laMakom*) and those that speak of our duties toward our fellow human beings (*mitzvot bein adam lachaveiro*).[1] The first category involves matters of "ritual," while the second addresses our conduct in the social realm: court procedure, monetary law (property, damages, contract), business and commerce, social welfare, government, and everything that we customarily classify under the heading of "ethics." One significant difference between these categories is that while "ritual" mitzvot involve behaviors that are particular to Judaism, "ethical" duties seem to address all people. As aspects of our *particular* Jewish bond with God, the ritual mitzvot flow from the texts of Torah (written and oral) alone. Were it not for Leviticus chapter 23, for example, we would never have arrived at the mitzvot of dwelling in the sukkah or of taking the "four species" known as *lulav* and *etrog*. Ethical responsibilities, on the other hand, are *universal* in that they involve standards of good and evil that are based in the resources of reason, common sense, and experience available to all people rather than in Scriptures or teachings specific to the Jewish tradition. As the Talmud acknowledges (Babylonian Talmud, *Yoma* 67b), even if the commandments prohibiting murder and robbery and the obligation to do justice had not been written in the Torah, we human beings would have come up with them on our own. From this, we might conclude that there is nothing specifically "Jewish" about ethics; the ethical thing to do in any given situation ought to be the same for a non-Jew as well as a Jew.

Except, of course, that the texts of Torah have a great deal to say about justice and righteousness and are replete with teachings concerning interpersonal conduct and social behavior. And traditionally, when rabbis have been asked for concrete guidance on such issues, they have provided that guidance as scholars of Torah rather than as philosophical ethicists. They have derived their answers through the process of halachah, relying not so much upon the principles of universal ethical reason as upon what is written in the Bible, the Talmud and other classical Rabbinic writings, and the post-Rabbinic halachic commentaries, codes, and responsa. In other words, rabbinic writing approaches ethics in much the same way that it approaches ritual: it uses the tools of analogy and interpretation to identify from the texts an authentically *Jewish* answer to the question at hand. In this sense, we can say that the halachah does offer a specifically Jewish approach to ethical thinking. This, at any rate, is the way traditional responsa approach *sh'eilot* of an ethical nature.

It is also the way of Reform responsa. Like the traditional variety, Reform *t'shuvot* speak the language of halachah when addressing questions arising in the spheres of business, family, social and organizational life, medicine, and politics. The individuals or communities that submit these *sh'eilot* are interested in determining not only the right course of action but primarily the *Jewish* version of that right course of action. They want to know the best answer *according to Torah*, the literary record of our efforts to work out the terms of Israel's covenant with God. The answers take the form of halachah, an argument based upon that literary record, the texts to which Jews have always turned when seeking the best answer to any question of sacred practice, ethical as well as ritual. From this perspective, Reform responsa treat questions of ethics, as they treat questions of ritual practice, in the same way that all other rabbinic responsa do.

What makes Reform responsa unique is, as we've said before, that they are written by Reform rabbis, members of a religious community committed to a "modern" (or "liberal" or "progressive") moral outlook. Since we are full participants in the culture of modernity, we are just as likely (if not more so) to learn our ethics from the values of that culture as from the texts of Jewish tradition. And those values will certainly influence the way we read our texts and the lessons we derive from them. At times, they will lead us to reject the tradition's teaching as contrary to *our* best understanding of the mitzvot that demand justice and righteous conduct. This doesn't necessarily mean that modern ethical values are superior to traditional Jewish ones. Sometimes, as we'll see, Jewish tradition has a lot to teach modernity, offering a useful critique of our social practices. But it does mean that serious Reform Jews, and Reform responsa writers, will arrive at their ethical decisions by comparing, contrasting, and balancing what they learn from these two great sources of guidance.

As we read the next three responsa critically, we should ask how well they perform that balancing act, particularly given that each *sh'eilah* poses a hard question, one that admits of different plausible answers that pull in opposite directions.

The CCAR Responsa Committee received the following *sh'eilah* in 1996 (the responsum can be found on pages 234-44):

> I am in my late twenties and about to be ordained as a rabbi. My father has Huntington's disease, a genetically transmitted condition that begins to show itself when a person reaches his or her thirties or forties. If I test positive for the disease, am I obligated to inform my congregation and the Placement Commission? Would the Placement Commission be obligated to share this information with any prospective congregation that would be interested in hiring me? Given that I fear employment discrimination should I test positive, am I obliged to be tested at all?[2]

The responsum begins with a brief description of the etiology and symptoms of Huntington's disease as these were understood at the time (and to a great extent still are).[3] This establishes for the readers what the rabbinical student who submitted the question already knows—namely that Huntington's is "a debilitating condition, the symptoms of which would render it impossible for you to discharge the duties of a congregational rabbi." The question, then: "does Jewish tradition require you to reveal this damaging information to a congregation or to any other institution at which you are employed or with which you may be interested in contracting for your rabbinical services?" At first glance, this simply restates the *sh'eilah*. On second glance, however, we see that the text wants us to think of that as a particularly *Jewish* question, to be answered according to the teachings of the "Jewish tradition." Our job as critical readers is twofold. First, as always, we need to consider whether the responsum's reading of the Jewish tradition is a correct or persuasive one. And second, we should ask whether its approach leads to a uniquely Jewish answer. That is, do the texts of Torah, as interpreted by this responsum, lead to an answer that differs from the one we might reach were we to think about the question as one of general or universal ethics, to be solved by resort to the values and techniques of reasoning available to all in our society?

The *t'shuvah* divides its analysis into three parts, a structure that reveals how it frames the *sh'eilah* and its strategy for resolving it. The juxtaposition of part 1 ("Personal Integrity and the Prohibition against Deception") and part 2 ("Jewish Tradition and the 'Right to Privacy'") suggests that the rabbinical student confronts a conflict between two Jewish (and also universal) ethical values: the duty to disclose and the right to keep private information private. Since these values make claims upon us that pull us toward different responses, we are once again to understand this question as a "hard" one for which there is no one obviously correct answer. The title of the third section ("Fixing the Balance: To Disclose or to Conceal?") implies that neither of these obligations overrides the other, so that the best resolution involves an accommodation between them.

Personal Integrity and the Prohibition against Deception
The Torah, of course, condemns falsehood, and the Rabbis turn this into a general prohibition against deceptive behavior. They call it *g'neivat daat*, which as the responsum tells us carries the sense of "theft" (*g'neivah*). The language conveys the idea that deception is not only an ethical lapse on the part of the deceiver but also, like an act of robbery, a trespass upon or violation of the person of the deceived. This prohibition is something close to absolute, particularly in the marketplace, "even when the act of deception does not result in any monetary loss to the buyer." In this case, the student's potential employers are the "buyers." To hide important information from them would be to create a false impression in their minds, an act of *g'neivat daat* that our tradition clearly forbids.

Except, of course, when it doesn't. What the responsum doesn't tell us is that the tradition recognizes that there are times when it is better to shade the truth, to withhold important details, or even to lie. This lesson is driven home in two famous texts that do not appear in this *t'shuvah*.

The first is found in the Babylonian Talmud, *K'tubot* 16b–17a:

> The Rabbis taught: What is the proper way to praise the bride when dancing in her presence at the wedding?
> The school of Shammai says: We describe her as she is. The school of Hillel says: "What a lovely and graceful bride!"
> The school of Shammai said to the school of Hillel: Suppose she is lame or blind. Do we still say "What a lovely and graceful bride"? Doesn't the Torah tell us, "Keep far from a lying word" (Exodus 23:7)?

> The school of Hillel said to the school of Shammai: Apply your logic to the following case. Suppose a person makes a bad purchase in the marketplace. Should we praise it to him or degrade it to him? Obviously, we ought to praise it. This is why the Sages say: One should always strive to be pleasing to other people [that is, to tell them what they want to hear; see Rashi].

Like many Rabbinic texts, this one does not adhere to our present-day standards of gender neutrality. Allowing for that fact, though, we can see that it concerns a question much like ours: does the obligation to tell the truth always takes precedence over other conflicting values? The scholars of the school of Shammai apparently think it does, given that the Torah explicitly instructs us to reject falsehood. The scholars of the school of Hillel know of that instruction, of course, but they think that the duty of truth-telling takes second place in at least some instances where expressing one's true opinion would cause embarrassment and shame to another. The halachic tradition rules here, as it usually does, in favor of the school of Hillel: "It is a mitzvah to rejoice with the groom and the bride and to dance in her presence, saying, 'What a lovely and graceful bride,' even if she is not lovely" (*Shulchan Aruch, Even HaEizer* 65:1).

The second text is from the Babylonian Talmud, *Y'vamot* 65b: "A teaching from the school of Rabbi Yishmael: How great is peace, for the sake of which even the Holy One resorted to falsehood, as in Genesis 18, where it is first written 'my husband is old' and is then written 'I am old.'"[4] In Genesis 18, which provides the background for this Talmudic passage, God informs Abraham that his childless wife Sarah is to have a son. Sarah overhears the conversation and scoffs at the news (verse 12): how is this thing possible when she is no longer of childbearing age "and my husband is old"—that is, has lost his sexual vigor? The very next verse tells us that God overhears Sarah's words and reports them to Abraham: "Why does Sarah laugh, saying, 'Shall I really bear a child, as old as I am?'" Notice that God's report conveniently omits Sarah's comment about *Abraham's* old age. From this, the Talmudic text deduces that God has shaded the truth—okay, let's be blunt: has *lied*—to preserve peace (specifically, *sh'lom bayit*, "peace within the household") by shielding Abraham from embarrassment and shame similar to that which the school of Hillel wishes to spare the bride.

We learn, therefore, that the rule against deception is *not* absolute. Like many (most?) ethical rules, there are exceptions to it, and we have to ask why the responsum doesn't mention them. We can imagine at least two plausible explanations. The first is that the responsum omits these exceptions for tactical (which is to say rhetorical) reasons. The text wishes to show that the sources of Jewish law "establish a strong prima facie case in favor of full disclosure of your personal medical history," and to point out exceptions to the rule of honesty would tend to weaken that case. If this explanation is correct, of course, the responsum can fairly be accused of some deceptive behavior of its own. The second explanation, which reflects a more generous reading of the *t'shuvah*, is that its authors do not believe that this case qualifies as an exception to the rule. Remember that the texts we have just read justify the deceptive speech on two grounds: that it brings about positive results for other people *and* causes no real harm. In our case, by concealing the relevant medical information, the student benefits their own situation rather than helping others. As for the argument that concealing the information causes no harm to potential employers (the student may or may not test positive for Huntington's, and any disability resulting from the disease would take some years to manifest itself), the responsum counters in two ways. First, the lack of harm in the concealment is irrelevant. The question here involves an employment contract, a commercial matter, and the text has already indicated that deception in commerce is prohibited even when it would cause no financial loss to the other party. Second, the student's deception would cause harm in the long run. While rabbis are not a "special case" (to use the responsum's language) when it comes to honesty, they should know and accept that higher standards of conduct are expected of them. Moreover—and here's a point to which a committee of rabbis will be sensitive—the reputation of the rabbinate as a whole is damaged whenever an individual rabbi "is found to have violated the canons of truth and honesty in his or her dealings with the community," even if that lack of honesty causes no financial harm. For these reasons, perhaps, the responsum holds that this case is *not* an exception to the rule requiring honesty and full disclosure.

Jewish Tradition and the "Right to Privacy"

There is, however, another rule that might justify a decision not to disclose: the halachic guarantee of a "right to privacy." That is, while we are forbidden to practice outright deception, there are aspects of our personal lives to which other people are not granted access. Here, the "right to privacy" would mean that neither the Placement Commission nor potential employers have any business asking for the student's medical data.

Notice that the t'shuvah places quotation marks around the phrase "right to privacy." It does so because, as it concedes, the halachic sources never explicitly mention such a right. No wonder; the concept of "rights" in general is foreign to the halachah, which speaks a language of obligations—the duties we owe to others—rather than of rights—the legal protections to which we are entitled.[5] If so, how can we speak of a Jewish legal "right" to privacy or, for that matter, a "right" to anything? The responsum argues that we should consider the matter in reverse: obligations guarantee "protections" that other legal systems define as "rights." For example, the prohibitions against theft (Exodus 20:13 and Leviticus 19:11) can be seen as implying a right to ownership, even if the halachah never uses "rights" language. In a similar way, the t'shuvah makes clear that Jewish law forbids us from violating what we today think of as the personal space of others. That prohibition resembles a right to privacy, because its effect is to shield us "against the prying eyes of other individuals and of the community as a whole."

The text now draws together a number of halachic prohibitions that, it claims, are united by the general principle that "Judaism guarantees a significant range of protection to our private lives." This approach is reminiscent of the one employed by Samuel D. Warren and Louis D. Brandeis in what has been called "that most influential law review article of all."[6] When that article appeared near the end of the nineteenth century, American law did not explicitly recognize a right to privacy. Warren and Brandeis, however, argued that such a right did exist in fact, if not in name. They pointed to a number of existing legal provisions that offer protection to an individual's "thoughts, sentiments, and emotions," protections that, taken together, can and should be understood as a distinct, identifiable "right to be let alone." Brandeis, subsequently appointed to the US Supreme Court, extended that argument to American constitutional law, writing in a famous dissent that although the US Constitution does not mention a right to privacy, its framers "sought to protect Americans in their beliefs, their thoughts, their emotions and their sensations. They conferred, as against the government, the right to be let alone—the most comprehensive of rights and the right most valued by civilized men."[7] Whether Warren and Brandeis succeeded in their efforts is controversial, at least as a matter of legal theory. Some scholars say "no," on the grounds that the "right to privacy" constitutes nothing new in the law but is simply a descriptive label for a set of protections that already exist. Others insist that privacy is indeed a separate right, based upon a principle of human dignity rather than upon a right to property, as is true of the older protections in the common law.[8] Either way, it's difficult to dispute that the Warren and Brandeis article significantly transformed the legal discussion among scholars and the public at large. With it, "privacy" and all matters related to that idea become an indelible component of the conversation that constitutes the law.[9]

Academic scholars of Jewish law have applied the Warren-Brandeis approach to the halachic tradition, arguing that it also recognizes something akin to a right to privacy.[10] The responsum follows that path here. It identifies various rules of classical Jewish law that, when combined, indicate a more general prohibition against the violation of personal privacy. These include the prohibition against a lender entering a borrower's home to take the latter's pledge (Deuteronomy 24:10–11); the halachic concept of *hezeik r'iyah*, damage caused by our unwanted gaze into a neighbor's property, which is considered "real" (actionable) damage; the medieval *takanah* (legislative edict) banning the unauthorized reading of another's mail; and the various prohibitions against gossip, talebearing, and slander. To be sure, the text acknowledges, "Rabbinic Judaism is not a libertarian philosophy," and its guarantee of privacy is not absolute. For example, halachah requires that we intervene into the affairs of others when we see them committing a serious transgression. Nonetheless, "our 'right' to take an active interest in the affairs of others is to be balanced against the halachic demand that one's home be shielded from the gaze of neighbors and that one's name and reputation be protected from violation by others, however well-meaning they may be." Ultimately, "all of us, created in the divine image, are possessed of a dignity that at some critical point requires that all others leave us be and let us alone," that last phrase a possible allusion to Warren and Brandeis's "the right to be let alone." At any rate, if such a right exists—if according to halachah "our lives are not an open book" and employers are not "entitled to know everything about us that they might wish to know"—then the rabbinical student has a good argument for choosing not to reveal information about their medical situation.

Fixing the Balance: To Disclose or to Conceal?
The responsum therefore frames this *sh'eilah* as a clash between the requirement to tell the truth and the prohibition against violating the privacy of another. To balance the conflicting demands of these mitzvot, it turns to sev-

eral earlier rulings that it sees as precedents. In those decisions—one involving a counselor's duty of confidentiality to her client, the second dealing with compulsory testing for HIV, and the third discussing conversations between spouses—the Responsa Committee found that "respect for privacy"—a concept, remember, that is not native to Jewish law and that the responsum has just introduced—"takes precedence over the sharing of personal information in most cases." According to this "rule of thumb," anyone seeking information about another person "must meet a fairly rigorous burden of proof" in order to be entitled to it.

In this case, the responsum judges that *"at this time"* (italics in original) the burden of proof has not been met. The student bears no obligation to disclose that they may one day test positive for Huntington's disease, because that nonexistent information—the responsum calls it "conjecture, possibility, and 'what-if'"—has no bearing upon the student's professional competence, particularly during the first term of employment. Nor is the student obligated to be tested for the Huntington's gene (though for personal reasons they may wish to be tested), for even a positive result would not guarantee that the disease would in fact develop. Since the medical information is irrelevant to the student's ability to perform the duties of a rabbi, neither the Placement Commission nor a potential employer is entitled to it, and their demand for it would be forbidden as an invasion of the student's privacy. Of course, as the phrase *"at this time"* has indicated, should the rabbi someday develop symptoms that do affect their ability to function on the job, that information ceases to be "a purely private matter," and the rabbi would bear a duty to disclose it.

One question we ought to ask of the responsum is whether the argument leading to its decision is needlessly complex. The text could have omitted the discussion about the "right" to privacy and reached the same conclusion by focusing solely on the mitzvah of truth-telling. The prohibition against deception (*g'neivat daat*), specifically in a commercial or employment negotiation, entails that we do not withhold from the other party any information that is relevant to the transaction. This has never been understood as an obligation to reveal *irrelevant* details, and common sense explains why. For example, if I am selling my car, I have a duty to disclose—and therefore I am forbidden to conceal, let alone to lie about—my legal ownership of the car, the year it was made, its mileage, repair history, and any other information *about the car* that the buyer has good reason to know. But the prohibition of *g'neivat daat* does *not* oblige me to reveal to the buyer my age, marital status, religion, place of employment, or any other information *about me* rather than the car. The buyer may wish to know some of these things, but since they are irrelevant to the condition of the car, I have no duty to disclose them, and my failure to disclose them does not constitute an act of deception. In every such transaction, of course, we must determine just which facts are relevant and ought to be disclosed. That requires an act of judgment, and like all such acts it will be open to criticism. The point is that the responsum could have centered entirely upon that judgment: is the possibility that the student will develop Huntington's disease in the future relevant at this time to the Placement Commission or to a potential employer? If the answer is "no"—and that, of course, is the answer the responsum reaches—then it could have simply concluded that the mitzvah of truth-telling and the prohibition of *g'neivat daat* do not require the student to reveal that information. In other words, the long discussion of privacy is extraneous to the question; the *t'shuvah* does not need it in order to justify its answer to this *sh'eilah*. This leaves us to ask what purpose that discussion truly serves here.

To answer that question, we should remember that a responsum does not always restrict itself to the *sh'eilah* that it has been asked. Frequently, its author(s) will look beyond that specific question to address other, perhaps broader concerns. This *t'shuvah* seems determined to make the argument that Jewish law recognizes something akin to a right to privacy, even though the existence of such a "right" is not essential for answering the present *sh'eilah*. It does so, perhaps, out of pure academic interest, but practical motivations may also be involved. The section "Jewish Tradition and the 'Right to Privacy'" could potentially serve as a precedent for future questions, raised by readers who will want to know what Jewish law might have to say about personal privacy and its infringement in an age of digital media, electronic surveillance, and 24/7 connectivity. Reform responsa writers who field those questions may find this discussion useful. Or maybe they won't; it is possible that future generations will find this discussion outdated and irrelevant to their technological environment. But even if future responsa writers disagree with this *t'shuvah*'s argument, they will have to contend with it; they will have to join the conversation and show just where the predecessors got it wrong. Either way, we see that in crafting its answer, this responsum speaks to the future as well as to the present *sh'eilah*, a feature we should keep in mind when we read a responsum and seek to understand how it makes meaning.

CHAPTER NINE
THE HALACHAH OF SOCIAL JUSTICE
The Synagogue and Organized Labor

Our RELIGIOUS AND ETHICAL VALUES, as we know, make very real demands upon us—upon our time and energy, of course, but frequently upon our pocketbooks as well. We recognize these financial demands as legitimate—is a religious or ethical value truly "valuable" to us if we are not prepared to pay for it?—but we also know that there must be limits to them. How do we set those limits? This question lies at the heart of a 2001 inquiry to the CCAR Responsa Committee from a Reform congregation in New Jersey (the responsum can be found on pages 244-52):

> Our congregation is in the process of cost-estimating some new construction to our synagogue facility. Our cost estimators suggested that we can save some $300,000 by using nonunion as opposed to unionized labor. Do Jewish law and ethics offer us guidance in making this decision?[1]

The congregation and its leadership wish to spend their resources in a way that affirms their ethical and political values, but acting on those values turns out in this case to be a very expensive proposition. This is a universal ethical problem, familiar to all people of conscience; one need not be Jewish to recognize the difficulty that this *sh'eilah* describes. Yet the congregation, seeking "guidance" from "Jewish law and ethics," wants a particularly Jewish answer to that difficulty. The responsum answers by identifying two inherently Jewish values that speak to the issue. But as we have seen with several of the *t'shuvot* we've read so far, each of these values would tend to support a different conclusion. Once again, a responsum frames its *sh'eilah* as a hard question. And once again, should we accept that framing, we'll be likely to agree with the responsum that the solution lies not in deciding for one value over the other, but in giving each side of the dilemma its proper due, so as to "resolve their conflict in a reasonable manner."

Organized Labor and Jewish Law

The *t'shuvah* begins with the claim that "Jewish law supports the right of workers to organize into unions in order to protect and further their economic and social interests." We should greet a sweeping statement like this with attention and, perhaps, a degree of skepticism. Do the sources in fact support it? The concept of a "labor union" is not found in the Talmud, the ultimate proof text for all halachic argument. Nonetheless, the responsum traces a line of rabbinic interpretation that both affirms the right of workers to unionize and endorses their decision to do so. That line begins with the following two Talmudic passages. First: "Our Rabbis taught: . . .The residents of a community [*b'nei ha-ir*] are entitled to units of measurement, the prices of commodities, and the wages paid to workers; they are also entitled to punish those who violate these rules" (Babylonian Talmud, *Bava Batra* 8b).This formula—"Our Rabbis taught" (*tanu rabanan*)—signals that the text is a *baraita*, a non-Mishnaic text that emanates from the Land of Israel during the first two centuries of the Common Era. On the surface, it establishes nothing more than a community's power to regulate commercial activity within its jurisdiction. The key question, though, is just who are the *b'nei ha-ir*, literally "the residents of the community"?

As we see from the second text, which recounts a case litigated in fourth-century Babylonia, the Rabbis give that term a special definition:

> Two butchers entered into a mutual agreement whereby should one of them work on a day reserved for the other, the skin of his animal would be torn. It so happened that one butcher did work on the day reserved for his fellow, and (accordingly) the skin of his animal was torn.
>
> They came before Rava for judgment. Rava ordered those who tore the skin to compensate its owner.
>
> Rav Yeimar bar Shelemya challenged Rava: "Doesn't the text say that 'the residents of a community [*b'nei ha-ir*] . . . are also entitled to punish those who violate these rules'"?
>
> Rava did not reply to him.
>
> Rav Papa said, "Rava was correct in not replying to him. The power to punish violators applies only when there is no person of stature [*adam chashuv*] in the community. But when there is such a person in the community, [the butchers] have no right to punish those who violate their agreement." (Babylonian Talmud, *Bava Batra* 9a)

These Babylonian rabbis understand the *baraita*'s term *b'nei ha-ir* to refer not only to the residents of a town but also to the members of a trade association, in this instance a contractual relationship between two butchers specifying the days on which each would be allowed to work. Thus, we learn that the members of a trade association wield powers similar to those of a town council. As Maimonides (Rambam) formulates the law in his twelfth-century code, the *Mishneh Torah* (*Hilchot M'chirah* 14:10–11):

> Members of a trade may agree to rules and regulations governing the conduct of their work and to punish those who violate that agreement.
>
> The above applies only to a community in which there is no sage of stature [*chacham chashuv*] to oversee the community and safeguard its welfare.[2] But if there is such a person in the town, the tradespeople are not entitled to make such agreements or to punish those who violate them unless they do so with his consent.

Rambam is clearly relying upon the two Talmudic texts we have read. Note that he replaces the ambiguous term *b'nei ha-ir* with the more specific *anshei umaniyot*, "artisans" or "practitioners of a trade." The theory behind this translation is offered by the thirteenth-century Spanish sage Rabbi Sh'lomo ben Adret: "It is settled law that the community may enact ordinances [*takanot*] as they see fit. Such ordinances enjoy the force of Torah law, and the community is empowered to punish those who violate their provisions.... Similarly, the local members of a particular trade, such as butchers, dyers, and sailors, may regulate the affairs of their trade. For any group united by a common interest is like a community unto itself.... All this, provided that a sage or community official agrees to these regulations" (*Responsa Rashba* 4:185). By the Middle Ages, then, Jewish law already recognized the right of tradespersons "united by a common interest" to organize to promote that interest, subject to the oversight of those governmental bodies or commissions ("a person of stature") established by law to oversee labor-management relations.

To be sure, these sources speak of trade associations that resemble guilds of merchants and skilled artisans, rather than unions that encompass laborers as well. Moreover, none of them says explicitly that unionization is a social good—something that we all should support, let alone be willing to pay for. But as our responsum notes, a number of twentieth-century *poskim* (Orthodox halachic authorities) take those extra steps, asserting that "Jewish law does not merely permit workers to form unions but positively encourages them to do so." Let's focus upon one that the responsum cites: Rabbi Benzion Ouziel (d. 1954), the first Sephardic chief rabbi of the State of Israel. Ouziel's responsum is actually a letter addressed in 1938 to the governing council of HaPoel HaMizrachi, the labor wing of the Orthodox Zionist movement in Mandatory Palestine:

We read in the Talmud (*Bava Batra* 9a): "Two butchers entered into a mutual agreement, etc." From here, the halachic authorities learn that the members of any trade are empowered to make such rules and that they enjoy the legal status of "the residents of the community" [*b'nei ha-ir*] with respect to their work. This is a clear and undisputed halachah. . . . Our Sages recognize the authority of regulations adopted by an organized trade association or a union of blue-collar laborers [*po-alim*] or white-collar workers [*p'kidim*], whether in the form of a single general union or of individual professional associations.

And this is only logical and just [*v'kach hadin notein*], lest the individual worker be left on his own, isolated, forced to hire himself out for a pittance that can scarcely feed and house him and his family. So that he might protect himself [from destitution], the law grants him the right to organize a union, to make rules governing the relationships among its members, and to win the respect of his employer and a decent wage for his labor so that he and his family might achieve a standard of living equivalent to that of his fellow citizens. It is reasonable that this union should provide [cultural and medical services], along with an insurance fund that can assist the worker in his old age or should he become disabled. . . . None of these goals can be accomplished in the absence of a union of workers. For this reason, Jewish law [*Torat Yisrael*] grants to workers the right to organize, even though this might result in financial loss to employers.[3]

We've quoted at length from Ouziel's responsum because it offers a wonderful example of how modern-day readers, through creative interpretation, can make old texts speak to contemporary reality. Take, for instance, the first paragraph, seemingly a restatement of the discussion in the Talmud and the medieval writers. Notice that Rabbi Ouziel inserts the words *po-alim* and *p'kidim* into that "restatement," indicating that *both* blue-collar laborers and white-collar office workers enjoy the right of unionization, even though the sources on which he relies do not use those terms. Ouziel likely presumes that the sources mean to include all workers among those who are entitled to form trade associations. The sources, however, do not say this explicitly; it is Ouziel who makes them say it. In the second paragraph, Rabbi Ouziel declares in no uncertain terms that Jewish law regards unionization as a positive good. Once again, the texts upon which he relies do not explicitly endorse the formation of labor unions, which means that his conclusion is not required by the literal meaning of those texts. It rather reflects his own judgment ("this is only logical and just"): if unionization is the most effective way for workers to achieve the goals to which human dignity entitles them, then the Torah must not only permit it but approve of it. We may well agree with his judgment, but like all judgments it is subject to argument. For example, we know that some mainstream economists contend that unionization is actually a bad deal for workers, in that it drives up labor costs (Ouziel himself concedes that it "might result in financial loss to employers"), leading to increased unemployment and ultimately to depressed wage levels. Many other economists disagree, of course, but that's the point: the correctness of Ouziel's judgment is a matter of economic argument, one that depends upon data that our sacred texts do not supply and over which rabbis have no special expertise. Rabbi Ouziel, for his part, does not analyze data here. Perhaps, because he's not an economist, he feels ill-equipped to do so. Perhaps, because he is addressing a pro-labor audience that obviously agrees with him, he thinks that data-based economic argument is irrelevant. Either way, he translates this economic question into a moral and ethical (which is to say halachic) one, and he presents his decision as reflecting the clear and unambiguous message of Torah when in fact it rests upon creative reading and inherently controversial judgment.

Does that mean that Rabbi Ouziel's decision is *wrong* as a matter of law? Not at all. It should rather remind us that the ruling of a rabbi on a question of halachah is not always a matter of "black letter law," where the answer seems dictated by the unambiguous logic of the legal texts. When it comes to hard questions, particularly to questions arising out of changing realities that the authors of those texts did not explicitly address, the answer is more likely the product of the rabbi's claim of meaning upon those texts and upon the Jewish tradition, a claim supported not only by what the texts literally say but also (and principally) by the value affirmations that the rabbi brings to the act of reading them. There's no avoiding this; reading sacred texts through the lens of our values is the essence of what we have traditionally called "interpretation." While it's true that Rabbi Ouziel adds new understandings to the previously existing halachic texts—and for that reason we can call his reading "creative"—there's no way for a rabbi to understand the texts and to apply them to the contemporary world in the absence of such interpretation.

At any rate, the CCAR responsum uses these traditional sources and their "creative" interpretation to support its argument that Jewish tradition looks with favor upon labor unionization. To these voices it adds that of "our own Central Conference of American Rabbis," which has issued numerous pro-labor resolutions over the course of many decades. This record testifies that the North American Reform rabbinate has made the same claim of meaning, namely that Torah and halachah endorse the cause of organized labor. The most recent of these resolutions "calls upon the constituent agencies of the Reform movement . . . to give consideration to the establishment of programs and projects to further these ends." The responsum understands "the language of this resolution" as a demand "that we as Reform Jews work to put the expressed ideals of our movement into concrete practice." It follows that "the synagogue bears an ethical responsibility to hire unionized workers when they are available."

A word about CCAR resolutions. In one sense, because these statements are adopted by the entire CCAR at its conventions, they are more "authoritative" as expressions of rabbinic opinion than CCAR responsa, which are issued by a small committee of the CCAR. At the same time, neither resolutions nor responsa possess "obligatory" authority; individual Reform rabbis and laypersons are free to disagree with them. Like Reform responsa, CCAR resolutions are best understood as a means through which a group of rabbis exercise their role as teachers of Torah. And like responsa, their authority lies ultimately in the degree to which their words are persuasive and can elicit the assent of their intended audience. Whether the resolutions that the responsum cites are truly persuasive is for their readers to decide. But for the responsum itself, they create a most persuasive demand for ethical consistency: "We who have championed the cause of organized labor for so many decades can hardly exempt our own institutions from the ethical standards we would impose upon others." From this vantage point, that of Jewish tradition and the teachings of our own Reform Movement, it's obvious that a Reform synagogue has an ethical duty to employ union labor for its construction project.

Fair Price and Jewish Law
Now for the other side of this hard question. If Jewish law promotes the right of workers to organize for their economic benefit, it also protects consumers against unfair pricing. Among the sources the responsum cites are the following:

> Price fraud [*onaah*] is defined by an overcharge of four silver coins out of the twenty-four that make up a *sela*; that is, one-sixth of the purchase price. Until when may the buyer revoke the sale? Until they can show the item to a merchant or to a relative (in order to ascertain its fair market value).

Both the buyer and the seller are entitled to raise claims of *onaah*. (*Mishnah Bava M'tzia* 4:3-4)

The *beit din* [the court, the governing authority] is obligated to appoint officials who will supervise prices, so that no merchant is entitled to a profit greater than one-sixth (over the wholesale cost of the item plus his expenses). . . . Whoever unfairly raises prices is subject to whatever punishment the *beit din* deems fair. (*Shulchan Aruch, Choshen Mishpat* 231:20-21)

The Jewish law on pricing and fair business practices is much more complex and nuanced than these two texts indicate. But they serve the responsum as proof that "the halachah displays a general tendency to supervise the stability of prices in the marketplace, and it looks askance upon factors that upset this stability to the detriment of consumers." One of these factors is wage inflation, which, as one leading commentator argues, is the reason for the Talmud's requirement that a "person of stature" (*adam chashuv*) arbitrate labor disputes: "The reason for this requirement is that by raising their prices the workers cause a financial loss to their customers. Thus, their decision has no legal force unless it is approved by that community official [appointed to supervise prices]" (Rabbi Nissim Gerondi [fourteenth-century Spain], *Commentary to Bava Batra* 9a). True, no such system of compulsory arbitration exists in our communities today. Yet this text shows that the halachah recognizes the "valid interest [of consumers] in maintaining a reasonable level of prices . . . including the cost of labor." The synagogue tells us that it would have to spend an extra $300,000 to hire union workers for their job. Is that a "reasonable" demand to place upon its budget?

One more consideration on behalf of that budget: the Talmudic principle *haTorah chasah al mamonam shel Yisrael*. Translated literally as "the Torah protects the property of Israel," it expresses the idea that we should be spared unnecessary expense when we perform mitzvot. As the responsum notes, the principle is not absolute—sometimes, indeed, we are encouraged to spend liberally for the sake of mitzvot—and the Rabbis do not apply it in every case where Jews are required to undertake financial expense. Still, this is one more consideration to think about before we decide that the synagogue is required to pay a significant premium to hire union labor for its construction project.

Tzedakah: The Demands of Social Justice
So we have a hard question. Jewish tradition offers strong support for orga-

nized labor, but that support does not automatically override concerns for price stability and the synagogue's financial bottom line. Rather, we confront two important Jewish legal values that, in this case at least, stand in conflict. "To reconcile the conflict" the responsum invokes the mitzvah of *tzedakah*, which it translates as "social justice." That's a crucial move. The word *tzedakah* is often rendered as "charity," from the Latin *caritas* (love, affection), a freewill gift of the heart. But "charity," of course, does not capture the meaning of *tzedakah*, which, derived from the Hebrew, *tzadi-dalet-kof*, is better understood as "justice" or "righteousness." The difference, the responsum argues, is vast. "As justice, *tzedakah* is obligatory conduct, not a voluntary contribution"—a tax that we owe, rather than a contribution we might or might not decide to make—and as a legal obligation, it is subject to enforcement. Thus we read:

> Every person is obligated to give *tzedakah*. Even the poor who are supported by *tzedakah* are obligated to give from the sum that they have been given.
> If one gives less than the amount deemed proper for him, the *beit din* may coerce him physically until he gives the amount that has been assessed for him. The authorities may also attach his property and seize the amount he is obligated to give. (*Shulchan Aruch, Yoreh Dei-ah* 248:1)

By translating "social justice" as *tzedakah,* the responsum identifies it as a mitzvah, a duty that, like many other such obligations, can be legally enforced. Obviously, this halachic enforcement power no longer exists. The *Shulchan Aruch* and its Talmudic sources (Babylonian Talmud, *K'tubot* 49b and *Bava Batra* 8b) are speaking of a time when the Jewish community possessed its own legal autonomy and like any government wielded the power to compel its members to meet their obligations. Our Jewish community today is a voluntary association that lacks the legal capacity to enforce its decisions. Still, this text communicates the unequivocal seriousness with which our tradition takes *tzedakah.* To repeat: *tzedakah* is a mitzvah, an obligation—a moral if no longer a legal one—that we ought to fulfill, even though we can no longer be compelled to do so.

Tzedakah now becomes the frame through which we view the conflict between our two conflicting values. The reasoning begins with the identification of the cause of union labor with social justice/*tzedakah*, a duty we have no right to ignore. From that vantage point, the text argues that while unionization raises wages and therefore the cost of goods and services to consumers, this higher level of wages is in fact the "just" price, and the nonunion pay scale is "unreasonably" low. If so, then by hiring nonunion workers and driving down the level of wages, we arguably commit price fraud (*onaah*) upon workers in general. (Remember that both buyers *and* sellers are entitled to claim *onaah*.) The responsum likewise refutes the objection from the principle that "the Torah protects the property of Israel." That principle has never meant that "we are exempt from performing the mitzvah merely because it is expensive." Many mitzvot—to build a sukkah, to obtain matzah for Pesach and wine for *Kiddush*, to support Jewish education and the synagogue, to perform deeds of *tzedakah* and social justice—require that we spend more money than we otherwise would. The issue boils down to this: how do we determine that a particular expense is "unnecessary" to the successful performance of a mitzvah? While hiring union labor does involve a greater expense to consumers, the responsum argues that those higher wages are the *necessary* means to fulfill the mitzvah of social justice. As the text puts it, if hiring nonunion workers actually "frustrates" that mitzvah, then "our own value commitments require that our institutions show a decided preference for hiring union labor."

Yet is that really so? The critical reader might object that the mitzvah of social justice/*tzedakah* does not necessarily require the hiring of union labor. This is because, as the responsum concedes, there exist "other visions of *tzedakah* than the one we have sketched here." Following one of these alternative visions, the reader could argue that the goal of justice is better served by hiring *nonunion* labor, since by holding down labor costs we tend to create more jobs for the unemployed. In some ways this is an example of the economic argument that we have already encountered, but it's also a moral argument because it is at least plausible that by raising the cost of labor and limiting the number of available jobs, unionization effectively prices the poor out of the labor market. If we interpret the demands of social justice in this alternative, nonunion direction, we could just as logically decide the congregation's *sh'eilah* the other way, that "social justice" requires that the synagogue hire *non*union workers for its construction project.

Our critical reader has put a finger on a serious problem. High-sounding value terms like "justice" are *equivocal*: they have no one objective definition. Indeed, the philosophical argument over "what is justice?" is as old as philosophy itself, and the answers provided by the great thinkers—Plato, Aristotle, Kant, Bentham and the utilitarians, the laissez-faire economists, Marx, the redistributionists—differ from and conflict with each other in crucial respects.[4] The responsum acknowledges this: "Suffice it to say that a general concept such as 'social justice' can be meaningless in the absence of some substantive vision that gives it content." To put this another way: if the universal ethical value called "social justice" is to mean anything at all, if it is to be of any use in solving real-life ethical dilemmas, we have no choice but to *choose* a particular definition for that value from among the available alternatives. For its part, this responsum chooses "the understanding of that term that makes the most sense to us . . . the vision put forth by the CCAR and by the prominent *poskim* whose words we have cited." It is this particularly *Jewish* definition of social justice that equips that ethical value with substantive bite. This definition, which involves "the empowerment of workers to control their destiny," is not the only possible definition; that's what makes it a choice. It is not, however, an *arbitrary* choice, a mere flip of a coin. It is the choice that the authors believe best accords with what our tradition means by *tzedakah*. And, significantly, that belief is supported by the weight of precedent—by the writings of generations of rabbis, both Reform and otherwise. The responsum can therefore contend that it has located a specifically Jewish approach to a question of universal ethics, the substantive vision of *tzedakah* that we Reform Jews—and the Jewish tradition generally—have been teaching and preaching for a long time. And "if we believe what we preach, it is our duty to practice the same."

Conclusion

Given all this, it's no surprise that the responsum calls upon the congregation to "make every effort to hire union labor for your construction project." Yet the Responsa Committee hedges its ruling with words of caution: "we cannot tell your congregation what it 'must' do." The difficulty, it tells us, lies with two caveats. First, $300,000 is a lot of money, and no committee of rabbis can tell *this* congregation in *this* instance that such an expense is sustainable, prudent, or a reasonable premium to pay in order to fulfill the mitzvah of social justice. And second, labor unions have not always been paragons of virtue. Some unions, we know, are corrupt, and we do not fulfill the mitzvah of social justice by signing a contract with such an organization. Indeed, in such cases we might better fulfill that mitzvah by hiring nonunion workers. The responsum does not wish to say that we must always employ union workers. Each case must be judged on its own merits.

Do these reservations indicate that the Responsa Committee lacks the confidence to issue a clear and straightforward ruling? Perhaps. But before we draw that conclusion, let's recall that the authors of this *t'shuvah* have chosen to frame this *sh'eilah* as a hard question, one that involves a close contest between conflicting values. They could always have chosen differently, to frame the question as an easy one, in which one of our two conflicting values obviously takes precedence. In that event, the answer, too, would have been obvious. By framing this as a hard question, the responsum prepares its readers for a middle-ground solution, a compromise between or reconciliation of these conflicting values. Yes, the mitzvah of *tzedakah*/social justice tilts that reconciliation in the direction of "a decided preference" for hiring union labor, but that preference must be tested in the crucible of the real-life factors that govern each specific case.

Another way to say this is that the responsum's "ideal audience" is one that can live with a reasonable degree of ambiguity. It is an audience that recognizes the Jewish tradition is replete with complexity and nuance and that its values can and do conflict, pulling us as they do here in the direction of opposing answers. If we require that *one* of those answers be obviously correct, the clear and indisputable message of Jewish tradition, we are bound to be disappointed. But *our* audience, the one to which this responsum seems to speak, does not make that demand. Rather than give us a single "right" answer, the *t'shuvah* offers its readers a two-step model for thinking through the dilemma of conflicting values. First, we study carefully the texts that relate to both values; perhaps we shall find that one of them does outweigh the other in importance and so dictates the answer to the question. Second, if we find that neither value obviously takes precedence—that the arguments seem to go both ways so that their resolution is not clear—we seek a balance, a way to reconcile the two conflicting values by giving each of them its due. This find-a-middle-ground approach, with all its uncertainty and moderation, may not entirely satisfy us. It surely will frustrate our desire for clear and definitive answers. But it may be the best we can do. And *that*, the responsum tells its intended audience, is not such a bad thing.

CHAPTER TEN

POLITICS AND REFORM HALACHAH
Hunger Strike: On the Force-Feeding of Prisoners

As WE'VE SAID BEFORE, we like to think that the two great traditions in which we Reform Jews participate—the specifically Jewish tradition and the tradition of modern Western civilization—yield similar guidance on questions of ethical behavior. Sometimes, however, we find these two sources in conflict. What do we do then? Do we reject the teaching of one tradition and embrace that of the other? Or can we identify a solution that affirms both of them? The following responsum (which can be read in full on pages 252–64) takes the latter approach:

> What would be the Jewish view of force-feeding (strapping somebody to a chair and putting a tube down their nose in as painless a fashion as possible) a mentally stable prisoner who desires to starve himself to death to make a political statement?[1]

The phrase "mentally stable prisoner" might refer to any prisoner in any prison. But the date of the *sh'eilah* (5766 = 2006) indicates, as the responsum comments in its opening sentence, that the questioner is thinking about "the treatment of detainees imprisoned at the US naval base at Guantanamo Bay, Cuba," prisoners taken during the American military operations in Afghanistan beginning in 2001. That conflict, along with the much larger Second Iraq War that commenced in 2003, was part of the "war on terror" that the American government initiated following the terrorist attacks of September 11, 2001. Whatever popular support the military response enjoyed at its outset, by 2006 it had become, in the responsum's words, a subject of "intense political controversy."

These words point to a significant problem confronting this responsum. If the "war on terror" itself was politically controversial, so too were a host of issues arising from the conduct of that war, including the treatment of prisoners. A responsum on any such issue, which might have to decide in favor of or against a policy of the US government, could well be viewed as a political statement. Now there's nothing wrong with rabbis making political statements; they do it all the time. A responsum, though, claims to be something other than a political statement. It claims to represent not the opinion of an individual rabbi or group of rabbis but the voice of Jewish tradition on the question at hand—a voice that is not biased by any particular partisan attachment or ideological bent. The authors of this responsum make precisely this claim in the second paragraph: they intend "to set the politics aside and to view this *sh'eilah*, as we do all others, as a *Jewish* one, involving the interpretation and application of values central to our religious tradition." This claim of political neutrality is also the responsum's claim of authority: you, the reader, can trust this *t'shuvah* because it *is* a *t'shuvah*—a rabbinic opinion that conforms to the best understanding of what our texts and sources teach us. The text declares that it will confine itself to the discourse of Jewish law and will speak equally to all readers, regardless of their attitude toward the war.

To this, the critical reader might—and should—object that we *can't* set the politics aside. We human beings do not approach questions of war and peace from a stance of pure objectivity. Our life experience, education, beliefs, and values have everything to do with our perception of the social and political world, and they necessarily shape the way we interpret our religious tradition. It follows that there is no such thing as a politically neutral "voice of Jewish tradition" that speaks to questions like this one, because our prior political commitments already predispose us to hear that voice in different ways. This is why political liberals and conservatives can read the same biblical or Rabbinic texts and arrive at very conflicting understandings of "what Judaism says" about matters of social justice or politics. (The previous chapter, on labor unionization, is a good example.) It also follows that a responsum, as the product of human beings who necessarily work from within some established set of social values and political commitments, will inevitably be informed by those values and commitments. That's the way we think; there's no avoiding it, and we shouldn't pretend otherwise.

The difficulty with this objection is that, should we accept it, we question the scholarly reliability of any responsum on any question that touches however remotely on a political or social question. For that matter, we risk giving the impression that *any* rabbinic interpretation of or teaching derived from Jewish tradition on any controversial public issue is driven by ideology and is nothing *but* politics. In all probability, we don't believe this. We more likely think that Jewish tradition does have something of substance to say about matters of political and social concern. When considering such questions, our goal must be to recognize and to filter out our political biases as best we can, so that the conclusions we draw would be valid regardless of whatever partisan tendencies we might have. This responsum, for its part, insists that it *is* possible to strip away the political elements of this issue and reduce it to its ethical (and Jewish ethical) core. And indeed, the text does strive throughout to maintain a nonpolitical tone. Nowhere does it overtly express a pro or con position concerning the war or an opinion concerning the justification (or lack thereof) for the detentions at Guantanamo. Its discussion is nonpolitical, too, in that it focuses exclusively upon the use of force-feeding to break a hunger strike by *any* imprisoned person. This supports the responsum's claim that the question is not "about" the prisoners taken as part of the "war on terror"; instead, it is a question of ethics, not politics. We'll return to this claim at the end of our discussion; how well it succeeds in supporting that claim is, of course, a judgment left to the reader.

Arguments in Favor of Force-Feeding
Even if we can imagine this question as apolitical, the responsum concedes that it is a difficult one, for "the Jewish view" of force-feeding "is far from obvious." The responsum therefore will examine the arguments on both sides, to "do justice to the genuine complexity of the case." This promise of a thorough and impartial analysis comes to reinforce the t'shuvah's claim of authority: you, the reader, can trust this t'shuvah's answer because it will be based on a discussion that is thoughtful, evenhanded, and free of bias.

The Jewish case in favor of force-feeding proceeds from the mitzvah of *pikuach nefesh*, the duty to save human life. As is well-known, this obligation takes precedence over virtually every other moral requirement recognized by Jewish law. But it is less well-known that this mitzvah—one our tradition views as a clear and undisputed obligation—is derived from a rather forced midrash (interpretation) of a Torah verse that seemingly has nothing to do with the saving of life: "You shall keep My statutes and My laws, which a person shall perform and *live by them* [*vachai bahem*]; I am the Eternal" (Leviticus 18:5). The literal sense (*p'shat*) of the italicized phrase is that by following God's mitzvot, the Israelites will attain the blessing of life, while the alternative path—rejecting the mitzvot—will bring death. That is, after all, the obvious consequence of the covenant with God that the people entered into while standing at Sinai. Some traditional commentators, especially the ones who emphasize the *p'shat* in their approach to the biblical text, explain the verse that way.[2] But the halachic sense of the verse is set by a midrash, cited a number of times in Rabbinic literature, that understands the Leviticus statement "to live by them" to mean that we should not *die* by them.[3] In other words, if by performing any mitzvah we would incur significant risk to life and limb, we set that mitzvah aside, because the commandment to preserve life takes precedence over it. Or as Rashi explains the idea, one shall observe the mitzvot in such a way that the observance poses no danger to one's life.[4] One famous example is the principle that *pikuach nefesh docheh et haShabbat*, saving human life takes precedence over the laws prohibiting "work" on the Sabbath (Babylonian Talmud, *Yoma* 85a–b). (There are, as we shall see, some exceptions to this rule of self-preservation.) In addition to *pikuach nefesh*, there is the positive ("thou shalt") commandment to rescue those whose lives are threatened. The Rabbis learn this obligation, too, by way of a creative interpretation of a biblical text by interpreting Leviticus 19:16, which cautions *lo taamod al dam rei-echa*, often translated as "Do not stand by the blood of your fellow." The meaning of the Hebrew is "uncertain,"[5] but the Rabbis read the word *taamod*, "stand," as "to stand idly by and do nothing": "From where do we learn that one who sees his fellow drowning in the river, attacked by a wild beast, or threatened by robbers is obliged to save him? From the verse 'do not stand *idly*' (Leviticus 19:16) when your neighbor's life is at risk" (Babylonian Talmud, *Sanhedrin* 73a).

These two ideas combine to support the case in favor of force-feeding. Since the duty of *pikuach nefesh* involves preserving one's own life as well as the life of another, the prisoners are in the wrong to undertake a hunger strike that jeopardizes their lives and health. The prison officials are therefore required to fulfill the duty of rescue, which in this case presumably requires the use of force-feeding to break the strike.

This is a straightforward and logical argument, but it has its weaknesses. We might object that these prisoners are not bound to obey the rule of *pikuach nefesh* because under the precepts of their own religion they have every right (and perhaps even an obligation) to die as martyrs for their cause. To this, the responsum could answer that the *sh'eilah* asks for "the Jewish view" of the issue, and our goal is therefore to determine what *Jewish* law (and not, for example, what Islamic law) has to say about it. A stronger objection would be that martyrdom is recognized as legitimate in *Jewish* law: that is, according to halachah we have a duty in some cases to surrender our lives for our faith, a duty that overrides the mitzvah of *pikuach nefesh*. The Babylonian Talmud defines this requirement in *Sanhedrin* 74a: "If one is told to transgress a prohibition of the Torah or be killed, one should transgress that mitzvah and save one's life, with the exception of the prohibitions against idolatry, adultery and incest, and murder." Those exceptions define the scope of martyrdom under Jewish law: one must accept a martyr's death rather than violate any of those prohibitions. The response to this would be that the situation of the Guantanamo prisoners doesn't involve any of these prohibitions, so Jewish law would not require that they sacrifice their lives. But then the question arises: may we *volunteer* for martyrdom, choosing to die for our faith even in situations where Jewish law does not obligate us to do so?

The responsum anticipates this question when it cites Maimonides (Rambam) to the effect that "one is not entitled to choose martyrdom in order 'to make a political statement.'" This is based on his ruling that says, "If the case is one in which the Torah says, 'Transgress the commandment and save your life,' the one who chooses to die rather than transgress the commandment is culpable for one's own death."[6] Yes, the responsum notes, the Torah does demand martyrdom in some cases, "but the circumstances in which this demand applies are strictly limited." In all other cases, such as the one described in the *sh'eilah*, martyrdom is *forbidden*: that is, according to "the Jewish view" of the issue, these prisoners are endangering their lives for no acceptable reason. That's the law—or, at least, that's the law according to Rambam. But other halachic authorities hold that in cases where the Torah does not require martyrdom, an individual may as an act of pious stringency volunteer to die "to sanctify the divine name."[7] It's a complex issue in the halachah. We may think that Maimonides's position is the stronger one, particularly because we take the demands of *pikuach nefesh* with the utmost seriousness. But the prisoners *do* have a good halachic argument in support of their action. Those "other halachic authorities" are no slouches, and the responsum should have mentioned their view. Had it done so, it could have answered that given the uncertainty over which view of "voluntary martyrdom" is correct, the better and safer course is to be stringent: to deny the prisoners the right to endanger their lives, and to break their hunger strike.

Arguments against Force-Feeding

The responsum now moves to arguments supporting the other side of the question. The obvious difficulty: if you want to make a case within the realm of Jewish law and tradition, how do you argue against *pikuach nefesh*, the obligation to protect human life that outweighs virtually all other considerations? We might say, a bit irreverently, that *pikuach nefesh* is the eight-hundred-pound gorilla of halachic argumentation: when one cites it, one expects all counterarguments to scurry quickly out of the way. The best move, then, is to frame the *sh'eilah* in such a way that it does *not* involve *pikuach nefesh*. The responsum does this by claiming that "this is a political, not a medical question." The prisoners have undertaken their hunger strike in order to demonstrate their frustration at their confinement, to bring pressure upon the prison officials, and "not necessarily to kill themselves or to cause themselves irreparable physical harm." If so, their lives are not really in danger, and we should therefore set aside those weighty concerns about *pikuach nefesh* and decide the question on other grounds. To be sure, the responsum's authors cannot prove that the hunger strike posed no serious danger to the prisoners' health. Still, this argument successfully places the burden of proof for this matter upon the prison officials. Those officials, by the way, seem to "concur in [the] assessment" that the strikers do not want to die but are making a political statement (see responsum endnote 14). All of this supports the point that the responsum makes at the beginning of this section: "Answers are frequently dictated by the way in which we frame the questions." When we view this question as a political issue rather than a medical one, arguments based on *pikuach nefesh*—the entire case in favor of force-feeding—lose their immediacy and relevance.

On the other hand, not all efforts at framing are successful. Sometimes, the suggested framing strikes us as weak, debatable, or transparently one-sided. Take, for example, the *t'shuvah*'s example of the hunger strike undertaken in the 1990s by "a number of Orthodox rabbis" in protest of the Oslo peace accords. Responsum endnote 17 tells us that those rabbis defended their action on the grounds that it is similar to a *taanit yachid*, a fast voluntarily undertaken by an individual. In drawing this analogy, those rabbis want us to frame the question as involving an act of religious devotion, something entirely permissible and perhaps even praiseworthy, rather than an act of reckless self-endangerment, prohibited under the rule of *pikuach nefesh* and the sort of thing that good rabbis would never condone. If this analogy is persuasive, the prisoners in our case could use this reasoning to justify their hunger strike according to Jewish law. But *is* the analogy persuasive? Here is how the halachah defines the *taanit yachid*: "Just as the community fasts in order to pray for relief from its troubles [*tzarot*], so may individuals fast and pray for relief from their troubles. For example, if one has a relative who is ill or lost in the wilderness or in prison, one may engage in a fast to pray for that person. But one may not engage in such a fast on Shabbat, festivals, Chanukah, Purim, or Rosh Chodesh" (*Shulchan Aruch, Orach Chayim* 578:1).

There are some similarities between an individual's fast and a hunger strike, but there are important differences as well. Like all fasts other than those of Yom Kippur and Tishah B'Av, a *taanit yachid* generally lasts from sunrise to sundown, thereby presenting few if any significant health risks, while a hunger strike lasts indefinitely. The "troubles" cited to justify the fast are personal rather than political in nature. And as we learn in the authoritative *Mishnah B'rurah* commentary to the *Shulchan Aruch* passage, individuals undertake fasts "because fasting is one of the paths of repentance [*t'shuvah*] and submission [*hachnaah*], and individuals are obligated to consider their sins and return to God." That is, one undertakes a *taanit yachid* in an attitude of humility and awareness of one's sinfulness, which is most definitely *not* the attitude of these hunger strikers, who are not repenting for their own sins but protesting the putative sins of others. Still, the fact that some rabbis have made this analogy reminds us of the critical importance of *framing* as a rhetorical tactic. If you, the speaker or the writer, can bring your audience to accept your portrayal of the subject—say, "the act described in this *sh'eilah* is a religious act, one that faithful and righteous Jews have always performed"—then you have gone a long way toward persuading them that your case is correct.

The second argument against force-feeding is that the procedure "is widely regarded as torture." Such is the view of "enlightened medical-ethical opinion" expressed in resolutions adopted by medical associations and human rights organizations around the world. Positions taken by these groups tend to carry significant weight with Reform Jews, and a community that defines itself as "progressive" would certainly not wish to countenance a tactic that these highly respected bodies define as torture. A Reform responsum, then, ought to take this criticism of force-feeding quite seriously.

The matter, however, is not so simple. As the *t'shuvah* explains (in the paragraph beginning with "Before we reach that conclusion"), these organizations base their stance upon the principles of patient autonomy and informed consent, which dominate bioethical thought in the contemporary Western world. Consider the language of the World Medical Association's Tokyo Declaration of 1975 (and last amended in 2016) that prohibits physicians from cooperating in the use of "torture" against prisoners and detainees: "Where a prisoner refuses nourishment and is considered by the physician as capable of forming an unimpaired and rational judgment concerning the consequences of such a voluntary refusal of nourishment, he or she shall not be fed artificially."[8] The declaration defines force-feeding as "torture" not (or not only) because it involves an act of violence, but principally because it denies the autonomous, rational prisoner the right to make an informed decision to refuse food and water. (Whether prisoners detained under the conditions prevailing at Guantanamo could indeed make an "informed" decision is another matter; see responsum endnote 26.) The declaration makes no exception for cases in which the hunger strike poses a substantive danger to life or health, aside from the provision that "the consequences of the refusal of nourishment shall be explained by the physician to the prisoner."

None of this is surprising, considering the dominant theory of bioethics—based on patient autonomy and informed consent—in the contemporary Western world. That principle wins out over its main competitor, the principle of beneficence, which requires that we act for the patient's benefit or best interests (however we define these) even against the patient's own wishes. A medical system operating upon the beneficence principle would be paternalistic ("doctor knows best") in nature; as a leading bioethicists textbook puts it, "Paternalistic interventions are seldom justified, because the right to act autonomously almost always outweighs obligations of beneficence toward the autonomous agent."[9] Hence, the right of the prisoners to say "no" to nutrition supersedes our concern for their physical well-being. And here is where Jewish tradition dissents, holding that the fundamental duty to protect and preserve human life will at times override a patient's rational choice. "In the traditional Jewish view, the patient has no right to make a decision, however 'informed,' for suicide, and the physician, who like every person bears a positive duty to save life, has no right to sit passively and watch the patient die." It turns out that the principle of *pikuach nefesh*, an expression of the exalted commandment to "choose life" (Deuteronomy 30:19), might in some cases *support* force-feeding. The *sh'eilah* therefore poses a direct clash between the two great traditions of bioethics—the modern Western one and the traditional Jewish one—from which Reform responsa draw guidance. Which one shall the responsum choose to follow on this question?

The answer is "neither" or "both." "We do not believe that the contemporary Western model of bioethics is any more exalted, noble, or humane than the Judaic approach." The responsum does not want to make the choice for one of these traditions at the expense of the other. We learn much from each of them, and "as heirs to *both* the classical Jewish tradition *and* the culture of modernity, we would not wish to live in a society that rejects *either* source of ethical value." The responsum, in other words, asserts an equality between them. The "classical Jewish tradition" of bioethics is not necessarily *better* than its modern secular counterpart, but it is also not *inferior* to it. Thus, the conclusions reached by contemporary secular ethicists should not be accepted uncritically. We should instead remain open to conflicting insights drawn from our own Jewish tradition, for "we reject the notion that 'modern, progressive, and Western' culture enjoys a monopoly upon moral truth."

Let's take note here that the responsum does not attempt to prove the ethical superiority of the traditional Jewish approach to bioethics, based upon a commitment to *pikuach nefesh* above all, over the modern approach in which the principle of patient autonomy is predominant. Does that constitute a weakness in its argument? Probably not; in fact, the responsum does not need to prove this point one way or the other. By asserting that both systems are equal in moral value—by declaring a tie—it effectively shifts the burden of proof to the other side. Those who wish to break the tie and claim that the Western autonomy-based bioethics is morally superior to the Jewish one must now argue and prove *their* point. That would certainly be an interesting argument, but the responsum does not engage in it, possibly— again—because it doesn't have to. Its argumentative strategy here is a much simpler one, namely to cause its Reform Jewish readers—full participants in "modern, progressive, and Western" culture who are generally sympathetic to that culture's bioethical approach—to question that approach as it relates to this question. We should not simply presume that the "enlightened medical-ethical opinion" necessarily has it right. We are Jews, after all, the heirs of another great tradition, and we should at least take interest in what that tradition, the halachah, has to say. When we do, the responsum implies, we will come away with a respect for what that tradition teaches about the sanctity of human life and about our overriding duty to protect and preserve it. And on that basis, we will be likely to agree with the responsum's conclusion in this section that "as Jews, we cannot apply the label 'torture' to a procedure designed to save the life of prisoners in our custody, even if they seem bound and determined upon suicide."

Accordingly, if we want to make a case against force-feeding, we must do so on undeniably *Jewish* grounds, from Jewish texts and values, and not simply from the principle of patient autonomy. The text therefore argues that "force-feeding transgresses against Jewish ethical principles." In particular, while Jewish law would mandate that the prisoners end a hunger strike that endangers their lives and health, it would not necessarily authorize the use of physical force to make them comply with that obligation. In this case, it is certainly difficult to read about the "harsh, violent measures" employed to feed the Guantanamo detainees against their will. And although one could invoke *pikuach nefesh* to justify such gruesome treatment, the responsum cites the ruling of the eminent Orthodox halachist Rabbi Moshe Feinstein that pointedly rejects the use of force to coerce a patient to accept lifesaving treatment.[10] He reasons that such measures will stir the patient's fear, which, "even though it be irrational, may itself cause him harm or even kill him." Or as the CCAR Responsa Committee has held, "To the extent that a medical procedure causes significant harm to a patient, it may be said to lose its therapeutic value and therefore its standing as 'medicine' that the patient would be obligated to accept."[11] Force-feeding, when administered through violent means such as the ones described, ceases to be a "medical" intervention, its only possible ethical justification.

Both Rabbi Feinstein and the CCAR Responsa Committee are struggling against the difficulty with which we began this section: how do you place limits upon the mitzvah of *pikuach nefesh*? The inherent logic of that "supreme" mitzvah would dictate that we take all measures necessary, including the use of force, to fulfill it, even when those measures adversely affect the patient's emotional well-being or "human dignity" (*k'vod hab'riyot*). Both rulings remove the difficulty by arguing that because measures involving physical force cause harm to the patient, they are therefore not to be defined as legitimate medicine and are not obligatory. This approach, however, has its problems: part of the nature of medicine is that many drugs and therapies involve harmful side effects, yet we still hold them to be "lifesaving"—and therefore obligatory under the rubric of *pikuach nefesh*—despite the damage they cause. A better strategy would be to acknowledge that yes, force-feeding may save lives, but while *pikuach nefesh* is the highest Jewish moral value, it is not the *only* such value. It always operates within a context of other duties that we Jews recognize. This context means that any one of our moral values, including *pikuach nefesh*, must coexist with all the others and that its reach is necessarily modified and limited when it conflicts with them. We believe in *pikuach nefesh*, but we also believe that physical violence in the name of "medicine" is demeaning and dehumanizing, a cure quite possibly worse than the disease. Whether in any individual case these concerns justify a decision to reject an otherwise lifesaving treatment is a difficult call to make. But it must be made, for there are things we simply will not do to coerce patients—or prisoners—to accept lifesaving medical treatment.

Toward a Conclusion

Our responsum, like others we have read in this book, recognizes the power of the arguments on both sides of the question. It seeks a solution that does not reject either the "pros" or the "cons" but finds a way to unite them. The responsum pitches this path as sensible and realistic. The danger, of course, is that, like all middle-ground solutions, this one might strike readers as wishy-washy and uncertain. The responsum's authors seem to agree. That they entitle this section "Toward a Conclusion" rather than simply "Conclusion" may suggest a hesitancy on their part, a sense that they have not found an answer that adequately resolves the issue. Perhaps no such answer exists.

The first step "toward" the conclusion reflects the arguments in favor of force-feeding. *Pikuach nefesh* "is the overriding Jewish moral concern," and when push comes to shove, it must take precedence over our commitment to patient autonomy. The responsum supports this by turning (in endnote 38) to Dr. Shimeon Glick, a professor of medicine at Ben-Gurion University in Israel. If Glick is correct that patients in extreme situations, even though considered legally competent, may not be capable of entirely "rational" judgment, then much of the argument against force-feeding collapses.[12] The second step, proceeding from the arguments against force-feeding, is similarly supported by a quotation buried in responsum endnote 39 (don't overlook those endnotes!). It's a famous quotation from a US Supreme Court ruling concerning a police interrogation measure "that shocks the conscience" even though employed for a positive end (the prosecution of crime). The responsum's inference is that force-feeding, by its nature "a violent, even brutal tactic," is easily abused, becoming "a tool for punishment or discipline" rather than lifesaving medical treatment. Its use must be restricted to cases "when it is obviously necessary to save the life of the hunger striker."

The responsum locates a "proper balance" in the regulations that have already been adopted by the US Federal Bureau of Prisons. According to those rules, force-feeding of hunger-striking prisoners is permissible, but only when competent medical authority determines (to the point of "reasonable medical certainty") that continuation of the strike would pose an "immediate" threat to a prisoner's life or "permanent" damage to the prisoner's health. The goal is to limit the use of harsh tactics such as those described in this responsum to situations of real medical emergency and to ensure they are not employed for political reasons. In Jewish terms, we might say that the goal is to limit the use of the *pikuach nefesh* justification to cases where life and health are truly in serious danger, so as to protect this highest of Jewish moral values from the distortion it suffers when (as may have occurred in this case) it is employed as a cover for actions that *ought* to shock the conscience.

One Final Note
The responsum ends with two suggestions. First, drawing upon the Bureau of Prisons' policies, it urges that any force-feeding undertaken upon military detainees be videotaped, and second, it recommends that the procedure be supervised by "outside observers who do not represent the prison system or the military." The goal is that despite "the secrecy that currently surrounds the activities at the Guantanamo prison camp," the government might thereby "demonstrate its commitment to 'humane' and 'compassionate' treatment of the detainees in the face of severe international criticism." Whatever we think about the wisdom or practicality of these ideas, it isn't difficult to read them as an echo of that "severe international criticism." At the very least, the responsum's language indicates that it finds the treatment of the Guantanamo hunger strikers to be distasteful (if not *in*humane and *un*compassionate). Does it also indicate a negative disposition toward the internment policies of the "war on terror" or, for that matter, toward the conduct of that war in general? The answer is, of course, a matter of interpretation. But the very fact that we can ask it casts doubt upon the responsum's claim of political neutrality. In this "final note," the responsum may be expressing (if ever so delicately) its authors' political commitments. That is a legitimate object of criticism, especially but not only from readers who hold different commitments with respect to the war.

Perhaps this outcome is inevitable. Perhaps the text's stated goal "to set the politics aside" and to examine the question on strictly "Jewish" grounds is an unrealistic aspiration. Perhaps the imaginary critical reader we quoted at the beginning of this chapter is right: you *can't* set politics aside when you deal with a question rooted in a political reality. It is certainly difficult to do so, especially when we are talking about questions of war and peace and human life and human dignity. Remember that this is a *rabbinic* opinion. Can we reasonably expect our rabbis, when they teach Torah on these issues, to check their deeply held political beliefs and social justice commitments at the door? And even if they could, would we want them to? What we *can* reasonably expect is that when our rabbis speak in the name of Torah, when they bring us "the message of Jewish tradition" on these questions, they will do their best to distinguish between their own politics or ideology and what the texts actually say. That's difficult, too, because "what the texts actually say" is largely a product of our reading of them, and we tend to read them through the lens of our beliefs, politics, and ideology.

At the end of the day, the best check upon potential political or ideological bias in rabbinic responsa is for a literate audience to read them critically. In this case, if they suspect that the responsum's authors opposed the "war on terror" or the US government's policies regarding the imprisonment of that war's detainees, those readers should ask of the *t'shuvah* whether it could have been written—that is, could the same arguments and analysis and decision have just as readily been made—by a rabbi or group of rabbis who supported the war, its aims, and its conduct. That's a test that can only be applied by the *t'shuvah*'s readership. And that just goes to show once again that a responsum, no matter how well-written and argued, is incomplete without an audience that accords it a respectful—and critical—reading.

CONCLUSIONS

IN THE INTRODUCTION to this book, I suggested that we try to read Reform responsa *critically*—that is, as a form of literature. And as I put it there, the goal of this kind of reading is "to inquire as to how responsa make meaning and create Torah." Now that we've applied this sort of reading to some fifteen responsa over these ten chapters, it's right to ask: what has this effort taught us? The answer to that question, of course, is mainly up to you, the reader. But I do hope that some conclusions will be evident to all, and I'd be remiss if I didn't mention them here.

The first conclusion: I hope that it's become plain that Reform responsa are *halachic* texts, with roots planted firmly in the Jewish legal tradition. The *t'shuvot* we've read demonstrate the different ways in which this is true. All of them use traditional halachic sources as a key element in their decision-making process. And more than simply citing those sources, Reform responsa engage them in conversation. That is to say, they participate in the *shakla v'tarya*—the traditional Talmudic-style discourse that characterizes much of the halachic literature and especially the responsa. In chapter 1, we see how Rabbi Freehof subjects the Orthodox arguments against Friday-night Torah reading to halachic analysis and finds them wanting. He concludes that they are based not in halachah, which does not prohibit this practice, but in ideology—what he calls the "Orthodox mood." In chapter 4, the Reform responsum surveys a centuries-old scholarly dispute over the authenticity of Rambam's responsum permitting the reading of Torah from a ritually defective scroll and actually takes part in the debate, offering its own solution to a problem that has occupied halachic scholars for centuries. In chapter 9, the CCAR responsum joins with a prominent Orthodox *poseik* in an act of "creative interpretation" to find that the halachah permits workers to unionize in order to secure better pay and working conditions. All of this suggests that Reform responsa look to halachic texts from ancient to contemporary times as an indispensable resource of meaning and that they want their readers to do the same. It's true that some Reform Jews contend that because the halachah is not "binding" upon us, we have no business speaking in its name and using its texts to help us answer our questions. Reform responsa, by their manner of thought and speaking, argue against that contention. The very existence of Reform responsa makes a claim that halachah is not foreign to us, that it plays a legitimate role in Reform Jewish thinking.

The second conclusion would be that our "conversation" with the halachic sources is very much a two-way street. Reform responsa do not merely consult the texts but talk back to them. For one thing, they do not hesitate to break with halachic tradition when they find it necessary to do so. For example, the three responsa in chapter 5 acknowledge Reform Judaism's rejection of the traditional Rabbinic definition of prohibited Shabbat "work" (*m'lachah*), even as they attempt to forge an acceptable "Reform" version of that concept. In chapter 3, Reform responsa written in 2006 and 1974 both affirm that cremation is an acceptable option for the disposal of human remains, despite the consensus view among Orthodox authorities that the halachah forbids the practice. These responsa, and many others that have been issued over the years, demonstrate what we mean when we—channeling Rabbi Freehof—say that the halachah serves us as "guidance" rather than "governance." The second way that the responsa "talk back" to tradition is by transforming it into something new, deriving meanings from the old texts that the authors of those texts most assuredly did not imagine. In chapter 2, the responsum applies the story of an ancient halachic *machloket* (scholarly dispute) toward resolving a contemporary Orthodox-versus-Reform dispute over the limits of Jewish religious pluralism. The responsum in chapter 7 takes several biblical, Talmudic, and medieval halachic sources and constructs from them a theory of "the secular," the realm of social and cultural experience that all citizens of a state, no matter their religion, share. And in chapter 8, the *t'shuvah* draws together a number of halachic rules and texts to argue for the existence of a "right to privacy" in Jewish law. We learn from these *t'shuvot* that while the literature of traditional halachah does play a central role in our Reform religious thinking, it does not constrict what we are able to say. On the contrary: the halachah offers us material we can use to craft creative *and* authentically Jewish answers to the questions of our time. Reform responsa do not regard the halachah as a body of fixed rules but rather as a language for ongoing argument, an argument in which today's generation, no less than those of the past, is entitled to speak in the name of our texts.

The third conclusion: though they stand within the tradition of halachic literature, Reform responsa are thoroughly *Reform* in their nature, style, and purpose. Some of them deal with questions that arise within a uniquely

Reform Jewish context. It is difficult to imagine that a contemporary Orthodox community would submit to a rabbi a *sh'eilah* about the acceptability of Friday-night Torah reading (chapter 1). The same is true, obviously, of the issue concerning whether an Orthodox minyan should be permitted in a Reform synagogue (chapter 2). Similarly, the congregation that asks whether it is proper to read publicly from a ritually defective "Holocaust" Torah scroll (chapter 4) is looking for a specifically *Reform* answer, one that must consider the reality that Reform Jews may not feel bound by the halachic rules that traditionally govern the practice. These responsa are uniquely Reform, too, in that they are part of a specifically *Reform* halachic tradition. Unlike responsa written by Orthodox rabbis, our *t'shuvot* consult existing Reform responsa and statements and resolutions adopted by Reform Jewish organizations as authoritative guidance for their own discussions. Cases in point: the responsum on cremation (chapter 3); the *t'shuvot* concerning the display of national flags in the synagogue sanctuary (chapter 6); and the responsum on the synagogue and organized labor (chapter 9). If the halachic tradition is an ongoing conversation with the sources of the past, *our* version of that conversation includes texts bequeathed to us by the leaders and teachers of our own movement.

Finally, these responsa are "Reform" because, written by Reform rabbis and directed toward a Reform audience, they are acts of *advocacy*: each one sets forth a particular vision of Reform Judaism and its religious observance that it invites its readers to share. At times, this vision supports our existing practices. In chapter 1, we read Rabbi Freehof's argument that the halachah does not forbid the reading of the Torah on Friday nights, a widespread Reform custom. In chapter 3, the responsum shows that both those who permit cremation and those who oppose it can draw support from halachah and from the history of Reform rabbinic thought. In such cases, the responsa offer a vision of Reform Judaism's authenticity: *our* observance, no less than that of our Orthodox brothers and sisters, fully concurs with the halachic tradition, the source of all Jewish religious practice. At other times, the vision poses a challenge to received ways of thinking and acting. In chapter 2 (Orthodox minyan in a Reform synagogue), the responsum asks its readers to resist the assumption that a Reform congregation must choose between the ideals of Jewish pluralism and Reform Jewish integrity. The Rabbinic tradition, it asserts, teaches that there is no necessary contradiction between them. It also calls upon them to respond to the request of an Orthodox Jew in the spirit of liberality and tolerance rather than of simple (rough?) justice; we need not do unto them as they would do unto us. The *t'shuvah* in chapter 4 argues that the halachic rules governing the ritual fitness of a *sefer Torah* are relevant and important for Reform Judaism, a claim that, it acknowledges, many Reform Jews will at first glance find controversial. The responsa in chapter 5 propose that even if we no longer observe the traditional definition of prohibited Shabbat "work," we ought to take the concept of Shabbat prohibitions—the mitzvah of *sh'mirat Shabbat*—with all seriousness, and they turn to the halachic literature for guidance (if not governance!) in constructing a Reform standard of practice. The responsa in chapter 6 (national flags in the synagogue sanctuary) urge us to think critically about our received assumptions concerning national patriotism and Zionism. The responsum on the force-feeding of prisoners (chapter 10) asks us to confront the limitations of the contemporary Western version of medical ethics, challenging the all-too-common presumption that the ethical approach of modern culture is always superior to that which we learn from Jewish tradition. Each approach has its strengths as well as its weaknesses, and each has something to teach us. Our answer, therefore, should attempt to do justice to both.

Have these acts of advocacy won your assent? The law of averages would suggest that you've found some of them persuasive and others . . . well, not so much. And that's only to be expected. As we've seen throughout this book, when Jews submit a *sh'eilah* to a rabbi or to a committee of rabbis, it tends to be a hard question—one that admits of more than one plausible answer. They seek a *t'shuvah* that not only answers the question but provides arguments as to why *this* is the right answer or at least a better answer than the plausible alternatives. Those arguments may win the reader to the responsum's point of view. Then again, maybe they won't, for it is in the nature of argument that it frequently provokes counterargument, debate, *machloket*. But this hardly counts as a weakness of the responsa literature; indeed, it is the *point* of the responsa literature. For if argument leads to disagreement, it is also the only way to *resolve* disagreement, the only way for the members of a community to understand their differing perspectives and, hopefully, work toward consensus. Thus, we ought to accept disagreement as a *good* thing, an essential building block of a healthy culture of argument. "Healthy" means that the arguments themselves are cogent and well-grounded in the sources and that the parties conduct their *machloket* with mutual respect, generosity, and in a common language—one composed of the shared value commitments that bind them together as a community of purpose. Responsa are a literary embodiment of the culture of argument that has both divided *and* united the Jewish people since the days of the Talmud.

By writing our own responsa, we Reform Jews claim our place in that culture. We write halachic responsa because the Jewish legal tradition is and has been the foundation of that culture and because the interpretation of halachic texts is and has been the focal point of that argument. Reform responsa testify to our conviction that this tradition and these texts belong to *us* no less than to other Jews who do not share our religious and cultural outlook. If that tradition has consisted of two thousand years of argument over just how the Torah, speaking through the texts of halachah, would have us respond to the call of Sinai, then our responsa are evidence that we do not cede to other Jews the exclusive right to decide what those texts mean. When we write responsa, we accept upon ourselves the historic responsibility of all students of Torah to take our part in the debate over just what those age-old texts and tradition are saying to us.

NOTES

Introduction

1. Menachem Elon (*Jewish Law: History, Sources, Principles*, trans. Bernard Auerbach and Melvin J. Sykes [Philadelphia: Jewish Publication Society, 1994], 1462) estimates the number of known responsa at three hundred thousand, collected in some three thousand volumes, which makes them by far the largest genre of Jewish legal writing.

2. The best-known collection is the Responsa Project of Bar-Ilan University, a searchable and steadily growing database housing over one hundred thousand *t'shuvot*, at https://www.responsa.co.il.

3. Examples of these early changes include the recitation of synagogue prayer in the vernacular language, specific changes in the wording of the prayers, the shortening of the service, and the introduction of a sermon, among others. See Jakob J. Petuchowski, *Prayerbook Reform in Europe: The Liturgy of European Liberal and Reform Judaism* (New York: World Union for Progressive Judaism, 1968), 84-104.

4. The best study of Freehof's work in the field of responsa is Joan S. Friedman's *"Guidance, Not Governance": Rabbi Solomon B. Freehof and Reform Responsa* (Cincinnati: Hebrew Union College Press, 2013).

5. This collection of Reform responsa can be found at www.ccarnet.org/rabbinic-voice/reform-responsa.

6. This is the most common etymology of the term *halachah*. Some, however, link it to an ancient Akkadian legal term; see I. Tzvi Abusch, *"Alaktu and Halakhah:* Oracular Decision, Divine Revelation," *Harvard Theological Review* 80, no. 1 (January 1987): 15-42.

7. For more on this, see especially Chaim Saiman, *Halakhah: The Rabbinic Idea of Law* (Princeton, NJ: Princeton University Press, 2018), 8.

8. "Codes" is in quotation marks because while codes in other legal systems are *legislative* acts, created by some law-making authority (the emperor, the elected legislature, etc.), halachic "codes" are acts of interpretation. Their authors do not make the law but rather set forth in some organized form their understanding of the law as it already exists.

9. In this book I follow the definition of "hard cases" offered by Ronald Dworkin in *Taking Rights Seriously* (Cambridge, MA: Harvard University Press, 1986), 255-56; see also chapter 2 of this book.

10. On what follows in this paragraph, see my chapter, "The Woodchopper Revisited: On Analogy, *Halakhah*, and Jewish Biothics," in *Medical Frontiers in Jewish Law*, ed. Walter Jacob (Pittsburgh: Freehof Institute of Progressive Halakhah, 2012), 1-62, https://www.freehofinstitute.org/uploads/1/2/0/6/120631295/the_woodchopper_revisited.pdf.

11. See Tom L. Beauchamp and James F. Childress, *Principles of Biomedical Ethics*, 3rd ed. (New York: Oxford University Press, 1989), 134–50.

12. The concept "interpretive community" was pioneered by Stanley Fish, *Is There a Text in This Class? The Authority of Interpretive Communities* (Cambridge, MA: Harvard University Press, 1980).

13. Alasdair MacIntyre, *After Virtue*, 2nd ed. (Notre Dame, IN: Notre Dame University Press, 1984), 222.

14. For an extraordinarily insightful description and analysis, see Haym Soloveitchik, "Rupture and Reconstruction: The Transformation of Contemporary Orthodoxy," *Tradition* 28, no. 4 (1994): 64–131, https://traditiononline.org/rupture-and-reconstruction-the-transformation-of-contemporary-orthodoxy.

15. For the term "post-halachic" see Neil Gillman, *Doing Jewish Theology: God, Torah, and Israel in Modern Judaism* (Woodstock, VT: Jewish Lights, 2010), 182; and Jack Cohen, *Judaism in a Post-Halachic Age* (New York: Academic Studies Press, 2010).

16. Eugene Borowitz, *Renewing the Covenant: A Theology for the Postmodern Jew* (Philadelphia: Jewish Publication Society, 1991), 281.

17. For a more detailed discussion, see section II in my chapter, "*Kiddushin* as a Progressive Halakhic Concept: Toward a Theory of Progressive *Halakhah*," in *The Modern Family and Jewish Law*, ed. Walter Jacob (Pittsburgh: Freehof Institute of Progressive Halakhah, 2018), https://www.freehofinstitute.org/uploads/1/2/0/6/120631295/kiddushin_as_a_progressive_halakhic_concept.pdf.

18. Borowitz, *Renewing the Covenant*, 222. See, in general, his chap. 16.

19. Solomon B. Freehof, *Reform Responsa* (Cincinnati: Hebrew Union College Press, 1960), 15–16.

20. The years that witnessed "the widest swing of the Reform pendulum away from traditional Jewish belief and practice"; Michael A. Meyer, *Hebrew Union College–Jewish Institute of Religion: A Centennial History 1875–1975*, rev. ed. (Cincinnati: Hebrew Union College Press, 1992), 264, and see in general 264–95.

21. Freehof, *Reform Responsa*, 16.

22. "Platforms," Central Conference of American Rabbis, https://www.ccarnet.org/rabbinic-voice/platforms.

23. At least, those Jews who stand within the Rabbinic tradition—the "heirs of the Pharisees" (Jakob J. Petuchowski, *Heirs of the Pharisees* [New York: Basic Books, 1970]). Though this definition excludes the Karaities and other groups, it represents the preponderance of contemporary Jewry.

24. Friedman, *Guidance, Not Governance*.

25. "Since argumentation aims at securing the adherence of those to whom it is addressed, it is, in its entirety, relative to the audience to be influenced" (Chaim Perelman and Lucie Olbrechts-Tyteca, *The New Rhetoric: A Treatise on Argumentation* [Notre Dame, IN: Notre Dame University Press, 1973], 19).

26. See Elon, *Jewish Law*, 983–85; and my article "Taking Precedent Seriously: On *Halakhah* as a Rhetorical Practice," in *Re-Examining Progressive Halakhah*, ed. Walter Jacob and Moshe Zemer (New York: Berghahn Books, 2002), 1–70, https://

www.freehofinstitute.org/uploads/1/2/0/6/120631295/taking_precedent_seriously.pdf.

27. James Boyd White, "What's an Opinion For?," *University of Chicago Law Review* 62, no. 4 (1995): 1366-67, https://chicagounbound.uchicago.edu/uclrev/vol62/iss4/7.

28. Harold Bloom, *How to Read and Why* (New York: Scribner, 2000), 19.

29. Robert Ferguson, "The Judicial Opinion as Literary Genre," *Yale Journal of Law and the Humanities* 2, no. 1 (1990): 208.

30. White, "What's an Opinion For?," 1366.

Chapter 1

1. Solomon B. Freehof, "Torah Reading on Friday," in *Modern Reform Responsa* (Cincinnati: Hebrew Union College Press, 1971), 14-17, https://www.ccarnet.org/ccar-responsa/mrr-14-17.

2. On the Sunday service issue, see Kerry M. Olitzky, "The Sunday Sabbath Movement in American Reform Judaism: Strategy or Evolution?," *American Jewish Archives Journal* 34, no. 1 (1982): 75-88; Michael A. Meyer, *Response to Modernity: A History of the Reform Movement in Judaism* (New York: Oxford University Press, 1988), 290-92; and Solomon B. Freehof, *Reform Jewish Practice and Its Rabbinic Background* (New York: Ktav, 1976), 19-22.

3. This practice is officially sanctioned in the prayer books published by the CCAR. The *Union Prayerbook, Newly Revised* edition (1959) includes a Torah service for Shabbat evening (pp. 94-97). In *Gates of Prayer* (1975), the note "The Rituals for Reading of Torah begin on p. 415" appears at the conclusion of the *T'filah* in each of its ten Shabbat evening services. A similar note appears at the conclusion of Shabbat evening *t'filot* in *Mishkan T'filah* (2007).

4. Rabbi Stanley R. Brav (1908-92) was founding rabbi of Temple Sholom in Cincinnati (https://templesholom.net/about-us/temple-history).

5. See Babylonian Talmud, *B'rachot* 33a; and Maimonides, *Mishneh Torah, Hilchot B'rachot* 1:15. This is not a universally held viewpoint in the halachah. Others explain the prohibition of *b'rachah l'vatalah* as Rabbinic, rather than Toraitic, in origin (*Hilchot Rabbeinu Asher ben Yechiel, Kiddushin* 1:49).

6. Rabbi Berlin's argument could be challenged on two grounds:
1. He learns that it is prohibited to read the Torah on nontraditional days from a commentator to the *Shulchan Aruch* (*Magen Avraham* to *Orach Chayim* 144:5), who mentions the custom of one community for a *chatan* (bridegroom) present at services on the Shabbat immediately after his wedding to read some verses from a second Torah scroll after the reading of the weekly portion. From this, Berlin concludes, "Since this was done only on a day of a scheduled Torah reading, we learn that there must be some prohibition against the public reading from a Torah scroll on a day not traditionally scheduled for Torah reading." That's an argument from silence. The fact that a congregation observed this practice on Shabbat does not necessarily entail that we may not schedule a public Torah reading at another time.
2. A congregation might avoid the *b'rachah l'vatalah* problem by reading the Torah

without reciting the blessings. Berlin objects to this on the basis of a passage in the Jerusalem Talmud (*B'rachot* 7:1), which tells us that the blessings *must* be recited over the public Torah reading. He concedes that the more authoritative Babylonian Talmud (*B'rachot* 21a) reaches the opposite conclusion, but "nonetheless, we ought to take account of the Jerusalem Talmud's position" and never read the Torah in public without a *b'rachah*. Needless to say, Rabbi Berlin *chooses* to rule this way; he could just as easily have followed long-standing halachic tradition to rule according to the Babylonian Talmud in cases where it conflicts with the Jerusalem Talmud. His decision reflects nothing more than his personal opinion. He's entitled to it, but it is hardly binding upon those who do not share it.

7. See Freehof, *Reform Jewish Practice*, 20–21, where he uses this reasoning to justify the practice of those congregations that hold their major weekly service on Sunday morning.

8. The best discussion is Alexander Guttmann, *The Struggle over Reform in the Rabbinic Literature during the Last Century and a Half* (Jerusalem: World Union for Progressive Judaism, 1976), who sets forth the halachic arguments on both sides with an English translation of the leading texts. On the "innovative" nature of Orthodox halachic theories, see my article "Halakhah in Translation: The Chatam Sofer on Prayer in the Vernacular," *CCAR Journal* 51 (Summer 2004): 127–48, https://www.academia.edu/2946939/_Halakhah_in_Translation_The_Chatam_Sofer_on_Prayer_in_the_Vernacular.

9. A pun on *Mishnah Orlah* 3:9, which says, "New [produce] is prohibited by the Torah."

10. See my article "Halakhah in Translation." The noted social historian Jacob Katz argues strongly (in *The "Shabbes Goy": A Study in Halakhic Flexibility* [Philadelphia: Jewish Publication Society of America, 1989], 378) that the Orthodox response to the Reformers' innovations, led by Rabbi Moshe Sofer and others, quickly became an expression of ideological and theological (as opposed to strictly halachic) opposition. The phrase "sanctification of the tradition" is Katz's.

11. Well, maybe not *all* changes. Orthodox Jewish practice itself has changed in significant ways over the past several decades, particularly in its embrace of more stringent standards of observance; see Haym Soloveitchik, "Rupture and Reconstruction: The Transformation of Contemporary Orthodoxy," *Tradition* 28, no. 4 (1994): 64–131, https://traditiononline.org/rupture-and-reconstruction-the-transformation-of-contemporary-orthodoxy. The "novelties" to which Freehof refers are innovations introduced by non-Orthodox movements.

12. To oversimplify: a gap exists whenever the legal sources do not clearly lead to or require one uniquely correct answer to a question of law. According to some thinkers (see H. L. A. Hart, *The Concept of Law*, 2nd ed. [Oxford: Clarendon Press, 1994], 128; and Joseph Raz, *The Authority of Law* [Oxford: Clarendon Press, 1979], 70), a "gap" means that there *is* no law on that question, so that the judge's decision is a matter of discretion or choice; the decision *creates* new law. Others, notably Ronald Dworkin (*Taking Rights Seriously* [Cambridge, MA: Harvard University Press, 1986]) and John Finnis (*Natural Law and Natural Rights* [Oxford: Clarendon Press, 1980]),

deny that law has "gaps": the law does recognize a correct answer to every legal question, even though that answer may have to be derived through legal interpretation.

Chapter 2

1. CCAR Responsa Committee,"Orthodox Minyan in a Reform Synagogue," CCAR responsum 5758.12, in *Reform Responsa for the Twenty-First Century: Sh'eilot Ut'shuvot*, ed. Mark Washofsky (New York: CCAR Press, 2010), 1:3–12, https://www.ccarnet.org/ccar-responsa/rr21-no-5758-12.
2. See the introduction, 6–9.
3. The word "coherent" reflects the approach of the legal theorist Ronald Dworkin. In his view, the judge's task when confronting a hard case is to decide it with "integrity": the judge's opinion must give a *coherent* account of the law, one that encompasses all or nearly all of the relevant legal data, rules, and precedents that comprise "the brute facts of legal history." See Ronald Dworkin, *Law's Empire* (Cambridge, MA: Harvard University Press,1986), esp. 255–56. Also see endnotes 1 and 2 of the responsum.
4. Alan Ryan, *The Making of Modern Liberalism* (Princeton, NJ: Princeton University Press, 2012), 8. Pluralism is grounded in what the political theorist Isaiah Berlin called "negative liberty," the freedom from social constraint that autonomous individuals require in order to choose their own ends or goals. See Isaiah Berlin, *Four Essays on Liberty* (Oxford: Oxford University Press, 1969), esp. 172–74.
5. A reference to Exodus 23:2, interpreted to mean that in cases of dispute we follow the majority opinion among the Sages.
6. See Jeffrey H. Tigay, *The JPS Torah Commentary: Deuteronomy* (Philadelphia: Jewish Publication Society, 1996), 136.
7. See endnote 10 of the responsum. Though this decision is disputed among the authorities, the note argues that Rava's view is the better interpretation.
8. Stanley Fish, *Is There a Text in This Class? The Authority of Interpretive Communities* (Cambridge, MA: Harvard University Press, 1980).
9. See the introduction, 7–8, as well as my article "The Woodchopper Revisited: On Analogy, *Halakhah,* and Jewish Bioethics," in *Medical Frontiers in Jewish Law*, ed. Walter Jacob (Pittsburgh: Freehof Institute of Progressive Halakhah, 2012), 1–62, https://www.freehofinstitute.org/uploads/1/2/0/6/120631295/the_woodchopper_revisited.pdf

Chapter 3

1. The word "burial" in this chapter refers to intact burial and *not* to the burial of cremains.
2. CCAR Responsa Committee, "When a Parent Requests Cremation," CCAR responsum 5766.2, in *Reform Responsa for the Twenty-First Century: Sh'eilot Ut'shuvot*, ed. Mark Washofsky (New York: CCAR Press, 2010), 2:193–208, https://www.ccarnet.org/ccar-responsa/nyp-no-5766-2.

3. Solomon B. Freehof, "Family Disagreement over Cremation," in *Contemporary Reform Responsa* (Cincinnati: Hebrew Union College Press, 1974), 228–31, https://www.ccarnet.org/ccar-responsa/corr-228-231.
4. See CCAR responsum 5766.1, "When a Parent Instructs a Child Not to Say Kaddish" by CCAR Responsa Committee, in Washofsky, *Reform Responsa for the Twenty-First Century*, 2:185–92, https://www.ccarnet.org/ccar-responsa/nyp-no-5766-1 .
5. The interpretation here follows *Sifra* on Leviticus 19:3. Rashi (Babylonian Talmud, *Y'vamot* 5b, s.v. *kulchem*) holds that the modification is based upon the final part of the verse ("I am the Eternal your God") rather than upon the commandment to observe the Sabbath.
6. The rules are codified in *Shulchan Aruch, Yoreh Dei-ah* 242.
7. Responsa writers commonly use the names of biblical personalities (especially the names of Jacob's sons and wives) as pseudonyms.
8. *Responsa Rashba* 1:369.
9. See endnote 8 in the responsum.
10. At endnote 25 in the responsum.
11. See "The Second Festival Day and Reform Judaism," CCAR responsum 5759.7 by CCAR Responsa Committee, in Washofsky, *Reform Responsa for the Twenty-First Century*, 1:49–64, https://www.ccarnet.org/ccar-responsa/rr21-no-5759-7.
12. See especially endnote 29 in the responsum.
13. Robert M. Cover, "Forward: *Nomos* and Narrative," *Harvard Law Review* 97 (1983): 4–5 (footnotes omitted). The essay ranks as the sixteenth most frequently cited law review articles of all time (out of 1.4 million articles in the database!). See Fred R. Shapiro and Mary Pearse, "The Most-Cited Law Review Articles of All Time," *Michigan Law Review* 110 (2012): 1489.

Chapter 4

1. CCAR Responsa Committee, "A Defective 'Holocaust' Torah Scroll," CCAR responsum 5760.3, in *Reform Responsa for the Twenty-First Century*, ed. Mark Washofsky (New York: CCAR Press, 2010), 2:59–70, https://www.ccarnet.org/ccar-responsa/nyp-no-5760-3/.
2. The term is never given a precise definition in the Talmud, which satisfies itself with various examples of things that in its view insult *k'vod tzibur,* the congregation's honor or dignity. One particularly infamous example: "All are included among the seven who read from the Torah on Shabbat [i.e., who are called to the Torah, who receive *aliyot*], even a child, even a woman. But the Sages said: A woman should not read from the Torah, for this would insult the dignity of the congregation" (Babylonian Talmud, *M'gillah* 23a). Liberal congregations, obviously, reject that notion.
3. *T'shuvot HaRambam*, ed. Yehoshua Blau, vol. 2 (Jerusalem: Mekitzei Nirdamim, 1960), no. 294.
4. For an explanation of the concept, see endnote 22 in the responsum.
5. See endnote 25 in the responsum.
6. "Gravitational force" refers to the degree of influence that earlier rulings exert upon

the thinking of a judge in a present-day case; see Ronald Dworkin, *Taking Rights Seriously* (Cambridge, MA: Harvard University Press, 1977), 111–12.

7. Solomon B. Freehof, *Reform Responsa* (Cincinnati: Hebrew Union College Press, 1960), 23.

8. CCAR Responsa Committee, "A Non-Traditional Sukkah," CCAR responsum 5755.4, in *Teshuvot for the Nineties: Reform Judaism's Answers for Today's Dilemmas*, ed. W. Gunther Plaut and Mark Washofsky (New York: CCAR Press, 1997), 91–96, https://www.ccarnet.org/ccar-responsa/tfn-no-5755-4-91-96/ .

9. See Emil Fackenheim's *The Jewish Return into History* (New York: Schocken Books, 1978) and *God's Presence in History: Jewish Affirmations and Philosophical Reflections* (New York: New York University Press, 1970). The critics include Jacob Neusner's *Stranger at Home: "The Holocaust," Zionism, and American Judaism* (Charlottesville: Scholars Press, 1997); and Michael Wyschograd's "Faith and the Holocaust," *Judaism* 20 (1971): 286–94.

10. The *b'rachot* are recited over the mitzvah of *k'riat haTorah* itself; they should not be recited over the reading from the second scroll, which occurs after the mitzvah has been fulfilled.

Chapter 5

1. For Rambam, the prophets (including Moses) had the status of "sage" or "rabbi," an expounder of the Torah and a legislator of *takanot*, ordinances that supplemented the inherited body of Torah law.

2. Rambam, *Mishneh Torah*, *Hilchot Shabbat* 29:1, based upon Babylonian Talmud, *P'sachim* 106a. "Remember" is understood as a requirement that we pronounce words that declare a separation of that day from the week that preceded it and from the week that is to follow.

3. See Babylonian Talmud, *Shabbat* 49b.

4. Tellingly, these Orthodox rabbis disagree as to just *which* category of forbidden *m'lachah* electricity belongs. Some analogize it to kindling a flame (*mavir*), others to building a structure (*boneh*), and still others call it an act of completing the construction of an object (*makeh bapatish*), all of which are listed as prohibited labors in *Mishnah Shabbat* 7:2. In addition, some Orthodox rabbis describe this action as a form of *molid*, of creating a new thing, prohibited on Shabbat by Rabbinic decree rather than by the Torah's prohibition of "work."

5. Joan S. Friedman, *"Guidance, Not Governance": Rabbi Solomon B. Freehof and Reform Responsa* (Cincinnati: Hebrew Union College Press, 2013), 121.

6. W. Gunther Plaut, *A Shabbat Manual* (New York: CCAR Press, 1972); and Mark D. Shapiro, *Gates of Shabbat: A Guide for Observing Shabbat* (New York: CCAR Press, 2016; first published in 1991).

7. Solomon B. Freehof, "Gift Corner Open on the Sabbath," in *Reform Responsa* (Cincinnati: Hebrew Union College Press, 1960), 51–55, https://www.ccarnet.org/ccar-responsa/rr-51-55.

8. Freehof acknowledges that a Conservative rabbi might "make a strong effort to

find a legal justification" for the transgressive act. His point is that the Conservative rabbi, like an Orthodox rabbi, would regard the halachah and its procedural rules as authoritative.

9. Alongside such other sources as interpretation and legislation. See Menachem Elon's *Jewish Law: History, Sources, Principles*, trans. Bernard Auerbach and Melvin J. Sykes (Philadelphia: Jewish Publication Society, 1994), 2:881–944.

10. Solomon B. Freehof, *Reform Jewish Practice and Its Rabbinic Background* (New York: Ktav, 1976), 7.

11. While much of the law may in fact have evolved from preexisting customary practice, the Jewish legal system has always distinguished between *minhag*—law based in custom—and halachah—law identified through the interpretation of the authoritative texts or from the ordinances presumably enacted by the ancient Sanhedrin. See Friedman, *"Guidance, Not Governance,"* 54–59, 217–18; and Elon, *Jewish Law*, 1:881–94.

12. See Jacob Katz, *The "Shabbes Goy": A Study in Halakhic Flexibility* (Philadelphia: Jewish Publication Society, 1989), 231.

13. Chaim Perelman and Lucie Olbrechts-Tyteca, *The New Rhetoric: A Treatise on Argumentation* (Notre Dame: Notre Dame University Press, 1973), 19.

14. As Freehof notes, he discusses the halachah at greater length in "Congregational Meeting on the Sabbath," in *Reform Responsa*, 46–50, https://www.ccarnet.org/ccar-responsa/rr-46-50 .

15. Maimonides, *Mishneh Torah, Hilchot Shabbat* 24:1.

16. *Magid Mishneh* (Rabbi Vidal Di Tolosa, fourteenth-century Spain), to *Hilchot Shabbat* 24:5.

17. CCAR Responsa Committee, "Delayed *B'rit Milah* on Shabbat," CCAR responsum 5755.12, in *Teshuvot for the Nineties: Reform Judaism's Answers for Today's Dilemmas*, ed. W. Gunther Plaut and Mark Washofsky (New York: CCAR Press, 1997), 165–68, https://www.ccarnet.org/ccar-responsa/tfn-no-5755-12-165-168.

18. On weddings, see "Marriage on Shabbat on Yom Tov," in *American Reform Responsa: Collected Responsa of the Central Conference of American Rabbis 1889–1983*, ed. Walter Jacob (New York: Central Conference of American Rabbis, 1983), 412–15, https://www.ccarnet.org/ccar-responsa/arr-412-415. For social action projects, see "Poverty Project and Shabbat," in *Contemporary American Reform Responsa*, ed. Walter Jacob (New York: Central Conference of American Rabbis, 1987), 265–67, https://www.ccarnet.org/ccar-responsa/carr-265-267; and "Communal Work on Shabbat," CCAR responsum 5753.22, CCAR Responsa Committee, in Plaut and Washofsky, *Teshuvot for the Nineties*, 169–70, https://www.ccarnet.org/ccar-responsa/tfn-no-5753-22-169-170.

19. CCAR Responsa Committee, "Presenting a Check for *Tzedakah* at Shabbat Services," CCAR responsum 5756.4, in *Reform Responsa for the Twenty-First Century*, ed. Mark Washofsky (New York: CCAR Press, 2010), 1:33–40, https://www.ccarnet.org/ccar-responsa/nyp-no-5756-4.

20. *Magid Mishneh. Hilchot Shabbat* 21:1.

Chapter 6

1. Israel Bettan, "National Flags at Religious Services," in *American Reform Responsa*, ed. Walter Jacob (New York: CCAR Press, 1983), 64–66, https://www.ccarnet.org/ccar-responsa/arr-64-66.

2. *Sefer Abudarham*, "Laws of Reading the Torah," end. Bettan cites p. 47c in the printed editions, but does not actually quote from the text in his responsum.

3. That prayer, found in many (though not all) traditional siddurim, often begins with the words *Hanotein t'shuah lam'lachim*, "May the One who grants victory to kings...."

4. Michael A. Meyer, *Hebrew Union College–Jewish Institute of Religion: A Centennial History 1875–1975*, rev. ed. (Cincinnati: Hebrew Union College Press, 1992), 293.

5. For this statement, see "Declaration of Principles: 1885 Pittsburgh Conference," https://www.ccarnet.org/rabbinic-voice/platforms/article-declaration-principles.

6. See *CCAR Yearbook* 8 (New York: CCAR Press, 1898), xli.

7. See Meyer, *Hebrew Union College–Jewish Institute of Religion*, 92.

8. On the history of the movement's relationship to Zionism, see Michael A. Meyer, *Response to Modernity: A History of the Reform Movement in Judaism* (New York: Oxford University Press, 1988), 293–95, 326–34, 355, 383–84; as well as Ephraim Tabory, "The Legitimacy of Reform Judaism: The Impact of Israel on the United States," in *Debates in Reform Judaism: Conflicting Visions*, ed. Dana Evan Kaplan (New York: Routledge, 2001), 221–34.

9. CCAR Responsa Committee, "Israeli Flag on a Synagogue Pulpit," in Jacob, *American Reform Responsa*, 66–68, https://www.ccarnet.org/ccar-responsa/arr-66-68.

10. See "The Guiding Principles of Reform Judaism," https://www.ccarnet.org/rabbinic-voice/platforms/article-guiding-principles-reform-judaism.

11. CCAR Responsa Committee, "Flags on the Bimah," CCAR responsum 5753.8, in *Teshuvot for the Nineties: Reform Judaism's Answers to Today's Dilemmas*, ed. W. Gunther Plaut and Mark Washofsky (New York: CCAR Press, 1997), 29–32, https://www.ccarnet.org/ccar-responsa/tfn-no-5753-8-29-32/.

12. CCAR Responsa Committee, "'HaTikvah' and 'The Star-Spangled Banner,'" CCAR responsum 5758.50, in *Reform Responsa for the Twenty-First Century*, ed. Mark Washofsky (New York: CCAR Press, 2010), 1:13–19, https://www.ccarnet.org/ccar-responsa/rr21-no-5758-10.

13. Officially entitled "Reform Judaism and Zionism: A Centenary Platform," in recognition of the one hundredth anniversary of the First Zionist Congress in Basel; https://www.ccarnet.org/rabbinic-voice/platforms/article-reform-judaism-zionism-centenary-platform.

14. Alfred North Whitehead, *Process and Reality*, corrected ed., ed. D. Griffin and D. Sherburne (New York: Free Press, 1978), 39: "The safest general characterization of the European philosophical tradition is that it consists of a series of footnotes to Plato."

Chapter 7

1. CCAR Responsa Committee, "St. Valentine's Day and Other 'Secular' Holidays," CCAR Reform responsa 5775.2 (2015), https://www.ccarnet.org/ccar-responsa/57752.

2. The standard printed editions read *ha-ovdei kochavim*, "idolaters," in places of *hagoyim*, "gentiles." The responsum follows the reading in the manuscripts and most early printed editions. See the responsum's endnote 7.

3. See Rashi to Genesis 26:5. The word *chok* traditionally designates *ritual* laws—"laws like the prohibition of pork or the wearing of *shaatneiz* that serve no rational purpose"—as opposed to *mishpatim*, monetary or criminal laws (do not murder; do not steal) that make rational sense, serve the purpose of social order, and are common to most societies.

4. See the summary in my article "Is There a Jewish Version of the 'Just War' Doctrine? Some Notes on the Nature of Halachic Interpretation," *CCAR Journal* (Spring 2019), 74–94.

5. See the literature cited in my article *"Halakhah* as Translation: On the Custody of Children in Jewish Law," in *The Modern Child and Jewish Law*, ed. Walter Jacob (Pittsburgh: Rodef Shalom Press, 2017), 1–3, https://www.freehofinstitute.org/uploads/1/2/0/6/120631295/halakhah_as_translation.pdf.

6. Lawrence Lessig, "Fidelity and Constraint," *Fordham Law Review* 65 (1997): 1371 (italics in original).

7. See endnote 17 of the responsum.

8. *Responsa Ig'rot Moshe, Orach Chayim* 5:20, sec. 6.

9. In his *t'shuvah*, cited in the previous note, Rabbi Feinstein describes Thanksgiving (and, presumably, other non-Jewish and nonreligious holidays) as "nonsense" (*hevel ush'tut*)—the same label that, as we saw in chapter 6, he applies to national flags displayed in the synagogue sanctuary.

10. As opposed to the rule in the Land of Israel, where such commerce is forbidden for three days prior to the non-Jewish festival as well as on the festival day itself (*Mishnah Avodah Zarah* 1:1).

Chapter 8

1. This precise terminology is a product of medieval authors. The earliest Rabbinic sources speak of "transgressions [*aveirot*] of an individual against God" and "transgressions of an individual against a fellow human being." See *Mishnah Yoma* 8:9.

2. CCAR Responsa Committee, "Privacy and the Disclosure of Personal Medical Information," CCAR responsum 5756.2, in *Reform Responsa for the Twenty-First Century*, ed. Mark Washofsky (New York: CCAR Press, 2010), 1:331–42, https://www.ccarnet.org/ccar-responsa/nyp-no-5756-2.

3. See National Institutes of Health, "Huntington's Disease," MedlinePlus, August 30, 2017, https://medlineplus.gov/huntingtonsdisease.html.

4. The immediately preceding text in *Y'vamot* 65b gives examples of human beings telling lies for the sake of peace. The Hebrew word *af* emphasizes that *even* God is willing to do so.

NOTES TO CHAPTER EIGHT   167

5. The concept of rights is not foreign to contemporary *Israeli* law, which uses the term *z'chuyot* (singular: *z'chut*) to refer to legal rights of various kinds. Israeli law is *not* identical with "Jewish law" or halachah but based primarily on the legislation of the Knesset and decisions of Israeli courts. Israeli jurists have adopted the language of "rights" from other legal traditions, particularly that of Anglo-Saxon common law, which held sway in Palestine during the Mandatory period.

6. Samuel D. Warren and Louis D. Brandeis, "The Right to Privacy," *Harvard Law Review* 4 (1890): 193–220. The quotation is from Harry Kalven, "Privacy in Tort Law: Were Warren and Brandeis Wrong?," *Law and Contemporary Problems* 31 (1966): 326–41, at 327.

7. Olmstead v. United States, 277 U.S. 438 (1928), 478.

8. Readers may note that the right to privacy figures prominently in American constitutional law as well as in the tradition of Anglo-American common law that was the subject of the Warren and Brandeis article. Here, too, that right is not mentioned explicitly in the constitutional text, and for that reason some legal scholars argue that it doesn't exist. Over the years, however, the US Supreme Court has derived the right to privacy by way of interpretation of other "enumerated" rights, in much the same fashion that Warren and Brandeis derive the existence of that right in the common law . . . and in much the same way that the authors of this responsum and other writers (see note 10) derive something akin to a "right" to privacy in Jewish law.

9. See my article "Internet, Privacy, and Progressive *Halakhah*," in *The Internet Revolution and Jewish Law*, ed. Walter Jacob (Pittsburgh: Rodef Shalom Press, 2014), 90–94, http://www.freehofinstitute.org/uploads/1/2/0/6/120631295/the_internet_privacy_and_progressive_halakhah.pdf.

10. The most extensive work is Nachum Rakover, *Hahaganah al Tzin'at Hap'rat* (Jerusalem: Ministry of Justice, 2006). See also Norman Lamm, *Faith and Doubt*, 3rd ed. (New York: Ktav, 1986), 299–312; Alfred S. Cohen, "Privacy: A Jewish Perspective," *Journal of Halacha and Contemporary Society* 1, no. 1 (Spring 1981); and Washofsky, "Internet, Privacy, and Progressive *Halakhah*."

Chapter 9

1. CCAR Responsa Committee, "The Synagogue and Organized Labor," CCAR responsum 5761.4, in *Reform Responsa for the Twenty-First Century*, ed. Mark Washofsky (New York: CCAR Press, 2010), 2:345–54, https://www.ccarnet.org/ccar-responsa/nyp-no-5761-4.

2. While Rambam's term *chacham* suggests a rabbi or Torah scholar, the commentaries to the Talmud and the *Mishneh Torah* understand this to mean any official who is specifically appointed to adjudicate public business.

3. *Responsa Piskei Ouziel B'sh'eilot HaZ'man*, no. 46.

4. For a thorough and accessible summary, see Michael Sandel, *Justice: What's the Right Thing To Do?* (New York: Farrar, Straus and Giroux, 2009).

Chapter 10

1. CCAR Responsa Committee, "Hunger Strike: On the Force-Feeding of Prisoners," CCAR responsum 5766.3, in *Reform Responsa for the Twenty-First Century*, ed. Mark Washofsky (New York: CCAR Press, 2010), 2:381–95, https://www.ccarnet. org/ccar-responsa/nyp-no-5766-3.

2. See especially Rabbi Sh'muel ben Meir (Rashbam). Rashi, following the traditional Aramaic *Targum* (translation) of the Torah and an alternative midrashic reading, understands the phrase to refer to eternal life, as does Rabbi Yitzchak Abarbanel.

3. For example, see Babylonian Talmud, *Yoma* 85b, *Sanhedrin* 74a, and *Avodah Zarah* 54a.

4. Rashi to Babylonian Talmud, *Yoma* 85b, s.v. *d'shmuel*.

5. See the note to the verse in the translation of the *JPS Hebrew-English Tanakh* (Philadelphia: Jewish Publication Society, 1999).

6. Maimonides, *Mishneh Torah, Hilchot Y'sodei HaTorah* 5:4. See also responsum endnote 11.

7. Rabbi Yosef Karo, author of the *Shulchan Aruch*, cites this opinion in his *Kesef Mishneh* commentary to Rambam's *Mishneh Torah* (*Hilchot Y'sodei HaTorah* 5:4), in the name of "many great scholars." It is a prominent view among leading Ashkenazic halachists in the high Middle Ages. For discussion, see Haym Soloveitchik, "*Halakhah*, Hermeneutics, and Martyrdom in Medieval Ashkenaz (Part I of II)," *Jewish Quarterly Review* 94, no. 1 (Winter 2004): 77–108.

8. "WMA Declaration of Tokyo: Guidelines for Physicians Concerning Torture and Other Cruel, Inhuman or Degrading Treatment or Punishment in Relation to Detention and Imprisonment," World Medical Association, September 6, 2022, paragraph 8, https://www.wma.net/policies-post/wma-declaration-of-tokyo-guidelines-for-physicians-concerning-torture-and-other-cruel-inhuman-or-degrading-treatment-or-punishment-in-relation-to-detention-and-imprisonment/.

9. Tom L. Beauchamp and James F. Childress, *Principles of Biomedical Ethics*, 3rd ed. (New York: Oxford University Press, 1989), 247.

10. Rabbi Moshe Feinstein, *Responsa Ig'rot Moshe, Choshen Mishpat* 2:73, section 5.

11. CCAR Responsa Committee, "On the Treatment of the Terminally Ill," CCAR responsum 5754.14, in *Teshuvot for the Nineties: Reform Judaism's Answers for Today's Dilemmas*, ed. W. Gunther Plaut and Mark Washofsky (New York: CCAR Press, 1997), 337–63, https://www.ccarnet.org/ccar-responsa/tfn-no-5754-14-337-364.

12. Shimeon Glick, "Unlimited Human Autonomy: A Cultural Bias?," *New England Journal of Medicine* 366, no. 13 (1997): 954–56.

APPENDIX
Full Text of Responsa

Reform responsa have a lengthy history, going back to the nineteenth century. Some of the responsa below may not reflect contemporary thinking or language and may no longer represent today's CCAR and Reform Movement. Citations and the spellings of some Hebrew transliterations have been updated for consistency, unless such a change would impact the meaning, contextual understanding, or impact of a responsum. To preserve the historical context, no further edits have been made.

CHAPTER 1: EMBRACING REFORMS
Torah Reading on Friday

QUESTION:

At one of the smaller American colleges, because of the heavy student schedule it seems impossible to have services other than on Friday night. The students, therefore, have services at that time and also read the Torah. The local rabbi prohibits the reading of the Torah on Friday night (which is not a traditional Torah-reading time) and declares that reading the Torah at this traditionally unauthorized time would make the Torah unfit for proper use at regular services. Is this judgment of the rabbi justified by the legal tradition? (Rabbi Stanley R. Brav, Cincinnati, Ohio)

ANSWER:

Before going into the legal question involved, it is worthwhile calling attention to a remarkable coincidence with regard to this question and to the geographical source of the enquiry. Naftali Zvi Berlin, the famous head of the Volozhin Yeshivah, was asked almost the identical question by a rabbi from Cincinnati in the United States (see Berlin's responsum 16 in *Meshiv Davar*).

The question from Cincinnati that was sent to Volozhin two generations ago was as follows: The synagogue was celebrating the dedication of a new Ark of the Law, and the chief celebration took place on Sunday morning. The Torahs were carried around in procession. A lay leader in the congregation was not content merely with the fact that the Torahs should be carried around in procession; he also wanted to have the Torah opened and read in regular fashion as part of the celebration. The rabbi objected on the ground that it is a sin to add to the requirements of the law as it stands now (*bal tosif*), and he based his objection against this Sunday morning reading on the statement of the [*Sefer*] *Mordechai* to *M'gillah*, chapter 1,¹ objecting to reading the *M'gillah* one day later than the authorized date on the fourteenth of Adar.

In answer to this objection Berlin says that there is no sin of "unauthorized addition" (*bal tosif*) involved here. He calls attention to the fact that on the eighth day of the holidays that are not authorized in Scripture, we read the Torah and recite blessings. Since the public reading of the Torah is not a biblical requirement, but a Rabbinic one, it is not a sin to add to the readings. The sin of adding (*bal tosif*) applies only to biblical commandments. However, although it is not prohibited, he is against it as a novelty and also because it involves reciting a blessing unnecessarily (*b'rachah l'vatalah*). He admits that the Babylonian Talmud and the Jerusalem Talmud are at variance with each other and that we ought to lean over in the direction of strictness because reciting the blessing might be a blessing in vain (*l'vatalah*). But even so, he is not too firm on the matter, since he asks the rabbi whether the lay leader is a learned man. If he is, then he may have a reason for this or some other precedent. But if the man is ignorant, he should be brushed aside for wanting such a novelty.

It can be seen from the above responsum that it is far from certain in the mind of this great scholar whether the reading of the Torah and the recital of the Torah blessings are really prohibited. He admits the possibility that the man who wanted it may have had some justification. But, of course, in accordance with the general Orthodox mood, he objects to any unauthorized novelty (that is, if it really is unauthorized).

On the basis of the above, it is clear that the rabbi in the college town has no basis for being so sure that the Torah may not be read at any other than the customary times. As for his statement that the reading of the Torah on Friday night will make the Torah unfit for use at other times, that statement, with all due respect to him, is absurd. A Torah is unfit for use (*pasul*) if it is incorrectly written, or if it is punctuated, or if written by a heretic. The various conditions under which a Torah is unfit are all clearly defined (cf. *Shulchan Aruch, Yoreh Dei-ah* 274 ff.). But to say that reading the Torah at unauthorized times makes it unfit (*pasul*) for reading at authorized times is totally unjustified. It is hard to believe that he actually made such a baseless statement. I would say to him exactly what Naftali Berlin said concerning the layman in

Cincinnati: If he is a learned man (and in the case of a rabbi, we assume he is), then we would like to know the reason for his statement that the Torah can be made unfit by an irregular reading. In general, one must say with regard to such a dire possibility that in Jewish traditional law the Torah is considered remarkably resistant to being spoiled. Any unclean person may read the Torah because of the general principle that the Torah is proof against uncleanness (see Babylonian Talmud, *B'rachot* 22a). The Torah scroll that is, according to older custom, taken out to be read to a bridegroom (not at the regular reading hours), the Torah that may be read by any unclean person and the blessings recited by him or her, is not so easily made unfit.

To sum up: While Orthodoxy naturally objects to any new custom, it is far from clear (judging by Naftali Berlin's response) that it is forbidden to read the Torah at other than the regular times. As for making the Torah unfit if it is so read, there seems to be no justification at all for such a decision.

—Rabbi Solomon B. Freehof, "Torah Reading on Friday," in *Modern Reform Responsa* (Cincinnati: Hebrew Union College Press, 1971), 14–17.

NOTE:
1. *Sefer Mordechai* is a halachic work, authored by Rabbi Mordechai ben Hillel, late thirteenth-century Germany. The citation here refers to the *Mordechai* to Babylonian Talmud tractate *M'gillah*.

CHAPTER 2: PRINCIPLES IN CONFLICT
Orthodox Minyan in a Reform Synagogue

SH'EILAH:

A few years ago a young man converted to Judaism at our congregation, which is the only one in the city. He subsequently underwent an Orthodox conversion, left the community, and attended yeshivah in New York. During a recent visit to Jackson, he requested the use of our facilities for an "Orthodox" minyan. By this he means that women, though they may attend the service, will not count as part of the minyan and will be denied any opportunity to participate in the service.

My initial response to this request was "no," on the grounds that the minyan would not be egalitarian and therefore contrary to our communal custom (*minhag hamakom*). On the other hand, I wonder if the Judaic value of hospitality to guests (*hachnasat orchim*) argues in favor of accommodating

Orthodox visitors? Does the answer differ when these visitors ask for space for a minyan that meets on a regular or permanent basis? How forthcoming should we be, especially in view of the numerous incidents at the Western Wall, where, to put it mildly, no accommodations are made for liberal practice and "mixed" minyanim? (Rabbi James Egolf, Jackson, Mississippi)

T'SHUVAH:

1. *A Hard Case.* There is an old saying that hard cases make bad law.[1] This may or may not be true;[2] what is clear, however, is that hard cases, questions for which the existing law offers no single clear and obviously "correct" solution, are unavoidable. We confront hard cases all the time, not only in the law but also in the other traditions in which we participate, such as ethics and religion, when the applicable rules, principles, and precedents of that tradition pull in conflicting directions. And when we do, we have no choice but to think our way toward an answer that, while recognizing the ambiguities of the situation, nonetheless represents our best and most coherent understanding of that tradition as a whole.

This *sh'eilah* presents just such a hard case. It involves a fundamental tension between two important Reform Jewish principles, both of which we proudly affirm. Each of these principles represents a range of values and commitments that express themselves throughout our personal and communal observance. And each of them would seem to argue for a contradictory response to our question. For the purposes of this *t'shuvah*, we designate these principles by the labels "Jewish pluralism" and "Reform Jewish integrity."

By "Jewish pluralism," we mean our recognition as *liberals* that there are a number of different and even conflicting paths that Jews might legitimately walk in response to the call of Torah.[3] As Reform Jews, we demand the right to make our own religious decisions, and we reject any effort to impose upon our communities an "Orthodoxy" that claims that there is but one correct way to believe, to pray, and to practice our faith. And simple fairness requires that, just as we assert this freedom for ourselves, we must grant it to others. We acknowledge that all Jews are entitled to observe their Judaism in a manner that speaks to them and suits their spirit. Accordingly, we do not insist that they adhere to our own version of "the correct way."

This commitment would lead us to provide this young man and those who would join him with space to worship according to their custom. True, our congregation already offers religious services to which visitors are welcome, and we might think that in making these services available we have fulfilled toward them our duty of *hachnasat orchim* (if, indeed, that mitzvah can be said to apply to our case).[4] Yet by defining themselves as an Orthodox community, these individuals declare that they cannot meet their liturgical needs by participating in our own communal worship. As liberals who affirm Jewish pluralism, we do not wish to compel them to do so. Nor do we wish to bar our doors to them, to tell them that unless they are willing to follow our rules they shall have to assemble elsewhere. To do so smacks of rank intolerance, a narrow-mindedness that ill-befits a liberal movement such as ours. On the contrary: we who affirm the positive value of Jewish religious diversity would prefer that they gather in our synagogue, which might then serve its true purpose as a "house of prayer for all Jews," a place where Jews of differing religious approaches may worship as they see fit.

By "Reform Jewish integrity," on the other hand, we express our conviction that Reform Judaism is based upon certain fundamental affirmations that define and distinguish us as a religious community. These affirmations constitute our core values, the irreducible content of our approach to Judaism, a content we cannot compromise without surrendering our integrity, without denying who and what we are. We are prepared, to be sure, to make some adjustments in our practice out of respect to Jewish diversity. In the present case, we would not oppose a request by a group to hold in our building a service at which a traditional siddur is used.[5] We would object, however, when this group identifies itself as an *Orthodox* community, for Orthodox Judaism espouses fundamental affirmations of its own that are incompatible with ours. One of these is its denial of ritual equality to women; thus, female members of our congregation would not be counted in this minyan and would be excluded from equal participation in its service. Another is Orthodoxy's refusal to recognize the halachic validity of conversions supervised by Reform rabbis, on the grounds that our rabbis are incapable of constituting a valid *beit din* (rabbinical court); thus, the Orthodox group would not accept our Jews-by-choice as Jews at all. Our objection, in other words, is not that Orthodox practice differs from ours but that Orthodoxy disenfranchises well over half our membership and proclaims that Reform is not a legitimate expression of Judaism. To permit this group to assemble in *our* building is to transmit the message that its theology is somehow acceptable to us. We must not send that message.

Although we affirm Jewish religious pluralism as a great value, it is not our *only* value. Acceptance of diversity can never be allowed to call our other basic Judaic commitments into question. Put simply, there are limits to our pluralism. These limits are set by those standards that form the essence of our Jewish outlook, standards that can be violated only at the cost of our Reform Jewish integrity. For all our tolerance, we would never permit a group of Jews for Jesus or other apostates to hold their worship services in our facility. Nor would we allow a group to organize an "alternative" Jewish service that denies as a matter of religious principle the right of participation to any Jew on the basis of gender. No religious community, no matter how liberal, could possibly exist if it were unable to draw lines, to set boundaries, and to agree upon at least the most minimal definitions of what it does and does not believe.[6] Our commitment to gender equality and our affirmation of our own Jewish religious legitimacy are examples of such boundaries; indeed, they are in the category of *minimal* standards, values without which "Reform Judaism" as we know it could scarcely exist. Our congregations dedicate themselves to the furtherance of these values and to the observance of these standards. To allow space to groups that repudiate them is to act in contradiction of our very purpose as a religious community.

2. *A Halachic Precedent.* We cannot resolve this issue, therefore, simply by invoking "Reform religious principles," because more than one such principle speaks to it and because those principles draw us in contradictory directions. How then shall we proceed in this situation, in which Jews deeply divided over matters of religious outlook and practice seek to live together within the same institutional framework?

Our tradition offers us guidance in the form of a helpful precedent. We refer to the Talmud's discussion of one of the halachic conflicts that divided the early Rabbinical "schools" of Hillel and Shammai.[7] The question arises: although the halachah generally follows the view of the school of Hillel,[8] did the school of Shammai ever put its theoretical viewpoint into concrete practice? Some, the Talmud suggests, answer this question in the affirmative. Yet to say this raises a problem: would not such an act violate the prohibition, derived from Deuteronomy 14:1, "do not divide yourselves into separate sects"?[9] This rule, if applied literally, seems to demand that those holding the minority or rejected legal viewpoint yield in practice to the majority or accepted opinion. The Talmud responds that the rule "do not divide yourselves" applies only to the context of a single *beit din* (rabbinical court), so that once a decision is rendered its judges do not express public dissent over it; however, "in a case of two separate rabbinical courts within the same community, the rule does not apply."[10] Each "court" is a distinct religious institution that enjoys its own halachic integrity and is entitled to practice as it sees fit. The schools of Hillel and Shammai are equivalent to two separate "courts" within the same community; thus, each may practice according to its own understanding of the halachah.

This passage reminds us of two important points. It teaches us, first of all, that the Rabbinic tradition indeed places a high value upon unity in religious practice. We are, after all, one people, in possession of one Torah, who ought to be united in service to the one God. Divisiveness in practice should be discouraged, for it suggests that we have failed to study the Torah properly and are therefore unable to agree on its message for us; such disagreement makes it appear that we are following "two Torahs" instead of the one.[11] Yet the existence of conflicting "schools" of Jewish thought and practice reminds us that diversity is inevitable. We Jews have never agreed on all questions of belief and observance, nor is it likely that we ever will. "Majority" and "minority" views will always exist among us; we cannot enforce a unity of religious life that, however ideal, is illusory in reality.[12] Our text therefore suggests a compromise that pays allegiance to both these goals. Opposing viewpoints ("courts"; "schools") may coexist within the same institutional framework ("city"), so that each "court," while accepting the existence of the other, possesses a distinct identity. *Unity* is preserved both as a theoretical goal and because each "school" retains the practical authority to determine its own standards. *Diversity* is acknowledged because each "school" is granted Jewish legitimacy within its own realm.

Our case, we believe, closely resembles the situation that obtained between the "schools" of Hillel and Shammai. We Reform Jews define our religious outlook in a particular way, and we want our synagogues and other institutions to reflect this definition. For this reason, we might well insist upon the rule "do not divide yourselves into separate sects" and require that those who meet to worship in our facilities do so according to our own standards of liturgical practice. Yet so long as the nascent Orthodox minyan enjoys a separate organizational identity from our own, there is no need to enforce this artificial unity. Like the school of Shammai, the Orthodox minyan is and can be seen by all to be a distinct entity—a *beit din*, "court" or "school"—

whose practices and doctrines are not to be confused with those of the larger Reform congregation. This group can coexist within our "city," alongside our Reform "court," so long as the separate existence of each group is acknowledged and made clearly visible to all. By facilitating this coexistence, we most certainly do not endorse the religious views of the Orthodox minyan, any more than the coexistence of the schools of Hillel and Shammai meant that either *beit din* endorsed the conflicting decisions of the other. Our Reform Jewish integrity therefore remains intact. We say rather that Jewish unity *and* diversity—integrity *and* pluralism— are equally worthy goals and that our tradition would have us make room for both.

We are aware of the irony of this position. We know that, were the situation of our *sh'eilah* to be reversed, an Orthodox congregation would not likely grant permission to a Reform group to hold services in its synagogue building. This is because Orthodox Judaism is not a liberal creed. It proclaims that there is but one correct version of Jewish practice and that Reform Jewish worship is not an acceptable variation of that correct version. They do not regard our disagreements as similar to the conflict between the schools of Hillel and Shammai, two legitimate if conflicting interpretations of the same Torah. On the contrary: they condemn us as heretics, they cast us outside the pale, they deny the Jewish validity of our practice. It may be tempting to respond in kind, to reject them in return, to deny them space within our precincts as they would surely deny it to us. Yet our religious principles forbid us the path of retaliation. The conduct of the Orthodox Jews who drive us from our rightful place at the Western Wall cannot serve as a model for our own behavior. If they are not liberals, *we* are; if their conception of Judaism cannot make room for diversity, ours does and must. We look upon Orthodox Jews not as enemies but as friends. We greet them not as aliens and heretics but as our brothers and sisters. And whether or not they would do the same for us, our liberal Jewish faith demands that we reach out to them in a spirit of fellowship and generosity.

Conclusion. A Reform congregation may provide space within its facility for an Orthodox congregation to worship, provided that the latter maintains a separate and distinct identity. In this way, all will know clearly that our synagogue, while reaching out in friendship to our fellow Jews, in no way endorses those aspects of their religious practice that are offensive to us.

How might we best maintain this "separateness" as we host the Orthodox congregation? On this point, the members of the Committee differ.

Some of us feel that the necessary separation can be maintained only by insisting that this arrangement be temporary. They are willing to provide space to the Orthodox minyan for a strictly limited period, to enable them to find suitable quarters of their own; should this prove impossible, it would be evidence that the community as a whole cannot support a separate Ortho- dox congregation. In any case, we will have done our duty to assist them.

Others are willing to allow the Orthodox minyan to meet in our building on a permanent basis, provided that they do not assemble for worship in our sanctuary. The sanctuary has been dedicated to Reform Jewish worship, in which all members of our congregation are accepted as equals. An Orthodox minyan would exclude many of us from equal participation. To permit them to assemble in our sacred space would amount to an insult, a lessening of its sanctity.

The majority of us, however, would permit the Orthodox group to meet on a permanent basis in our building, including the sanctuary; we do not agree that the worship service of any legitimately Jewish congregation affects the holiness of that space. We would place two provisos upon our permission. First, the Reform congregation must be acknowledged as the *baal habayit*, the owner of the building. This means that the Orthodox group may use our facilities *only* so long as their usage does not conflict with our own services and other events. A clear and binding written agreement specifying the restrictions placed upon their usage of our facilities is a necessity. Second, it is best that this Orthodox group formally and legally constitute itself as an independent congregation, so that it not appear to be a *chavurah* or sub- group of our own. Moreover, we should charge them rent for the use of our facilities, although this rent might well be set at a purely symbolic amount. In this fashion, it will be evident to all that the two groups, their congrega- tion and ours, are separate and distinct entities, so that each may pursue— together yet independently of the other—its chosen path to Judaism and Torah.

> —CCAR Responsa Committee, "Orthodox Minyan in a Reform Synagogue," CCAR
> responsum 5758.12, in *Reform Responsa for the Twenty-First Century: Sh'eilot
> Ut'shuvot*, ed. Mark Washofsky (New York: CCAR Press, 2010), 1:3–12.

NOTES

1.   A legal maxim of uncertain origin. The definition of "hard cases" here follows that of the legal philosopher Ronald Dworkin; see his *Law's Empire* (Cambridge, MA: Belk-

nap/Harvard Press, 1986), 255–56. As such, it represents a change from the original understanding of the term: "judicial decisions which, to meet a case of hardship to a party, are not entirely consonant with the true principle of the law. It is said of such: 'hard cases make bad law'" (J. R. Nolan and J. M. Nolan-Haley, eds., *Black's Law Dictionary*, 6th ed. [St. Paul: West Publishing Co., 1990], 717, taken from *Corpus Juris* 29:213 [1922]). On the difference between the "new" and "old" definitions, see note 2, below.

2.　Actually, the maxim makes sense only if we accept the original definition of a "hard case" as one in which law and equity, conceived of as two separate realms not to be mixed, are at loggerheads. In such an instance, it might be claimed that an equitable decision makes "bad law" by introducing non-legal considerations into the legal system. The definition adopted by Dworkin better refers to what we might call a "difficult case," and as Richard A. Posner points out, "only difficult cases make law, good or bad. Cases that are easy to decide are so by virtue of being controlled by existing law"; see his *The Problems of Jurisprudence* (Cambridge, MA: Harvard University Press, 1990), 161, n. 1.

3.　Note the phrase "a number of different and even conflicting paths." By this, we mean a not-unlimited "number." No plausible interpretation of Jewish pluralism requires us to recognize every conceivable version of "Judaism" as legitimate. None of us, for example, would dissent from the thoughts expressed below concerning the Jews for Jesus.

4.　On the source of the mitzvah of hospitality, see Babylonian Talmud, *Shabbat* 127a–b, where it is listed among the things "whose fruits one consumes in this world and whose principal remains available for one in the world-to-come," an example of *g'milut chasadim* (acts of loving-kindness). Maimonides classifies such acts under the rubric of "love your neighbor as yourself" (Leviticus 19:18; *Mishneh Torah, Aveil* 14:1). This obligation, however, is traditionally understood in the more literal sense as hospitality to travelers, hosting and feeding them in one's home or in some other suitable location. We know of no interpretation of this mitzvah that calls a congregation to modify its liturgical practice in order to accommodate a visiting group within its midst. On the contrary: normative practice is for the visitors to accommodate themselves to the *minhag* of the host synagogue.

5.　If there are objections as to the content of the siddur, we might respond that those passages that offend our religious sensibilities can either be reinterpreted or, if necessary, excised from the service.

6.　For a fuller version of this point, see introduction to *Teshuvot for the Nineties*, especially xvii–xxi.

7.　*Mishnah Y'vamot* 1:1–3 and Babylonian Talmud, *Y'vamot* 13a–14a. This particular dispute centers upon the institution of levirate marriage (*yibum*), the requirement that the widow of a childless man be married to her brother-in-law in order that she might raise up a child in the name of her deceased husband (Deuteronomy 25:5–10). Both schools agree that should the widow be forbidden to her brother-in-law as an *ervah*, one of the sexual unions prohibited in Leviticus 18, she is exempt from both the requirement of *yibum* and the legal ceremony of *chalitzah* that releases that requirement. The school of Hillel go farther, holding that if the deceased had two wives, then both of them were equally forbidden as an *ervah* to the brother of the deceased. The school of Shammai disagreed; they held that the "second" wife in such a case had to submit to *yibum* or *chalitzah* if she were not actually an *ervah*. According to the school of Hillel, the child born of that union—permitted and required by the school of Shammai—is a *mamzer*. As we can see, therefore, this dispute was hardly a matter of superficial importance.

8. By virtue of the decision of the *bat kol*, the "heavenly voice," which proclaimed that "the views of both schools are in accord with divine teaching [*eilu v'eilu divrei Elohim chayim heim*], but the halachah follows the school of Hillel" (Babylonian Talmud, *Eiruvin* 13b).

9. From the phrase *lo titgod'du*. The literal meaning of these words, of course, is a prohibition against making gashes in one's body with sharp instruments (Rashi to Deuteronomy 14:1; *Mishneh Torah, Avodat Kochavim* 12:13). The Talmud here resorts to a fanciful midrash and reads the words as: *lo tei-asu agudot agudot*, "do not divide yourselves into separate sects." As the discussion in Babylonian Talmud, *Y'vamot* 13b–14a makes clear, the "separateness" referred to here is not a purely theological matter but one of separate standards of halachic observance.

10. This is according to the opinion of Rava in Babylonian Talmud, *Y'vamot* 14a, which is cited as halachah in *Hilchot HaRosh, Y'vamot* 1:9 (see also Rabbi Menachem HaMeiri, *Beit HaB'chirah, Y'vamot* 14a). It differs from the opinion of Abayei, who declares that the prohibition does not apply in the case of two courts in *two* separate cities but does apply to two courts in the same city. Maimonides (*Mishneh Torah, Avodat Kochavim* 12:14) follows Abayei, a ruling that puzzles his commentators, since according to the normal rules of halachic decision-making, the law follows Rava in virtually all cases when he is disputed by Abayei. Rava's position, moreover, is presented by the Talmud as the conclusion of the *sugya*, another fact that indicates its predominance. And his view is clearly superior to that of Abayei, for it more effectively answers the difficulty raised against those who argue that the school of Shammai actually practiced according to their "incorrect" opinion. It has been suggested that Maimonides gives evidence here of his distaste for *machloket* (dispute): he thus decides according to Abayei because Rava's view is the more lenient and tolerant of dispute. See Rabbi David ibn Zimra, *Responsa Radbaz*, no. 1384.

11. Thus Rashi (on Babylonian Talmud, *Y'vamot* 13b, s.v. *lo taasu*) explains the prohibition against dividing into "separate sects": "*denirin k'nohagin sh'tei torot.*"

12. See the remark of Rabbi Menachem HaMeiri, *Beit HaB'chirah, Y'vamot* 14a: "So long as we are dealing with two separate courts, even though they reside in the same city, each one holding to its own understanding of the law, they do not violate the rule 'do not divide yourselves.' For it is impossible that everyone should always agree to follow the same opinion."

CHAPTER 3: REFORMING REFORMS, EMBRACING TRADITION
When a Parent Requests Cremation

SH'EILAH:

A man, who is approaching death, has instructed that his body be cremated. His children are very uncomfortable with this request. They ask whether, under Jewish tradition, they are obliged to honor it, or are they entitled to bury him intact, in contradiction to his express wishes? Rabbi Solomon B. Freehof has ruled that in such a case we apply the Talmudic dictum "It is a mitzvah to fulfill the wishes of the deceased" (Babylonian Talmud, *Gittin* 40a and elsewhere). I wonder, however, if a more nuanced approach is better suited to a case such as this, where the children have strong religious objections to their father's instruction? (Rabbi David Katz, Binghamton, New York)

T'SHUVAH:

In the responsum that our *sho-eil* mentions, Rabbi Freehof rules that "we should urge" the family to carry out a father's wish to be cremated.[1] He acknowledges that the principle "It is a mitzvah to fulfill the wishes of the deceased" is not absolute; we are in fact *forbidden* to fulfill the wishes of the deceased if he or she instructs us to commit a transgression against Jewish law.[2] Thus, an Orthodox rabbi would surely rule against the request: "Since cremation is contrary to Jewish law, the man's wish contravenes the law and may not be carried out." However, since the question has been posed to a Reform rabbi, "the answer cannot be so clear-cut." For us, cremation does *not* necessarily "contravene the law"; the Central Conference of American Rabbis (CCAR) resolved in 1892 that "in case we should be invited to officiate" at a cremation, "we ought not to refuse on the plea that cremation be anti-Jewish or irreligious."[3] Rabbi Freehof notes that there is no clear and obvious prohibition against cremation in the sources of Jewish law and that "the Orthodox agitation against cremation actually began about a century ago" in response to the growing movement toward cremation in Western societies. Indeed, "when one studies the (Orthodox) arguments adduced against cremation, one can see that they are forced." On this basis, Rabbi Freehof concludes that Reform Jews can have no principled religious objections to cremation. In the instant case, unless the man's family is Orthodox, we should counsel them to honor his instruction. "Surely, if we officiate at a cremation, we cannot refrain from fulfilling or encouraging the fulfillment of a man's wish for this type of disposal of his body."

We have quoted at length from Rabbi Freehof's responsum because we do not want to minimize the challenge that faces us. Our *sho-eil* is asking that we rule against our teacher, and we are ordinarily reluctant to do so.[4] We would argue, though, that the times demand a different response. For one thing, the situation is no longer "so clear-cut"; the Reform position on cremation is more complex today than it was when Rabbi Freehof wrote his *t'shuvah*. We also think that our attitude toward the maintenance and encouragement of traditional forms of Jewish observance has changed quite a bit over the last several decades. For these reasons, we hold that the children in this case may well be entitled to act upon their own religious beliefs and *not* to fulfill their father's request.

In order to make this argument, we shall have to consider, first of all, the attitude of Jewish law and tradition toward cremation as a means of the disposal of human remains. We shall then look at the developing Reform Jewish attitude toward cremation as expressed in the literature of the CCAR. Finally, we shall consider this particular case in the context of Jewish tradition, Reform Jewish practice, and the ethical obligations that the children may owe to their dying father.

1. *Cremation in Jewish Law.* There is no explicit requirement in the biblical text that the dead be buried rather than cremated. The sources make clear that burial was the normative practice in ancient Israel,[5] but nowhere do we find an express prohibition of the burning of the corpse. The Rabbis understand burial to be a requirement of Torah law, derived from Deuteronomy 21:23.[6] Maimonides codifies the law as follows: "If the deceased gave instructions that his body not be buried, we ignore him, inasmuch as burial is a mitzvah, as the Torah says (Deuteronomy 21:23), 'You shall surely bury him.'"[7] Yet like the Bible, the Talmud and the classical halachic literature contain no explicit prohibition of cremation. The subject seems almost never to have come up, most likely because cremation was simply not practiced by the Jews and no one thought to ask whether it was permitted or forbidden.[8] The silence lasted until the nineteenth century, "when cremation became an ideal that was agitated for through many societies in the western lands."[9] At that time, the leading halachic authorities condemned cremation as a transgression against Jewish law, an opinion that remains the consensus viewpoint.[10] This prohibitive opinion rests primarily on two halachic grounds. First, cremation does not fulfill the commandment to bury the dead, based as we have seen

on Deuteronomy 21:23. Burial of the cremains would not rectify this, since the mitzvah of burial applies to the body itself and not to its ashes.[11] Second, Jewish tradition mandates *k'vod hameit*, that we treat the corpse with honor and respect, and it regards the burning of a body as an act of *nivul* (or *bizayon*) *hameit*, contemptible treatment of a corpse.[12] Other arguments include the prohibition against imitating gentile customs (*chukot hagoyim*)[13] and the contention that cremation is tantamount to an act of heresy in that it denies the belief in *t'chiyat hameitim*, the physical resurrection of the dead.[14]

These arguments may or may not be "forced," as Rabbi Freehof describes them. Some of them may be more persuasive than others. What is certain, though, is that Orthodox authorities are united in the opinion that cremation violates traditional Jewish law, an opinion shared by Conservative[15] and Reform[16] writers.

2. *Cremation in the Literature of the CCAR.* The CCAR has published a number of statements with respect to cremation.

   a. The 1892 resolution, referred to above, declares that "in case we should be invited to officiate as ministers of religion at the cremation of a departed co-religionist, we ought not to refuse on the plea that cremation be anti-Jewish or anti-religion."[17] The resolution followed upon the report of a special committee, chaired by Rabbi Bernard Felsenthal, that had been appointed to study the issue. The report made two essential points. First, it demonstrated at some length that the practice of cremation was contrary to Jewish law and tradition.[18] Second, it sought to avoid the substantive issue of whether to endorse cremation as a method for disposal of human remains. "The writer of this does not wish to be understood that he pleads for cremation. He also does not oppose it." Since a rabbi is not "a competent expert" in the matter of whether cremation is "preferable" to burial, the only motion "in order in a rabbinical conference" is one that calls upon rabbis, whatever their position concerning cremation, to provide pastoral care for those of their people who do choose the procedure.[19]

   b. The 1961 *Rabbi's Manual*, recounting the 1892 resolution, states, "Since that time, most Reform Jews have gone beyond this cautious tolerance and have accepted cremation as an entirely proper procedure. A number of leading Reform rabbis have requested

that their bodies be cremated."[20] In its section on funeral liturgy
the *Manual* contains a prayer suggested for recitation when "the
body is to be cremated."[21]

c. The 1974 responsum of Rabbi Freehof discussed at the beginning
of our *t'shuvah*.

d. *Gates of Mitzvah*, a guide to Reform Jewish life-cycle observance published in 1979, stresses that "while both cremation and
entombment in mausoleums are acceptable in Reform Judaism,
burial is the normative Jewish practice."[22]

e. In 1980 the CCAR Responsa Committee appended a comment to
the 1892 resolution. It notes that the resolution "remains unchal-
lenged policy within [the CCAR]," but adds, "In this generation of
the Holocaust we are sensitive to terrible images associated with
the burning of a body. Rabbis may, therefore, choose to discourage the option of cremation. The practice remains permissible,
however, for our families."[23]

f. The current *Rabbi's Manual*, published in 1988, states, "We continue to stress that burial is the time-honored Jewish way of disposing of the dead. . . . However, the practice of cremation has
lately spread, for a number of reasons. We would reiterate that it
ought to be discouraged if possible, especially in our generation,
which has seen the murderous dispatch of millions of our people
by way of crematoria. If, however, cremation has been decided
upon by the family, we should not refuse to officiate. It is suggested in such cases that the service be held at an appropriate
place and not at a crematorium."

g. A 1990 responsum notes, "Reform Jewish practice permits cremation . . . although . . . we would, after the Holocaust, generally
discourage it because of the tragic overtones."[24]

The record of these statements suggests a perceptible shift of attitude
toward cremation within North American Reform Judaism during recent
decades. While our earlier pronouncements accept cremation as permissible or even as "entirely proper," the CCAR since 1979 has pulled back from
that affirmative stance. Although acknowledging that the 1892 resolution
remains on the books and that Reform Jewish practice "permits" cremation,
our more recent statements call upon rabbis to actively "discourage" the

practice. This negative position is based upon two threads of argument: that burial is the normative traditional Jewish practice and that, after the Holocaust, cremation has become associated with one of the darkest periods in Jewish and human history.

These threads of argument, in turn, reflect two important transformations in the way that many Reform Jews have come to think about their religious lives and decisions. The first has to do with the positive reevaluation of "tradition." In the past, the fact that a particular observance was "traditional" or accepted Jewish practice did not in and of itself recommend that observance to Reform Jews. Indeed, we were quite ready to dispense with any such practices that were "not adapted to the views and habits of modern civilization" and that "fail to impress the modern Jew with a spirit of priestly holiness."[25] It is for this reason that Rabbi Felsenthal could argue *both* that cremation was a transgression against traditional Jewish law *and* that this fact was irrelevant to Reform Jewish thinking on the subject:

> Joseph Karo's Code is of no obligatory authority to you. The Talmud is of no obligatory authority to you. Even the laws of the Bible as such are of no obligatory authority to you. . . . Shall we for the sake of the living inquire of the dead? Shall we for the sake of the living open the old folios, and submit to what they have said hundreds of years ago under quite different conditions of life? Shall we learn there whether or not cremation is in accord with the spirit of Judaism?[26]

Rabbi Felsenthal's words remain an eloquent expression of a central article of Reform Jewish faith. To this day, we affirm our right to define the "spirit of Judaism" and to abandon, alter, or replace old practices that we no longer find religiously meaningful. In this view, we cannot declare to Reform Jews that cremation ought to be forbidden solely because it runs counter to the halachah or to the customs of our ancestors.

In recent decades, however, a new attitude has taken hold within our community. We have described it as follows:

> Many of us have reclaimed ritual observances abandoned by previous generations of Reform Jews, from the generous use of Hebrew in the liturgy, to the wearing of *kippah*, tallit, and *t'fillin*, to the dietary laws (kashrut), to the ceremonies surrounding marriage and conversion. These examples—and more could be cited—testify that our approach to traditional ritual practice differs significantly from that of our predecessors. This difference stems, no doubt, from the divergent religious agenda that we have set for ourselves. If our predecessors regarded their acculturation into the surrounding society as a pre-

dominant objective, we who benefit from the social and political gains that they achieved are more concerned with taking active measures to preserve our distinctive Jewishness. Thus, where they may have viewed many ritual observances as barriers to social integration and as obstructions to "modern spiritual elevation," we may find them an appropriate and desirable expression of our Jewish consciousness.[27]

This is what we mean by the positive reevaluation of "tradition." The point is not that traditional practices exert, to use Rabbi Felsenthal's words, "obligatory authority" upon us. The point, rather, is that we take the Bible, the Talmud, and even "Joseph Karo's Code" more seriously than we did in his day as positive influences upon our own religious behavior. We are now more inclined than ever before to adopt or to preserve a ritual observance precisely because it is "Jewish." We are more likely to regard a practice's traditional pedigree as a reason for maintaining it, especially when there are no compelling moral or aesthetic arguments against that practice. We are therefore today more likely—though not obligated—to oppose cremation on the grounds that burial is a mitzvah, the "normative" Jewish way of disposing of human remains.

We might in a similar way explain our differences over whether cremation constitutes an act of *nivul hameit* (contemptible treatment of a corpse). A Reform Jew is certainly entitled to define this term in a way that is "adapted to the views and habits of modern civilization." Cremation is widely accepted in Western culture as an honorable way of treating human remains. We are therefore under no obligation to regard it as an act of *nivul hameit* solely because some Rabbinic texts portray it as such. Yet to say that we are not obligated to adopt the traditional definition does not entail that we are *forbidden* to do so. It is true that concepts such as "honor" and "disgrace" do not admit of objective definition. All this means, however, is that such terms can only be defined from within a particular social context; to reach these definitions, we must choose to work within a particular culture's set of values and affirmations. The particular culture that is Jewish tradition declares the burning of the corpse to be an act of *nivul* or *bizayon*. A Reform Jew today who finds special and satisfying meaning in the values and affirmations of Jewish tradition is thus entitled—though, again, not obligated—to adopt this definition precisely because it flows from the religious and cultural heritage of our people.

The second transformation in our religious thinking concerns our sensitivity to the experience of the Shoah (Holocaust). There is, to be sure, all the difference in the world between the Nazi crematoria and the freely made choice of cremation for ourselves and our loved ones. We should, moreover, be wary of invoking the memory of the Shoah as a facile justification for decisions concerning religious practice.[28] Yet for all that, the Jewish world *is* a different place now, "after Auschwitz," than it was before. Neither we nor our religious consciousness has emerged unchanged from our confrontation with that event. And one such change, as the recent statements of the CCAR affirm, has to do with our attitude toward the machinery of cremation. The images of fire, ovens, and smokestacks, which we recall so vividly when we contemplate the mass murder of our people, can and do persuade many liberal Jews that today, after Auschwitz, the consigning of our dead to the flames is not the proper Jewish way to honor them.[29]

We emphasize that we are dealing here with general trends. To speak of transformations in our religious thinking is to *describe* what is happening within large segments of the Reform Jewish community rather than to *prescribe* a correct course of action in a specific instance. Not all Reform Jews are affected in the same way by these trends, and not every Reform Jew will draw from them the same conclusions concerning his or her religious observance. As a noted jurist once remarked, "General propositions do not decide concrete cases."[30] Yet in this particular concrete case, the CCAR has moved decisively away from its previous acceptance of cremation. The members of the CCAR Responsa Committee reiterate this stance. Although we, like our more recent predecessors, continue to acknowledge that the 1892 resolution remains the formal policy of the CCAR, we would continue to call upon our rabbis to discourage the practice of cremation among our people. We do so for three primary reasons. First, burial is the normative traditional Jewish practice; as such, it is a mitzvah that exerts a strong persuasive force upon us. Second, we note the absence of convincing moral or aesthetic objections to the practice of traditional burial that would move us to abandon it.[31] Finally, we concur with our predecessors that today, after the Shoah, the symbolism of cremation is profoundly disturbing to us as Jews.

3. *The Question before Us.* How should the children of whom our *sh'eilah* speaks respond to their father's request? Considering all the above, we would counsel the following.

a. The North American Reform Movement does not regard cremation as a "sin." The 1892 resolution of the CCAR calls upon rabbis to officiate at cremation services, and despite our reservations concerning cremation, we hold that the procedure does not "contravene the law." Therefore, the children are not forbidden to honor this request, and they may arrange for cremation in response to the mitzvah to honor our parents and to the dictum that we should seek to fulfill the wishes of the deceased.

b. Nonetheless, the children are not *obligated* to honor their father's request. The CCAR discourages the choice of cremation; it supports the choice of traditional burial; and Reform thought today recognizes the right of our people to adopt traditional standards of religious practice that previous generations of Reform Jews may have abandoned. The commandment to honor one's parents does not apply in such a case, for a parent is not entitled to compel his or her children to violate their sincerely held Judaic religious principles.[32] Thus, when a Reform Jew has serious and substantive religious objections to cremation, he or she may refuse a loved one's request for it.

c. By "traditional burial," we do not mean to endorse many of the practices that, although associated with burial in the public mind, would be deemed as excessive or inappropriate by many of us. Among these are such elaborate and unnecessary steps as embalming, expensive caskets, and the like. Jewish tradition emphasizes simplicity and modesty in burial practices; individuals should not feel driven to choose cremation in order to avoid the expense and elaborate display that all too often accompany contemporary burial.[33]

d. It is essential that families speak about such matters openly, honestly, and before the approach of death. When the child fails explicitly to say "no" to a parent's request for cremation, the parent will justifiably think that the child has agreed to carry out that instruction. In such a case, the child quite likely has made an implied promise to the parent and thus bears an ethical responsibility to keep it. Therefore, if the children have objections to cremation, they should make their feelings known to their parents sooner—much sooner—rather than later.

—CCAR Responsa Committee, "When a Parent Requests Cremation," CCAR responsum 5766.2, in *Reform Responsa for the Twenty-First Century: Sh'eilot Ut'shuvot*, ed. Mark Washofsky (New York: CCAR Press, 2010), 2:193–208.

NOTES

1. Solomon B. Freehof, "Family Disagreement over Cremation," in *Contemporary Reform Responsa* (Cincinnati: Hebrew Union College Press, 1974), 228–31, https://www.ccarnet.org/ccar-responsa/corr-228-231.

2. See the midrash cited in Babylonian Talmud, *Y'vamot* 5b. Leviticus 19:3 says, "You shall each revere your mother and your father, and keep My Sabbaths." The midrash explains that the second clause comes to limit the scope of the first: we "revere" our parents (i.e., we fulfill their wishes) so long as they do not instruct us to contravene the laws of the Torah, of which Shabbat is an example. See also *Mishneh Torah*, *Mamrim* 6:12; and *Shulchan Aruch*, *Yoreh Dei-ah* 240:15.

3. "Cremation from the Jewish Standpoint," in *American Reform Responsa*, 341–48, https://www.ccarnet.org/ccar-responsa/arr-341-348. A much more complete version of the debate that led to the adoption of this resolution can be found in *CCAR Yearbook* 3 (1893): 53–68.

4. We have on occasion differed with Rabbi Freehof. Often, this is due to transformations in the religious outlook of Reform Jews from his day to ours. Such changes are inevitable over the course of time, so that by responding to them we do not believe that we do any dishonor to Rabbi Freehof's teachings or to his accomplishments in the field of Reform responsa, a genre he did so much to develop. In fact, we think he would be pleased that we, his successors, continue his work in the spirit of free and critical inquiry, an ideal that he always championed and to which our movement has long pledged loyalty. On the other hand, we are aware that were he with us Rabbi Freehof would no doubt offer cogent responses to our objections. We don't do this lightly; after all, as the Talmud cautions, "Do not contradict the lion after his death" (Babylonian Talmud, *Gittin* 83b).

5. "There is no evidence that corpses were cremated in Palestine, except in days long before the coming of the Israelites, or among groups of foreigners; the Israelites never practiced it" (Roland de Vaux, *Ancient Israel* [New York: McGraw-Hill, 1965], 1:57). See also *Encyclopedia Mikra-it*, 7:4–5: "It is clear that [cremation] was not generally practiced." This doesn't mean that it never happened. Amos 6:10 speaks of the *m'sareif* who comes to the house during time of plague to collect the bones of the dead, presumably for burning (*s-r-f*). Scholars, however, are unsure of the precise explanation of the term; see F. I. Anderson and D. N. Freeman, *The Anchor Bible: Amos* (New York: Doubleday, 1989), 572, 574. Then there is the burning of the corpses of Saul and his sons by the men of Yavesh-Gilead (I Samuel 31:12–13). This detail causes some obvious perplexity and embarrassment to later writers; the Chronicler (I Chronicles 10:12) omits it entirely, and the traditional Jewish commentators are at pains to explain it away. From this, we can learn two important points: first, that cremation was not unheard of in ancient Israel, and second, that later Jewish tradition did not derive any positive support for the practice of cremation from these isolated references.

6. Although that verse speaks of the body of an executed offender, its requirement of burial is interpreted to apply to all the dead. See Babylonian Talmud, *Sanhedrin* 46b, which cites the verse as a *remez* (a hint; an indication) to the fact that burial is a Toraitic obligation.

7. *Mishneh Torah, Aveil* 12:1. See also Rambam's *Sefer HaMitzvot*, positive commandment number 231. In the Babylonian Talmud (*Sanhedrin* 46b) we find a dispute over whether the purpose of burial is to safeguard the corpse from contemptible treatment (*mishum bizyona*) or to effect atonement (*kaparah*) for the deceased. If the latter is the case, the Talmud suggests that the deceased would be within his rights to instruct his heirs not to bury him, since he is entitled to refuse atonement for himself. The dispute is not firmly resolved (*Hilchot HaRosh, Sanhedrin* 6:2); therefore, say some authorities, we ought to rule strictly and require burial, inasmuch as the Torah mentions it (*Sefer Or Zarua, Hilchot Aveilut*, chap. 422). Rabbi Yosef Karo (*Kesef Mishneh, Hilchot Aveil* 12:1 and *Beit Yosef, Yoreh Dei-ah* 348) arrives at a similar conclusion, which he attributes to Nachmanides. The *Lechem Mishneh* (*Mishneh Torah, Aveil* 12:1) argues that this dispute is relevant only for those who hold that the mitzvah of burial is of Rabbinic origin. Maimonides, quite clearly, holds that it is a Toraitic commandment. In any event, we find no evidence in the traditional halachah that one is in fact entitled to instruct his heirs not to bury him.

8. In the thirteenth century, Rabbi Sh'lomo ben Adret permitted mourners, who wanted to transport their father to a family plot, to put quicklime on the corpse in order that the flesh be consumed rapidly and to spare it the dishonor (*bizayon*) of rotting (*Responsa Rashba* 1:369; see Isserles, *Yoreh Dei-ah* 363:2). Does this serve as a precedent to allow cremation? Most likely, the answer is no. For one thing, not everyone would be persuaded that fire is analogous to quicklime. For another, subsequent interpreters have limited Rashba's decision to precisely this sort of case: the exhumation and transport of a corpse for permanent burial. See the eighteenth-century Rabbi Yaakov Reischer (*Responsa Sh'vut Yaakov* 2:97), who permits quicklime in a case where the alternative to transporting the corpse would be to bury it in a place where it could not be protected and would necessarily suffer *bizayon*. See also *Aruch HaShulchan, Yoreh Dei-ah* 363, paragraph 2. This line of thinking, in other words, deals with exceptional circumstances and not with the use of cremation as a regular means of disposing of human remains.

9. Freehof, "Family Disagreement over Cremation," 230. Does this mean, as Rabbi Freehof suggests, that cremation is considered a transgression *only* because of the nineteenth-century Orthodox "agitation" against it? Not necessarily. It is just as likely that cremation would have been explicitly prohibited had the question been raised during the seventeenth century, or the thirteenth, or earlier. The question was not considered until the practice became widespread in the West.

10. Rabbi Yitzchak Shmelkes, *Responsa Beit Yitzchak, Yoreh Dei-ah* 2:155; Rabbi David Zvi Hoffmann, *Responsa Melamed Leho-il*, 2:113-14; Rabbi Chaim Ozer Grodzinsky, *Responsa Achiezer* 3:72; Rabbi Avraham Yitzchak HaKohein Kook, *Responsa Daat Kohen*, no. 197; Rabbi Yaakov Breisch, *Responsa Chelkat Yaakov, Yoreh Dei-ah*, no. 203; Rabbi Yekutiel Greenwald, *Kol Bo al Aveilut*, 53-54; Rabbi Yechiel M. Tykocinski, *Gesher HaChayim* 16:9.

11. Hoffmann (see note 10) learns this from Jerusalem Talmud, *Nazir* 7:1 (55d): Deuteronomy's commandment to "bury him" applies to the entire body (*kulo*, or at least to the major part of the body) and not to a small portion of it (*miktzato*). He points

as well to the fact that the ashes of a burnt human corpse, unlike the corpse itself, are not a source of ritual impurity (*Mishnah Ohalot* 2:2; *Mishneh Torah, Tumat Meit* 3:9–10). In other words, burnt remains are not a "body" such as requires burial under the law. Grodzinsky (note 10) notes simply that ashes are not the "body" of the dead person. Although it may be proper (*ra-ui*) to bury the ashes of those who have been accidentally burned in a Jewish cemetery, he concludes, no actual obligation is fulfilled thereby.

12. Among other proof texts, the authorities point to the law that permits the removal of a corpse on Shabbat from a courtyard in which a fire has broken out. Transferring the corpse under normal conditions would violate the rules concerning the moving of objects on Shabbat, but it is permitted in this case because it would be a disgrace (*bizayon*) to the body were it consumed in the fire. See *Shulchan Aruch, Orach Chayim* 311:1 and commentaries (the latter make it clear that the permit to remove the body extends to transferring it to another *r'shut*). Although the *Magen Avraham* commentary to that passage (no. 3) suggests that burning would not be a case of *bizayon hameit* (or, at least, not enough of a *bizayon* to warrant setting aside the restrictions of Shabbat), his opinion is rejected by virtually all other commentators.

13. Leviticus 18:3 and 20:23. On the issue, see "Blessing the Fleet," CCAR responsum 5751.3, in *Teshuvot for the Nineties*, 159–64, https://www.ccarnet.org/ccar-responsa/tfn-no-5751-3-159-164.

14. See Freehof, "Family Disagreement over Cremation," 230. This point does appear in the writings of some of the authorities cited in note 10. It is, however, a somewhat tangential argument. The *poskim* do not spend much time developing it, nor do they present it as the major focus of their objection to cremation. It is unfortunate, therefore, that Rabbi Freehof cites this contention as his only example of the "arguments adduced (in the last century) against cremation," which he describes as "forced." This might give the reader the erroneous impression that Orthodox opposition to cremation is founded mainly upon a doctrine that we Reform Jews have long since rejected, at least in its literal form. In fact, the Orthodox writers invest a great deal more intellectual effort into the halachic arguments that we have noted, namely that cremation does not fulfill the mitzvah of burial and that it constitutes an act of *bizayon hameit*.

15. See the responsum authored by Rabbi Morris N. Shapiro, "Cremation in the Jewish Tradition," issued in 1986 by the Committee on Jewish Law and Standards of the Conservative Movement's Rabbinical Assembly (https://www.rabbinicalassembly.org/sites/default/files/assets/public/halakhah/teshuvot/19861990/shapiro_cremation.pdf).

16. See at notes 18 and 19, below.

17. See note 3, above.

18. This was in response to a paper delivered at a previous conference by Rabbi Max Schlesinger (*CCAR Yearbook* 2 [1892–93]: 33–40). Schlesinger's argument, namely that cremation was "the primitive custom among the Hebrews" (p. 36), was thoroughly refuted by Felsenthal and his committee.

19. *CCAR Yearbook* 3 (1893): 67–68.
20. *Rabbi's Manual* (New York: CCAR, 1961), 140.
21. *Rabbi's Manual*, 90.
22. Simeon J. Maslin, ed., *Gates of Mitzvah* (New York: CCAR Press, 1979), 56–57 (C-11).
23. Found at the conclusion of "Cremation from the Jewish Standpoint."
24. "The Ashes of a Couple in a Single Urn," in *Questions and Reform Jewish Answers*, 304–5, https://www.ccarnet.org/ccar-responsa/narr-304-305.
25. The "Pittsburgh Platform" of 1885, paragraphs 4 and 5, https://www.ccarnet.org/rabbinic-voice/platforms/article-declaration-principles.
26. *CCAR Yearbook* 3 (1893): 66.
27. "The Second Festival Day and Reform Judaism," CCAR responsum 5759.7, in *Reform Responsa for the Twenty-First Century*, 1:49–64, https://www.ccarnet.org/ccar-responsa/rr21-no-5759-7.
28. An argument in this vein can be found in "A Defective 'Holocaust' Torah Scroll," CCAR responsum 5760.3, in *Reform Responsa for the Twenty-First Century*, 2:59–70, https://www.ccarnet.org/ccar-responsa/nyp-no-5760-3.
29. The above paragraph reflects the ways in which the CCAR, through the publications we have cited, has described this particular "transformation in our religious thinking." Rabbi David Lilienthal, a corresponding member of the CCAR Responsa Committee, notes that the reaction of survivors of the Shoah may be quite different. His work in Europe with many survivors and children of survivors indicates that some may be inclined to choose cremation for themselves as a sign of solidarity with murdered family members. Other members of our committee report that they have detected no such tendency among survivors and descendants. In any event, we stress again that we are referring here to general trends and that, when it comes to the perception of the symbolic meaning of particular ritual acts, one community may well differ from another.
30. Justice Oliver Wendell Holmes, Jr., dissenting in the case of *Lochner v. New York* (198 U.S. 45, 76). He continues, "The decision will depend on a judgment or intuition more subtle than any articulate major premise."
31. This is not to say that such objections cannot be raised but rather that they do not persuade us that there is a compelling reason to adopt cremation as the standard procedure for the disposal of human remains. Individuals, of course, may be impressed by arguments to this effect, but we as a committee are not. Although this is not the place for a lengthy discussion of specific issues, we think that the ecological and economic criticisms that are raised from time to time against traditional burial can be addressed in ways that do not entail the choice of cremation. See the article by our colleague Daniel Schiff, "Cremation: Considering Contemporary Concerns," *Journal of Reform Judaism* 34, no. 2 (Spring 1987): 37–48, and see below in the text at note 33.
32. See "When a Parent Instructs a Child Not to Say Kaddish," CCAR responsum 5766.1, in *Reform Responsa for the Twenty-First Century*, 2:185–92, https://www.ccarnet.org/ccar-responsa/nyp-no-5766-1.
33. See *Gates of Mitzvah*, 55. We should follow the example of Rabban Gamliel, who

instructed that he be buried in simple linen shrouds rather than expensive ones to demonstrate that burial need not impose a crushing financial burden upon the mourners (Babylonian Talmud, *Mo-eid Katan* 27b).

CHAPTER 4: HONORING MEMORY AND HALACHAH
A Defective "Holocaust" Torah Scroll

SH'EILAH:

Our congregation possesses one of the Czech Torah scrolls that were taken by the Nazis and then rescued and cared for by London's Westminster Synagogue Memorial Trust. There are over one thousand scrolls now on "permanent loan" to synagogues around the world. Ours comes from the town of Kolin, near Prague. Some synagogues have scrolls that are fragmentary or incomplete. Our scroll is a complete *sefer Torah*, but sections of script have flaked away. A *sofer s'tam* (i.e., a scribe qualified to write Torah scrolls, *t'fillin*, and mezuzot) has told us that the parchment will not hold new ink. The scroll, since it cannot be repaired, is technically *pasul*, disqualified for public reading.

Our congregation has decided to use the scroll for Shabbat Torah readings, in places where the script is perfect or at least very clear. In addition, we have allowed many *b'nei mitzvah* to read their *parashah* from the scroll. This enables our youngsters to make a tactile connection between themselves and the vanished community of Kolin. We have taken synagogue and youth trips to Kolin and have prayed at its synagogue, which still stands. The scroll and its history have therefore become a significant part of our congregation's life.

A question has been raised: is it proper for us to read from this scroll, inasmuch as it has been declared *pasul*? How shall we answer this question, in light of both our tradition and the value we have found as a congregation in the public reading of the scroll? (Rabbi Mark S. Shapiro, Glenview, Illinois)

T'SHUVAH:

This *sh'eilah* poses a conflict between two profoundly important Jewish religious values. On the one hand, the honor due to the *sefer Torah* is a matter of great consequence in our tradition,[1] which as we shall see demands that the formal public reading of the Torah (*k'riat haTorah*) be performed from a *sefer Torah kasher*, a scroll that meets the strict requirements of ritual fitness. On the other hand, the events of the Shoah have left a profound imprint upon the Jewish mind and heart, and the remembrance of that tragedy has taken on for us the character of a religious duty.[2] Many congregations have acquired Torah scrolls that were rescued from the Nazis, and by reading from these scrolls they demonstrate in a concrete and moving way the continuity of the Jewish people and faith. How do we accommodate these two religious values, both of which make powerful claims upon our attention?

1. *The Reading of the Torah from a Ritually Unfit Scroll.* In his great code of Jewish law, Maimonides (Rambam) offers a list of twenty defects that render the scroll *pasul*.[3] The fifteenth item reads: "If the form of one letter should be diminished to the point that it cannot be read at all or so that it resembles another letter, whether this occurred at the original writing or through a perforation, a tear, or fading [of the text]." The Czech Torah scroll described in our *sh'eilah* is clearly *pasul* according to this definition. The proper response would be to repair the scroll and to restore it to kashrut, a ritually acceptable condition.[4] Since this is not possible in our case, tradition prescribes that the scroll be buried or stored away in a *genizah*.[5] In any event, it may not be used to fulfill the required ritual reading (*k'riat haTorah*). As Maimonides writes, "Should any one of these defects be present, the scroll is reduced to the status of a *Chumash*[6] that is used for the teaching of children; it is not to be read before the congregation."[7] The reason for this prohibition, according to the Talmud, is that to perform the reading from a *Chumash*—that is, from a scroll that is anything less than a complete *sefer Torah*—is an affront to the dignity of the congregation.[8]

   The issue, however, is not as cut and dried as it seems. The very same Maimonides is the author of a responsum that rules to the opposite effect.[9] His correspondents ask whether a community that does not possess a *sefer Torah* may perform the public reading from *Chumashim* and recite the blessings before and after the reading, or should they abstain from reading the Torah altogether? Similarly, may the blessings be recited over a *sefer Torah* that is ritually defective? Rambam answers without hesitation: *mutar l'vareich*, it is permitted to recite the blessings over the reading from a *sefer Torah pasul*. This is because we recite the blessings over the *reading* itself and not over the scroll; thus, one may recite the blessings whether the reading is performed from a scroll that is *kasher*, from a scroll that is *pasul*, or even if one recites without reading from a text at all.[10] Rambam offers two proofs for this theory. He first refers us to the beginning of the morning service (*Shacharit*), where one recites the blessing *asher bachar banu mikol haamim*—the same blessing recited prior to the reading of the Torah—before reciting passages of Scripture and rabbinic literature.[11] The worshiper says this *b'rachah* even though he does not recite the passages from a *sefer Torah*. "Thus, the actual mitzvah is the pronunciation [*hagayah*] of the words of Torah, and the blessing pertains to that pronunciation." Second, Rambam cites the Talmudic passage, mentioned above, that forbids congregational reading from *Chumashim*.[12] A *Chumash*, he notes, is the supreme example of a defective Torah scroll;[13] still, it is not prohibited *because* it is defective but rather because to read from it is an affront to "the dignity of the congregation." This suggests that a defective scroll is not disqualified per se for the congregational reading, but simply that it would be unseemly to use such a scroll for that purpose. The reading itself is therefore not invalid, and to recite a blessing over such a scroll is not an instance of *b'rachah l'vatalah* (a misplaced or unnecessary benediction).

This permissive ruling remains very much a minority view. Other leading authorities reject Rambam's arguments outright.[14] First, they write, Rambam's permit cuts against the grain of accepted Talmudic and halachic thought, which holds that a defective *sefer Torah* is not to be used for public reading even if no other Torah scroll is available.[15] Second, the benedictions are in fact recited over the scroll and *not* (as Rambam suggests) over the reading itself. Otherwise, we would be able to fulfill the requirement of *k'riat haTorah* by reciting the Torah portion orally; yet the ancient Rabbinic ordinance that established the practice[16] requires that the portion be read from a scroll and not from memory.[17] Third, while the Talmud's language might support Rambam's leniency with respect to a *Chumash*—that is, one of the Torah's five books written correctly on a separate scroll—the disqualification of a Torah scroll whose writing is defective or worn away appears to be absolute.[18] Indeed, it is arguable that a scroll lacking even one letter is not considered a *sefer Torah* at all,[19] so that the reading from it does not "count" toward the fulfillment of the mitzvah of *k'riat haTorah*.[20]

These are serious objections. Rambam's ruling seems to contradict everything the tradition has to say on the use of ritually unfit Torah scrolls. It most certainly contradicts the position of his own *Mishneh Torah* on the subject. It is therefore not surprising that some subsequent authorities sought to account for this problematic responsum by questioning its validity or authenticity.[21] Still, we think it possible to explain this *t'shuvah* without excising it from the literature of Jewish law. Near the conclusion of the responsum, Rambam declares, "It is proper for every community to possess a Torah scroll that is *kasher* in all respects, and it is preferable [*l'chat'chilah*][22] to read from that scroll. If this is not possible, however, let them read in public even from a *pasul* scroll and recite the blessings, on the basis of the reasoning I have supplied." In other words, Rambam holds that the preferable, optimal standard of observance demands a *kasher* scroll, and the ruling in the *Mishneh Torah* reflects that view.[23] The responsum, meanwhile, conveys Rambam's understanding of the minimally acceptable standard of observance: when the optimal standard cannot be met, the reading from a *sefer Torah pasul* suffices to fulfill the mitzvah of *k'riat haTorah*.[24] A community that does not possess a *sefer Torah kasher* may perform the reading from a *pasul* scroll, presumably so that (in the words of a later authority) "the practice of reading the Torah not be forgotten" there.[25]

2. *The Issue from a Reform Jewish Perspective*. We could make a good case to support this congregation's desire to conduct its Shabbat Torah readings from the Czech scroll. We have seen that Jewish law does not clearly forbid the reading from a *pasul* scroll; the responsum of Maimonides may be a minority opinion, but it is not necessarily "wrong" on that account.[26] We Reform Jews, at any rate, certainly see nothing wrong with adopting a minority opinion as the basis of our own practice, particularly when that opinion expresses an uplifting and "liberally affirmative" interpretation of Jewish tradition.[27] In the present case, we might say that there is no reason to forbid the use of this scroll. To read from it most certainly does not offend the dignity of the congregation. On the contrary: reading from this *sefer Torah*, which symbolizes the horrific events of the Shoah and our people's determination to survive all attempts to destroy us, is a deeply meaningful religious experience. Thus, just as Rambam and others were concerned that the practice of Torah reading would not be "forgotten" in small communities, we are motivated to use this *pasul* scroll by our determination that the Shoah never be forgotten.

Yet this "good" case is insufficient, for it fails to consider the central role that the reading of the Torah plays in our practice. *K'riat haTorah* is more than simply one religious observance out of many. It is the reenactment of the drama of Sinai, a reaffirmation of the covenant that binds God and Israel. We observe this mitzvah, as do all other Jews, by reading from a Torah scroll. By this we mean that we use a *scroll*, not a printed book,[28] a scroll, moreover, that is written and constructed according to the requirements set forth in Jewish law for a proper *sefer Torah*. These requirements, it must be stressed, are not mere technicalities, nor are they standards of "Orthodox" practice that we Reform Jews are free to ignore. Rather, they are standards of *Jewish* practice, the rules that define what a *sefer Torah* is, rules universally observed in all Jewish communities, including our Reform congregations. If Rambam permits the reading from a scroll that does not meet these requirements, he does so as a temporary measure; he is speaking, after all, to a community that has no *kasher* scroll available. To exalt this stopgap device to the status of a permanent and weekly observance is to say that it makes no difference to us that a Torah scroll is defective rather than *kasher*. It is to suggest that we are satisfied with an ersatz standard of Jewish practice, that appearances count more than reality, that we are perfectly content to read from a scroll that looks like—but is not—a real *sefer Torah*.[29] This is not the sort of statement that *any* Jewish community, Reform or otherwise, ought to make;[30] we should consider it an affront to the dignity of our congregation. Let us keep in mind, too, that the Czech synagogue from which this *sefer Torah* originates would never have read it publicly in its ritually unfit state. Like observant Jews everywhere, they would have done the proper thing: either to repair the scroll or to consign it lovingly to a *genizah*. It is not a little ironic that we should seek to perpetuate the memory of that community by means of an act that they themselves would have rejected as an affront to the dignity of *their* congregation.

It might be argued, of course, that our duty to remember the Shoah outweighs the need to adhere to the rules and regulations concerning the *sefer Torah*. Yet the reading from this scroll is by no means the only way for us to remember the Shoah in our ritual observance. References to the victims and the events of the Nazi persecutions figure prominently in our liturgy, in our liturgical calendar, and in our synagogue architecture and furnishings. We have frequent opportunity, in other words, to remember the Shoah, even if we do not read from this scroll. More than that: we must take great care *how* we remember the Shoah. In particular, we must not allow that memory to supersede our devotion to the laws, customs, and practices that comprise our Judaism. That the Nazis murdered millions of our brothers and sisters is a fact that has seared its way deeply into our collective consciousness, but it is no reason—indeed, it is precisely the *wrong* reason—to alter the contours and content of our religious practice. To change, detract from, or abandon essential religious observances *because* of the Shoah, to read from a *pasul* Torah scroll—something we would otherwise not do—*because* the Nazis murdered the Jews who once possessed it, is to proclaim that the crimes of Hitler take precedence over the "voice of Sinai," the proper conduct of Jewish religious life. This, too, is a statement we should not make. It is surely the wrong message to send to our young people on the day when, called to the Torah for the first time, they symbolically accept the responsibilities and commitments of Jewish adults.

We should insist, instead, that our regular weekly, Shabbat, and holiday Torah portions be read from a *sefer Torah kasher*. This is the standard bequeathed to us from Jewish tradition. This was the standard observed by the Czech community from which the scroll in question originated. And it remains the standard that informs Reform Jewish life, the standard to which we educate our children and to which we ought to aspire.

The above does not mean that the congregation should *never* read from its Czech *sefer Torah*. The point is that we should not allow the Shoah to cause us to detract from or alter the nature of our most important observances; the regular, statutory reading of the Torah, therefore, should not be accomplished from a scroll that is ritually unfit for that purpose merely because that scroll survived the Nazis. On the other hand, it is entirely permissible to *add* to the body of our observance in response to the Shoah. The institution of Yom HaShoah, a special day of memorial for the victims and the survivors of the death camps, is an obvious example of such a creative endeavor. We therefore may read from the *pasul* scroll *after* we have read the regular Torah portion for that day from a *kasher* scroll. This should be done in such a way as to distinguish it from the reading of the first scroll. The rabbi should announce that this is an additional reading, and the appropriate benedictions should *not* be recited over the *pasul* scroll. In this manner, the traditional objections to the reading from a *pasul* scroll are removed.[31] The congregation can observe the laws and customs that define the mitzvah of the reading of the Torah while at the same time honoring the memory of those who perished in the Shoah.

An overriding concern for all the members of this Committee is that the reading from the *pasul* scroll should be seen as an exceptional occurrence. The too-frequent use of this scroll would likely upset the careful balance we seek to draw between commemorating the Holocaust and focusing our people's attention upon the enduring content of Jewish life. Most of us urge that the *pasul* "Holocaust" scroll be read only on special occasions that have an obvious connection to the Shoah; the Shabbat closest to Yom HaShoah, Kristallnacht, and the *yahrzeit* (i.e., the date of the destruction) of the community from which the scroll originates are possible examples.[32] On those occasions, some of us feel that the *pasul* scroll may be used for the regular reading, with no distinctions; thus, the *b'rachot* may be recited over it.[33] Others among us hold that even on these special occasions the *pasul* scroll should be used only for an "additional" reading (that is, not the statutory portion for the day) and that no *b'rachot* should be recited over it.[34] All of us agree, however, that the *pasul* scroll should not be read every week.

Conclusion. A congregation may read from a *sefer Torah pasul* in remembrance of the Shoah. This should be done, however, only on appropriate special occasions, and then in such a way as to emphasize that the reading of the Torah ought to be accomplished from a scroll that is, in all respects, a proper *sefer Torah*.

> —CCAR Responsa Committee, "A Defective 'Holocaust' Scroll," CCAR responsum 5760.3, in *Reform Responsa for the Twenty-First Century: Sh'eilot Ut'shovot*, ed. Mark Washofsky (New York: CCAR Press, 2010), 2:59–70.

NOTES

1. The rules concerning the honor due to the *sefer Torah* are summarized in *Shulchan Aruch, Yoreh Dei-ah* 282.
2. The chief expression of this duty is the observance of Yom HaShoah. "It is a mitzvah to remember the six million Jews who were murdered in the Shoah by attending special memorial services" (*Gates of the Seasons*, ed. Peter S. Knobel [New York: CCAR Press, 1983], 102–3). See *CCAR Yearbook* 87 (1987): 87.
3. *Mishneh Torah, Sefer Torah* 10:1.
4. Babylonian Talmud, *K'tubot* 19b; *Mishneh Torah, Sefer Torah* 7:12; *Shulchan Aruch, Yoreh Dei-ah* 279:1.
5. Babylonian Talmud, *M'gillah* 26a; *Mishneh Torah, Sefer Torah* 10:1; *Shulchan Aruch, Yoreh Dei-ah* 282:10.
6. A *Chumash* here refers to one of the five books of the Pentateuch, written as a separate scroll; Babylonian Talmud, *Gittin* 60a, and Rashi s.v. *bachumashin*; *Mishneh Torah, Sefer Torah* 7:14 and *Kesef Mishneh* ad loc.
7. *Mishneh Torah, Sefer Torah* 10:1.
8. Babylonian Talmud, *Gittin* 60a: *ein korin bachumashin b'veit hak'neset mishum k'vod tzibur.*
9. The responsum is found in the traditional collections of Rambam's *t'shuvot* (*P'eir*

HaDor, 9, and *Kovetz T'shuvot HaRambam*, no. 15) as well as in both of the two twentieth-century critical editions: *T'shuvot HaRambam*, ed. Aron Freimann (Jerusalem: Mekitzei Nirdamim, 1934), no. 43; and *T'shuvot HaRambam*, ed. Yehoshua Blau, vol. 2 (Jerusalem: Mekitzei Nirdamim, 1960), no. 294.

10. The blessings surrounding the Torah reading, Rambam writes, differ from those we recite over such mitzvot as sukkah and *lulav*. In those instances, should the object itself be *pasul* we would not recite the appropriate *b'rachah*, because "the mitzvah is the taking of a *lulav* or the dwelling in a sukkah, and the blessing is recited over those objects. Should they be ritually unfit [i.e., should they not meet the requirements for a valid *lulav* or sukkah], one does not perform the mitzvah [when using them]." The blessing would therefore be an improper one, a *b'rachah l'vatalah*. By contrast, the blessings surrounding the Torah reading are said over the reading and *not* over the Torah scroll itself.

11. See *Shulchan Aruch*, *Orach Chayim* 47:5, which lists the three *b'rachot* recited during the beginning of the morning service (*Birchot HaShachar*) over the study of Torah. Our own prayer book omits the third of these blessings, *asher bachar banu*; see *Gates of Prayer* (New York: CCAR Press, 1975), 52.

12. Babylonian Talmud, *Gittin* 60a.

13. Rambam's reason for saying this is not altogether clear. Presumably, he means that a *Chumash*, unlike other "defective" scrolls, does not even resemble a proper *sefer Torah*.

14. This is especially true of Rabbi Sh'lomo ben Adret (Rashba; Barcelona, d. 1310), whose ruling is not found in the extant collection of his responsa but is cited at length in two early fourteenth-century works—*Orchot Chayim*, *Sefer Torah*, no. 5 and *Kol Bo*, 13b-c—and referenced by the fifteenth-century Rabbi Yosef Kolon (*Responsa Maharik*, no. 69) and Rabbi Sh'lomo ben Shimon Duran (*Responsa Rashbash*, no. 11) and the sixteenth-century Rabbi Yosef Karo (*Beit Yosef*, *Orach Chayim* 143).

15. This, says Rashba see note 14), is derived by the Talmud's language concerning the defective scroll: *ein korin bo*, "it is not to be read (before the congregation)"; this, he argues, implies an absolute disqualification and not, as Rambam thinks, a provisional disqualification to be waived when no other scroll is available. See also *Responsa Rashba* 1:487. Moreover, the same language—*ein korin bo* or *al yikra bo*— is used in Tractate *Sof'rim* with respect to a *sefer pasul*, and the disqualification there appears to be absolute. See, e.g., *Sof'rim* 3:7 and 9.

16. Rabbinic tradition holds that the formal, public Torah reading was established by Moses and Ezra through a series of *takanot*, or legislative enactments. See Babylonian Talmud, *Bava Kama* 82a and *Mishneh Torah*, *T'filah* 11:1.

17. This argument is less than airtight. Maimonides could respond that, if the reading is *supposed* to be carried out from a scroll *mishum k'vod tzibur*, "due to the dignity of the congregation," this does not imply that a reading done without the scroll is not valid *b'diavad*, or "after the fact." Yet Rashba makes the point that if the Rabbis ordain that blessings be recited over the performance of a mitzvah, they should be said *only* when that mitzvah is carried out in its intended form; thus, the *b'rachot*

should not be said over anything but a proper (*kasher*) Torah scroll.

18. See Babylonian Talmud, *Gittin* 60a: while *Chumashim* are not read in the synagogue because of "the dignity of the congregation" (implying that the congregation may waive its "dignity" and allow the reading to take place), a defective scroll is simply "not read" (*ein korin bo*), presumably even if the reading would not offend the congregation's dignity.

19. See Babylonian Talmud, *Bava Batra* 15a, on Deuteronomy 31:26, and Rabbi Yosef Karo, *Kesef Mishneh* to *Mishneh Torah, T'fillin* 1:2.

20. Thus, according to "most" opinions (*daat rov haposkim; Mishnah B'rurah* 143:13), when an error is discovered in a *sefer Torah* during the congregational reading, the reading must be repeated from a *kasher* scroll from the beginning of that day's appointed section. See Rabbi Asher ben Yechiel, *Responsa HaRosh* 3:8; and *Migdal Oz* to *Mishneh Torah, T'fillin* 1:2, in the name of Rabbi Meir Abulafia, Rabbi Avraham ben David of Posquières, Ramban, and Rashba. This rule is not universally accepted; see below, note 26.

21. Thus Rashba (cited at note 14) proposes that the responsum represents the opinion of Maimonides "in his youth," while the *Mishneh Torah* expresses his more considered and mature viewpoint. Rashbash (cited at note 14) raises the possibility that Rambam is not the actual author of the responsum. He writes that, inasmuch as we cannot be certain that the *t'shuvah* was in fact written by Rambam ("is his signature upon it?"), it is wiser to follow the opinion of the *Mishneh Torah*, of which his authorship is not doubted.

22. The word *l'chat'chilah*, a technical term of Jewish law, signifies the optimal standard of observance, the practice that *ought* to be followed if one has a choice. Yet if an individual or community cannot adhere to that standard, they can still fulfill the requirements of the mitzvah provided that they have met the minimally acceptable standard of observance (*b'diavad*).

23. That is, although a congregation's "honor" dictates that it should not read from a ritually unfit Torah scroll, the reading therefrom is not invalid; otherwise, it would be unacceptable even *b'diavad*, as a "minimally acceptable" standard. The wording of *Mishneh Torah, Sefer Torah* 10:1 suggests that Rambam, unlike Rashba, draws no distinction between the *Chumash* and the defective scroll on this point; see at note 18.

24. This line of thought is indicated by none other than Rashba in a responsum (1:805). The Talmud (Babylonian Talmud, *Gittin* 60a) declares that we do not read from *Chumashim* on the grounds that to do so affronts the dignity of the congregation. This implies that, as a matter of technical law, it is permitted to perform the public reading from a *Chumash* (*min hadin mutar*), though by all means a proper *sefer Torah* ought to be used. See also Rabbi Yoel Sirkes (seventeenth-century Poland), *Responsa HaBach HaChadashot*, no. 42.

25. See *Magen Avraham* to *Shulchan Aruch, Orach Chayim* 143:2, and see note 31, below.

26. In addition, Rambam's "rejected" *t'shuvah* retains a great deal of influence over Jewish ritual practice. See *Shulchan Aruch, Orach Chayim* 143:4 and *Yoreh Dei-ah*

279:2: if an error is found in the text of a *Sefer Torah* during the reading, another scroll is brought from the ark and the reading continues from the place in the text where the error was found. In other words, that part of the reading already performed from the *pasul* scroll "counts" toward the fulfillment of the mitzvah. This ruling is, on the surface, a curious one: if a Torah scroll is ritually unfit, it stands to reason that none of its text can be utilized for the performance of the mitzvah. That, indeed, is the opinion of "most" authorities (see note 19). Rabbi Yosef Karo, who notes that this custom originated with his colleague Rabbi Yaakov Berav of Safed, justifies it on the basis of Rambam's *t'shuvah*: "even though we do not follow Rambam's ruling, we rely upon it after the fact in order to accept the reading" that was already performed from the *sefer Torah pasul* (*Beit Yosef, Yoreh Dei-ah* 279).

27. On the tendency of Reform responsa to seek the "liberally affirmative" answer, see *Reform Responsa*, 23. For a more recent, systematic account of the principles of liberal halachah, see Rabbi Moshe Zemer, *Evolving Halachah* (Woodstock, VT: Jewish Lights, 1999).

28. This is not to say that we are forbidden to read the Torah portion from a printed *Chumash* during our services. Sometimes, there is no alternative to doing so; see note 31, below. But the act of reading from a printed *Chumash*, however valuable in and of itself, does *not* meet the definition of the act of *k'riat haTorah*. That mitzvah, a ritual observance that meets its own particular requirements, is accomplished only through the reading from a *sefer Torah*.

29. See at note 19, above.

30. On the use of "substitutes" for ritual observance, see "A Non-Traditional Sukkah," CCAR responsum 5755.4, in *Teshuvot for the Nineties*, 91–96, https://www.ccarnet.org/ccar-responsa/tfn-no-5755-4-91-96/.

31. It is not forbidden to read in public from a non-*kasher* Torah scroll; the point is that such a reading does not fulfill the mitzvah of *k'riat haTorah*. The blessings, which pertain to that mitzvah, are therefore inappropriate. It follows that to read from the scroll without pronouncing the blessings is permitted, so long as we do not think we are fulfilling the mitzvah thereby. See Isserles, *Orach Chayim* 143:2 and *Magen Avraham* ad loc.: a community that does not possess a *sefer Torah kasher* may read from a printed *Chumash* provided that the blessings are not recited. And see *P'ri Megadim* to *Orach Chayim* 143, Eshel Avraham no. 2: "In a community too small to gather a minyan, perhaps it is proper to read from the *sefer Torah* without the accompanying *b'rachot*, so that the practice of *k'riat haTorah* not be forgotten."

32. There are others. Our colleague Rabbi David Lilienthal, of the Liberal Jewish congregation in Amsterdam, reports that his community reads from its own *pasul* "Shoah" Torah scroll on two occasions during the year: Shabbat Zachor (Deuteronomy 25:17–19, "Remember what Amalek did to you...") and Shabbat Shuvah (Deuteronomy 32, *Parashat Haazinu*).

33. Here following the theory of Rambam's responsum: the reading from a *sefer Torah pasul* does fulfill the mitzvah of *k'riat haTorah*, and the reading from it on these special occasions is not to be considered an affront to the congregation's "honor."

34. On the grounds that even on these special occasions the congregation should

respond to the Shoah by observing this mitzvah in the form that we generally think proper. The *pasul* scroll, though used for the "additional" reading, will still leave a moving impression upon the congregation.

CHAPTER 5: THE CHANGING REFORM "MOOD"
Three Responsa on Shabbat

Responsum 1: Gift Corner Open on the Sabbath

SH'EILAH:

The congregational gift corner provides books and prayer books, candles and candlesticks, Chanukah menorahs; in other words, it serves a religious purpose. Should this fact not justify keeping the gift corner open on Friday night? It is only on Friday night that large numbers of people coming for the Sabbath service can conveniently make use of the gift corner. (Rabbi David Polish, Chicago, Illinois)

T'SHUVAH:

This question would evoke a complete and immediate negative from an Orthodox rabbi. There cannot possibly be any way of justifying by traditional law any of the processes involved in keeping the gift corner open after sundown on Friday evening. It is unnecessary to enumerate the various prohibited actions that would be involved, such as writing down orders, receiving money, giving change, and carrying purchased objects home from the synagogue. Thus, the question is so simple in Orthodoxy that it would not even be asked.

But in a Reform (and for that matter in a Conservative) congregation the question is no longer simple and may well be inquired into and considered. The Sabbath laws of prohibited work are no longer clear with us. They are undergoing constant change. As far as the rather undefined mood of Reform is concerned, certain Sabbath prohibitions have simply ceased to be actual among us. No one in a Reform community considers it a violation of the spirit of Judaism to ride to the temple on the Sabbath and to drive the car oneself, nor is it violative of our feelings to carry objects on the Sabbath from one place (*reshus*) to another. No one objects to the cooking of food on the Sabbath, nor for that matter, if it became necessary, to the purchasing of food. These things are no longer contrary to our general Sabbath mood. But there is a difference between us and the Conservatives on this matter, although they generally are equally nonobservant with regard to these Sabbath laws. The Conservatives might try to reestablish the observance of these laws or, failing that, they would make a strong effort to find a legal justification for the new situation. Clearly, our attitude is different. Generally we feel that those observances that are gone cannot now be easily restored. The effort to restore them would require an overemphasis on ritual matters. However, what we can preserve, and without too much overemphasis restore as a natural mood of the people, that we would endeavor to do.

Therefore we are justified in making a distinction between what the people do outside the temple with regard to Jewish observance and what we would permit on the Sabbath or on other occasions on the temple premises. Thus, for example, while people do drink liquor at home and at parties, many congregations do not permit hard liquor at temple celebrations. There is, indeed, an inconsistency in this, but that is due to the fact that we want the temple to be an example and an influence in certain special directions. The people readily recognize that certain types of celebrations or observances that they follow elsewhere are not appropriate at the temple. It is from this point of view that we must consider the question of keeping the gift corner open on Friday night.

Is there any justification for this particular enterprise being open on the Sabbath in the temple? Is any sort of business permitted in the temple on the Sabbath? We know, for example, that it is a long tradition that certain of the privileges with regard to taking out and being called to the Torah were not only sold, but auctioned off at the highest price during the service itself. No one has strongly objected to this procedure. It has had many defenders (see the entire discussion in the CCAR responsum "Congregational Meeting on the Sabbath"). The reason that this auctioning of *mitzvos* could become so established as a fixed custom is due to a clear distinction made in the Talmud (Babylonian Talmud, *Shabbat* 150a) between personal business and public business, especially with regard to the money needed for charity and for communal good. The Talmud calls attention to the fact that Isaiah (58:13) warns against "pursuing thy business" (that is, one's own private affairs) on the Sabbath. Therefore, it concludes, we may make money calculations for a mitzvah, we may determine on money matters relating to charity for the poor on the Sabbath, and we may go to the synagogue to supervise the affairs of the community on the Sabbath. This permission to discuss matters involving money is codified as a law by Maimonides (*Hilchot Shabbat* 24:5) and by

Joseph Karo and Isserles in *Shulchan Aruch* (*Orach Chayim* 306:6).

Is the gift corner, or Judaica shop, to be considered a business for "the benefit of the community," which is permitted on the Sabbath? To a large extent it is. The providing of prayer books, menorahs, candlesticks, and books of Jewish study certainly promotes the observance of our religion. Even the purchase of nonreligious objects contributes to the income of the Sisterhood and not only makes possible its own work, but helps provide contributions from the Sisterhood to building funds and to general maintenance. The gift corner may therefore be considered to be the type of public work that is permitted on the Sabbath. However, even in the public work that is permitted by the law, the definitely prohibited actions, such as handling of money, et cetera, were of course never permitted (see *Maggid Mishnah* to the law in Maimonides, cited above). What, then, is the good of permitting the opening of the gift corner if the transactions involved are violative of the mood of the Sabbath, especially in the synagogue?

Of course, if there is no particular pressure for the opening of the gift corner on Friday night, the simplest thing is to keep it closed. But since the question has been asked, it is evident that there are some in the congregation who would like it open and, very likely, some others who have certain objections to its being open. The solution, therefore, must be a matter of judgment, depending upon the mood of the particular congregations involved. It would seem that the best procedure, under our present vague relationship with the Sabbath laws, would be somewhat as follows:

The gift corner may well be kept open, but a clear distinction should be made between its management on the Sabbath and on other days of the week. On Sunday, when parents bring their children to Sunday school, on weekdays when there are sewing groups and other meetings, the gift corner is open for complete business as any other place of business. On the Sabbath, however, although the gift corner is open, there should be no exchange of money, but people may come in to select what they want. People do that all the time in department stores; they choose what they want, and delivery and payment come later. It is not likely that the business of selecting and ordering in the gift corner will be so great and complex that it cannot be carried in mind by the committee members, and matters of delivery and payment can easily be arranged.

This distinction between the gift corner's procedure on the Sabbath and on weekdays would rather tend to strengthen the consciousness of the Sabbath in the lives of our people. It would serve to remind them of the Sabbath traditions and perhaps influence them to do less purchasing in general on the Sabbath, whenever such self-restraint is practical.

—Rabbi Solomon B. Freehof, "Gift Corner Open on the Sabbath," in *Reform Responsa* (Cincinnati: Hebrew Union College Press, 1960), 51–55.

Responsum 2: Delayed *B'rit Milah* on Shabbat

SH'EILAH:

The *b'rit milah* of a newborn baby was delayed past his eighth day. His parents now wish to schedule that ceremony on a Shabbat, since Shabbat is a day when family and friends can attend the *simchah*. According to tradition, a delayed *b'rit milah* may not take place on Shabbat. Is that the position of Reform Judaism as well? (Rabbi Eric Slaton, Lexington, Kentucky)

T'SHUVAH:

This question, as we understand it, concerns the nature and standing of both *b'rit milah* and Shabbat as they are observed or ought to be observed in our communities. Is the celebration of the mitzvah of circumcision, truly a powerful Jewish moment, so important and central that it should supersede the restrictions that customarily define Shabbat? Or does the reverence we accord Shabbat demand that other mitzvot, should they interfere with its observance, be set aside? Our answer will consist of two parts: first, a brief survey of the halachah on the timing of the *b'rit milah*, and second, a look at the issue from the standpoint of our own Reform Jewish tradition.

Milah on Shabbat in Jewish Law. The Torah states twice that the ritual circumcision (*b'rit milah*) of a Jewish boy is performed at the age of eight days (Genesis 17:12 and Leviticus 12:3). The latter verse reads, "On the eighth day [*uvayom hash'mini*] the flesh of his foreskin shall be circumcised," from which the Rabbis deduce that the circumcision must take place *on that very day*, even if it happens to fall on Shabbat.[1] The traditional expression is *milah biz'manah dochah Shabbat*, "circumcision at its proper time supersedes the Shabbat": that is, we do the procedure even though it requires actions that otherwise violate the prohibitions against doing work (*m'lachah*) on the Sabbath. It follows that a circumcision done prior to or later than a boy's eighth day (*milah shelo biz'manah*) does not supersede the Shabbat and may not take place on that day.[2]

Of particular interest is the precise way in which circumcision at its proper time may take place on Shabbat. The Mishnah records a famous dispute over the issue.[3] According to Rabbi Eliezer, since one is permitted to perform the circumcision itself, one may also perform a variety of other actions normally prohibited on Shabbat in order to prepare for the *milah*. Thus, one may carry the *izmil*, the mohel's knife, through the public thoroughfare; one may even make a knife if none is available. Rabbi Akiva, however, forbids these actions according to his rule: any labor that could have been performed before Shabbat does not supersede Shabbat, and any labor that could *not* have been performed earlier does supersede Shabbat. Thus, it is forbidden to carry or prepare the knife on Shabbat, even though the circumcision cannot be performed without it, since the knife could have been brought the day before. The halachah follows Rabbi Akiva's more stringent position.[4] And through that determination, the tradition teaches an important point: though the performance of a mitzvah may entitle us to take actions that normally violate Shabbat, we are to keep those actions to a minimum.[5] Even if it is the day of a boy's circumcision, it remains Shabbat for the entire community; Shabbat continues to make its legitimate demands upon the Jew, demands that cannot be ignored or forgotten.[6]

Reform Approaches. This committee has consistently held to this position in questions that have come before us. Like Rabbi Akiva, we have held that Shabbat is a sacred span of time, an institution of Jewish life that makes its own legitimate demands upon us. The fact that Shabbat "conflicts" with another mitzvah or worthy cause does not mean that it is *Shabbat* that must give way. Indeed, the reverse is often the case. Put differently, Shabbat is more than merely a good day on which to schedule good deeds. It is *Shabbat kodesh*, a *holy* day; we do not violate or trespass upon it, even for the sake of mitzvot, unless those mitzvot must be performed on it.

In 1977, for example, the committee was asked whether weddings might take place on Shabbat or festivals. Theoretically, there might be any number of practical reasons why a couple would wish to schedule their wedding on Shabbat, and one could even argue that, as a holy day, Shabbat is an especially meet time to hold the ceremony of marriage, which is in our tradition an act of consecration (*kiddushin*). Yet the committee, concerned with "the sanctity of Shabbat as understood and encouraged by the Reform Movement," recommended that the traditional prohibition against weddings on that day be maintained. "We encourage our members to make Shabbat a 'special' day upon which we do not carry out duties and acts performed on other days. Countenancing marriages on Shabbat would detract from this objective and weaken our efforts."[7] In 1986 and again in 1993, the Responsa Committee declared that Reform synagogue groups ought not to participate in *tzedakah* projects, such as the building of houses for the poor, that take place on Shabbat. Although the importance of social action in Reform Jewish thought can hardly be overstated, the importance of Shabbat as a refuge from activity defined as work is also a sacred value to us. Since the *tzedakah* work is not an emergency and since it could be performed on another day, it ought to take place on a day other than Shabbat.[8] Our attitude has been similar with respect to *b'rit milah*. We have ruled that circumcision ought to take place on the eighth day, even if another day might be more convenient to the family.[9] And we have recommended that a *b'rit milah* not be scheduled at night, inasmuch as tradition calls for circumcision to be performed only in the daytime.[10] In these cases, we have argued that *b'rit milah* is to be distinguished from "circumcision." The latter is a mere surgical procedure; the former is a ritual act whose parameters are discerned in the rules set down in the Jewish tradition. It is precisely when we conduct it according to those rules that we transform the surgical procedure into a religious observance.

There are times, of course, when *b'rit milah* must occur on Shabbat. This, however, is not one of those times. We recognize that it would be more convenient for the family to schedule their son's circumcision on Shabbat. But if convenience is the only justification for their request, it is, in our view, an insufficient reason to accede to it. If we are serious, as we say we are, about keeping Shabbat and observing *b'rit milah* within our Reform communities, we have no choice but to respect and revere the lines that define them as religious acts.

—CCAR Responsa Committee, "Delayed *B'rit Milah* on Shabbat," CCAR responsum 5755.12, in *Teshuvot for the Nineties: Reform Judaism's Answers for Today's Dilemmas*, ed. W. Gunther Plaut and Mark Washofsky (New York: CCAR Press, 1997), 165–68.

NOTES
1.   Babylonian Talmud, *Shabbat* 132a. The word *uvayom* seems superfluous; the verse would bear the same sense had it read *uvash'mini*. The Rabbis reason, therefore, that the word comes to teach another detail, i.e., "on that day, even Shabbat."

2.   *Mishneh Torah, Hilchot Milah* 1:9; *Shulchan Aruch, Yoreh Dei-ah* 266:2.

3.   *Mishnah Shabbat* 19:1.

4.   See note 2.

5.   Similarly, when one needs to eat or drink on Yom Kippur, "we feed him little by little," i.e., the minimal amount necessary to sustain him, so as to avoid a wholesale abandonment of the commandment to fast on that day; *Hilchot HaRosh, Mishnah Yoma* 8:13; *Shulchan Aruch, Orach Chayim* 618:7-8.

6.   For the sake of thoroughness, it should be noted that even Rabbi Eliezer, who assumes a more lenient position in the mishnah, would answer our *sh'eilah* in the negative. The circumcision may not take place on Shabbat, since that is not the child's eighth day.

7.   "Marriage on Shabbat or *Yom Tov*," in *American Reform Responsa*, 412-15; see Marc Dov Shapiro, ed., *Gates of Shabbat: A Guide for Observing Shabbat* (New York: CCAR Press, 1991), 58. The latter work, in particular, is evidence of our rabbinate's commitment to the observance of Shabbat as a holy day within Reform communities.

8.   The responsa are, respectively, "Poverty Project and Shabbat," in *Contemporary American Reform Responsa*, 265-67, and "Communal Work on Shabbat," CCAR responsum 5753.22, in *Teshuvot for the Nineties*, 169-70.

9.   "Circumcision Other Than the Eighth Day of Birth," in *American Reform Responsa*, 143-44; "Circumcision Prior to the Eighth Day," in *American Reform Responsa*, 145-46.

10. See Babylonian Talmud, *M'gillah* 20a, *Y'vamot* 72b; *Mishneh Torah, Hilchot Milah* 1:8; *Shulchan Aruch, Orach Chayim* 262:1; "*Berit Milah* in the Evening," in *Questions and Reform Jewish Answers*, 159-61.

Responsum 3: Presenting a Check for *Tzedakah* at Shabbat Services

SH'EILAH:

Our congregation plans a special Shabbat service to honor the work of a charitable agency. As we have raised funds for that cause, we wonder whether it would be permissible to give a check to a representative of that agency during the service. (Rabbi Lawrence Englander, Mississauga, Ontario)

T'SHUVAH:

The observance of Shabbat is a complex and challenging issue for Reform Jews. On the one hand, we dispense in our practice with many of the traditional prohibitions associated with the day. Put differently, we tend to be more comfortable with *zachor*, the various rituals that enable us to "remember" the Sabbath, than with *shamor*, the requirement that we refrain from a multitude of activities as the proper means to "observe" the Sabbath. On the other hand, it is inaccurate to say that we Reform Jews have no concept of Shabbat observance. The seventh day is for us, as it is for other Jews, *Shabbat kodesh*, a sacred time, possessing a character that differentiates it from other days. An inescapable component of this sanctity is the recognition that certain activities ought not to be performed on Shabbat, for to indulge in them would violate the essence and spirit of the holy day as we perceive these to be. Our list of "forbidden activities" may differ from and be markedly smaller than that maintained by the traditional halachah, but the spirit behind these prohibitions demonstrates that we regard the issue of Shabbat observance with the utmost seriousness.[1]

In the case before us, we are asked whether a congregational gift to *tzedakah* is one of these "forbidden activities." The *sh'eilah* demands that we balance a traditional observance, that which prohibits the making of gifts on Shabbat, against an action which reflects a community's commitment to social justice, one of the highest values in Reform Jewish thought. Is the making of this donation compatible with our conception of Shabbat observance? The answer to this question requires that we consider the nature of the halachic prohibition, the extent to which it continues to speak to us as Reform Jews, and the possibility that a gift to *tzedakah* counts for us as an exception to the rules laid down by Jewish law and tradition.

1. *Commercial Activity (Sale and Gift) on Shabbat.* Although buying and selling (*mekach umimkar*) are not numbered among the thirty-nine categories of work (*m'lachah*) prohibited on Shabbat,[2] commercial activity is nonetheless forbidden on that day.[3] The authorities differ over the textual basis of this rule. Some trace it to biblical verses, whether Isaiah 58:13 ("if you refrain from trampling the Sabbath, from pursuing your affairs on My holy day . . . if you honor it and go not your ways, nor look to your affairs . . ."),[4] Nehemiah 13:15–22,[5] or Leviticus 23:24.[6] Others explain the prohibition as a Rabbinic ordinance (*sh'vut*), a preventive measure aimed at reducing the temptation to write on the Sabbath.[7] In any event, the sources agree that business transactions are prohibited, not because they constitute "work" but because they violate the spirit of Shabbat. The making of a gift is also prohibited on Shabbat on the grounds that, since it involves a transfer of ownership, it is analogous to buying and selling.[8]

In declaring these acts forbidden, the halachic sources teach us that the observance of Shabbat is much more than the mere abstinence from that which is formally defined as "work." Shabbat, as idea and experience, demands that we separate ourselves from other inappropriate preoccupations as well. In the words of one commentator, "Although the Torah prohibits the various kinds of work [*m'lachot*] in all their details, a person might still toil all day long at those things that do not fall into that category. It is to forestall this possibility that the Torah says: 'you shall rest.'"[9] The Rabbis, that is to say, acting at the Torah's behest, prohibit on Shabbat a number of activities that, though not *m'lachah*, are deemed incompatible with the nature of the day. Commercial transactions clearly fall under this rubric. They may not transgress, in a formal sense, the prohibition against "work." Yet they are prohibited because they comprise a realm of effort, of striving after gain, which is out of place on a day devoted to holiness, destructive of the goal of *m'nuchah*, of Shabbat rest and spiritual renewal.[10]

The prohibition against the giving of gifts is not absolute. One may make a gift on Shabbat or on a festival in an indirect manner, through a variety of legal devices that allow one to avoid transgressing the letter of the law. Thus, one may formally transfer the ownership of the item to the recipient prior to the onset of Shabbat, even though the recipient takes physical possession of it on Shabbat itself. Alternately, one may instruct the recipient not to intend to assume ownership of the gift until after Shabbat has ended.[11] Moreover, under certain circumstances it is entirely permissible to make a gift directly on Shabbat. These include gifts made "for the sake of Shabbat or the festival" or "for the sake of a mitzvah."[12] An example of this is the act by which a person gives his *lulav* to another so that the other may fulfill the mitzvah of *n'tilat lulav* on the first day of Sukkot.[13] Similarly, since it is a mitzvah to rejoice with the bride and groom, we give them gifts on the Shabbat during their wedding week.[14] And no less an authority than Rabbi Moshe Sofer permits a congregation to give a gift to a rabbi on Shabbat, "for this honors the Torah and glorifies the mitzvah."[15] Yet the tradition does not extend this permissive line to gifts of money. While a community may discuss matters of *tzedakah* and other public business and even decide upon *tzedakah* appropriations on Shabbat,[16] it is nonetheless forbidden to make monetary donations, even to a worthy cause, on that day.[17]

2. *Shabbat Observance and Reform Judaism.* Does this prohibition apply to our case, in the context of a contemporary Reform congregation? A good argument can be made that it does not. It is well-known, after all,

that Reform Judaism does not strictly observe the traditional prohibitions connected with the Sabbath. While we accept the traditional conception of Shabbat as a day on which we "rest" and do no manner of "work," we do not believe that the structure of m'lachah and sh'vut framed by the ancient Rabbis represents the final word on Jewish practice. We exercise the freedom to continue their work for our own time, to "develop definitions of work and rest that resonate with the needs of contemporary Jews."[18] We may set aside the traditional prohibitions when we find them irrelevant to our conception of Shabbat or when we believe that the sanctity of the day will be nurtured and encouraged thereby.

If so, why should a Reform Jew or congregation be prevented from making a charitable donation on Shabbat? We have already seen that the halachic tradition permits gifts on Shabbat when these enhance the day's holiness or when they enable us to perform a mitzvah. In the case before us, the gift is to be made to tzedakah, surely one of the most exalted of the mitzvot. Tzedakah, moreover, plays a vital and central role in the practice of Reform Judaism, which has distinguished itself by its dedication to the cause of social justice. A gift to tzedakah in the context of a worship service would serve to strengthen in our congregants the sense of holiness and the commitment to Jewish life. Thus, while halachah prohibits the transfer of money on Shabbat, this prohibition should perhaps be waived when the recipient of the money is a person or organization that will use it for the sake of tikkun olam.

Yet this argument fails to register the other side of our attitude toward religious observance. Though we are free to depart from traditional practices, we are not free to ignore them altogether. The tradition serves us as an indispensable starting point, the standard by which we measure our perception of "the needs of contemporary Jews" against the collective religious experience of the Jewish people throughout its history. It is our goal "to balance our creativity in practice with the desire to conserve and adapt what speaks to us from the past."[19] This conception implies that we are not neutral and dispassionate in our attitude toward traditional standards of practice. Rather, we seek actively and affirmatively to "conserve" and to "adapt" those traditions whenever possible. In practical terms, traditional observances ought to enjoy a considerable presumptive weight in our thinking. As liberal Jews who seek affirm our connection to our people in all lands and all ages, we should maintain the traditional practice in the absence of a compelling reason to abandon or alter it.[20]

The Responsa Committee has long followed this approach with respect to questions on the observance of Shabbat. We have stressed time and again that Shabbat is a mitzvah in its own right, one that makes its own legitimate demands upon us, demands that often take precedence over other worthy causes.[21] We maintain the prohibition against performing weddings and funerals on the Sabbath, even though both of these ceremonies enjoy the status of mitzvah in the Jewish tradition.[22] We strongly discourage the scheduling of congregational meetings and synagogue fundraising projects on that day, even though it is a mitzvah to support the community.[23] In each of these cases, we have found that the traditional practice expresses a sense of the sanctity of Shabbat that maintains its attraction to Reform Jews. We have therefore favored that practice over an alternative, more "innovative" standard.

We have also urged that social action and *tzedakah* projects involving traditionally prohibited labor not be held on Shabbat. *Tzedakah* is indeed a mitzvah, but then, so is the observance of Shabbat; and generally, "we do not perform a true mitzvah if it is done by transgressing another command."[24] In light of our movement's increasing efforts during recent decades to strengthen Shabbat observance among our people,[25] we must acknowledge that while a social action project may be scheduled on a weekday, "the seventh day is the Sabbath; it belongs to *Adonai* your God" (Exodus 20:10; Deuteronomy 5:14). Shabbat is not simply a day on which we do good deeds. It is *Shabbat kodesh*, a holy day, a refuge from many of the activities associated with the weekday world of building and planting, sowing and reaping, getting and spending. We do not trespass upon Shabbat, even for the sake of mitzvot, unless those mitzvot must be performed on that very day.

Conclusion. In the case before us, we would ask a simple question: must the donation be made to the charitable organization on Shabbat? Clearly, the answer is "no." This is not an emergency situation; there is no consideration of *pikuach nefesh* (the saving of a life) that demands an immediate response. We see no reason why the gift cannot be made, and do just as much good, on Friday or Sunday. It is true that a gift to *tzedakah* does not count as a "commercial activity" and is therefore less offensive to our religious sensibilities than an ordinary business transaction. Still, we doubt that any good purpose is served by abandoning the traditional prohibition against the transfer of money on the Sabbath. Indeed, the opposite is the case. By not making the gift at the service, by pointedly calling attention to the fact that we do not transfer money on this day, we remind our community that Shabbat is a holy day, a day set aside for the pursuit of its own very special purposes.

The congregation may by all means devote the theme of its Shabbat services to *tzedakah* or to the work of the organization in question. And a representative of the congregation may certainly announce that a gift has been made (or will be made at the conclusion of the Sabbath) to the agency. In this way, the community can achieve its goal of instilling and reinforcing the value of *tzedakah* in its members. And by not making the actual donation at the service, it can demonstrate its commitment to another, no less important value: that Shabbat, no less than *tzedakah*, is a mitzvah in its own right.

—CCAR Responsa Committee, "Presenting a Check for *Tzedakah* at Shabbat Services," CCAR responsum 5756.4, in *Reform Responsa for the Twenty-First Century: Sh'eilot Ut'shuvot*, ed. Mark Washofsky (New York: CCAR Press, 2010), 1:33–40.

NOTES

1. For an attempt to define a Reform Jewish approach to the prohibition against "work" on Shabbat, see Marc Dov Shapiro, ed., *Gates of Shabbat: A Guide for Observing Shabbat* (New York: CCAR Press, 1991), 49–59.
2. *Mishnah Shabbat* 7:2.
3. *Shulchan Aruch, Orach Chayim* 306:1ff.
4. Babylonian Talmud, *Shabbat* 113a–b; *Tosafot*, 113b, s.v. *shelo*; Babylonian Talmud, *Beitzah* 37a, and Rashi, s.v. *mishum mekach umimkar*; *Aruch HaShulchan, Orach Chayim* 306:17.
5. Rashi, Babylonian Talmud, *Beitzah* 27b, s.v. *ein poskin damim*.
6. Nachmanides to the verse.
7. *Mishneh Torah, Hilchot Shabbat* 23:12; Rashi, Babylonian Talmud, *Beitzah* 37a, s.v. *mishum mekach umimkar*, second explanation; *Mishnah B'rurah* 306:32.
8. *Mishneh Torah, Hilchot M'chirah* 30:7.
9. *Magid Mishneh* to *Mishneh Torah, Hilchot Shabbat* 21:1, Maimonides' citation of Exodus 23:12: "Six days shall you occupy yourself with all your affairs [*maasecha*], but on the seventh day you shall rest."
10. See Nachmanides to Leviticus 23:24, who derives this point from the word *shabbaton*.
11. In this fashion some authorities permitted the giving of gifts to a boy on the day of his bar mitzvah celebration. See Rabbi Y'hudah Aszod (nineteenth-century Hungary), *Responsa Y'hudah Yaaleh, Orach Chayim*, no. 83; Rabbi Yechiel Yaakov Weinberg (twentieth-century Germany and Switzerland), *Responsa S'ridei Eish* 2:26, and Rabbi Yonah Metzger (twentieth-century Israel), *Responsa Miyam HaHalachah* 2:80.
12. *L'tzorech mitzvah; Beit Yosef, Orach Chayim* 527, in the name of the *Mordechai*;

Magen Avraham, Orach Chayim 306:15; *Mishnah B'rurah* 306:33; *Aruch HaShul-chan, Orach Chayim* 306:17.

13. See Leviticus 23:40 (*ul'kachtem lachem*) and Babylonian Talmud, *Sukkah* 41b; *Shulchan Aruch, Orach Chayim* 658:3–4: on the first day of Sukkot, one fulfills the mitzvah only with one's own *lulav*, not a borrowed one.

14. *Aruch HaShulchan, Orach Chayim* 306:17.

15. *Hagahot HaChatam Sofer* (eighteenth- to nineteenth-century Hungary), *Shulchan Aruch, Orach Chayim* 306, to *Taz*, no. 2.

16. Isaiah 58:13 (see at note 4, above) is understood as prohibiting us from pursuing our own affairs on Shabbat; the pursuit of "heaven's business" (*tzedakah*, the pub-lic welfare), by contrast, is permitted. Babylonian Talmud, *Shabbat* 150a; *Shulchan Aruch, Orach Chayim* 306:6.

17. See *Shulchan Aruch, Orach Chayim* 310 on the restrictions concerning contact with money on Shabbat.

18. Shapiro, *Gates of Shabbat*, 57. And see Rabbi Israel Bettan's responsum from 1952: "To hark back to the puritanic rigors of the Rabbinic Sabbath is to call into question the relevancy of religion to modern life" (Rabbi Israel Bettan, "Sabbath Observance," in *American Reform Responsa*, 117, https://www.ccarnet.org/ccar-responsa/arr-114-117/).

19. Shapiro, *Gates of Shabbat*, 57.

20. This affirmation is evident in numerous decisions rendered by the CCAR Responsa Committee in recent years. In this, we have followed the guidance of our teacher, Rabbi Walter Jacob: see his *Questions and Reform Jewish Answers*, nos. 4, 67, 95, 99, 100, and others.

21. See "Delayed *B'rit Milah* on Shabbat," CCAR responsum 5755.12, in *Teshuvot for the Nineties*: "The fact that Shabbat 'conflicts' with another mitzvah or worthy cause does not mean that it is Shabbat that must give way. Indeed, the reverse is often the case."

22. On the prohibition of weddings on Shabbat, see "Marriage on Shabbat or *Yom Tov*," in *American Reform Responsa*, 412–15, http://ccarnet.org/responsa/arr-412-415/: "We encourage our members to make Shabbat a 'special' day upon which we do not carry out duties and acts performed on other days. Countenancing marriages on Shabbat would detract from this objective and weaken our efforts."

23. "Gift Corner Open on Shabbat," in *Reform Responsa*; "A Holiday Gift Wrapping Project and Shabbat," in *Contemporary American Reform Responsa*, 267–68, https://www.ccarnet.org/ccar-responsa/carr-267-268/. See also "Fund Raising on Shabbat," in *Questions and Reform Jewish Answers*, 97–98, http://ccarnet.org/responsa/narr-97-98/, who notes that the availability of Sunday as a non-work day in our culture virtually eliminates the need to discuss communal business on Shabbat.

24. "Communal Work on Shabbat," CCAR responsum 5753.22, in *Teshuvot for the Nine-ties*, 169–70, http://ccarnet.org/responsa/tfn-no-5753-22-169-170/; see also "Pov-erty Project and Shabbat," in *Contemporary American Reform Responsa*, 265–67, http://ccarnet.org/responsa/carr-265-267/.

25. Testimony to this emphasis is found in many recent publications of the Central Conference of American Rabbis: *Gates of Shabbat; Gates of the Seasons* (1983), 15–33; and *Shabbat Manual* (1972).

CHAPTER 6: NATIONALISM, ZIONISM, AND REFORM
Flags on the Bimah

Responsum 1: National Flags at Religious Services

QUESTION:

In our temple we have two flags on the pulpit: one is the United States flag and the other is the flag of Israel. Some members of the congregation seem much disturbed by the practice. They feel that these flags have no place in the auditorium where religious services are held and should therefore be removed to the social hall. The matter has been referred to our Committee on Religious Practice. We are anxious to avoid unnecessary emotional conflicts among our members. We should like to bring to them a proposal that would rest on sound principle and could be followed by all factions.

ANSWER:

In Judaism, devotion to the welfare of the country in which one lives has long assumed the character of a religious duty.

When, in the sixth century BCE, the people of Judah had been carried into captivity by the Babylonian conqueror, it was the prophet Jeremiah who proclaimed God's message to the captives in the following words: "And seek the peace of the city whither I have caused you to be carried away captive, and pray unto the Eternal for it; for in the peace thereof shall ye have peace" (Jeremiah 29:7).

Centuries later, when the Roman emperors ruled over many kingdoms, including Palestine, it was the Rabbis who pronounced the same religious principle. "Pray for the welfare of the government," they said, "since but for the fear thereof men would swallow one another alive" (*Mishnah Avot* 3:2).

Accordingly, a special prayer for the ruling power soon found its way into the fixed liturgy of the synagogue (*Abudarham*, 47c). On the Sabbath day, during the morning services, immediately after the scriptural lesson, the prayer for the welfare of the government is recited in all the synagogues of the world. In every country the Jew thus affirms his faith from week to week that loyalty to the institutions of the particular country of which he is a citizen is a solemn religious obligation.

The presence of the American flag in the synagogues of the land, far from being an intrusion, may well serve to strengthen in us the spirit of worship. Symbolizing, as it does, the duties we owe to our country, obedience to its laws, and zealous support of its rights and interests, our national flag speaks to us with the voice of religion and partakes, therefore, of the sanctity of our religious symbols.

What the American flag is to the American Jew, the British flag is to the British Jew; the French flag is to the French Jew; and the Israeli flag, to the citizens of Israel. The American flag has no proper place in the synagogues of Israel, even as the Israeli flag is quite out of place in an American synagogue.

The United States Army regulations governing the display of any national flag other than our own—and these regulations have now become the standard civilian practice as well—are quite broad and adequate. While frowning on the practice of habitually flying a foreign flag alongside the American flag, these regulations provide that (1) in the presence of a visiting dignitary of a foreign land or (2) on some notable anniversary of that land, its national flag may be displayed as a token of respect.

American Jewish congregations, if they so desire, may therefore display the Israeli flag when a representative of the State of Israel is present in their midst, or when the State of Israel celebrates a special anniversary, such as the Day of Independence.

—Rabbi Israel Bettan, "National Flags at Religious Services," in *American Reform Responsa: Collected Responsa of the Central Conference of American Rabbis*, ed. Walter Jacob (New York: CCAR Press, 1983), 64–66.

Responsum 2: Israeli Flag on a Synagogue Pulpit

QUESTION:

Should an Israeli flag be displayed on the pulpit of an American Reform synagogue? In this case, an American flag is already so displayed. (Rabbi R. Goldman, Chattanooga, Tennessee)

ANSWER:

The six-pointed Star of David is now commonly recognized as a symbol of Jews and Judaism throughout the world, both by ourselves and by our non-Jewish neighbors. There is no clear distinction between Jews and Judaism, between our religious and our national aspirations.

Since the Babylonian diaspora, our prayers have constantly contained petitions for the return to Zion and the reestablishment of Israel. In the traditional Shabbat morning Torah service, we find in addition a prayer (a) for the academies in Israel, Babylonia, and the Diaspora, (b) for the local congregation, and (c) for the gentile government under which we live (*Abudarham*, 47b; *Machzor Vitry*; Rokeach). These prayers have been part of the service either since the Talmudic period or, at the latest, since the fourteenth century. In other words, the service has for a long time contained side-by-side prayers expressing the desire for a return to the Land of Israel, gratitude for the land in which we live, and hope for the welfare of our own communities. The flags of the United States and Israel on a pulpit might be said to symbolize the prayers that have always been said in the synagogue. For this reason, there is no religious objection to placing an American flag on the pulpit, nor to placing an Israeli flag alongside it. (Of course, there are specific secular regulations about the placement of such flags that should be followed.) It might be helpful to look at the historical background, especially as there is no ancient record of a Jewish flag or symbol for the entire people of Israel.

The six-pointed star was rarely used by the early Jewish community. It is found carved on a stone in the Capernaum synagogue and also on a single tombstone in Tarentum, Italy, which dates from the third century. Later kabbalists used it, probably borrowing it from the Templars (Ludwig Blau, "Magen David," *Jewish Encyclopedia*, vol. 8, 252). It is also found in some non-kabbalistic medieval manuscripts. None of these usages, however, was widespread.

The first time a Jewish flag is mentioned was during the rule of Charles IV of Hungary, who prescribed in 1354 that the Jews of Prague use a red flag with David's and Solomon's seal. Also, in the fifteenth century, the Jews of that city met King Matthias with a red flag containing two golden six-pointed stars and two five-pointed stars. Aside from this, we have no record of the use of a flag by any Jewish community, and, of course, the six-pointed star now so commonly used was rarely used as a Jewish symbol before the late eighteenth century and early nineteenth century. In that period, the newly emancipated Jewish community wished to possess an easily recognizable symbol akin to that of Christianity and so adopted the six-pointed star, which was then used frequently on books, synagogues, cemeteries, tombstones, etc. The star soon became recognized as a sign of Judaism. In 1799 it was already used in antisemitic literature. In 1822, the Rothschilds utilized it for their coat of arms, and it was adopted by the Zionist Congress in Basel in 1897 as its symbol. Subsequently, the State of Israel has used it in its national flag, although the official symbol of Israel is the menorah. Naturally, all of us also remember that the Nazis used the six-pointed star on their badges that identified Jews.

If you wish for detailed information about this material see Matthias Gruenewald, "Ein altes Symbol . . . ," *Jahrbuch fuer juedische Literatur*, 1901, 120ff; Ludwig Blau, "Magen David," *Jewish Encyclopedia*, vol. 8, 25f; and Gershom Scholem, "Magen David," *Encyclopedia Judaica*, vol. 11, 687ff.

Various synagogues have found other solutions to the desire for honoring both the United States and Israel. Thus, some have placed both flags in the foyer of the community hall, but have no flags on their pulpits. In any case, both the loyalty of our communities to the United States and our common concern for Israel are clear with or without the placement or possession of flags.

> Walter Jacob, *Chairman*
> Stephen M. Passamaneck
> W. Gunther Plaut
> Harry A. Roth
> Herman E. Schaalman
> Bernard Zlotowitz

—CCAR Responsa Committee, "Israeli Flag on a Synagogue Pulpit," in *American Reform Responsa: Collected Responsa of the Central Conference of American Rabbis*, ed. Walter Jacob (New York: CCAR Press, 1983), 66–68.

Responsum 3: Flags on the Bimah

SH'EILAH:

It is customary in many synagogues to place flags on the bimah, both the national flag and that of the State of Israel. Is it appropriate for Reform synagogues to exalt national symbols to the same rank as the symbols of Jewish worship? Specifically, does this practice border upon idolatry (*avodah zarah*)? (Rabbi Philip Bentley, Huntington Station, New York)

T'SHUVAH:

Our sources regard the synagogue as a sacred place. The rules concerning the proper use of the synagogue,[1] discussed in the third chapter of the Mishnah's tractate *M'gillah*,[2] are linked to Ezekiel 11:16: "I have become for them a small sanctuary [*mikdash m'at*]." This midrash, of course, is not to be taken literally. Clearly, many of the rules that apply to the Sanctuary in Jerusalem (for example, those dealing with priestly status and access, ritual purity and defilement) do not apply to the synagogue. Yet in many significant respects the synagogue is patterned after the Temple. The synagogue bimah is customarily adorned with the *ner tamid*, the *aron hakodesh*, and the menorah, symbols that evoke the original Sanctuary. None of the appurtenances of the Sanctuary, moreover, were connected with what we would view as the cult of nationhood. The only symbolism permitted there was that devoted to the worship of the God of Israel.

The point is obvious: God is to be exalted above all kings and nations. Israel, to be sure, is a nation, but it exists only to serve God; that is the essence, perhaps the entirety of its national identity. To have included purely national symbols within the Sanctuary would have invited the suspicion that we were equating devotion to the nation with the service of God. This, in turn, would have been seen as idolatry, for God alone is worthy of worship.[3]

We might well draw the same conclusion with regard to our "small Sanctuary" and forbid the placement of national flags on the bimah as an improper invasion of the secular into the realm of the sacred.

Jewish tradition, however, does not draw that conclusion. The Talmud[4] reports that four sages prayed in a synagogue in Babylonia that contained a statue of the king. From this we might infer that the presence of a national symbol, even a graven image that might otherwise create the suspicion of idolatry, is not necessarily prohibited in a synagogue on the grounds of *avodah zarah*, idolatry.

Our specific question, that of national flags, is the subject of several contemporary responsa.

Rabbi Moshe Feinstein sees them as purely secular symbols (*chulin*), which, unlike those associated with idolatry, are not forbidden in the sanctuary. He writes: "These flags are not set up in the synagogue because they are regarded as sacred symbols but rather as indications that the congregation's leaders love this country and the State of Israel and wanted to display their affection in a public place."[5]

This committee has explicitly supported the custom to place national flags on the bimah. Writing in 1954, Rabbi Israel Bettan[6] argued that the presence of the national flag is the symbolic equivalent of the prayers that we have long recited for the welfare of the government and its leaders.[7] A separate opinion, from 1977, finds "no religious objection" to placing a national flag on the pulpit.[8] Given such precedents, and given the fact that it has become a widespread *minhag* (customary observance) among Reform congregations to place flags in their sanctuaries, we would certainly not urge their removal.

At the same time, we see nothing wrong with a congregation's desire to reconsider this practice. The mere fact that the presence of flags on the bimah violates no ritual prohibition does not mean that they ought to be there, that to place national flags in the sanctuary is a positive good that achieves some high religious purpose.[9] Indeed, the opinions we have cited differ widely over this issue. Feinstein, for example, declares that it is "improper" (*lo min hara-ui*) to put secular symbols in a sacred space, especially next to the ark. It would be best to remove these objects of "nonsense" (*hevel ush'tut*) from the synagogue. In his opinion, this is particularly true of the flag of Israel, a nation founded by nonobservant Jews (*r'shaim*) who have rejected the Torah. Still, since there is no actual prohibition against them, the flags should not be removed if doing so would lead to community strife and dissension.

Bettan, by contrast, believes that the display of the national flag performs a vital religious function, that "it may well serve to strengthen in us the spirit of worship." He declares that the flag symbolizes our loyalty to our country and our "zealous support of its rights and interests." The flag "speaks to us with the voice of religion and partakes, therefore, of the sanctity of our religious symbols." The 1977 responsum strikes a different chord and does not make this comparison. It simply reminds us that gratitude for one's land, hope for its welfare, and concern for the Jews of the Land of Israel are valid Jewish religious sentiments that can be symbolized through the placement of flags in the sanctuary. Some congregations, however, choose to express these sentiments by placing flags in the social hall rather than on the pulpit; still others do not place flags in their buildings at all. "In any case, both the loyalty of our communities to (our country) and our common concern for Israel are clear with or without the placement or possession of flags."

This committee reaffirms the ruling and the attitude expressed in the 1977 responsum. As Reform Jews we believe that our acceptance of the responsibilities and privileges of citizenship, our devotion toward the prophetic ideals of social justice, and our love for the State of Israel imply a more positive disposition toward national flags than that assumed by Feinstein. We care deeply about the welfare of our societies; their symbolic representations must not be dismissed as "nonsense."

At the same time, the committee believes that the language employed by Bettan no longer reflects the precise relationship of many, and perhaps most, Reform Jews to their national state. We are properly suspicious of rhetoric equating "God and King" or "God and Country." While it may have been proper at one time to speak of the flag as a religious symbol, and while such language may not be, strictly speaking, a case of idolatry, it connotes for many of us today some of the most disturbing historical tendencies of our time: chauvinism, racism, and ethnic intolerance. If it is true that God alone is worthy of our religious worship, we ought to avoid language that, rightly or wrongly, suggests otherwise.

We would therefore say rather that, for us, the flag serves as an expression of a religiously legitimate devotion, a devotion that may be expressed, should the congregation so choose, by the placement of national flags in the sanctuary or in some other location within the synagogue building.

—CCAR Responsa Committee, "Flags on the Bimah," CCAR responsum 5753.8, in *Teshuvot for the Nineties: Reform Judaism's Answers to Today's Dilemmas*, ed. W. Gunther Plaut and Mark Washofsky (New York: CCAR Press, 1997), 29–32.

NOTES

1. See *Shulchan Aruch, Orach Chayim* 151.
2. The same arrangement is preserved in the *Talmud Yerushalmi*. In the Babylonian Talmud, however, this material—*perek "B'nei Ha-ir"*—comprises chapter four, 25b ff. The midrash discussed here is located in Babylonian Talmud, *M'gillah* 29a.
3. Cf. *Gates of Prayer* (New York: CCAR Press, 1975), 75: "We are Israel: our Torah forbids the worship of race or nation, possessions or power."
4. Babylonian Talmud, *Rosh HaShanah* 24b.

5.   Responsa *Ig'rot Moshe, Orach Chayim* 1:46. The opinion was written in 1957.
6.   Rabbi Israel Bettan, "National Flags at Religious Services," in *American Reform Responsa*, 64–66.
7.   Both in the Diaspora and in Israel, elements of the "civil religion" have assumed a prominent place in Jewish ritual practice. See "Blessing of the Fleet," CCAR responsum 5751.3, in *Teshuvot for the Nineties*, 159–64, https://www.ccarnet.org/ccar-responsa/tfn-no-5751-3-159-164/. In Israel, these issues are exemplified by the debates over the observance of Israel Independence Day in synagogues. While the subject is controversial, many observant Jews do recognize this national festival as a religious holiday. See Nahum Rakover, ed., *Yom Ha-Atsma'ut ve-Yom Yerushalayim: Berurey Halakhah* (Jerusalem: Ministry of Religions, 1973).
8.   "Israeli Flag on a Synagogue Pulpit," in *American Reform Responsa*, 66–68. This *t'shuvah* extends the approval to the placing of the Israeli flag in the sanctuary, a practice that Rabbi Bettan regarded as inappropriate in a Diaspora synagogue except on special occasions.
9.   Indeed, while the four sages prayed in the presence of the king's image (see note 4, above), that passage does not in any way suggest that such statuary should be placed in synagogues.

Responsum 4: "HaTikvah" and "The Star-Spangled Banner"

SH'EILAH:

It is the custom at our congregation to conclude our Yom HaAtzma-ut service with the singing of "HaTikvah." In addition, since this past year was the fiftieth anniversary of the founding of the State of Israel, three *b'nei mitzvah* as well as our confirmation class requested that "HaTikvah" be sung at their services. The vice president of the synagogue criticizes this practice on the grounds that "HaTikvah," as the national anthem of a foreign country, should always be accompanied by "The Star-Spangled Banner." Is it proper for us to sing "HaTikvah" unaccompanied by our own national anthem? (Rabbi Lance J. Sussman, Binghamton, New York)

T'SHUVAH:

Of Flags and Anthems. Reform responsa have not spoken to the issue of national anthems at religious services. There does exist, however, a line of decisions with respect to the placement of national flags in the synagogue sanctuary and on the bimah. Flags, to be sure, are not a perfect analogy to national anthems. A flag is an item of synagogue ornamentation, usually a permanent presence, while an anthem tends to be sung only on occasion, in connection with a particular religious observance. Still, they are similar to the extent that they raise the issue of our spiritual and emotional attachment to our own country and to the State of Israel, the way in which these attach-ments can take on religious significance for us, and the potential conflicts that these attachments are said to involve.

Writing in 1954, Rabbi Israel Bettan[1] permitted the placement of the American flag in an American synagogue on the grounds that in Judaism, devotion to the welfare of one's country, as expressed through the prayers we recite on behalf of the government, "has long assumed the character of a religious duty." Far from being a secular intrusion into the world of religion, "the presence of the American flag . . . may well serve to strengthen in us the spirit of worship . . . (partaking) of the sanctity of our religious symbols." As the emblem of a foreign state, meanwhile, an Israeli flag would be "quite out of place in an American synagogue." A congregation might display an Israeli flag only on those occasions specified by US Army regulations and civilian practice that govern "the display of any national flag other than our own": to honor a visiting dignitary of a foreign land, or in observance of some notable anniversary (such as Yom HaAtzma-ut) of that land.

Rabbi Bettan's view contrasts sharply with an Orthodox perspective dat-ing from 1957 by Rabbi Moshe Feinstein,[2] who regards all national flags as purely secular symbols possessing no religious value whatsoever. Indeed, he calls them "nonsense" (*hevel ush'tut*), which by rights should not be placed in the sanctuary. This is particularly true of the flag of Israel, a state founded by nonobservant Jews (*r'shaim*) who in Feinstein's view had abandoned the path of Torah. On the other hand, since the presence of the flags does not vio-late a ritual prohibition and does not invalidate the synagogue as a place of prayer, the congregation is not required to remove them, especially if to do so would be the cause of needless dissension (*machloket*) among its members.

A 1977 responsum[3] by this committee, permitting the display of an Israeli flag in an American Reform synagogue, effectively reversed the Bettan deci-sion. It is true, the committee wrote, that we recite prayers in the synagogue for the welfare of the country in which we live. It is also true, however, that Jews have long prayed for the return to the Land of Israel and the reestab-lishment there of Jewish national life. Thus, "the flags of the United States and Israel on a pulpit might be said to symbolize the prayers that have always been said in the synagogue." The flag of Israel, moreover, is dominated by the six-pointed Star of David, which "is now commonly recognized as a symbol of Jews and Judaism throughout the world." Since "there is no clear distinction between Jews and Judaism, between our religious and our national aspirations," the display of this Jewish national symbol cannot be objectionable on Judaic religious grounds. This does not mean that the flag *must* be displayed. As the responsum noted, our synagogues have varying policies on this matter, so that "in any case, both the loyalty of our communities to the United States and our common concern for Israel are clear with or without the placement or possession of flags."

In its most recent statement,[4] this committee reaffirmed the 1977 decision: the national flag serves as an expression of a religiously legitimate devotion that *may* be expressed, should the congregation so choose, by placing the flag in the sanctuary. It also made explicit that our national flag is not a religious symbol and therefore should not be described as such. We therefore put a firm if respectful distance between ourselves and the tone of Rabbi Bettan's responsum: "We are properly suspicious of rhetoric equating 'God and King' or 'God and Country.'" Such talk, we wrote, may not meet the technical definition of "idolatry,"[5] but the historical experience of the last several decades leads us to associate the language of uncritical nationalism with such disturbing phenomena as chauvinism, racism, and ethnic intolerance. In stressing the secular—that is, religiously neutral—nature of political nationhood, the responsum adopts a view resembling that of Rabbi Feinstein on that issue. On the other hand, "our acceptance of the responsibilities and privileges of citizenship,[6] our devotion to the prophetic ideals of social justice, and our love for the State of Israel imply a more positive disposition toward national flags than that assumed by Rabbi Feinstein. We care deeply about the welfare of our societies; their symbolic representations must not be dismissed as 'nonsense.'"

These responsa speak not only to the specific issue of national flags but also to the more general one of patriotism, of our sense of commitment to our own countries and to the State of Israel. Our observations on this larger issue, of which the question of national flags is but a concrete manifestation, may be summarized as follows:

a. Since Jews have always "prayed for the welfare" of the government, it is appropriate for us to express our love and concern for our country in a concrete way as part of our synagogue ritual.

b. The nation, its government, and the symbols representing them are secular rather than religious matters. We are under no obligation to bring these symbols into our synagogues or insert them into our religious practice. In any event, our loyalty to and concern for our country are beyond doubt even should we choose not to incorporate its national rituals into our buildings or services.

c. The State of Israel is the political embodiment of the age-old Jewish dream of national redemption, a dream that we have expressed in our prayers for two millennia. The survival and welfare of the Jewish state are therefore matters of our utmost religious as well as political concern. It follows that the symbols of the Israeli state are not simply Israeli symbols; they reflect and convey a powerful Jewish meaning to us. Should we choose to display the Israeli flag in our synagogues, we do not thereby declare political allegiance to the Israeli state; we rather affirm that the Jewish ideas and ideals that that flag symbolizes are present in the religious life of our community.

"HaTikvah": The National Anthem of a "Foreign" State? Given the above, we find it entirely permissible for a Reform congregation in the Diaspora to sing "HaTikvah" at a worship service or other event. Like the flag of Israel, "HaTikvah" is not simply the national symbol of the Israeli state but the longstanding anthem of the Jewish national movement. It thus expresses, quite literally, our hope for the restoration of our people to Zion, which we have seen is a central and quite legitimate theme of Reform Jewish worship. And just as our loyalty and love for our own countries are not called into question when we display the Israeli flag, they remain open and obvious as well when we sing "HaTikvah," whether or not we accompany it with our own national anthem.

The objection raised by the vice president of this congregation, we might add, seems based upon an ideology that we categorically reject. Yes, it is technically the case that Israel is a "foreign" country and that "HaTikvah" is its anthem. Yet to conceive of Israel solely in this manner is to define our Judaism in a way that is surely foreign to us. Let us consider an illustration. Were our community to host the ambassador of, say, the Czech Republic, it would be proper to honor him or her with the playing of the Czech national anthem, which by common custom would be followed with our own. Such is proper behavior in the presence of a representative of a foreign state. But when we sing "HaTikvah," we do not do so in order to show respect for or loyalty to a foreign political entity. We do it because "HaTikvah" celebrates the symbolic role of the State of Israel in defining our religious and cultural identity as Jews, not our political identity as Israelis. As Jews, we are *Am Yisrael*, the Jewish *people*, rather than simply Americans or Canadians of the Mosaic persuasion. *Eretz Yisrael*, the Land of Israel, is the homeland of this people. And *M'dinat Yisrael*, the State of Israel, is the political structure through which this people unites to give concrete expression to its national existence. "HaTikvah," like the flag of Israel, is to us a powerful representation of that nexus of meanings.

The Reform Movement in North America has long recognized these facts of contemporary Jewish identity, and we have time and again expressed that recognition through our acknowledgment of the religious significance of the Zionist movement and of the State of Israel. The Columbus Platform of 1937 declared that "in the rehabilitation of Palestine, the land hallowed by memories and hopes, we behold the promise of renewed life for many of our brethren. We affirm the obligation of all Jewry to aid in its upbuilding as a Jewish homeland." The Centenary Perspective of 1976 notes that "we are bound to that land and to the newly reborn State of Israel by innumerable religious and ethnic ties. . . . We see it providing unique opportunities for Jewish self-expression. We have both a stake and a responsibility in building the State of Israel, assuring its security and defining its Jewish character." Our most recent and comprehensive statement is the "Platform on Reform Religious Zionism," adopted by the Central Conference of American Rabbis in 1997.[7] In that document, we proclaim that the establishment of the State of Israel "after nearly two thousand years of statelessness and powerlessness represents an historic triumph of the Jewish people." Israel "is therefore unlike all other states . . . [serving] uniquely as the spiritual and cultural focal point of world Jewry." Yom HaAtzma-ut, Israel Independence Day, has been established as "a permanent annual festival in the religious calendar of Reform Judaism,"[8] and our prayer book contains a liturgy for Yom HaAtzma-ut.[9] We consider it "a mitzvah for every Jew to mark Yom HaAtzma-ut by participation in public worship services and/or celebrations that affirm the bond between the Jews living in the Land of Israel and those living outside."[10] Those services and celebrations have become the norm, the accepted *minhag* in our congregations and communities.

Israel, in other words, is emphatically not a "foreign" country to us. It may not be the sovereign entity of which we are citizens and to which we owe our political allegiance. But it is, in the most deeply Jewish sense, our *own*, in our devotion to its well-being and in our identification with the history and experience that its national symbols represent.

We may therefore sing "HaTikvah" at our religious services, whether or not we choose to accompany it with our own national anthems.

> —CCAR Responsa Committee, "'HaTikvah' and 'The Star-Spangled Banner,'" CCAR responsum 5758.10, in *Reform Responsa for the Twenty-First Century: Sh'eilot Ut'shuvot*, ed. Mark Washofsky (New York: CCAR Press, 2010), 1:13–19.

NOTES

1. Rabbi Israel Bettan, "National Flags at Religious Services," in *American Reform Responsa*, 64–66.
2. *Responsa Ig'rot Moshe, Orach Chayim* 1:46.
3. "Israeli Flag on a Synagogue Pulpit," in *American Reform Responsa*, 66–68.
4. "Flags on the Bimah," CCAR responsum 5753.8, in *Teshuvot for the Nineties*, 29–34.
5. See "Flags on the Bimah," 30, citing Babylonian Talmud, *Rosh HaShanah* 24b.
6. We stress "citizenship" for a reason. It is quite possible that the age-old tradition of praying for the welfare of the government originated not out of love of country and fellow-feeling with its other inhabitants, but rather out of the desire to demonstrate our loyalty to a skeptical regime and to protect ourselves against an all-too-often hostile population. As *citizens* of our countries, we are active and equal participants in its democratic governance. "Our" country today is truly *ours*, in a way that our ancestors could never claim for the nations in whose midst they resided.
7. Published along with its Hebrew text (*HaYahadut haReformit vehaTziyonut*) in *CCAR Yearbook* 106 (1997): 49–57.
8. *CCAR Yearbook* 80 (1970): 39.
9. *Gates of Prayer* (New York: CCAR Press, 1975), 590–611.
10. Peter S. Knobel, ed., *Gates of the Seasons: A Guide to the Jewish Year* (New York: CCAR Press, 1983), 102.

CHAPTER 7: JEWISH FAITH AND SECULAR CULTURE
St. Valentine's Day and Other "Secular" Holidays

SH'EILAH:

Is it acceptable for Jews to participate in the customs and celebrations of St. Valentine's Day and other non-Jewish holidays that are currently regarded as "secular" but that originated as religious observances? (Rabbi David Vaisberg, New York, New York)

T'SHUVAH:

The quick and easy way to answer our *sh'eilah* would be to say: "Go and see what the people are doing," that is, let the *minhag*, the widespread custom, indicate the correct standard of practice.[1] In this case, we would discover that Jews in our communities take full part in the activities of such non-Jewish holidays as St. Valentine's Day, Halloween, Thanksgiving, New Year's, and Mardi Gras, and we would therefore conclude that the answer to our *sh'eilah* is "yes." But it is the task of rabbis not simply to accept the existence of a custom as a fait accompli but, at times, to submit that custom to careful Judaic scrutiny. Even if our people participate in these non-Jewish holidays, we should inquire as to whether our sources raise any objections to that participation. We should ask, as well, as to the line that we must draw between those non-Jewish holidays that are acceptable to us and those that we feel Jews ought not to observe.

1. *The Prohibition of* Chukot HaGoyim. This most obvious potential objection to Jews' participation in non-Jewish holidays is rooted in the biblical injunction (Leviticus 18:3) *uv'chukoteihem lo teileichu*, "you shall not follow their laws." While the verse refers explicitly to the "laws" of the Egyptians and the Canaanites, the Rabbis interpret it as a prohibition against the imitation and adoption of the customs of all gentiles.[2] Jews realized early on that the forbidden "laws" could not encompass every existing behavior of the surrounding society, since it was impossible not to adopt at least some of those behaviors. As the midrash explains, the verse cannot mean that we are forbidden to build buildings and to engage in agriculture merely because the gentiles do the same! Rather, the prohibition applies only to the sorts of religious[3] and social practices (*nimusot*)[4] that distinguish one culture from another.[5] As Maimonides codifies the rule:[6]

> We are not to follow the laws of the gentiles[7] or seek to resemble them in their manner of dress, haircut, and the like. . . . Rather, the Jew should remain separate from them, recognizable (as a Jew) by his manner of dress and by his other deeds, just as he is recognizable by his philosophy and his beliefs.

Over time, halachah came to permit significant exceptions to the prohibition of *chukot hagoyim*. An early example is the tannaitic statement that the rule does not apply to those who are *k'rovim l'malchut*, Jews who are "close to the government," who must deal constantly with the authorities and who therefore must follow the latter's expectations of appropriate grooming and dress.[8] More to the point here, despite the prohibition, medieval Jewish communities adopted any number of the cultural practices of their neighbors—even some that were specifically religious in nature—and adapted them to their own needs. If some rabbis sought to protest against such borrowing, others were supportive. Addressing the custom in one community for mourners to visit the cemetery every morning during the seven days following the funeral, the eminent fourteenth-century *poseik* Rabbi Yitzchak bar Sheshet urged his correspondent not to interfere with the practice, even though the Jews had apparently learned it from their Muslim neighbors. If we wish to forbid the custom for that reason, he wrote, "we might as well prohibit the eulogy, since the gentiles, too, eulogize their dead."[9] Rabbi Yosef Colon (Maharik; fifteenth-century Italy) permitted Jewish physicians to don the distinctive robes worn by their gentile colleagues. The prohibition against adopting "gentile laws," he argued, covers only two categories of "laws": (1) customs that offend the rules of modest behavior; and (2) cultural practices that are unique to the gentiles and serve no other rational and acceptable purpose (*taam*), so that the Jew would adopt them only because they wish to imitate the non-Jewish culture.[10] Maharik's approach, though not accepted by all,[11] was codified by Rabbi Moshe Isserles in the *Shulchan Aruch*[12] and is followed by many in the halachic community today. Thus, leading Israeli Orthodox authorities have approved the sounding of a siren on Yom HaZikaron and Yom HaShoah, even though this custom was "borrowed" from the memorial practices of other nations, because it serves the acceptable purpose of rendering honor to the dead.[13]

2. *"Secular" versus "Religious" Celebrations.* Our Reform Jewish approach to Leviticus 18:3 is based upon the conviction that the prohibition of *chukot hagoyim* does not apply to aspects of our contemporary surrounding culture that we experience as secular. Since the term "secular" is a broad one, difficult at times to define with precision, we will explain what we mean in detail.

First, in the negative sense, that which is secular is "nonreligious" or, perhaps better, "nonsectarian" in nature. This helps us determine just how far we may go in adopting non-Jewish modes of expression to serve our own specifically religious needs. For example, it is well-known that the style of our public worship—the architecture of our prayer spaces, our modes of liturgical music, our approaches to the leadership of communal prayer—are heavily influenced and have been so throughout history by the styles we have encountered in the surrounding culture. With respect to the content of our public worship, however, we have drawn the line. Thus, this committee has cautioned against borrowing non-Jewish prayers and hymns, both because they are identified with other religions and because our own Jewish liturgical tradition is sufficiently rich to afford us abundant resources for worship.[14] Since we regard it a mitzvah to preserve the distinctly Jewish elements of our identity, particularly as this touches upon our religious practice, inappropriate borrowing from other religions runs afoul of the prohibition against the imitation of non-Jewish customs and ceremonies.

Second, in the positive sense, that which is secular in our culture is that which all citizens of the community can share in common and in which they can participate on an equal footing with all their fellow citizens. To put this in traditional Jewish terminology, in a liberal democracy all of us should be considered *k'rovim l'malchut*, for we *are* the *malchut*; the government and the culture belong to us, they are of us, and we do not regard them as alien entities. Secular customs, as the common space in which all of us can meet, serve the "rational and acceptable purpose" (to use Maharik's terminology) of uniting the members of a disparate and multicultural society into a common bond.

For these reasons, we have no objections to Jews' participation in national patriotic holidays. These special days are secular in both the senses we have described: they are nonreligious, and they speak equally to all the citizens of the state. True, these holidays are major events in the calendar of what has been called the "civil religion," the set of beliefs, texts, rites, and ceremonies by which the citizens express their collective national identity.[15] The civil religion, one could argue, is a religion, a sort of nonsectarian "faith" (the "cult of the nation," of "God and country") and is therefore not secular at all. We, however, resist this conclusion; as we have written elsewhere, participation by Jews in their nation's civil religion "is a proper expression of their full participation in the life of the general community."[16] Although patriotism can be and all too often has been twisted into the form of a quasi-religion,[17] we see national holidays as occasions that, in Maharik's words, serve the "rational and acceptable purpose" of uniting the citizens of the state and of reminding them of their social and ethical duties toward each other. They are secular observances precisely because they belong to us all, and for that reason they cannot be dismissed as *chukot hagoyim*.

For these reasons, too, we see no reason why Jews should be prohibited from participating in holidays we deal with here: Valentine's Day, Halloween, Thanksgiving, New Year's, Mardi Gras. Although these holidays originate in Christian practice,[18] they are now secular observances; neither we nor the vast majority of our fellow citizens perceive them as religious festivals. They are in this regard easily distinguishable from Christmas, Easter, and other obviously religious holidays that it is clearly inappropriate for Jews to celebrate.[19] And here is where we depart from the stance taken by some of our Orthodox colleagues. For example, Rabbi Moshe Feinstein, the leading American Orthodox halachic authority of the twentieth century, has famously ruled that Jews are forbidden to take part in the "festivities" (שמחות, s'machot) and "feasting" (סעודות, seudot) of American Thanksgiving, not, to be sure, because he thinks of Thanksgiving as a religious holiday—he doesn't—but because he defines it as the sort of "gentile custom" that Leviticus 18:3 forbids Jews to observe.[20] The wording of his argument suggests that Rabbi Feinstein does not recognize the existence of the cultural realm that we have defined as "secular." We, by contrast, do recognize the existence of the secular; Thanksgiving and these other holidays pertain to the culture that we share with all others in the society and in which we participate as full and equal members. As such, they are not "gentile" festivals, and we would not prohibit them on that basis.

3. *Secular versus Religious Holidays.* We have stated that secular non-Jewish holidays are "easily distinguishable" from "Christmas, Easter, and other obviously religious holidays." An obvious objection to this is the claim that for many non-Jews in our society these holidays have become nonreligious celebrations, so that by the logic of this *t'shuvah* Jews should be permitted to participate in their observance. We acknowledge that the line separating "religious" from "secular" is not a hard and fast one. As the examples of St. Valentine's Day and Halloween demonstrate, and as the Rabbis of the Talmud were aware, holidays with religious origins can lose their religious connotations over time.[21] But other holidays are and remain essentially religious in nature. By this we do not mean that everyone in the non-Jewish population celebrates them as religious festivals, but rather that they retain their central role in the doctrine and practice of non-Jewish faiths. It is our task to distinguish between these two categories. That requires a careful act of judgment, and judgments, of course, can be controversial. Still, we feel quite confident in saying that, despite all the tinsel and reindeer and Santa Claus and bunny-

and-egg displays, Christmas and Easter retain a status in Christian thought and practice that is quite different from that enjoyed by Halloween and St. Valentine's Day. The religious meaning of those days is still central in the eyes of many of our Christian neighbors, who would rightly feel insulted were we to declare those days—wrongly—to be "secular" observances.

4. *A Final Note.* We do find it sadly ironic that we are talking about Jews taking part in secular non-Jewish holidays while the level of our community's observance of many of our own holidays leaves much to be desired. We state therefore for the record: there is a difference between permission and encouragement. Jews are certainly permitted to participate in secular and national holidays, but they ought as well to take part in the full range of observances that mark our Jewish calendar. Our communities should never ignore the task of strengthening the specifically Jewish nature of our Reform Jewish life.

Conclusion. It is permissible for Jews to take part in the celebration of St. Valentine's Day and other secular holidays, even if these originated in other religious traditions. As part of the common culture in which we all participate, these days are not to be thought of as "alien" and "foreign"—much less "Christian"—so as to fall under the terms of Leviticus 18:3.

> —CCAR Responsa Committee, "St. Valentine's Day and Other 'Secular' Holidays," CCAR responsum 5775.2 (2015), https://www.ccarnet.org/ccar-responsa/57752.

NOTES

1. The Talmudic phrase is פוק חזי מאי עמא דבר, *pok chazi mai ama davar*, which occurs in Babylonian Talmud, *B'rachot* 45a and *Eiruvin* 14b as the answer to the question: What is the halachah?
2. And not only those of the Egyptians and the Canaanites to whom the verse explicitly refers; *Sifra, Acharei Mot, parashah* 9, chap. 12.
3. This insight flows from the word that the verse uses for "law"—חוק, *chok*—which the Rabbis tend to interpret or translate as ritual obligations (e.g., rules covering forbidden foods, manner of dress, and the Temple service) that cannot be derived by human reason; they are obligatory solely because God has enjoined them upon Israel. By contrast, an obligation that is derivable through human reason is indicated by the word משפט, *mishpat*. See Rashi to Leviticus 18:4.
4. *Sifra, Acharei Mot, parashah* 9, chap. 13, and see Onkelos and Rashi to Leviticus 18:3. The word *nimusot* is the Rabbinic Hebrew translation of the Greek *nomos*.
5. This definition allows for some useful distinctions. See, for example, Babylonian Talmud, *Avodah Zarah* 11a: When a king of Israel dies, it is permissible as part of

the funeral ritual to burn his bed and his personal property, even though gentiles mourn their kings in the same way. Why? The burning is not a "law" (*chukah*), the sort of religious practice we are not permitted to copy, but simply a sign of respect.

6. *Mishneh Torah, Hilchot Avodat Kochavim* 11:1. See also Rambam's *Sefer HaMitzvot*, negative commandment no. 30.

7. We adopt the reading הגוים, *hagoyim*, "gentiles," preserved in the edition of the *Mishneh Torah* edited by Rabbi Yosef Kafich (Jerusalem, 1983), in place of the printed version's העובדי כוכבים, *haovdei kochavim*, "idolaters." Kafich based his edition upon Yemenite manuscripts widely considered to be more faithful to Rambam's original text than is the printed version.

8. Babylonian Talmud, *Bava Kama* 83a; *Mishneh Torah, Hilchot Avodah Zarah* 11:3.

9. *Responsa Rivash*, no. 158.

10. *Responsa Maharik*, no. 88. The wearing of a uniform identifying one as a physician is clearly a rational and purposeful act, and it is certainly not an immodest one.

11. See Rabbi Eliyahu, the Gaon of Vilna, *Biur HaGra, Yoreh Dei-ah* 178, no. 7.

12. Moshe Isserles, *Shulchan Aruch, Yoreh Dei-ah* 178:1. See also Rabbi Mordechai Yaffe, *L'vush, Yoreh Dei-ah* 178:1.

13. Rabbi Chayim David Halevy, *Responsa Aseh L'cha Rav* 1:44 and 4:4; Rabbi Tzvi Y'hudah Kook, *T'chumin* 3 (1982): 388; Rabbi Y'hudah Henkin, *T'chumin* 4 (1983): 125–29.

14. See "The Lord's Prayer," CCAR responsum 171, in *Contemporary American Reform Responsa*, 256–57, http://ccarnet.org/responsa/carr-256-257; and "Amazing Grace," CCAR responsum 5752.11, in *Teshuvot for the Nineties*, 21–22, http://ccarnet. org/responsa/ccarj-fall-1992-65-66-tfn-no-5752-11-21-22.

15. Although the term "civil religion" originates with Jean-Jacques Rousseau (*The Social Contract*, chap. 8, book 4), the concept as presently understood by sociologists traces back to a famous article by Robert Bellah, "Civil Religion in America," *Daedalus* 96, no. 1 (1967): 1–21, http://www.robertbellah.com/articles_5.htm. Bellah speaks to the experience of the United States, and it is controversial whether his observations extend past its borders; see, for example, Andrew E. Kim, "The Absence of Pan-Canadian Civil Religion: Plurality, Duality, and Conflict in Symbols of Canadian Culture," *Sociology of Religion* 54 (1993): 257–75, and John von Heyking, "The Persistence of Civil Religion in Modern Canada," *Cardus*, October 21, 2010.

16. "Blessing the Fleet," CCAR responsum 5751.3, in *Teshuvot for the Nineties*, 159–64, http://ccarnet.org/responsa/tfn-no-5751-3-159-164.

17. We must be vigilant to maintain the lines that distinguish religion from patriotism; otherwise, religion will inevitably be drafted into the service of the cult of state power. As we have written elsewhere: "We are properly suspicious of rhetoric equating 'God and King' or 'God and Country.' While . . . such language may not be, strictly speaking, a case of idolatry, it connotes for many of us today some of the most disturbing historical tendencies of our time: chauvinism, racism, and ethnic intolerance. If it is true that God alone is worthy of our religious worship, we ought to avoid language that, rightly or wrongly, suggests otherwise" ("Flags on the

Bimah," CCAR responsum 5753.8, in *Teshuvot for the Nineties*, 31, http://ccarnet. org/responsa/tfn-no-5753-8-29-32).

18. We will not enter the controversy over the source of Halloween: did it originate as a Celtic and probably pagan festival that was subsequently adapted into the Christian calendar, or was it a Christian festival to begin with? Suffice it to say that in its present form, as "the eve of All Hallows' / All Saints' Day," its Christian associations are obvious.

19. See below, section 3. We leave aside here the often-vexing question of whether and to what extent Jews may take part in the apparently nonreligious aspects of Christmas and Easter: office parties, gift exchanges, watching parades, etc. Clearly, as members of a religious minority that does not seal itself off from its environment, we will participate in at least some of these. When we say that it is "inappropriate" for Jews to celebrate these days, we have in mind the introduction of holiday observances, decorations and the like into our own homes. We do not think it unreasonable to insist that the Jewish home be a "Christmas-free zone" during the holiday season.

20. *Responsa Ig'rot Moshe*, *Orach Chayim* 5:20 (1981), section 6.

21. See Babylonian Talmud, *Avodah Zarah* 11b: the Babylonian sage Rav Y'hudah permits his students to engage in commerce with pagans on one of the latter's festival days. Although this contradicts the prohibition set forth in *Mishnah Avodah Zarah* 1:1, Rav Y'hudah permits the activity on the grounds that the festival in question is not permanently fixed on the calendar and is therefore not a truly serious pagan observance (see Rashi, *Avodah Zarah* 11b, s.v. *d'la k'via*).

CHAPTER 8: MODERN VALUES, JEWISH TRADITION
Privacy and the Disclosure of Personal Medical Information

SH'EILAH:

I am in my late twenties and about to be ordained as a rabbi. My father has Huntington's disease, a genetically transmitted condition that begins to show itself when a person reaches his or her thirties or forties. If I test positive for the disease, am I obligated to inform my congregation and the Placement Commission? Would the Placement Commission be obligated to share this information with any prospective congregation that would be interested in hiring me? Given that I fear employment discrimination should I test positive, am I obliged to be tested at all?

T'SHUVAH:

Huntington's disease is an inherited, chronic, and progressive disorder of the nervous system, the onset of which generally occurs in midlife. It is characterized by involuntary movements, cognitive decline, and emotional disturbance. Those afflicted exhibit what physicians term "movement disorder," which may include facial twitching, unsteadiness in gait, and spasticity. The disease severely affects the patient's speech, to the point that he or she will ultimately become unintelligible. Other manifestations include poor impulse control, depression, delusions, and even psychosis. Although some experimental treatments appear promising, no therapy currently known can halt this disease.[1]

As the foregoing medical description makes abundantly clear, Huntington's disease is a debilitating condition, the symptoms of which would render it impossible for you to discharge the duties of a congregational rabbi. You are not presently diagnosed with this disease, nor have you taken the genetic test that would reveal whether you are "at risk" of contracting it.[2] Still, you are rightly concerned that should you test positive, the sharing of these results would adversely affect the prospects for your employment. Your question, then, is most sensitive and difficult on religious as well as personal grounds: does Jewish tradition require you to reveal this damaging information to a congregation or to any other institution at which you are employed or with which you may be interested in contracting for your rabbinical services?

1. *Personal Integrity and the Prohibition against Deception.* Judaism, as we know, places a great emphasis upon honesty in human conduct. The Torah cautions us against lying (Leviticus 19:11) and bearing false witness (Exodus 20:13; Deuteronomy 5:17)[3] and admonishes us to "keep far from falsehood" (Exodus 23:7).[4] The Rabbis teach that truth is the very seal of God, the signature of the Divine;[5] it follows that we, who are instructed to imitate God's ways in our own lives,[6] must comport ourselves with the highest respect for the truth.[7] As Maimonides puts it, "One should not say one thing and mean another. Rather, let one's outer expression reflect the person within, so that one speaks what is truly in one's heart."[8] Expressed in negative language, this emphasis upon truth becomes a prohibition against the practice of deception, or *g'neivat daat.*[9] This Hebrew term is taken from the word *g'neivah*, which expresses the idea of "theft"; hence, one who deliberately creates a false impression in the mind of another is guilty of an act of trespass, of quite literally "robbing the mind" of that person.[10] *G'neivat daat* occurs frequently in connection with deceptive business practices, which our tradition expressly forbids.[11] Significantly, however, the prohibition applies even when

the act of deception does not result in any monetary loss to the buyer.[12]

These texts and teachings, to which more could easily be added, establish a strong prima facie case in favor of full disclosure of your personal medical history. First of all, the very act of concealing these facts suggests a transgression against the standards of personal honesty and integrity that our tradition demands from us in our everyday social conduct. In addition, this concealment would form an integral part of a business transaction, the process by which you will seek employment as a rabbi. The possibility that you may one day develop Huntington's disease and be rendered unable to fulfill your duties as a congregational rabbi is unquestionably a matter of great relevance to the Placement Commission and to the communities you might serve. To withhold this pertinent information from them is quite possibly an act of *g'neivat daat*, especially since, as you note in your *sh'eilah*, knowledge of your medical history is likely to be a critical factor in a congregation's decision as to your employment.

You could, of course, argue that inasmuch as you have not yet tested positively for the Huntington's gene, you have no "pertinent" medical information to reveal. Even in the worst case, moreover, the onset of the disease is some years away. The congregation would therefore suffer no harm by offering you a contract now, since in all probability you will be able to fulfill your duties as their rabbi. These arguments fail, however, because in the final analysis they are offered in defense of deception, of *g'neivat daat*. Deceptive behavior is, in and of itself, the negation of integrity and a transgression against morality, quite apart from the damage it may or may not cause. And we have seen that Jewish tradition prohibits us from creating a false impression in the minds of others even when to do so causes them no financial harm.

Then, too, the fact that you are about to become a rabbi should play a crucial role in your thinking. We do not claim that a rabbi is a "special case" when it comes to morality; surely the Torah demands the same standard of ethical behavior from all of us, rabbis and laypersons alike. Yet those who would present themselves as spiritual leaders of the Jewish community must recognize that they are expected to exemplify that standard in their personal and professional lives. For you to secure your first congregational position by withholding relevant information from your employer—that is to say, for you to begin your rabbinical career on a falsehood—would do severe damage to your own reputation should the truth later be revealed. In a wider context, it would adversely affect the standing of the rabbinate as a whole. Our ability to serve the Jewish people as rabbis rests in large part upon their perception of us as men and women of character and integrity. And that perception is called into doubt each time a rabbi is found to have violated the canons of truth and honesty in his or her dealings with the community.

2. *Jewish Tradition and the "Right to Privacy."* All of this, however, must be balanced against the concern that our tradition voices for the privacy of the individual, the right to be shielded against the prying eyes of other individuals and of the community as a whole. Although Jewish law does not formally recognize a "right to privacy"—indeed, Judaism does not speak the language of "rights" in general—it does know of certain obligations whose observance would guarantee protections that other legal systems classify under this heading.

One of these obligations involves the prohibition against the unwarranted transgression of a person's private domain. The Torah states explicitly that "when you make a loan of any sort to your neighbor, you must not enter his house to take his pledge. You must remain outside, while the man to whom you made the loan brings the pledge out to you" (Deuteronomy 24:10-11). This prohibition applies to the bailiff of the court (*shaliach beit din*) as well as to the lender.[13] Mention should also be made of the concept *hezeik r'iyah*, harm caused by the prying eyes of neighbors, which the halachah defines as an actionable tort: "When neighbors own jointly a courtyard that is large enough to be divided, any one of them may require the others to erect a partition in the middle of it so that each one may use his portion of the courtyard without being seen by the others. We hold that damage resulting from sight [*hezeik r'iyah*] is real damage."[14] For this reason, a neighbor who wishes to install a window in his wall that opens upon another's property or upon a jointly owned courtyard can be prevented from doing so.[15]

Another privacy protection is guaranteed in the medieval enactment (*takanah*), attributed to Rabbeinu Gershom (*M'or HaGolah*, "the light of the exile," tenth-century Rhineland), forbidding one to read a letter written and sent by another person without that person's consent.[16] One who violated this *takanah* was subject to excommunication.[17]

Especially important to our discussion are the various kinds of prohibited speech. The Torah cautions us against gossip or "talebearing" (Leviticus 19:16), which is also understood as a violation of the personal domain of the individual.[18] Maimonides divides this law into three categories:[19]

a. One who gossips about another person (*holeich rachil; hameragel b'chavero*), even if his words are true and are not meant to harm the other. "Who is a gossiper? One who carries words from person to person, saying, 'Thus said so-and-so' or 'This is what I heard about so-and-so.' Even if what he says is true, he is a destroyer of the world." One who does this violates the commandment against tale-bearing (Leviticus 19:16).

b. One who practices *lashon hara*, who speaks negatively about another person even if what is said is true.

c. One who is *motzi shem ra*, who spreads falsehood and slander to damage another person's reputation.

Our tradition severely condemns these sins of speech; the ancient Rabbis went so far as to compare slander with leprosy.[20] In recent times, Rabbi Yisrael Meir HaKohein Kagan devoted his famous *Chafeitz Chayim*, one of the outstanding *musar* texts in Jewish history,[21] to the sins of gossip and slander, which he declares violate the negative commandment "do not hate your brother in your heart" (Leviticus 19:17) and the positive commandment to "love your neighbor as yourself" (Leviticus 19:18).[22] "Gossip" as a prohibited activity includes "tales carried from one person to another," even if the information transmitted is truthful, even if it is not meant disparagingly, and even if the person who is the object of the gossip would not deny the report were he or she asked about it.[23]

What do we learn from these facts of Jewish law, from the prohibitions against trespassing or spying upon a neighbor's abode, against reading another's private correspondence, and against engaging in gossip and slander? We learn, first and foremost, that Judaism guarantees a significant range of protection to our private lives. This, to repeat, does not imply that Jewish tradition knows of such a thing as a right to privacy, for Rabbinic Judaism is not a libertarian philosophy. On the contrary: in addition to the prohibitions just described, it includes doctrines such as the duty to "rebuke your neighbor [*hochei-ach tochiach et amitecha*]" (Leviticus 19:17)[24] and the assertion that "all Jews are responsible for one another,"[25] teachings that express the idea that each one of us has at some point the obligation to intervene into the "private life" of a fellow Jew, to be informed as to his or her personal behavior and, if possible, to set that person back on the path of Torah and mitzvot. Nonetheless, the halachic proscriptions of *hezeik r'iyah* and *r'chi-*

lut come to teach us that reasonable limits must be placed upon this sort of intervention. Our "right" to take an active interest in the affairs of others is to be balanced against the halachic demand that one's home be shielded from the gaze of neighbors and that one's name and reputation be protected from violation by others, however well-meaning they may be. There are aspects of our existence that are and must remain off-limits to the eyes and tongues of those among whom we live, and we are therefore under no moral or religious obligation to share with them information about ourselves that they have no legitimate reason to know. This conclusion drawn from our law may not be the exact equivalent of the "right to privacy" in other legal systems. But it does express, in language too clear to permit of misunderstanding, a commitment to the proposition that all of us, created in the divine image, are possessed of a dignity that at some critical point requires that all others leave us be and let us alone.

This means, in practical terms, that our lives are not an open book. We have a duty to be truthful in our dealings with others, including our employers, but this duty must be measured against our justifiable desire, endorsed by the halachah, to keep our private lives private. With respect to economic life, it means that our employers rightfully demand that we reveal to them information about ourselves that has a legitimate bearing upon our performance of the job for which we have contracted. They are not, however, entitled to know everything about us that they might wish to know. In the case at hand, the task you face is to determine just where to draw the line between these two conflicting obligations.

3. *Fixing the Balance: To Disclose or to Conceal?* At what point does the demand for truth override our legitimate concern for privacy and the prohibition against gossip? We might begin our analysis with the observation that danger to life quite obviously outweighs any expectation of privacy and confidentiality. The rule that "no consideration takes precedence over the preservation of life"[26] would certainly require that one who possesses information concerning a threat to the life of another must reveal that knowledge. This obligation is generally true even if one has taken an oath of confidentiality with respect to the person who is the source of that information.[27] In this context, "the preservation of life" has been broadened by our tradition to include rescuing another person from various kinds of danger or unfortunate circumstances.[28]

On the other hand, in cases where mortal danger is not clearly involved, the rule that we refrain from violating the dignity of others can preclude us from taking actions that would otherwise seem well intentioned. This committee, for example, has ruled that the presence in the general population of HIV, the virus that causes AIDS, does not warrant the institution of compulsory testing for that virus unless and until it poses a significant health risk to that population. To require testing in the absence of a greater degree of danger was seen as an unjustified intrusion into the private domain of the individual.[29] We have also found that *lashon hara* and gossip are inappropriate even when they are shared between husband and wife and are ostensibly aimed at improving the marital relationship.[30] From these decisions and from their supporting argumentation we would derive the following rule-of-thumb for cases such as this: respect for privacy takes precedence over the sharing of personal information in most cases. Those who seek to acquire and to make use of information concerning other persons must meet a fairly rigorous burden of proof in order to be permitted to do so.

In the case before us, we do not believe that either the Placement Commission or any potential employer at this time meets that burden of proof. You are obliged to share with them only that personal or family medical information that is relevant to your employment, and at present, no such information exists. You do not at this time suffer from Huntington's disease. That your father has the illness does not indicate with certainty that you are a carrier of the Huntington's gene, and even if you were a carrier it is not certain that you would develop the disease.[31] The ethical duty to reveal the truth to your potential employers refers specifically to *truth*, to matters of fact; it does not entail an obligation to reveal matters of conjecture, possibility, and "what-if." You need not inform them that you might at some unspecified future time develop Huntington's, for this is hardly news; at some point any person might develop a debilitating or terminal disease. You need only be able to assure them that, barring circumstances that cannot reasonably be foreseen, you are confident that no physical impairment will prevent you from fulfilling the obligations of your service during the period of your contract. The question is whether you can provide that assurance now. It seems to us that you can in all sincerity answer "yes" to this question, for even if you were to test positive for the gene it is by no means certain that you would develop the disease. Given your age, moreover, you would have good reason to believe that you were not likely to contract Huntington's disease during your initial term of employment.

This implies that you have no obligation to have yourself tested for the gene, although for personal reasons you may wish to do so. Nor is there any obligation on your part to share the results of that test with the Placement Commission or with potential employers, since those results cannot predict with certainty that you will develop the disease. In addition, should the Placement Commission possess that information, it would not be entitled to share it with potential employers, since it is not clear that even a "positive" test for the gene constitutes relevant medical information. The report in that instance would amount to gossip and the spreading of an evil report, the unwarranted revelation of details that ought to remain secret.[32]

On the other hand, should there arise a real and concrete indication that you may not be able to fulfill your rabbinical responsibilities—should you begin to exhibit the early signs of Huntington's disease—you are morally obliged to share this information with your employer. It is at that point that information concerning your medical condition ceases to be a purely private matter and becomes an issue that your employer is entitled to know.

Ultimately, you are the only person who can decide if and when that point has arrived. You and you alone can determine whether the time has come to reveal the facts of your personal medical situation to your employer. We trust that you will make the correct decision. And we pray that God grant you health, vigor, and many long years of service as a rabbi to your people.

—CCAR Responsa Committee, "Privacy and the Disclosure of Personal Medical Information," CCAR responsum 5756.2, in *Reform Responsa for the Twenty-First Century: Sh'eilot Ut'shuvot*, ed. Mark Washofsky (New York: CCAR Press, 2010), 1:331–42.

NOTES

1.   See J. Willis Hurst, ed., *Medicine for the Practicing Physician*, 4th ed. (Stamford, CT: Appleton and Lange, 1996), 1764–68. For another description, see the website of the US National Library of Medicine and the National Institutes of Health (http://www.nlm.nih.gov/medlineplus/huntingtonsdisease.html): "Huntington's disease (HD) is an inherited disease that causes certain nerve cells in the brain to waste away. People are born with the defective gene, but symptoms usually don't appear until middle age. Early symptoms of HD may include uncontrolled movements, clumsiness or balance problems. Later, HD can take away the ability to walk, talk or swallow. Some people stop recognizing family members. Others are aware of their environment and are able to express emotions. . . . There is no cure. Medicines can help manage some of the symptoms, but cannot slow down or stop the disease."

2. Hurst, ed., *Medicine for the Practicing Physician*, 1764–68. The test is administered to an individual whose parent suffered from the disease. A "positive" result on this test means that the person carries the gene that causes Huntington's and therefore is "at risk" of developing the condition.

3. We use the term "Jewish law" advisedly. In actuality, your relationship with a potential employer may be governed by the civil law in force within the relevant jurisdiction. You are therefore well advised to consult competent legal counsel prior to your interview.

4. Much Rabbinic commentary on this verse (see Babylonian Talmud, *Sh'vuot* 30b–31a) connects it expressly to conduct demanded of the *dayan*, the rabbinic judge. Hence, we might say that this verse is particularly relevant to issues involving a rabbi's dealings with his or her community.

5. *B'reishit Rabbah* 8:5 and 81:2; Babylonian Talmud, *Shabbat* 55a, *Yoma* 69b, and *Sanhedrin* 64a.

6. See Babylonian Talmud, *Sotah* 14a, on Deuteronomy 13:5: How is it possible to "follow after *Adonai* your God"? By adopting God's ways. Thus, just as God clothes the naked, so should you clothe the naked, etc. See also Rambam, *Sefer HaMitzvot*, positive commandment number 8.

7. See Babylonian Talmud, *Yoma* 86a: "'You shall love *Adonai* your God' (Deuteronomy 6:5): act so that God's name will be beloved because of you," that is, "make sure that your business dealings are conducted honestly."

8. *Mishneh Torah*, *Dei-ot* 2:6.

9. See Genesis 31:26 and II Samuel 15:6, where the root *ganav* signifies the act of deceiving others.

10. Babylonian Talmud, *Chulin* 94a; *Mishneh Torah*, *Dei-ot* 2:6. Some authorities hold that the prohibition of *g'neivat daat* is a Toraitic one, derived from Leviticus 19:11, which prohibits both robbery (*lo tignovu*) and lying; see *Chidushei HaRitva* to *Chulin* 94a. Since there is no midrashic evidence that the Rabbis read Leviticus 19:11 in this way, this interpretation represents a significant expansion of the legal content of the biblical verse by post-Talmudic tradition.

11. The general prohibitory statements are found in *Mishneh Torah*, *M'chirah* 18:1 and *Shulchan Aruch*, *Choshen Mishpat* 228:6. The texts cite numerous examples of deceptive commercial practices. One is forbidden to remove the chaff from the top of the storage bin, for this creates a false impression that the chaff has been removed from the entire bin. Similarly, one is forbidden to paint or ornament objects for sale in such a way as to create the impression that these are newer—and hence more valuable—than they really are. See *Mishnah Bava M'tzia* 4:12; *Mishneh Torah*, *M'chirah* 18:2, 4; *Shulchan Aruch*, *Choshen Mishpat* 228:9, 17.

12. *Sefer Mei-irat Einayim* to *Shulchan Aruch*, *Choshen Mishpat* 228:7; *Aruch HaShulchan*, *Choshen Mishpat* 228:3. A transaction involving financial loss falls under the rubric of *mekach ta-ut* and can be annulled. See *Mishneh Torah*, *M'chirah* 15:1ff.

13. Babylonian Talmud, *Bava M'tzia* 113a–b; *Mishneh Torah*, *Malveh V'Loveh* 2:2; *Shulchan Aruch*, *Choshen Mishpat* 97:6. Over time, this principle was modified in order to combat fraud on the part of the borrower. On the other hand, the principle

remains in force when it is clear that the borrower is a poor person. See Menachem Elon, *Cherut hap'rat b'darchei g'viat hachov bamishpat ha-ivri* (Jerusalem, 1964).

14. The citation is Maimonides (*Mishneh Torah, Sh'cheinim* 2:14). See *Mishnah Bava Batra* 1:1 and the Talmud ad loc.

15. *Mishnah Bava Batra* 3:7; Babylonian Talmud, *Bava Batra* 59b–60a; *Mishneh Torah, Sh'cheinim* 5:6 and 7:1ff.; *Shulchan Aruch, Choshen Mishpat* 154 and 160:1, 3.

16. The attribution is found in *Responsa Rabbi Meir* of Rothenburg (ed. Prague), no. 1022.

17. See in general *Shiltei Giborim* to Alfasi, *Sh'vuot*, fol. 17a, end.

18. See Rashi ad loc.: the talebearer (*holeich rachil*) is a kind of spy (*holeich r'gilah*) who enters the home of another to steal private information for use in gossip.

19. *Mishneh Torah, Dei-ot* 7:1ff.

20. See *Vayikra Rabbah* 16, which expands the biblical word *m'tzora* (leper) to *motzi shem ra* (slanderer).

21. Vilna, 1873. The book's title is suggested by Psalm 34:13–14, in which the one who "desires life" (*hechafeitz chayim*) is counseled to "keep your tongue from evil." See also *Vayikra Rabbah* 16:2. In fact, the word *musar* does not entirely do the book justice: its arrangement into sections, chapters, and halachot, much like Rambam's *Mishneh Torah*, suggests that its author takes his subject with all seriousness, seeing the topic as one of law as well as social propriety.

22. *Chafeitz Chayim*, Introduction.

23. *Chafeitz Chayim, Hilchot R'chilut* 1:1–3.

24. For the details of this mitzvah, see Babylonian Talmud, *Bava M'tzia* 31a; and *Mishneh Torah, Dei-ot* 6:7–9.

25. Babylonian Talmud, *Sh'vuot* 39a–b.

26. *Ein l'cha davar sh'omeid bifnei pikuach nefesh* (Babylonian Talmud, *K'tubot* 19a). See *Mishneh Torah, Y'sodei HaTorah* 5:1; and *Shulchan Aruch, Yoreh Dei-ah* 157:1.

27. See "Confidentiality and Threatened Suicide," CCAR responsum 5750.3, in *Teshuvot for the Nineties*, 283–88, https://www.ccarnet.org/ccar-responsa/tfn-no-5750-3-283-288/, and Rabbi Eliezer Waldenberg, *Responsa Tzitz Eliezer* 13:81, part 2, for analysis of the question whether a vow that requires one to violate a mitzvah (in this case, the duty to save life) is valid under Jewish law.

28. See *Responsa Chelkat M'chokeik* 3:136 (*Even HaEizer* 79), who rules that a physician is obligated to reveal to a woman the fact that her fiancé suffers from cancer. And see *Chafeitz Chayim, Hilchot R'chilut* 9:1ff.: to reveal information that spares a person from physical or monetary damage does not violate the prohibition against gossip.

29. "Testing for HIV," CCAR responsum 5750.1, in *Teshuvot for the Nineties*, 103–10, https://www.ccarnet.org/ccar-responsa/tfn-no-5750-1-103-110/. This conclusion is modified by two conditions. First, its validity is very much a matter of empirical evidence: should the incidence of AIDS in the general population grow to significant proportions, compulsory testing might well be warranted. Second, an individual who has engaged in behavior that places him/her at risk of being a carrier of HIV is indeed morally obligated to be tested or to reveal the facts of his/her sexual history

to potential sexual partners.

30. "Gossip between Husband and Wife," CCAR responsum 5750.4, in *Teshuvot for the Nineties*, 187–90, https://www.ccarnet.org/ccar-responsa/tfn-no-5750-4-187-190/.

31. We would add that, according to an established principle of Jewish law (*safeik s'feika l'kula* [Babylonian Talmud, *Kiddushin* 75a and elsewhere]), the presence of two elements of uncertainty in the facts of a case is held to warrant a lenient ruling. In the present instance, "leniency" means that you would not be required to reveal this information.

32. Based upon Proverbs 25:9, the Rabbis deduced a prohibition against the revelation of secrets; see *Mishnah Sanhedrin* 3:7. The discussion there centers upon courtroom procedure (see *Mishneh Torah*, *Sanhedrin* 22:7), but the analogy applies well to our case: the Placement Commission functions as an administrative (and hence quasi-legal) agency, governed by formal rules, whose decisions have a concrete impact upon the lives of those who fall under its jurisdiction. The members of the Placement Commission, like the judges of a court, have no business revealing secret information.

CHAPTER 9: THE HALACHAH OF SOCIAL JUSTICE
The Synagogue and Organized Labor

SH'EILAH:
Our congregation is in the process of cost-estimating some new construction to our synagogue facility. Our cost estimators suggested that we can save some $300,000 by using nonunion as opposed to unionized labor. Do Jewish law and ethics offer us guidance in making this decision? (Rabbi Stuart Gershon, Summit, New Jersey)

T'SHUVAH:
Jewish tradition does offer guidance toward answering your question. That guidance is divided, however, between the affirmation of two conflicting concerns. On the one hand, Jewish law supports the right of workers to organize into unions in order to protect and further their economic and social interests. In our Reform Jewish tradition, this support is very warm indeed. On the other hand, consumers also have interests that deserve protection. One of these is the legitimate desire to reduce costs by spending less for goods and services. Our goal in this responsum is to examine both of these concerns and to propose a way to resolve their conflict in a reasonable manner.

1. *Organized Labor and Jewish Law*. We read in the Talmud, "the residents

of a community [b'nei ha-ir] are entitled to establish the community's units of measurement, the prices of commodities, and the wages paid to workers; they are also entitled to punish those who violate these rules."[1] This passage is a major source of the Jewish law of takanot hakahal, the power of the community to govern itself by adopting legislation on a wide variety of matters.[2] The Talmud makes clear, moreover, that the term b'nei ha-ir (the residents of a community) applies not only to the local citizenry but also to the members of a specific commercial or trade group. Thus we read in a related passage that the butchers of a certain town adopted a rule that prohibited any one of them from doing business on a day that had been reserved for another.[3] Workers in other trades possess similar powers.[4] Medieval halachah, indeed, recognized that "any group whose members share a common economic interest" is endowed with the power of the b'nei ha-ir to legislate concerning wages, competition, and working conditions.[5] The regulations adopted by these groups are binding upon their members in much the same way as the laws adopted by the b'nei ha-ir are binding upon all the residents of the community.[6] This position was affirmed by leading twentieth-century poskim, who rule that the halachah permits workers to organize in support of their economic interests.[7]

Some authorities go farther. In their view, Jewish law does not merely permit workers to form unions; it positively encourages them to do so. In the words of Rabbi Avraham Yitzchak HaKohein Kook, unionization partakes of the Torah's insistence upon justice (tzedek), righteousness (yosher), and the betterment of society (tikkun olam). The existence of nonunion labor lowers the general wage rate and leads to inferior working conditions; therefore, such labor causes financial loss to all workers.[8] Rabbi. Ben Zion Ouziel regards unionization as a matter of simple justice and common sense. If workers were forbidden to organize, the individual worker would find himself isolated and alone, left to the mercy of market caprice, forced to hire himself out at starvation wages to the detriment of himself and his family. Halachah empowers workers to unionize, because it is through the power of organization that they can achieve decent wages, secure their economic dignity, and create institutions for cultural advancement and social support.[9] Our own Central Conference of American Rabbis has taken a similar stand. Frequently during our history we have resolved to support the right of labor to organize, to bargain collectively, and to secure fair wages and humane working conditions. As early as 1921, we resolved that "under the present organization of society, labor's only safeguard against a retrogression to former inhuman standards is the union."[10] We have endorsed progressive legislation, such as the Wagner National Labor Relations Act in the United States, that guarantees workers the right to form unions.[11] We have supported the unionization of social workers serving Jewish communal agencies.[12] In particular, we have championed the cause of farm workers, urging that they be allowed to organize to secure a decent standard of living and future for their children.[13] Summarizing this long history of support for organized labor, we declared in 1985 that "Trade Unionism traditionally is important to the well-being of America as a whole, and to minorities, including the Jewish community in particular. Primarily concerned with the large working class, it is perforce one of the strongest supports and most secure foundations of our democracy. . . . The CCAR reiterates its traditional support of organized labor and calls upon its members to help establish local conferences of religion and labor, and to remind their congregants of the importance of a strong, effective, and responsible labor movement to the health of American society. The CCAR calls upon the constituent agencies of the Reform movement and upon the Union of American Hebrew Congregations to give consideration to the establishment of programs and projects to further these ends."[14]

The language of this resolution requires that we as Reform Jews work to put the expressed ideals of our movement into concrete practice. This, too, is but a matter of simple justice and common sense. We who have championed the cause of organized labor for so many decades can hardly exempt our own institutions from the ethical standards we would impose upon others. When our "constituent agencies" hire nonunion labor in preference to union workers, we thereby help to depress the level of wages and deal a setback to the cause for which workers organize. We cannot in good conscience do this. If we believe that unionization aids the cause of workers by raising their standard of living and allowing them a greater say in their conditions of employment—and our resolutions clearly testify to this belief—then our support for unionized labor must begin at home. The synagogue bears an ethical responsibility to hire unionized workers when they are available.

2. *Fair Price and Jewish Law.* The question we face, however, is not as simple as that. Jewish tradition considers the interests of the consumer as well as those of the worker. This consideration is expressed through the law of *onaah* (price fraud), which specifies that buyers and sellers are entitled either to

compensation or to annul a sale when the amount paid diverges more than a specified amount from the fair market price for the object or service in question.[15] Unionized labor can be said to distort the market by forcing consumers to pay significantly more for labor than they would otherwise do. To be sure, the laws of *onaah* do not as a matter of technical halachah apply to wages paid to hired workers.[16] Still, the halachah displays a general tendency to supervise the stability of prices in the marketplace,[17] and it looks askance upon factors that upset this stability to the detriment of consumers. Some authorities, in fact, limit the power of trade groups to set prices and wages, since in the absence of controls these unions might cause unfair economic loss to the community.[18] Consumers, in other words, are entitled to protection against unreasonable economic demands from merchants and from workers. If such protection is not afforded them by the communal government, the consumers may boycott the providers of the goods and services, even when these pertain to religious observance, until the prices come down to appropriate levels.[19] Jewish law, in other words, recognizes that consumers have a valid interest in maintaining a reasonable level of prices for goods and services, including the cost of labor.

To this, we may add the Talmudic principle that "the Torah protects the property of Israel" (*haTorah chasah al mamonam shel Yisrael*).[20] That is, Jewish law seeks to spare us unnecessary expense in the observance of mitzvot. This principle motivates *poskim* toward finding leniencies in the law when a more stringent conclusion would involve significant financial loss.[21] It should be noted that this principle is not absolute. It is balanced by the counter-principle "there is no poverty in a place of wealth" (*ein aniyut b'mekom ashirut*): that is, price should be no object when it comes to the Torah and to determining the proper observance.[22] Various authorities over the centuries have sought to resolve the apparent conflict between these two principles.[23] At any rate, the fact that our tradition will at times take financial loss into account in assessing the precise level of religious duty suggests that we should be careful before demanding that a congregation incur a large expense when alternatives are available.

3. Tzedakah: *The Demands of Social Justice.* How then shall we attempt to reconcile the conflict between these two values, the one favoring unionization, the other protecting the consumer? The answer, it seems to us, rests with the demand of our Torah and our tradition that we do *tzedakah*. This

word, usually associated with "charity," is better translated according to its Hebrew root as "social justice." As justice, *tzedakah* is obligatory conduct, not a voluntary contribution; thus, the court can require an individual to contribute an amount that the court has determined is proper for that person.[24] To put this more bluntly, *tzedakah* is expensive. It is the nature of *tzedakah* that it costs money. If we want to work for social justice, we have to be prepared to invest of our time and our substance. And while there are limits to the amount that can be demanded of any person,[25] no Jew—and, we would add, no Jewish institution—can escape the duty of *tzedakah* on the grounds that it involves financial expense.

With this in mind, we can put our conflicting values into perspective. First, let us consider the concept of *onaah*. We noted above that a transaction may be canceled when its price exceeds by a specified amount the "fair market value" of the product in question. On this basis, we might conclude that if the cost of hiring organized labor significantly exceeds the cost of engaging nonunion workers, the "union price" is an example of *onaah* and we have no ethical obligation to pay our workers at that rate. We reject this conclusion. If, as we believe and as we have resolved on numerous occasions, unionization is an indispensable means of securing justice for workers in our society, then our dedication to *tzedakah* requires that we not set the "fair market value" of labor according to the wage level for nonunion workers. On the contrary: it is the nonunion wage rate that qualifies for the label *onaah*, for that rate depresses the market, lowering the wages and the standard of living that workers would otherwise achieve. Justice rather demands that we measure the "fair market price" for labor according to the accepted cost for *union* labor in a particular locale. It would be unjust and injurious to all workers were we to set the standard for "fair wages" according to lower, nonunion scale.

Similarly, the demand to do *tzedakah* modifies our understanding and application of the principle "the Torah protects the property of Israel." All that principle means is that financial considerations *may* be relevant in determining how we are to perform a mitzvah. It does not mean that we are exempt from performing the mitzvah merely because it is expensive.[26] Again, once we determine that nonunion labor frustrates the mitzvah of social justice, it becomes clear that our own value commitments require that our institutions show a decided preference for hiring union labor.

We acknowledge the existence of other visions of *tzedakah* than the one we have sketched here. We are aware that some will argue that nonunion labor in fact serves the cause of "social justice" for all by reducing the overall cost of goods and services and that lower wages mean that more jobs will be available for unemployed workers. We will not contest these issues here. Suffice it to say that a general concept such as "social justice" can be meaningless in the absence of some substantive vision that gives it content. Our particular vision of social justice, the understanding of that term that makes the most sense to us, is the vision put forth by the CCAR and by the prominent *poskim* whose words we have cited. It involves the empowerment of workers to control their destiny and to achieve goals (higher wages and benefits, better working conditions, a more secure future for workers and their families) that all of us want for ourselves and our children. This is the vision of "social justice" that the Reform Movement has proclaimed for many years. If we believe what we preach, it is our duty to practice the same.

In short, although Jewish tradition does recognize the legitimate interests of consumers, it does not teach us that consumers are always entitled to the lowest possible price for goods and services. Rather, it teaches that the interests of all of us are best served when we work together to build a just society. Our synagogues are indeed consumers of goods and services, but in their buying and selling, they ought to remember the higher purposes for which synagogues are established in the first place.

Conclusion. In the final analysis, we cannot tell your congregation what it "must" do. It is easy for us, who do not have to raise the $300,000 of which you speak, to tell you that you must incur that expense. We recognize, too, that your decision must be based upon local factors of which we are unaware. For example, it is sometimes the case that labor unions act in an unfair (to say nothing of an illegal) manner. Like all institutions, they can be corrupt, rapacious, or discriminatory. There are times, in other words, when cooperation with a labor union may *not* serve the public interest and the cause of *tzedakah*. All we can tell you is that, *in general*, Jewish tradition and our Reform Jewish interpretation of that tradition perceive unionization as an indispensable tool in the long struggle for social justice and the rights of workers. For that reason, your congregation should make every effort to hire union labor for your construction project.

—CCAR Responsa Committee, "The Synagogue and Organized Labor," CCAR responsum 5761.4, in *Reform Responsa for the Twenty-First Century: Sh'eilot Ut'shuvot*, ed. Mark Washofsky (New York: CCAR Press, 2010), 2:345–54.

NOTES

1. Babylonian Talmud, *Bava Batra* 8b and Rashi ad loc.

2. *Mishneh Torah, M'chirah* 14:9; *Shulchan Aruch, Choshen Mishpat* 231:27. On the subject of *takanot hakahal*, see "The Reform Rabbi's Obligations toward the UAHC," CCAR responsum 5758.1, in *Reform Responsa for the Twenty-First Century* 1:311–18, at notes 4–7, https://www.ccarnet.org/ccar-responsa/nyp-no-5758-1/.

3. Babylonian Talmud, *Bava Batra* 9a.

4. *Tosefta, Bava M'tzia* 11:12.

5. Rabbi Sh'lomo ben Adret, *Responsa Rashba* 4:185 (*she-kol chaburah she-hem benei inyan echad harei hem ke-ir bifnei atzmah . . .*). Rabbi Asher bar Yechiel, *Hilchot HaRosh, Bava Batra* 1:33, writes that "craftsmen" (*baalei omanut*) are empowered to set the regulations governing their trade, as does Rabbi Yitzchak ben Sheshet, *Responsa Rivash*, no. 399. The law is codified in *Shulchan Aruch, Choshen Mishpat* 231:28.

6. One difference between laws adopted by the citizenry as a whole and laws adopted by professional groups is that the latter are considered binding upon the group's members only if they meet with the approval of an *adam chashuv*, a "distinguished public figure" (Babylonian Talmud, *Bava Batra* 9a). The definition of this term, which in that Talmudic passage is applied to the *Amora* Rava, is the subject of some controversy. Some require that this person be a Torah scholar who serves as a leader in the local government (*parnas al hatzibur*; Rabbi Yosef ibn Migash and Rabbi Yonatan HaKohein of Lunel, cited in *Shitah Mekubetzet, Bava Batra* 9a; Rabbi Menachem HaMeiri, *Beit HaB'chirah, Bava Batra* 8b; *Magid Mishneh, Hilchot M'chirah* 14:11; *Shulchan Aruch, Choshen Mishpat* 231:28). Others do not require that this communal leader be a Torah scholar (*Responsa Rashba* 4:185). On the other hand, where there is no *adam chashuv* in place, the professional group may adopt whatever rules it sees fit and enforce them on its members. And at least one authority holds that the consent of the *adam chashuv* is required only to approve measures taken by the association that involve fines and penalties against its members; all other rules, including the setting of wages and salaries, may be adopted without such approval (Rabbi Moshe Feinstein, *Responsa Ig'rot Moshe, Choshen Mishpat* 1:58). In our own legal environment, of course, the secular authorities, who regulate union-management relations through legislation, fulfill this function.

7. Among these *poskim* are Rabbi Avraham Yitzchak HaKohein Kook, *N'tivah*, 11 Nisan 1933; Rabbi Ben Zion Ouziel, *Responsa Piskei Ouziel B'she-elot Haz'man*, no. 46 ("It is beyond all dispute that our Sages recognize the rules adopted by unions of craftsmen or laborers and by professional organizations"), and Rabbi Moshe Feinstein, *Responsa Ig'rot Moshe, Choshen Mishpat* 1:58 ("There is no basis in halachah for outlawing the formation of labor unions"). Rabbi Eliezer Y'hudah Waldenberg, *Responsa Tzitz Eliezer* 2:23, permits the formation and functioning of unions on the basis of local custom (*minhag ham'dinah*): laws governing labor-management relations are matters of communal authority, and the community is entitled through legislation to recognize labor unionization. See also Rabbi Katriel P. Techursh, *Keter Efraim*, no. 19; and Rabbi Chaim David Halevy, *Aseh L'cha Rav*, 2:64.

8. See note 7.
9. See note 7.
10. *CCAR Yearbook* 31 (1921): 44.
11. *CCAR Yearbook* 45 (1935): 79; *CCAR Yearbook* 50 (1940): 104, 105.
12. *CCAR Yearbook* 46 (1936): 78.
13. *CCAR Yearbook* 83 (1973): 109; *CCAR Yearbook* 86 (1976): 68; *CCAR Yearbook* 89 (1979): 102.
14. *CCAR Yearbook* 95 (1985): 239– 40.
15. See *Misnah Bava M'tzia* 4:3-7; *Mishneh Torah, M'chirah* 12; and *Shulchan Aruch, Choshen Mishpat* 427. The amount of divergence is set at one-sixth of the accepted market price for the object or service. If the price charged exceeds the market price by one-sixth, the buyer is entitled to a refund of the overcharge; similarly, if the price falls below the market price by one-sixth, the seller is entitled to compensation in that amount. Should the price charged diverge by *more* than one-sixth of the market price, the sale may be invalidated entirely.
16. *Shulchan Aruch, Choshen Mishpat* 227:33 (and see 227:29), derived from *Mishnah Bava M'tzia* 4:9.
17. Babylonian Talmud, *Bava Batra* 89a; *Mishneh Torah, G'neivah* 8:20 and *M'chirah* 14:1; *Shulchan Aruch, Choshen Mishpat* 231:2.
18. Rabbi Menachem HaMeiri, *Beit HaB'chirah, Bava Batra* 9a; Rabbi Yom Tov ben Ish-bili, *Chidushei HaRitva, Bava Batra* 9a; Rabbi Nissim Gerondi, *Chidushei HaRan, Bava Batra* 9a. The "controls" spoken of here refer to the concept of *adam chashuv* (see note 6). The "distinguished public figure" functions as an arbiter between the conflicting economic demands of labor and management or of merchants and consumers. A number of authorities suggest that all labor disputes must be submitted to the approval of the *adam chashuv*, in the form of a rabbinical *beit din* or a specially appointed court of arbitration, provided that such an agency exists within the community. These include Rabbi Ben Zion Ouziel (see note 7), Rabbi Chaim David Halevy (see note 7); Rabbi Shaul Yisraeli, *Amudim*, Nisan 5726 (1966), 223; and R. Sh'lomo Daichovsky, *HaTzofeh*, 9 Tevet 5733 (1973), 3.
19. See *Mishnah K'ritot* 1:7. Rabbi Menachem Mendel Krochmal (seventeenth century; *Responsa Tzemach Tzedek*, no. 28) cites that mishnah in permitting a consumer boycott against local fishmongers.
20. Babylonian Talmud, *Chulin* 49b and parallels. Rashi ad loc., s.v. *hatorah chasah*, links the principle to the *Sifra* on Leviticus 14:36. See also *Mishnah N'gaim* 12:5.
21. For example, Rabbi David Zvi Hoffmann (*Responsa M'lamed L'ho-il* 1:91) permits a Jew who owns stock in a restaurant to retain ownership of his shares, even though the restaurant remains open during Pesach and the Jewish stockholder therefore will profit from the sale of *chameitz*. He seeks a lenient answer, in part, "because the Torah protects the property of Israel."
22. See Babylonian Talmud, *M'nachot* 89a and parallels.
23. The most comprehensive summary of these discussions is Rabbi Chaim Chizkiah Medini's nineteenth-century *S'dei Chemed*, 1:128, p. 44. Among other passages, he cites Rabbi Moshe Sh'lomo ibn Habib's seventeenth-century work *Sh'mot BaAretz*

(section *yom t'ruah*, on Babylonian Talmud, *Rosh HaShanah* 27a). There, we read that the halachah does *not* determine in advance the conditions under which either principle must apply. That decision is rather left to the discretion of the sages in every generation.

24. Babylonian Talmud, *K'tubot* 49a; *Mishneh Torah, Matanot Aniyim* 7:10; *Shulchan Aruch, Yoreh Dei-ah* 248:1.

25. See *Shulchan Aruch, Yoreh Dei-ah* 249:1–2 for the ideal and practical levels of giving.

26. The responsum cited in note 21 is not an argument against this point. While Rabbi Hoffmann explained the search for a lenient answer on the grounds that *haTorah chasah al mamonam shel Yisrael*, that principle did not in and of itself justify the answer. The particular halachic question there was whether a stockholder in a corporation can be said to "own" its *chameitz* and therefore be found in violation of the Torah during Pesach. Hoffmann argues that the owning of stock in a company does not constitute "ownership" in that sense. If, on the other hand, he had concluded that stock shares do constitute "ownership," he would have required that the stockholders sell those shares despite the financial loss incurred.

Chapter 10: Politics and Reform Halachah
Hunger Strike: On the Force-Feeding of Prisoners

SH'EILAH:

What would be the Jewish view of force-feeding (strapping somebody to a chair and putting a tube down their nose in as painless a fashion as possible) a mentally stable prisoner who desires to starve himself to death to make a political statement? (Rabbi Joel Schwartzman, Morrison, Colorado)

T'SHUVAH:

This question arises with respect to the treatment of detainees imprisoned at the US naval base at Guantanamo Bay, Cuba. These detainees were captured during military operations beginning in 2001 against the Al Qaeda terrorist organization and the Taliban government of Afghanistan. During the summer and fall of 2005, they staged a hunger strike to protest their detention and treatment. In February 2006, various news organizations reported that prison officials were force-feeding the detainees, in a manner similar to that described by our *sho-eil*, as a means of breaking the strike. Military officials justified these harsh measures as necessary to save the lives of the hunger strikers. The prisoners themselves have charged that both the restraint and the insertion of the feeding tubes were accomplished through excessive violence.[1]

We compose this responsum in the summer of 2006, a time when the "war on terror" and the invasions of Afghanistan and Iraq are subjects of intense political controversy. We seek, however, to set the politics aside and to view this *sh'eilah*, as we do all others, as a *Jewish* one, involving the interpretation and application of values central to our religious tradition. With respect to this question, those values point us in different and conflicting directions. This is not an easy question for us; the "Jewish view," as our *sho-eil* puts it, is far from obvious. We will therefore set forth as thoroughly as we can the arguments both for and against force-feeding, in the hope that our answer will encompass the valid points raised by both sides and do justice to the genuine complexity of the case.

1. *Arguments in Favor of Force-Feeding.* Jewish tradition teaches that *pikuach nefesh*, the preservation of human life, is a mitzvah, a religious duty, and that it transcends and supersedes virtually all others.[2] The Rabbis derive this from Leviticus 18:5: "You shall keep My statutes and My laws, which a person shall perform and live by them." They interpret the words "and live by them" to mean "and not die by them."[3] Thus, "one is to perform the mitzvot in such a way that one's life is not subjected to danger."[4] The supreme value that Judaism places upon the safeguarding of life expresses itself in three related rules. First, we are forbidden to cause physical harm (*chavalah*) to ourselves[5] or to place ourselves in any unnecessary danger.[6] Second, the practice of medicine is itself a form of *pikuach nefesh* and therefore supersedes other conflicting religious obligations,[7] even such serious ones as the prohibitions surrounding Shabbat and Yom Kippur.[8] And third, we are forbidden "to stand idly by the blood" of another (Leviticus 19:16): that is, we bear a positive obligation to rescue the lives of those who are in danger.[9]

These teachings raise a sharp critique of the tactics of the hunger strikers. If there is a single, uncontested feature of the "Jewish view" of this question, it is that human life is sacred and that it must be treated with the utmost reverence. Yes, there are times when our tradition would permit and even demand that one die rather than violate a mitzvah, but the circumstances in which this demand applies are strictly limited.[10] In other words, one is not entitled to choose martyrdom in order "to make a political statement."[11] All of this would lead to the conclusion that the prisoners are forbidden to endanger their lives by engaging in a hunger strike and that the prison officials, who are ultimately responsible for the health and safety of those in their custody, are justified in taking strong action if necessary to bring the strike to an end.

That such action may involve force and violence is regrettable, but the blame for this unhappy result lies with the prisoners themselves. By refusing nourishment, it is they who are endangering their lives. The prison officials, by contrast, are simply following the dictates of Jewish law, which enjoins us to fulfill the obligation of *pikuach nefesh* quickly and diligently: "Whosoever delays in the performance of this mitzvah is guilty of bloodshed."[12]

2. *Arguments against Force-Feeding.* On the other hand, a case can be made that Jewish tradition does not warrant the force-feeding of prisoners who have undertaken a hunger strike. That case rests upon the following three points.

a. This is a political, not a medical question. Answers are frequently dictated by the way in which we frame the questions. If we define this question primarily as a medical one, we will tend to ask it as follows: "Under Jewish law, is a patient entitled to refuse life-sustaining medical treatment?" The answer, clearly, is "no": under the rule of *pikuach nefesh*, a patient is morally obligated to accept a remedy that consensus medical opinion regards as *r'fuah b'dukah* or *r'fuah vada-it*, one that offers a reasonably certain prospect of a successful therapeutic outcome.[13] If hunger is a disease, then food is a "sure remedy" for it. Yet we would note that the prisoners themselves do not see this as a medical question. They have chosen the hunger strike as a tactic to protest against the conditions of their captivity. Their goal is to bring pressure upon their jailors, not necessarily to kill themselves or to cause themselves irreparable physical harm. Indeed, the prison officials at Guantanamo concur in this assessment.[14] If so, then the forceful insertion of nasogastric tubes is arguably a political rather than a medical intervention, designed not to save lives but "to break the hunger strikes because they were having a disruptive effect and causing stress for the medical staff." If the strike and the attendant force-feeding both serve political goals, then the rules and principles that apply to a medical context may not be appropriate here.[15] In this connection, we would note that the prohibition against inflicting physical damage upon oneself, to which we refer above, is limited to cases in which the injury is done "in a contemptible manner" or for no good purpose.[16] Obviously, those who undertake a hunger strike in protest against prison conditions would say that the harm they inflict upon themselves does not fall into that category. We would add that a number of Orthodox rabbis participated in hunger strikes during the 1990s in protest of the Oslo peace accords between Israel and the Palestine Liberation Organization. Although the strikes were controversial, the fact that they took place suggests that the hunger strikers were able to distinguish, on Jewish grounds, between an action designed to endanger one's life and health (forbidden) and an action intended to "make a political statement" (permitted).[17]

b. Force-feeding is widely regarded as torture. This policy is set forth by the World Medical Association (WMA) in its "Declaration of Tokyo" concerning "torture and other cruel, inhuman or degrading treatment or punishment in relation to detention and imprisonment":[18]

> Where a prisoner refuses nourishment and is considered by the physician as capable of forming an unimpaired and rational judgment concerning the consequences of such a voluntary refusal of nourishment, he or she shall not be fed artificially. The decision as to the capacity of the prisoner to form such a judgment should be confirmed by at least one other independent physician. The consequences of the refusal of nourishment shall be explained by the physician to the prisoner.

The American Medical Association, a member organization of the WMA, has reaffirmed its endorsement of this clause of the Tokyo policy.[19] In March 2006, the British medical journal The Lancet published a letter of protest, signed by over 250 distinguished physicians from the United States and Europe, against the force-feeding at Guantanamo. The letter, which calls upon the US government "to ensure that detainees are assessed by independent physicians and that techniques such as forcefeeding and restraint chairs are abandoned forthwith in accordance with internationally agreed standards,"[20] has garnered the support of well-known human rights organizations.[21] We take these statements with the utmost seriousness. As Jews, we are heirs to a tradition that commands us to pursue justice (Deuteronomy 16:20) and to a Torah "whose ways are pleasantness" and "whose paths are peace" (Proverbs 3:17).[22] How then can we support a tactic that much of the world's enlightened medical-ethical opinion has castigated as a form of torture? To do so is arguably to perpetrate a chilul HaShem, a profanation of God's name, an offense we commit whenever we behave in a manner inconsistent with the high standards that the world expects of a people that lives in covenant with God.[23]

Before we reach that conclusion, however, let us consider that the Tokyo Declaration's opposition to force-feeding is based upon two principles that enjoy a dominant—some would say a "canonical"[24]—standing in contemporary secular bioethics. The first of these is patient autonomy, which holds that a medical procedure is ethical to the extent that a competent patient makes his or her own decision regarding that procedure in an autonomous manner, free of coercion. The second is informed consent: the patient agrees to a suggested treatment only when he or she has been supplied with all material information that a reasonable medical layperson would consider significant with regard to that decision.[25] Applied to our case, these principles suggest that when a prisoner makes a rational, informed decision that he does not wish to be fed, we are not permitted to feed him against his expressed will, even though the decision may result in his death.[26] Yet as we have seen, the classical Judaic approach to questions of life and death is founded not upon the affirmation of individual autonomy but upon the commitment to the sanctity of life and the duty to heal. In the traditional Jewish view, the patient has no right to make a decision, however "informed," for suicide, and the physician, who like every person bears a positive duty to save life, has no right to sit passively and watch the patient die.[27] The Jewish physician can therefore make a powerful argument that, when confronted by a situation such as the one described in our *sh'eilah*, his or her ethical responsibility is to save the patient's life rather than to respect the patient's autonomy.[28]

We do not believe that the contemporary Western model of bioethics is any more exalted, noble, or humane than the Judaic approach. In saying this, we do not mean to disparage modernity or its contributions to moral thought. We mean rather that as heirs to *both* the classical Jewish tradition *and* the culture of modernity, we would not wish to live in a society that rejects *either* source of ethical value. Thus, while we acknowledge that the modern affirmation of the dignity of the individual human being serves in our world as a bulwark against tyranny and oppression, particularly of the sort rooted in religious extremism, we reject the notion that "modern, progressive, and Western" culture enjoys a monopoly upon moral truth. On the contrary: we believe that contemporary secular civilization can learn a great deal from the Jewish tradition, especially in the realm of bioethics, where the Judaic approach can yield answers that might well be morally superior to those produced by secular thought.[29] As citizens of Western society and participants in its culture, we cannot ignore the fact that the predominant medical-ethical opinion in *our* society and culture defines the force-feeding of patients as an immoral act. But as Jews, we cannot apply the label "torture" to a procedure designed to save the life of prisoners in our custody, even if they seem bound and determined upon suicide.

c. Force-feeding transgresses against Jewish ethical principles. Yet even if we view this as a medical rather than a political question, the fact that a patient is obligated to accept life-sustaining treatment does not necessarily mean that we may force it upon her against her will. Here it is essential to consider just what force-feeding entails. As one Guantanamo detainee has described the procedure:

> The head is immobilized by a strap so it can't be moved, their hands are cuffed to the chair and the legs are shackled. They ask, "Are you going to eat or not?" and if not, they insert the tube. People have been urinating and defecating on themselves in these feedings and vomiting and bleeding. They ask to be allowed to go to the bathroom, but they will not let them go. They have sometimes put diapers on them.[30]

Another charges that "a lieutenant came to his isolation cell and told him that if he did not agree to eat solid food, he would be strapped into the chair and force-fed. After he refused to comply, he said, soldiers picked him up by the throat, threw him to the floor and strapped him to the restraint chair."[31] The nasogastric tubes, inserted forcibly against the prisoners' wishes, have been said to cause "unbearable pain."[32] We have no way, of course, to verify these statements, and we also know that the force-feeding has been defended by officials of the US Defense Department as "compassionate" and "humane."[33] Still, it is possible that these descriptions are accurate, and it is quite plausible that harsh, violent measures would be required to compel nutrients upon a prisoner who is determined to refuse them. And it is questionable whether Jewish tradition obligates us to resort to such violence even when the treatment is necessary to save a patient's life. Rabbi Moshe Feinstein, for example, has ruled that medical treatment, though compulsory under Jewish law, "must be administered in such a way that it does not frighten the patient. For fear, even though it be irrational, may itself cause him harm or even kill him. . . . It is therefore preferable that the physicians not administer treatment against the patient's will . . . and the physicians must consider this matter very carefully."[34] We would phrase this point somewhat differently: medical treatment can be considered obligatory only when it is *medicine*, that is, when it partakes of the mitzvah of healing (*r'fuah*). To the extent that a medical procedure causes significant harm to a patient, it may be said to lose its therapeutic value and therefore its standing as "medicine" that the patient would be obligated to accept.[35] We are, of course, in no position to draw a proper balance in this case between the "harm" caused to the detainee by the violent force-feeding and its obvious benefit of saving his life, *provided* that he was intent upon suicide in the first place. Nonetheless, the concern over the negative effects of these measures must give us pause before we assert that we are morally bound to administer them by force.

In addition, even if force-feeding could be said to have no objective and observable "negative effects," we would still have reason to oppose it. Violence against a patient, even when exercised by medical professionals convinced they are acting in the patient's best interests, is still violence.[36] It is the sort of treatment that offends against our most basic conceptions of *k'vod hab'riyot*, the essential dignity that all of us, including prisoners, possess as human beings created in the image of God.[37] Force is sometimes necessary in our dealings with others, but it should never be resorted to lightly. And when we do choose that path, we had best make sure that our actions are truly the only available means by which to achieve a vital purpose.

Toward a Conclusion. What is the "Jewish view" of force-feeding? As we have indicated, we think that there can be no simple, one-sided answer to this question. We have encountered powerful Judaic arguments both for and against the practice, arguments based upon Jewish legal and moral values that demand our respect and assent. Accordingly, our response acknowledges the wisdom of all these arguments in an effort to arrive at what we think is the most persuasive interpretation of the teachings of our tradition.

We begin from the obvious starting point: *pikuach nefesh*, the duty to preserve human life and to rescue those in danger, is the overriding Jewish moral concern. In any sort of "Jewish view," the obligation to save the life of a patient must take precedence over the desire to respect the patient's autonomously chosen decision to die. This is especially true given that a decision to embark upon a hunger strike must raise concerns as to the patient's ability to arrive at a truly rational choice based upon "informed consent."[38]

At the same time, force-feeding by its nature is a violent, even brutal tactic that "shocks the conscience"[39] and robs the prisoner of his fundamental human dignity. Although force-feeding can under extreme circumstances be justified on medical grounds, we think that prison authorities can abuse it all too easily for nonmedical purposes, as a tool for punishment or discipline. When they do so, we fully agree with those who condemn the measure as a form of torture. It is to be avoided in all cases except when it is obviously necessary to save the life of the hunger striker.

How do we draw a proper balance between these conflicting values and concerns? We find helpful guidance, surprisingly perhaps, in the regulations regarding hunger strikes adopted by the US Federal Bureau of Prisons.[40] These provide that a prisoner who embarks on a hunger strike is at first permitted to maintain that action. He is placed under careful medical supervision, and food is brought to his cell three times a day. Prison officials will make efforts to persuade him to abandon the strike, but they will not force him to do so until "a physician determines that the inmate's life or health will be threatened if treatment is not initiated immediately." The prisoner may be fed involuntarily only "if the physician is convinced to a reasonable medical certainty that there is an immediate threat to the inmate's life, or permanent damage to the inmate's health."[41] The words "immediate" and "permanent" are crucial here. They declare that the only acceptable grounds for force-feeding are medical and that those grounds must be sufficiently urgent to remove virtually all doubt that the feeding is medically necessary. These regulations, if adhered to in the case of the Guantanamo detainees, would prevent the misuse of force-feeding for other purposes, such as for maintaining prison discipline or for relieving "stress" upon the prison staff.[42]

One Final Note. The Bureau's rules also provide that when nasogastric tubes are inserted by force, "these events should be videotaped."[43] We cannot overemphasize the importance of this point for our *t'shuvah*. The force-feeding of prisoners must be carefully supervised, for only in that way can we hope to prevent excessive violence and other mistreatment. This supervision therefore should be performed by outside observers who do not represent the prison system or the military. Although this might interfere with the secrecy that currently surrounds the activities at the Guantanamo prison camp, we think it is the best way for the US military to demonstrate its commitment to "humane" and "compassionate" treatment of the detainees in the face of severe international criticism. In so doing, they would fulfill the spirit of the Mishnah's dictum that it is essential to display our innocence in the sight of people as well as in the sight of God.[44] It would also meet the high standard set by the United States Declaration of Independence, which proclaims the American people's "decent respect to the opinions of mankind."

—CCAR Responsa Committee, "Hunger Strike: On the Force-Feeding of Prisoners," CCAR responsum 5766.3, in *Reform Responsa for the Twenty-First Century: Sh'eilot Ut'shuvot*, ed. Mark Washofsky (New York: CCAR Press, 2010), 2:381–95.

NOTES

1. This description is culled from the following news sources: "Force-Feeding at Guantanamo Is Now Acknowledged," *New York Times*, February 22, 2006 (http://www.nytimes.com/2006/02/22/international/middleeast/22gitmo.html?ex=1298264400&en=7ea399aeaba6605e&ei=5090&partner=rssuserland&emc=rss); "Doctors Attack US over Guantanamo,"*BBC News*, March 10, 2006 (http://news.bbc.co.uk/1/hi/world/americas/4790742.stm); "Guantanamo Force Feeding Tactics Are Called Torture," *Washington Post*, March 1, 2006 (http://www.washingtonpost.com/wp-dyn/content/article/2006/02/28/AR2006022801344.html) .

2. The classical formulation of this rule is the phrase *yaavor v'al yehareg*, "one should transgress the commandment rather than be killed," in the event that a persecutor demands that a Jew either violate the mitzvah or forfeit his life. See Babylonian Talmud, *Sanhedrin* 74a and *Avodah Zarah* 27b; *Mishneh Torah, Y'sodei HaTorah* 5:1ff.; *Shulchan Aruch, Yoreh Dei-ah* 157:1. On the exceptions to this rule see note 10, below.

3. Babylonian Talmud, *Yoma* 85b, *Sanhedrin* 74a, and *Avodah Zarah* 27b; *Sifra* to Leviticus 18:5.

4. Rashi, Babylonian Talmud, *Yoma* 85b, s.v. *d'shmu'el leit leh pircha*.

5. Babylonian Talmud, *Bava Kama* 90b; *Mishneh Torah, Chovel Umazik* 5:1. But see below in the text.

6. Derived from Deuteronomy 4:9. *Mishneh Torah, Rotzei-ach* 11:4; *Shulchan Aruch, Choshen Mishpat* 427:8-10. On this basis, a number of contemporary Orthodox authorities have begun to prohibit smoking. See the discussion in "Responsum on Smoking," CCAR responsum 5753.23, in *Teshuvot for the Nineties*, 331-35, https://ccarnet.org/ccar-responsa/tfn-no-5753-23-331-335/ .

7. *Mishnah Yoma* 8:5; Nachmanides, *Torat HaAdam*, ed. Hayyim David Chavel (Jerusalem: Mosad Harav Kook, 1964), 41-42; *Tur* and *Shulchan Aruch, Yoreh Dei-ah* 336:1.

8. Thus, a person who rejects the instruction of a competent physician (*rofei baki*) on the grounds that the instruction involves prohibited labor on Shabbat is "a pious fool [*chasid shoteh*]. This is not an act of piety but of suicide. One is required to do what the physicians prescribe" (Rabbi David ibn Zimra [sixteenth- to seventeenth-century Egypt], *Responsa Radbaz* 1:1139.

9. Babylonian Talmud, *Sanhedrin* 73a: "From where do we learn that one who sees his fellow drowning in the river, attacked by a wild beast, or threatened by robbers is obliged to save him? From the verse 'Do not stand idly by the blood of your fellow.'" Rambam (*Mishneh Torah, Rotzei-ach* 1:14) codifies the rule as follows: "One who is able to save his fellow [from danger] and does not do so has transgressed against the mitzvah of Leviticus 19:16." See also *Shulchan Aruch, Choshen Mishpat* 426.

10. See the sources enumerated in note 2, above. Jewish tradition requires martyrdom in three specific cases; to put this differently, there are three mitzvot which one must never violate, even at the cost of one's life. These are idolatry, the sexual transgressions enumerated in Leviticus 18, and murder. These are formulated in the

sources as "exceptions" to the rule of *pikuach nefesh* established by the interpretation of Leviticus 18:5. Each exception is itself derived by way of midrash (textual interpretation) or *s'vara* (logical inference); see Babylonian Talmud, *Sanhedrin* 74a.

11. See *Mishneh Torah, Y'sodei HaTorah* 5:4: "If the case is one in which the Torah says, 'Transgress the commandment and save your life,' the one who chooses to die rather than transgress is culpable for his own death"; i.e., he has committed suicide. But see below in the text.

12. *Shulchan Aruch, Yoreh Dei-ah* 336:1.

13. See "On the Treatment of the Terminally Ill," CCAR responsum 5754.14, in *Teshuvot for the Nineties*, 337–364, at notes 38–40, https://www.ccarnet.org/ccar-responsa/tfn-no-5754-14-337-364/.

14. According to Maj. Gen. Jay W. Hood, commander of the prison camp at the Guantanamo naval base, the hunger strikers are not suicidal but are simply protesting their confinement. "In none of these [cases] have I ever gotten the impression that these guys want to die." See Susan Okie, MD, "Glimpses of Guantanamo: Medical Ethics and the War on Terror," *New England Journal of Medicine* 353, no. 24 (Dec. 15, 2005): 2529–34.

15. "Force-Feeding at Guantanamo Is Now Acknowledged" (see note 1, above). The quotation is attributed to two "Defense Department officials." See also "Guantanamo Medics Accused of Abusive Force-Feeding," *Boston Globe*, Oct. 15, 2005 (http://www.boston.com/news/nation/articles/2005/10/15/guantanamo_medics_accused_of_abusive_force_feeding), quoting Dr. Arthur Caplan, director of the Center for Bioethics at the University of Pennsylvania: "Medicine is supposed to remain neutral. When you start to become complicit in efforts to break resistance using medical expertise that should be there simply to protect the health of people, you're headed down the wrong track."

16. *Mishneh Torah, Chovel Umazik* 5:1: the phrase is *derech nitzayon* (or, in some readings, *bizayon*). See "Cosmetic Surgery," CCAR responsum 5752.7, in *Teshuvot for the Nineties*, 283–88, https://www.ccarnet.org/ccar-responsa/tfn-no57503-283-288/.

17. See Rabbi Menachem Feliks, "Ve'af al Pi Chen: Shevitat Raav," *T'chumin* 16 (1996/5756): 291–95. Feliks contends that the halachah permits an individual to undertake a voluntary fast (*taanit yachid*) in order to protest against policies of the Israeli government that, in the individual's opinion, endanger the Jewish people and state. He would not apply his argument, obviously, to the Muslim detainees at Guantanamo. From a liberal perspective, though, the notion that one may declare a fast in service to a "higher purpose" is a principle that should not be restricted to Jews.

18. The World Medical Association Declaration of Tokyo (1975, 2005, and 2006), paragraph 6 (https://www.wma.net/what-we-do/medical-ethics/declaration-of-tokyo/).

19. "AMA Reiterates Opposition to Feeding Individuals against Their Will," statement by Duane Cady, MD, chair, American Medical Association, cited by M. K. Wynia, "Should Doctors Force Feed Prisoners?," *MedGenMed* 9, no. 4 (2007): 5, http://www.medscape.com/viewarticle/563171.

20. David J. Nichol et al., "Forcefeeding and Restraint of Guantanamo Bay Hunger

Strikers," *The Lancet* 367 (March 11, 2006): 9513, http://www.thelancet.com/journals/lancet/article/PIIS0140673606683268/fulltext.

21. Among these are Physicians for Human Rights (https://phr.org/news/over-250-medical-leaders-condemn-brutal-force-feeding-methods-at-guantanamo/) and Amnesty International (http://www.amnesty.org.uk/news_details.asp?NewsID=16898).

22. Halachic authorities sometimes cite this verse as a guide for the interpretation of the Torah's laws according to its ultimate intent. Thus, Maimonides rules (*Mishneh Torah, Chanukah* 4:14) that, in the event one has only enough oil either for household illumination or for the Chanukah lamp, one should use it for household illumination, "for the sake of domestic peace" (*mishum shalom beito*). He adds, "Great is peace, for the entire Torah was given to bring peace to the world, as it is said, 'whose ways are pleasantness, etc.'"

23. For sources and discussion on *chilul HaShem*, see "Collection of Debts to the Congregation," CCAR responsum 5764.1, in *Reform Responsa for the Twenty-First Century*, 2:291–98, at notes 11–15, https://www.ccarnet.org/ccar-responsa/nyp-no-5764-1/.

24. The term is used by Rabbi Hamel, "The Reign of Autonomy: Is the End in Sight?," *Second Opinion*, January 1995, 75–79.

25. These definitions reflect the formulation of American law, represented especially by the leading case *Canterbury v. Spence*, 464 F.2d 772 (D.C. Cir. 1972). The classic formulation is perhaps that of Judge Benjamin N. Cardozo in *Schloendorff v. Society of N.Y. Hospital*, 105 N.E. 92 (N.Y. 1914): "Every human being of adult years and sound mind has a right to determine what shall be done with his own body, and a surgeon who performs an operation without his patient's consent commits an assault for which he is liable in damages." See, in general, Ruth R. Faden, Tom L. Beauchamp, in collaboration with Nancy M. P. King, *A History and Theory of Informed Consent* (New York: Oxford University Press, 1986).

26. See the statement from the WMA's Tokyo Declaration at note 18, above. It is, however, not certain that the Guantanamo detainees are able to make an "informed" decision under the conditions of their incarceration. See Okie, note 14 above, at 2530–31.

27. In this, Jewish tradition would dissent from the decision of the British authorities who allowed hunger-striking members of the Irish Republican Army to starve themselves to death while in prison in 1981. See Okie, note 14 above, 2530.

28. For an example of such a powerful argument, see Shimeon Glick, MD, "Unlimited Human Autonomy: A Cultural Bias?," *New England Journal of Medicine* 356 (March 27, 1997): 954–56 (https://www.nejm.org/doi/full/10.1056/NEJM199703273361312).

29. For an example, see "Live Liver Transplantation," CCAR responsum 5763.2, in *Reform Responsa for the Twenty-First Century*, 2:143–64, section 4 and following, https://www.ccarnet.org/ccar-responsa/nyp-no-5763-2/.

30. "Force-Feeding at Guantanamo Is Now Acknowledged" (see note 1, above).

31. "Force-Feeding at Guantanamo Is Now Acknowledged" (see note 1, above).

32. "Guantanamo Force Feeding Tactics Are Called Torture"(see note 1, above).

33. "Force-Feeding at Guantanamo Is Now Acknowledged" and "Doctors Attack US Over Guantanamo" (see note 1, above).

34. Responsa Ig'rot Moshe, Choshen Mishpat 2:73, part 5.

35. For a detailed analysis of this point, see "On the Treatment of the Terminally Ill," CCAR responsum 5754.14, in Teshuvot for the Nineties, 337–63, at section 3, https://www.ccarnet.org/ccar-responsa/tfn-no-5754-14-337-364/.

36. Some of these objections, it might be argued, can be removed simply by sedating the prisoners prior to force-feeding. While it is true that, as a matter of degree, sedation would reduce the amount of violence employed in force-feeding, it would still in its essence, as a forcible transgression of the patient's will, constitute an act of violence against him. As such, the Judaic principles cited in this paragraph would continue to apply. Needless to say, moreover, the procedure would still be defined as "torture" under the Tokyo Declaration (note 18, above).

37. Although it may sound like a lofty ethical principle with little substantive content, k'vod hab'riyot functions as a real consideration in halachah. In its general formulation, the rule is that considerations of "human dignity" may be great enough to supersede a conflicting Rabbinic ordinance (Babylonian Talmud, B'rachot 19b; Mishneh Torah, Shabbat 26:23 and Kilayim 10:29). In this case, of course, the conflicting ordinance is pikuach nefesh, which originates in the Torah (d'oraita), and one might argue that the saving of life surely overrides considerations of k'vod hab'riyot. But one leading poseik suggests that "dignity" (kavod) may in some cases override pikuach nefesh. See Rabbi Sh'lomo Kluger (nineteenth-century Galicia), Chochmat Sh'lomo to Shulchan Aruch, Choshen Mishpat 426:1.

38. See note 26, above, as well as Glick, "Unlimited Human Autonomy," 955: "One might perhaps see forcing people to undergo lifesaving therapy as an action that does respect their autonomy and for which they may ultimately be grateful; their judgment may be temporarily compromised by irrationality, although they remain within the bounds of legally defined competence."

39. This phrase is particularly appropriate here, in that it is the definition of "torture" adopted by the US Supreme Court in a case involving the seizure of evidence from a suspect by means of induced vomiting. The Court held that "the proceedings by which the conviction was obtained do more than offend some fastidious squeamishness or private sentimentalism about combating crime too energetically. This is conduct that shocks the conscience. . . . They are methods too close to the rack and the screw to permit of constitutional differentiation." Rochin v. California, 345 U.S. 165 (1952), at 172.

40. US Department of Justice, Federal Bureau of Prisons, Program Statement, no. P5562.05, July 29, 2005, https://www.bop.gov/policy/progstat/5562_005.pdf

41. Program Statement, 6.

42. See above at note 15. The goal of prison population control can be met in other ways. For example, the Statement provides that when a prisoner undertakes a hunger strike, he or she may be isolated in "a medically appropriate locked room" (p. 3). The formal justification for this rule is medical: isolation allows for close monitoring of the prisoner's physical condition. But it also addresses the concerns surround-

ing discipline (i.e., preventing the hunger strike from causing disturbances among the inmate population), thereby avoiding the resort to force-feeding as a means of breaking the strike.

43. *Program Statement*, 7.

44. *Mishnah Sh'kalim* 3:2, based upon Numbers 32:22.

GLOSSARY

aggadah: Talmudic or Rabbinic nonlegal literature; "lore" as opposed to "law."

Amoraim: Rabbinic sages who lived ca. 250–500 CE, who discussed Mishnaic law and whose teachings are included in the Gemara.

aron kodesh: The ark that contains a synagogue's Torah scrolls.

bal tosif: The halachic principle according to which we are not permitted to add to the Torah's commandments; derived from Deuteronomy 4:2.

baraita/baraitot: Rabbinic texts dating from the first and second centuries CE that were not included in the Mishnah.

beit din: A Jewish court of law.

Beit Din HaGadol: The ancient Great Court, sometimes known as the Sanhedrin. The Great Court also possessed legislative authority.

Beit HaMikdash: The ancient Temple in Jerusalem.

beit k'neset: "House of assembly"; synagogue.

bimah: The platform in a Jewish sanctuary from which prayers are led and the Torah is read.

b'nei ha-ir: "Residents of a community."

b'rachah l'vatalah: An improper or unnecessary blessing.

b'rit milah: "Covenant of circumcision"; the ceremony that formally initiates male babies into the covenant with God through the act of circumcision. Today there are also covenant ceremonies marking the birth of female babies.

chidush: A unique contribution, teaching, or halachic idea.

chol: "Secular"; the opposite of *kodesh*, "holy."

chuk/chukot: "Laws"; the term generally denotes those mitzvot of the Torah that have no clear rationale (*taam*).

Chumash: The five books of the Torah in book form, to be used for study or reading rather than public recitation. In ancient times, any one book of the Torah written separately on a scroll was called a *Chumash*.

d'oraita: A commandment derived from or attributed directly to the Torah.

d'rabanan: A commandment enacted by the ancient Rabbis.

etrog: Part of the four species—in this case, a citrus fruit—used during the observance of Sukkot.

Gemara: Commentary and expansion on the Mishnah from the second to fifth centuries CE. Together with the Mishnah, they compose the Jerusalem and Babylonian Talmuds.

g'neivah: "Theft."

g'neivat daat: Deceptive behavior.

hachnasat orchim: "Welcoming guests."

halachah/halachot: Jewish law/s.

Havdalah: "Separation"; the ceremony occurring at the end of Shabbat or a festival marking the separation between that day and the next.

kasher: Something ritually fit for use; the opposite of *pasul.*

Kiddush: A blessing recited on Shabbat and holidays over a glass of wine, marking the sanctification of the day.

kodesh: "Holy"; the opposite of *chol,* "secular."

kohein: Priest.

k'riat haTorah: "Reading of the Torah" before the congregation, part of the public worship service.

k'vod hab'riyot: "Human dignity."

k'vod sefer Torah: The honor due to a Torah scroll.

k'vod tzibur: The dignity of the congregation.

lulav: Part of the four species—specifically, branches of palm—used during the observance of Sukkot. The word *lulav* frequently includes two other species, branches of willow (*aravot*) and myrtle (*hadasim*).

machloket: "Disagreement"; a scholarly dispute.

Magen David: The Jewish six-pointed star, the symbol of the Jewish people.

mara d'atra: The local rabbi acting as the ultimate halachic decisor (*poseik*).

matzah: Unleavened bread.

meishiv: A responder, the author of a responsum.

menorah: "Candelabrum"; the seven-branched candelabrum that stood in the Temple and that is often symbolically included in a Jewish synagogue's decorations.

mezuzot: "Doorposts"; these are scrolls affixed to the doorposts of one's home with special boxes that contain specific verses of the Torah.

M'gillat Esther: "The Scroll of Esther."

midrash: Rabbinic exegesis on or expansion of Torah, documented in the Talmud as well as other Rabbinic books of Jewish teaching and interpretation.

Minchah: The afternoon prayer service.

minhag/minhagim: Custom/s.

minhag hamakom: "Custom of the place"; a local custom.

minyan: A group of ten Jewish adults required to recite public prayers.

Mishnah: "Repetition"; the first major Rabbinic written collection of Jewish law, redacted by Rabbi Y'hudah HaNasi, ca. 220 CE.

mitzvah/mitzvot: Commandment/s.

m'lachah: "Work," specifically the category of work that is forbidden on Shabbat.

m'nuchah: "Rest"; specifically, the rest required on Shabbat.

ner tamid: "Eternal flame"; the symbolic light in Jewish synagogues that is kept burning (or on, in the case of an electric light) at all times.

onaah: "Oppression"; specifically, price fraud.

parashah: "Portion"; usually refers to the weekly Torah portion. The Torah is divided into fifty-four portions to be read each week, though in some cases two portions are read on the same Shabbat.

pasul: Something that is ritually unfit for use; the opposite of *kasher*.

pikuach nefesh: The duty to save a human life, which overrides virtually all other mitzvot of the Torah.

poseik: The authority who makes a halachic decision.

p'sak: An authoritative halachic decision.

p'shat: "Simple"; the plain, literal meaning of a text. Often used as the opposite of *midrash* or *d'rash*, the meaning of the text created in Rabbinic exegesis.

sefer/sifrei Torah: "Torah scroll/s."

Shabbat kodesh: "Holy Shabbat."

Shacharit: The morning prayer service.

shakla v'tarya: An Aramaic phrase referring to the back-and-forth dialectical style of Talmud study.

sh'eilah: Question.

sh'eilot ut'shuvot: "Questions and answers"; Jewish responsa literature.

sh'lom bayit: "Peace in the home."

sh'mirat Shabbat: Observance of Shabbat.

Shoah: "Catastrophe"; the Hebrew term for the Holocaust.

sho-eil: A questioner.

shofar: The ram's horn blown on Rosh HaShanah.

Shulchan Aruch: "The Set Table"; sixteenth-century code of Jewish law written by Rabbi Yosef Karo. The work includes a set of authoritative glosses called the *Mapa* ("Tablecloth") by Rabbi Moshe Isserles.

sh'vut: An activity the Rabbis deemed inappropriate for Shabbat even though it does not fall into the category of *m'lachah*, "work."

simchah: "Joy" or "happiness"; a celebration or joyful moment.

sofer s'tam: A scribe specially trained to write *sifrei Torah*, *t'fillin*, and mezuzot.

sukkah: "Booth"; the open-air thatched hut erected during the holiday of Sukkot as a reminder of the time the Israelites wandered in the desert.

taanit yachid: "A personal fast."

Talmud: The Rabbinic collection containing both the Mishnah and Gemara. The Jerusalem Talmud, or *Talmud Y'rushalmi*, was redacted ca. 350 CE in the Galilee of the Land of Israel; the Babylonian Talmud, or *Talmud Bavli*, was redacted in Babylonia over the course of several hundred years beginning in the sixth century CE.

Tanna/Tannaim: A Jewish sage or sages who lived ca. 70–250 CE, whose teachings are recorded in the Mishnah and elsewhere.

tanu rabanan: "Our Rabbis taught"; a unique formula introducing a *baraita* in Rabbinic literature.

t'fillin: "Phylacteries"; black leather prayer boxes attached to the forehead and forearm with leather straps during morning weekday worship, which contain four passages from the Torah, including the first portion of the *Sh'ma* (Deuteronomy 6:4–9).

Torah Sheb'al Peh: The Oral Torah.

Torah Shebichtav: The Written Torah.

tradition: As this book understands it, tradition "is an historically extended, socially embodied argument, and an argument precisely in part about the goods which constitute that tradition" (Alasdair MacIntyre, *After Virtue*, 2nd ed. [Notre Dame: Notre Dame University Press, 1984], 222).

t'shuvah: Response by the *meishiv* to the question submitted by the *sho-eil*.

tzedakah: "Righteousness"; the term that describes an act of giving that other traditions call "charity."

tzitzit: "Fringes"; fringes tied with special knots affixed to each corner of a tallit, prayer shawl.

Y'hudah HaNasi, Rabbi: Rabbi Judah the Prince, also known as Rabbi, who codified the Mishnah ca. 200 CE.

yitur lashon: Superfluous or extra language in the Torah, which the Rabbis understood as conveying information in a midrashic sense.

REFORM RESPONSA PUBLICATIONS

Reform Responsa, by Rabbi Solomon B. Freehof, PhD. Cincinnati: Hebrew Union College Press, 1960.

Recent Reform Responsa, by Rabbi Solomon B. Freehof, PhD. Cincinnati: Hebrew Union College Press, 1963.

Current Reform Responsa, by Rabbi Solomon B. Freehof, PhD. Cincinnati: Hebrew Union College Press, 1969.

Modern Reform Responsa, by Rabbi Solomon B. Freehof, PhD. Cincinnati: Hebrew Union College Press, 1971.

Contemporary Reform Responsa, by Rabbi Solomon B. Freehof, PhD. Cincinnati: Hebrew Union College Press, 1974.

Reform Responsa for Our Time, by Rabbi Solomon B. Freehof, PhD. Cincinnati: Hebrew Union College Press, 1977.

New Reform Responsa, by Rabbi Solomon B. Freehof, PhD. Cincinnati: Hebrew Union College Press, 1980.

American Reform Responsa: Collected Responsa of the Central Conference of American Rabbis, edited by Rabbi Walter Jacob. New York: CCAR Press, 1983.

Contemporary American Reform Responsa, edited by Rabbi Walter Jacob. New York: CCAR Press, 1987.

Today's Reform Responsa, by Rabbi Solomon B. Freehof, PhD. New York: CCAR Press, 1990.

Questions and Reform Jewish Answers: New American Reform Responsa, by Rabbi Walter Jacob. New York: CCAR Press, 1992.

Teshuvot for the Nineties: Reform Judaism's Answers to Today's Dilemmas, edited by Rabbi W. Gunther Plaut and Rabbi Mark Washofsky, PhD. New York: CCAR Press, 1997.

Reform Responsa for the Twenty-First Century: Sh'eilot Ut'shuvot, volumes 1–2, edited by Rabbi Mark Washofsky, PhD. New York: CCAR Press, 2010.

Additional responsa have been published in the *CCAR Journal: The Reform Jewish Quarterly* (formerly titled *Journal of Reform Judaism*), by the Solomon B. Freehof Institute of Progressive Halakhah, or on the CCAR's website (www.ccarnet.org/rabbinic-voice/reform-responsa/).

All publications are available from CCAR Press as ebooks. The responsa are also available for free on the CCAR's website.

ABOUT THE AUTHOR

Rabbi Mark Washofsky, PhD, is an emeritus professor of Jewish law and practice at Hebrew Union College–Jewish Institute of Religion in Cincinnati, where he received his rabbinical ordination (1980) and his PhD (1987) and where he taught Talmud and Jewish legal literature from 1985 to 2021. He served as chair of the Responsa Committee of the Central Conference of American Rabbis from 1996 to 2017. He is currently the chair of the Solomon B. Freehof Institute of Progressive Halakhah. His publications include *Jewish Living: A Guide to Contemporary Reform Practice*; *Reform Responsa for the Twenty-First Century*, the latest printed collection of Reform responsa; and numerous articles on the development of halachah, the application of legal and literary theory to Jewish legal writing, and Jewish bioethics.